MOB MURDER
of America's
Greatest Gambler

Herb Marynell
with Steve Bagbey

ISBN:1479336149

ISBN 13:9781479336142

Library of Congress Control Number: 2012917428
CreateSpace Independent Publishing Platform
North Charleston, South Carolina

Chapter 1

THE BIG BANG

An unforgettable day began with a bang few knew was coming.

Rick Reed looked in the mirror, straightened his tie and made sure his briefcase was nearby.

It was a little after 1 p.m. on Tuesday, October 18, 1977, time to go to work as a bail bond and pre-sentence investigator for the Vanderburgh County Circuit Court in the Civic Center. He never complained about starting in the afternoon and staying late at night because he was hired with no experience and felt lucky to have the job.

Luck had been with him before. He had served in the U. S. Army, from 1971 to 1974, and twice had orders cut to go to Vietnam, but something always came up and he never was sent. Instead, he was assigned to the psychological warfare training school in Okinawa and then to the Army language school at Monterey, California, to learn Korean.

Now 25 years old and back in Evansville, Indiana, Reed had divorced earlier in the year and moved into the Chateau Village apartments on the city's East Side, living in a ground floor corner apartment with a picture window that looked out on the fence and parking lot of the Olympia Health Spa a few feet away. The view wasn't much and he spent little time at the window.

He reached to pick up his briefcase when he heard a thump. Suddenly, all hell broke loose.

The picture window blew out. A big hot hand picked Reed up and slammed his 5-foot 8-inch, 130-pound frame into an apartment wall five feet away. He thought he saw thousands of pieces of glass floating and weaving in slow motion across the living room toward him, crashing to the floor and showering him with shards. He smelled the heat; it was an odd odor.

Even in basic training at Fort Knox with heavy tanks firing their guns, Reed never experienced a blast like this. He thought a natural gas line had exploded. Stunned but not hurt, he took a few seconds to get his bearings then ran outside. In the spa parking lot there was a car or what once was a car. It was blown apart, the front end twisted, the hood and top missing. Black smoke billowed and flames shot into the air.

He looked again. There appeared to be someone sitting in the car, more like a crash dummy in the driver's seat with flames all around. The figure seemed totally black, but Reed wasn't sure. There was too much smoke.

Pieces of the vehicle were everywhere, some still burning. Reed looked helplessly at the driver again and slowly, ever so slowly, the figure slumped to the left toward what once was the driver's door. He had to be dead. *No one could survive that blast!* Reed thought.

People rushed from the spa. More came out of businesses and offices across the street and from nearby apartments, standing and looking, unwilling to rush to the car because of the intense heat, smoke and flames. People yelled, even screamed. Several other cars in the parking lot were smashed, tires flattened, windows knocked out.

A small electric substation just a few feet behind the burning vehicle was damaged by the blast, knocking out electricity to that part of the city. Reed never had gotten to Vietnam but thought he was seeing a bit of Vietnam in Evansville.

Three men approached the burning vehicle. One man was driven back by the flames but the remaining two dragged the lifeless figure from the vehicle with one leaning over to check if the victim was breathing. The other appeared to be saying a prayer.

Police cars and fire trucks roared up, an ambulance. More people crowded the sidewalks to gawk. Reed stood and watched for a long time, unable to walk away. He just stared, thinking he'd never seen anything like that before.

Finally, he decided to go to work. When he reached his MG Midget sports car in the apartment parking lot, he discovered the convertible top ripped.

Part of the burning car's grill was lying in the seat. It was still warm to his touch.[1]

---

1 Rick Reed later was hired by the county sheriff's department, working in the jail and in dispatch; then he joined the Evansville police department. He retired with the rank of sergeant, taught criminal justice classes at a local collage and wrote books about murders in Evansville.

Chapter 2

BEAUTIFUL DAY TURNED UGLY

Dorothy Mae Manion had worked as a maid at the elegant house at 600 Lombard Avenue for 30 years. She left her home blocks away in a predominately black neighborhood on that quiet Tuesday to get there in time to make breakfast for Ray Ryan and his wife Helen.

Eva Ball, who'd been with the Ryans for 20 years, normally did the cooking and downstairs cleaning but she was on vacation celebrating her 65th birthday, leaving the 72-year-old Manion to take over her duties.

It was a beautiful mid-October Indian summer day in southwestern Indiana, sunny, little wind, temperature in the mid-60s. Perfect. Activity at the house had picked up in the past few months after Ray returned to the United States in June from his annual visit at the plush Mount Kenya Safari Club in Africa. He joined Helen in visiting their daughter Rae Jean in Palm Springs, California, before both returned to Evansville.

At age 73, Ray was tanned and still handsome. He had picked up a few pounds in the last year and his once dark hair was gray. His presence that before dominated a room had faded and his zest for life was diminished by the nagging problems he constantly faced. He and his Evansville attorney George Barnett, Sr. had met at the Ryan home the night before to discuss the Internal Revenue Service case in Washington that had plagued Ray for years and to play cards, a game called Spite and Malice that Ray loved. The session broke up around midnight.

The IRS trial was scheduled for Nov. 15, a few weeks away. IRS attorneys had offered Ryan a compromise and were awaiting a counteroffer from Ray's attorneys. Rumors floated around that Ray would cut a deal and tell all he knew about organized crime figures and his past dealings with them to get out of the tax case. His attorneys said that wasn't true, but did the mob buy it?

After breakfast, Ray read the morning paper, talked by phone with an employee at his downtown Ryan Oil Company office and played a game of backgammon with Helen, a morning ritual. He planned to play backgammon with friends at the Petroleum Club that evening.

First he was going to the spa. Concerned about his weight, Ray had paid $89 in July for a three-month membership to the Olympia Health Spa located a mile east of his home. In August, he purchased another membership for his long-time friend Charles O'Curran, a Hollywood dancer/choreographer who visited often.

Ray didn't know until he signed up that Kenneth Newcomb had taken over Olympia earlier in the year. Kenny Newcomb and Ray had been friends for years and done oil leasing deals together. Newcomb's son, David, managed the facility. Ray had given the Newcombs a painting by an area artist named Glenn Robertson that now hung in the spa's lobby. The Newcombs planned to give Ray a life membership to the spa in two days, when his membership had to be renewed.

Ray left home shortly after 11 a.m. in his new Lincoln Continental Mark V, purchased two weeks earlier for him by Doyle Dressback, his Evansville oil company manager. Around his neck, Ray wore favorite necklace with a South African Kruger rand, a 20-carat gold piece and a gold Saint Christopher medal, the patron saint of travelers.

He went to the spa on Tuesdays, Thursdays, and Saturdays. This would be the fifteenth time Ray had gone there in a ten-week period and the sixth visit on a Tuesday.

He became predictable and that proved lethal.

Chapter 3

"LET'S WRAP IT UP"

The Olympia Health Spa opened in 1973 at 4920 Bellemeade Avenue near Green River Road, the city's growing commercial hub filled with stores, restaurants, and offices. The one-story masonry building drew retirees and office workers who came during their lunch hour or after 5. There was a workout area, sauna, an indoor pool and a smaller outdoor pool next to the parking lot.

On the south side of the two-lane Bellemeade Avenue were an assortment of neighborhood shops and offices. North and east of the spa were two buildings of the Chateau Apartments. The outdoor pool was afforded privacy by a chain link fence laced with green and white aluminum strips.

Ray Ryan arrived at 11:15 a.m., parked in a space near the door and went inside. He took off his necklace, handed it to David Newcomb, who put it in a lockbox, and went to locker 35 to change.

The spa started to fill. Mike Dubber, arriving at noon, guided his vehicle into the parking space next to the front door. Bruce Tabor got there a little later and parked on one side of Ray's car. Major Joe Irvine, the 59-year-old balding director of the local Salvation Army recently discharged from a hospital after suffering a heart attack, was dropped off at Olympia by his wife. Several other members arrived.

The Rev. Patrick Foster showed up around 1 p.m., parking his new Oldsmobile 88 in the remaining slot next to Ray's vehicle. Foster was proud of the Oldsmobile. It was the first new car the 47-year-old priest had owned and had only 6,000 miles on it. He had visited patients at Deaconess Hospital, one of the city's two East Side medical facilities, and couldn't stay long at the spa because he had a 3 p.m. appointment on the West Side. As he went in, Foster didn't notice Ray getting ready to leave, but later under hypnosis did recall an older man sitting on the couch by the door.

Before leaving, Ray talked a few minutes with Kenny Newcomb about property Newcomb had acquired. Ray wanted to look at the site and suggested they leave together, but Newcomb said he had an errand to run first and went to his car and drove away. That errand saved his life. "How lucky can I be?" Newcomb thought later. Ray collected his necklace and left.

Foster headed to the locker room and began removing his shirt. That's as far as he got. The explosion was deafening. It was 1:18 p.m. The building shook. Foster thought a water heater had exploded. David Newcomb, in the rear of the building, was knocked to the floor by the blast. *Something happened to my father* was David Newcomb's first thought.

Everyone rushed outside. Debris was everywhere. People were shouting. Pandemonium reigned. Flames engulfed a car in the lot, curling 60 feet into the air and dense black smoke soared 100 feet. Gerry Bender, filling a soft drink machine at his store across the street, saw the hood of an automobile sail 30 feet over the telephone wires. Small parts of the car were still landing. The blast was heard miles away. A couple of cars in the parking lot were burning, but the blast was centered at Ray's 4,652-pound Lincoln Mark V, which had been ripped to shreds.

More than 20 windows were blown out of the Chateau Apartments. Pictures fell from walls. The blast knocked a sleeping resident out of his bed. Outside, parts of the car fell like shrapnel from the sky onto streets and the tops of buildings.

The blast knocked out the back door of the health club, and blew windows and frames out of the wall and into the indoor swimming pool without breaking the glass. The shock wave cracked the outdoor pool that would still leak three decades later.

Sam Gates, a 26-year-old Evansville firefighter assigned to the "meat wagon," the department's emergency ambulance operation, was off duty and a block away at a Shell gas station when he heard the explosion. He quickly drove between the apartment buildings and the spa. He saw an elderly woman screaming near a trash container by the fence. Gates jumped out of his car, climbed a fence, and ran to the burning car.

Ray was still partially in the vehicle. Gates and Major Irvine, who had rushed out of the spa, tried to pull him from the vehicle, but his feet were stuck under the brake pedal. The interior of the car was burning, the tires blown out. Despite the intense heat, Gates and another person managed to untangle Ray's feet and pull him away from the car engulfed in fire. Ray's pants were burning, and Gates put the flames out with his hands.

Ray's gold chain was visible around his neck. His shoes were missing and Gates figured the blast knocked them off. Ray's face was blackened and the top layer of skin already was bubbling and peeling off. Gates thought the face, coated with blood, look grotesque.

The body was "red hot" to Gates. The heat burned his hands and it would take days for the skin to grow back. David Newcomb rushed out of the spa and knew the body wasn't his father when he saw the necklace.

Gates put his ear to the hot chest then to the mouth listening for breathing. He only heard a gurgling sound, a death rattle. The man didn't say any words.[2]

Gates saw a man approach with a sports coat over his arm with what appeared to be a walkie-talkie in his hand similar to what police officers carried. The man with the walkie-talkie offered no assistance, which Gates thought was odd. The flames grew hotter and Gates turned to ask for help to move the victim farther away, but the man with the walkie-talkie had vanished. Other people standing nearby helped move Ray.

Father Foster also rushed outside and knew the man lying on the parking lot was dead. The priest said a blessing. He then looked around the parking lot. The windows on his new Oldsmobile were shattered, the tires flat, the engine damaged beyond repair. Foster's car was a total loss.

Someone with a walkie-talkie would become part of the police investigation in the bombing.

---

2 Later FBI agents asked Gates to retract a news report that Ray was dead when pulled from the car, wanting the killers to believe Ray passed along valuable information before dying. Then an agent told Gates that after retracting the report, if he saw wires hanging from his car he should call the FBI. Remembering what Ray looked like lying on the pavement, Gates never told reporters the version the FBI wanted him to.

The next day attorney Robert Matthews told authorities he was driving in the area of Green River Road shortly before 1 p.m. listening to Channel 2 on the citizens band radio when he heard two male subjects talking back and forth. From the strength of the signal, Matthews knew the men had to be close. One male voice said "It's the third car in the parking place." The other man responded "Let's wrap it up and get out of here."

Ryan's car was in that third parking space.

Cops knew they had at least two people involved in the killing and that such an elaborate murder plot required more conspirators to pull off – lookouts, guys in cars ready to block off vehicles that may chase the actual bombers and someone to trail Ray for several days before the hit.

Investigators soon had hundreds of leads, but trying to find a cohesive pattern was like assembling a jigsaw puzzle of a thousand pieces mixed with pieces from another puzzle.

Few people gawking at the bombing site knew the man lying on the asphalt parking lot was Raymond John Ryan. He called Evansville home for nearly 40 years but hardly anyone in town had heard of him because he usually was gallivanting around the world.

They didn't know that he often won and lost more money in a day at casinos in America, Europe and the Far East than they would make in a lifetime or that his assortment of acquaintances included gangsters Frank Costello and Frank Erickson, and Hollywood stars like Clark Gable, Bill Holden, Dean Martin, Frank Sinatra, Phil Harris, Bruce Cabot, Jimmy Stewart, Bing Crosby and Bob Hope.

And what Ray had become – a multi-millionaire oilman, the highest of the world's high-stakes gamblers, a developer of Palm Springs, California and the man behind the Mount Kenya Safari Club in Africa – all started in Evansville.

Chapter 4

BAGBEY GETS A CALL

The detective office in the downtown Civic Center suddenly had turned quiet.

The large open room reeked of government-cheap metal desks and bland walls where the only color was gray water trails after inmates in the jail on the second floor clogged up and flushed the toilets in a temper tantrum, causing drains to overflow and the sewage to leak down the walls below.

At a desk, Steve Bagbey cranked a blank supplemental burglary report into the old Olivetti typewriter. A few minutes earlier, detectives heard over the radio scanner about an explosion on the city's East Side and took off, most thinking an auto parts store had blown up or a car caught fire and the gas tank ignited. A sergeant stayed in the office to man phones.

Steve wasn't asked to go along and didn't think that unusual. He was one of several patrolmen assigned to the detective office three years earlier to help combat a rash of burglaries and thefts.

He turned his attention to the burglary report he had to write. It was painful to watch Steve type, banging away with two fingers, hunting and pecking. Reports took a long time but he stuck with it.

Months ago his partners Don Erk and Ronnie Clark had popped off several keys on the typewriter and switched them. They watched as Steve typed a report, getting confused then frustrated as "f" appeared as "d" or "b" as "v." "Damn, I must be losing my mind," Steve said out loud. Erk, Clark and other veteran detectives roared with laughter at putting one over on "Bags."

Most cops liked Steve. He was far from being the smartest cop on the force, but he was a plugger, a nose-to-the-grindstone type who cleared his share of cases. If he was after a hard-ass criminal and the timing was right, he'd arrest them on Christmas Eve just to spoil their holidays, even if he had to work on his day off and not charge the city overtime.

Evansville was the only home Steve had known. His family, a mixture of Irish and German Catholics, originally lived on the city's West Side. His grandfather, Frank Riger, was a crane operator at Bucyrus-Erie who listened to Notre Dame's football games on the radio, fingering his rosary and crying for joy when Notre Dame scored.

The Bagbey family moved in 1956 to the city's southeast side where Steve, five years younger than Rae Jean Ryan, went to the same Catholic schools she had attended.

Steve had been a C and D student at Memorial High School. He did well enough in government, history, literature and religion classes to earn a diploma. The priests and lay teachers nurtured him through his family issues – an alcoholic father, a mother with health problems – and taught him to think, to reason and to communicate.

In November 1972, he joined the police department and now was taking classes at Indiana State University-Evansville (later to become University of Southern Indiana). His first semester grade-point average was 0.92, but he was starting to do better in school.

Steve was 29 years old, a couple inches shorter than six feet with dark hair starting to recede. He exercised to maintain a 175-pound frame with a 48-inch chest, and 36-inch waist. He had played football in high school until he blew out a knee but would keep involved in sports as a grade school football coach and as a high school and university referee.

He listened to the police radio chatter as he typed the report. The phones were ringing. The sergeant yelled to Steve that Lt. Gene Martin was on the phone.

"Bags, I need you here," Martin said when Steve answered.

"Where's here?" asked Steve.

"The Olympia Health Spa," Martin replied

"Whatcha you got?" asked Steve.

"Get your ass here," was Martin's curt answer.

Martin wasn't a guy for chit-chat or to be ignored. He wasn't big, but was in great shape from working out with weights. He was a professional wrestler on the side, wrestling across the country as Farmer Martin or the Masked Marvel and he owned an interest in the mid-South wrestling organization. When Martin spoke, cops listened. Steve listened and moved, and the events on Bellemeade Avenue would follow him the rest of his life.

Despite its impact, the car bombing wouldn't be the biggest news in Evansville over the next few months. Less than two months later on a Tuesday in December, a chartered National Jet Service DC 3 crashed seconds after taking off from the Evansville airport, killing 29 people including 14 players on the University of Evansville basketball team. Then in January, residents were shoveling out from 7.8 inches of snow – a record for a day. The city was paralyzed for days.

The university, the city and relatives of the victims grieved for the plane crash victims, a memorial was built and another team put together. The snow melted.

But, Ray's murder would rivet the city's attention for years as the investigation dragged on. People always remembered where they were when Raymond John Ryan was killed.

The police department had no files on Ray. Some cops knew that he was a wealthy oilman; others remembered movie stars coming to town to visit the Ryans.

A local FBI agent kept a loose track on Ray's whereabouts because of his trouble with the IRS and the Justice Department, but where Ray was on any given day wasn't high on the priority list – at least for the FBI.

Chapter 5

HELTER-SKELTER

The spa area was overrun with firefighters, police, FBI and U.S. Treasury Department's Bureau of Alcohol, Tobacco and Firearms (ATF) agents, state police and sheriff deputies by the time Steve arrived.

News traveled fast. Hundreds of residents descended on the area, wandering around, jostling each other on sidewalks for a better look at the destruction.

They watched as police officers dashed off to surrounding apartments and stores to interview people and collect nearby pay phone telephone numbers in hopes the killers might have used one. Cops went to car rental agencies to find out who recently rented vehicles, to hotels for lists of recent guests and to interview residents in the Ryans' neighborhood.

Arriving detectives were irate at what they saw – people picking up pieces that probably came from Ryan's car, pointing out where they found them, putting the items into car trunks as souvenirs. Even rescue workers and firefighters took some pieces.

Evansville Mayor Russell Lloyd and several city councilmen showed up and Police Chief David Jackson took them through the parking lot. A veteran patrol sergeant guided friends around the parking lot, snatching up pieces of twisted metal for them to hold.

Detectives knew the importance of preserving a crime scene, and wondered if anyone would tell the mayor and councilmen to remove their shoes to be tested for evidence. No one did. *This is a helluva way to begin an investigation,* one cop thought.

Barry Hart, a 31-year-old patrolmen also assigned to the department's detective unit, was shocked by the total destruction of the Mark

V. Debris was everywhere, part of the hood still hung on a power line, but only one person dead. He couldn't believe more people hadn't been killed.

Everyone realized the car bombing would be a big deal with lots of publicity. Gangsters, movie stars, a wealthy oilman all made for attention-grabbing headlines. That also would lead to friction between the FBI and ATF, a headache for local cops just wanting to solve a murder.

ATF agents began processing the bomb scene and the officers with the city police's ID crime scene unit were told to take a back seat. Investigators laid out 19 grids over the spa parking lot and scrupulously collected hundreds of pieces of debris. Officers climbed the roofs of apartment buildings and stores, scoured grassy areas, parking lots, sidewalks and neighborhood streets.

All items recovered were painstakingly logged and placed into evidence bags. One piece of the car was found 377 feet northeast of the bomb site. The spa outdoor swimming pool was drained and pieces of the car found in the bottom.[3]

Hart put together a chart of cars parked in the spa lot and along the street, looking for anything unusual – cars and people normally not in the area.

When Steve got to the spa, he saw Robert "Bob" Zoss Sr., an up-and-coming attorney in his late 20s who had risen to chief deputy prosecutor less than a year ago. The odor of burnt cars still lingered in the air as they looked at the hectic scene, knowing the local cops had no experience dealing with a professional car bombing.

Most murders in the city were committed by people using nothing more sophisticated than guns, knives, fists or a handy heavy object. Both were sure no one in Evansville could rig a bomb to cause the destruction before them.

Steve remembered reading about the June 1976 car bombing death in Phoenix of Don Bolles, the Arizona Republic reporter who had spent years writing about organized crime and land and fraud scams.

---

3 It took two days before federal agents were finished with the crime scene and Ray's car could be towed away. ATF agents told the Evansville police crime scene unit to collect samples from the bomb crater to send to the ATF national laboratory. A city garage worker used a jackhammer to pound through four inches of asphalt then a crowbar to lift the entire bomb crater out in one piece weighing over 100 pounds. It was the first time the ATF lab ever received an intact bomb crater.

Evansville needed help, and Phoenix seemed a good place to start. Bob went into the spa, telephoned the Phoenix police and got the name of a contact person that he passed on to city police. It was a start, he felt.

George Barnett Sr., Ray's Evansville lawyer who was in his mid-50s, arrived, smoking a cigarette in a shaking hand while fingers on the other hand nervously jingled coins in his pocket. Barnett usually was a cool customer, but not that day. His normally flushed face from frequent after-work drinking sorties was a ghostly white. He had planned to ride to the spa with Ray, but decided not to at the last minute. Barnett stood there thinking he could have been in that Lincoln.

Barnett asked police to get back with him later and headed to the Ryan home to await the arrival of Raymond Larroca, Ray's Washington, D.C. attorney.

Several times during the day, police asked various persons why Ray was targeted. The answers were the same – revenge for his testimony in the 1964 extortion case against Marshall Caifano, a well-known Chicago gangster, and lesser-known hood Charles Delmonico, whose father was veteran New Jersey gangster Charles "The Blade" Tourine.

But no one knew for sure.

Steve joined in canvassing the area residences and businesses until Lt. Martin pulled him aside and told him to get to the Ryan house and check out the vehicles until the arrival of Detective Ray Hamner, the department's only bomb technician. Steve had enough training to know what an explosive device looked like. He checked Helen Ryan's blue Cadillac, but found nothing.

He didn't know what to expect when he entered the Ryan house wondering if it would be garish, a display of glittering diamonds and gold furnishings. But the large home was well kept with expensive but tasteful furniture. The family's love for Africa was obvious in a main room decorated in African motif with wildlife tapestries, rugs of animal skins and African paintings.

Steve found Barnett, Helen, a housekeeper, ATF and FBI agents and one or two Ryan associates in the house. The telephone rang frequently as Helen handled calls from Dean Martin, John Wayne, Jerry Lewis and others offering their condolences. Ray's old friend Bing Crosby had died four days earlier of a heart attack while playing golf in Spain and Crosby's widow called Helen with words of sympathy. The investigators were amazed that Ray, who they knew little about, lived in such a world.

Doyle Dressback, manager of Ray's Evansville area business operations for a year, told them he had talked to Ray at about 10 that morning before leaving to check out Ray's Lake Malone Inn in Kentucky. Dressback hurried back after Kenneth Newcomb had reached him by phone and said there "had been a terrible tragedy."

Newcomb had thought Dressback's response was unusual. "Is it over with?" Dressback asked. When Newcomb said he believed Ray was dead, Dressback wanted to know for sure.

Those closest to Ray had lived for years knowing that he might be killed.

Barnett wanted police to wait until Larroca arrived from Washington before asking questions and interviewing Helen because she was so upset. James Canter, the local AFT agent, had a problem with that as did Richard Eisgruber, an Evansville FBI agent, because the wife usually is one of the first persons suspected when a husband is murdered, but the agents agreed to wait.

Barry Hart showed up with Hamner to check the Ryan house and vehicles for bombs. Hart knew nothing about bombs, and thought it was special to go along. Then he wondered what he would do if Hamner actually found a bomb.

In the car on the way over, Hart told him "if you find a bomb I'll back off and if it goes off, I want you to know I'll be taking copious notes." Hart wasn't sure if he was joking. Hamner checked the car and garage, but didn't find a bomb.

With interviews on hold, Lt. Martin pulled Steve aside. "Come with me. We got to go and see a guy who might know some information." They got into Martin's green Ford Torino and drove five minutes to the 1300 block of Lincoln Avenue.

Although on the police department only five years, Steve knew the house was the home of Hubert Cokes, the famed "Daddy Warbucks" or "The Giant."

Steve remembered veteran officers talking of going years ago to the Elks Club or a second floor downtown pool room to watch Cokes, Titanic Thompson, Rudolph "Minnesota Fats" Wanderone and other pool greats play.

Cokes was a throwback to the 1930s and 1940s when cities were wide-open for gambling. So was Evansville in those days. In the summer, passers-by could hear the clatter of the ticker tape machine, the calling of race winners, shuffling of cards or the roar from a dice table from the open windows of buildings. Cokes had hit gambling and pool halls across the nation and met a lot of underworld people. Martin figured if anyone in Evansville knew about Ray's troubles and those responsible for his death, it would be Cokes.

Cokes' wife met them at the door and Martin told her why they were there. "You boys go in. I'll make sure Hubert comes out. Hubert is not feeling well," she said. Steve sat down in the living room. On a wall was a drawing by the noted Evansville Press artist and cartoonist Larry Hill of Cokes as Daddy Warbucks.

A door opened and out walked a stooped figure wearing blue pajamas and a red silk smoking jacket and carrying a small French poodle. By 1977 time had passed Cokes by. He had the dead man's shuffle, slowly sliding along in his slippers in short steps.

Once a vigorous man, tanned, smartly dressed and usually with a cigar in his mouth, Cokes now was 79 years old and appeared several inches less than his usual six feet in height, a thin, frail man with white hair and silver-framed glasses.

Cokes and Martin called each other by their first names. Martin introduced Steve. "Yeah, I heard about him," said Cokes in a small, eerie voice that sounded like wind rushing from his body.

The voice sent shivers down Steve's spine. He reached his left hand to his waist to hold the handle of the .357 Magnum on his hip. *Christ, is this a mob guy or what,* Steve thought. Whatever he had heard about Cokes, he didn't expect this.

Martin asked Cokes to tell them about Ray and Marshall Caifano or Johnny Marshall, the other name Caifano was known by. "Well, Gene, old Johnny's a shooter, heh heh heh," Cokes said with a chuckle as he stroked the poodle wrapped in his arm. "He ain't no bomber; he's a shooter, Gene, heh heh heh."

Cokes then broke into a coughing fit. Steve hadn't been so nervous since he was a rookie cop. Cokes looked at Steve and continued speaking. "It will be a tough time solving it. Ray liked to cheat a lot of people. Ray didn't have a whole lot of friends, heh heh heh. You got to remember good old Johnny, old Johnny ain't a bomber. Johnny was a shooter, heh heh heh. If I think of anything else, I'll let you know."

Martin thanked Cokes and he and Steve stood to leave, watching as Cokes slowly shuffled out of the room. At the front door, Mrs. Cokes again reminded Martin and Steve that her husband "is not in the best of shape." She invited the officers to come back any time they wanted to talk to Cokes.

Martin and Steve got into the car and headed back to the bomb scene. That was the first and last time Steve saw Hubert Cokes. In four months Cokes would be dead.

Chapter 6

HUNDREDS OF TIPS

David Newcomb, the Olympia spa manager, was interviewed several times by different officers in the hours after the car bombing. It had been an unusual day with people coming in he hadn't seen before.

About 15 minutes after Ray arrived wearing Bermuda shorts with his necklace dangling around his neck, a man Newcomb had never seen entered the spa.

The man carried a black bag, was stocky, about six feet tall, dark complexioned with thin, stringy blond hair, a day-old beard and bushy sideburns. He wore black wing tip shoes, brown slacks, a gold Masonic ring and a cheap silver watchband. His eyes were serious; he didn't speak to anyone, but walked straight into the area where Ray was. After a few minutes, he left and wasn't seen again. Newcomb couldn't forget the guy because the man's movements were unusual.

A spa member also remembered seeing the visitor with an older stocky man and one of them saying "he's still here" as they left. Later, police sketches based on witnesses' descriptions turned out to be eerily similar to two suspects federal agents believed were part of a mob killing crew.

Another spa member, when he was languishing in the outdoor pool, noticed a figure on the other side of the lattice-work fence, a man with dark clothes and shoes like a police officer might wear. The fellow, whose face couldn't be seen through the fence, walked along the fence several times, sometimes turning and appearing to look toward the street.

When he was ready to go, Ray left the spa, got into the Lincoln, and started backing up the expensive car. As he was turning the wheels the bomb went off, apparently set off electronically by remote control, the mob's weapon of choice in those years.

It was a surgical strike by professional hit men intent only on killing the specific target. They had waited before setting off the bomb until Ray had backed the Lincoln far enough to avoid harming anyone in the outdoor pool.

The dynamite had been placed under the right side of the Continental near the catalytic converter. The Evansville dealership's chief mechanic later told police there were only a few places to place a bomb under the well-constructed chassis. Cops reenacted the placement of a bomb with another car and found it took only a few seconds.

Among hundreds of tips the police received, a woman said she saw a late model, yellow Chrysler Cordova with Pennsylvania plates at the spa shortly before noon with a dark, Italian-looking man wearing a grey business suit inside, looking like he had something in his hands.

Another woman saw a late model, dark blue Lincoln or Cadillac with Kentucky license plates parked in front of the spa. A white man, about six feet tall with a husky build and dark hair walked hurriedly from the parking lot and got into the car.

Other residents saw an older brown Lincoln driven by a white man traveling between the spa fence and the apartments shortly after the bombing, and a white Lincoln Continental with Illinois plates near the spa prior to the bombing.

Other witnesses saw a white male in his late 40s, over six feet tall, 180 pounds, with salt and pepper hair and wearing a gray suit near Ray's vehicle, a white husky male with dark hair and sunglasses wearing an expensive green three-piece suit walking away from the bomb scene while other people were rushing to it, and two well-dressed men near Ryan's body just after the bombing. They were whispering and one wrote something down on a piece of paper then walked away.

Those were some of the more pertinent, yet odd, tidbits passed on to the cops.

And there were more. Dozens of residents called police about other suspicious people in the city – a rough-looking man driving a Ford Thunderbird with Delaware license plates in several night spots the night before tipping waitresses with $50 and $100 bills, a man at the city's downtown hotel saying "something big was going down Tuesday" and a man looking like Elvis Presley driving a black with white top Cadillac bearing Texas plates.

Ryan's neighbors also had seen strangers around his Lombard Avenue home in recent months. One neighbor saw a man 40 to 50 years of age with a stocky build and gray felt hat parked outside her home during the day and another one saw a blond woman with a pony tail get out of a car and take photographs of the Ryan home.

An attorney who lived on Lombard told police that he approached a parked vehicle with two men inside while walking his dog. The men noticed him and quickly drove away. The neighbors thought the people they'd seen might have been Ray's customary bodyguards or federal agents keeping watch over the home and never called the police.

If they had, Ray Ryan might have avoided being killed.

Chapter 7

RAY'S FINAL HOUR

Raymond Larroca arrived late Tuesday evening and joined Barnett, Dressback and local police and federal agents in the basement of the Ryan home. The get-together was subdued and serious.

Dressback also said Charley O'Curran was flying in. O'Curran, nine years younger than Ray, had been one of Ray's closest friends since they first met a quarter century earlier in Palm Springs. O'Curran was a choreographer and director for Hollywood movies since 1943 and worked on several Elvis Presley movies, but his Hollywood career lagged after that.

He hung around Ray for years with Ray footing the bill wherever they were. Dressback liked it when O'Curran showed up because Ray constantly wanted someone to play poker, gin rummy, backgammon or Spite and Malice to keep his mind active.

Dressback devoted most of his time and energy to running Ray's local operation, with little left over for cards and games but when O'Curran arrived, he would take over keeping Ray amused and busy. Dressback always was amazed at Ray's mind, noting that after a few rounds of gin rummy, Ray would rattle off most of the cards Dressback had in his hand. Dressback wondered how he did it.

Dressback briefly filled in the investigators on Ray's background – born in Watertown, Wisconsin on January 9, 1904, married Helen Mary Kelley years ago, only child Rae Jean. Ray rarely went out socially when in Evansville except to the Petroleum Club or to the Knob Hill Tavern in nearby Newburgh for fiddlers. Since returning to Evansville, Ray had made trips to Chicago, Nashville, his inn at Lake Malone and to Lexington, Kentucky for an art show he sponsored for Glenn Robertson.

Ray, Barnett, O'Curran, Robertson and Dressback went on the Lexington trip where Ray rented the Bluegrass Suite at the Hyatt and constantly had a card game going on. The trip left Dressback with lasting memories of good times. They played Spite and Malice, cutting up and having fun. O'Curran was a lousy card player and Barnett and O'Curran planned to team up against Ray and throw the game to O'Curran. Dressback tipped Ray off about the plan.

"Ray had the best time with that," Dressback said. "They would holler and scream and cuss at each other. Ray got to losing and would fall under the table and mess the cards up. Ray loved it. The game went on and on until O'Curran and Barnett finally threw up their hands. Ray was a joy to be around. Damn, I wish he had been able to stay around a little longer."

A few days before the bombing, Dressback saw that Ray seemed troubled, but didn't know if it was from the legal wrangling over the tax case or the danger of being killed by the mob. No matter what Ray did each day, the fear that his life was on the line constantly nagged at him, lurked in the back of his mind. Ray never could put the thought aside. Dressback remembered Ray once casually remarking "when you stop running, they stop chasing." But Dressback wondered if that only meant the mob knew where to find Ray.

The 47-year old Larroca glibly navigated investigators through Ray's myriad dealings in oil, business developments overseas and in Palm Springs and elsewhere. About a month earlier, Larroca met in Chicago with Ray, O'Curran, Frank Hayden (the manager of Ray's West Coast developments) and a tax attorney to go over the tax case.

Larroca rattled off to Steve the names involved in the 1964 trial in California where Ray testified against hoodlums trying to extort money from him – Caifano, Delmonico, Felix "Milwaukee Phil" Alderisio, Allen Smiley and Nicholas Andrea "Nick the Greek" Dandolos. Larroca said Sam Giancana, a veteran mobster who eventually became the Chicago mob boss, and Johnny Rosselli, who had been the Chicago mob's representative on the West Coast and Hollywood, had urged Ray not to testify. After the trial, Ray hired as a bodyguard Joseph Calabrese, who Larroca and Barnett said had a checkered background.

Steve took notes, but he was unfamiliar with many of the names. He wrote a 19-page report of what he learned during the first three days of the investigation. Not everything made it into the report.

Left out was ATF agent Canter telling Larroca that the murder "will be solved. I guarantee it." Steve was still a young officer, but knew better than to promise that. He looked at FBI agent Eisgruber, who rolled his eyes. Larroca later told Steve that he knew no arrest would be made because it was a mob hit.

Also left out was Larroca saying that Ray was "a rounder" and "a player" when it came to women. Ray liked the ladies, Larroca said. He didn't go into any details. Steve left it at that.

Also left out of the report was Larroca saying that over the years Ray talked to people from the state department. Steve knew the "state department" meant the CIA, the Central Intelligence Agency. So Ray was a CIA contact? Steve could believe that. Ray traveled the world, talked to kings, ex-kings, government officials, aristocrats and business leaders at the highest level and top hoods across America. He could come up all sorts of interesting information in the process.

Hell, the CIA might have kicked in some dough to Ray in the process, Steve thought. But he didn't see how Ray's possible role as an informant fit into the investigation. Chicago was behind the car bombing. The CIA stuff went into a folder in Steve's head. Years later, he wished he had looked deeper into that aspect of Ray's life.

Larroca also confirmed that Ray obsessed over the IRS tax case but denied IRS and Justice Department allegations that Ray used Swiss bank accounts to launder his money – and perhaps the mob's money.

Larroca admitted Ray knew men like Erickson and Costello, but never had criminal dealings with organized crime members and always said he couldn't stand mobsters. The government's claims to the contrary weren't true, the attorney said.

That's why Helen and Larroca didn't trust the Feds. They would answer agents' question, but were more willing later to open up to Steve.

While the questioning was going on at the Ryan home, an autopsy was under way on the body lying on a metal table in a small room at the Ziemer Fountain Terrace Funeral Home a few miles away.

Barry Hart stopped by earlier to see at the body, which had been removed from the bomb scene before he arrived. With the bomb's destructive force, he expected the corpse to be ripped apart, but it was intact. There were a few blood spots, some singed areas of the face, a few apparent wounds to a leg and arm, but otherwise, Ray looked like someone who died in bed.

Patrolman Ed Biederwolf had a video tape recorder, two hours of tape, a 35-mm camera and rolls of color negative, color slide and black and white film to photograph the autopsy. County Coroner Dr. David Wilson and others from his office were there as Dr. Albert Venables conducted the autopsy. Autopsies by Venables usually didn't last long, but everyone knew this one would.

Biederwolf started video taping and taking photographs, surprised at the lack of damage to the body. There was superficial burning on the right cheek, forehead and nose. Brown-gray smoke deposits were over the neck, the right ear lobe partly destroyed, the hair on the top of the head singed, a deep laceration on the left arm and smaller cuts on the right thigh.

Venables made a V-shaped incision from near both shoulders to the sternum in the middle of the body. Another cut was made to the crotch, creating a Y-shaped incision through the skin and fatty tissue. He cut into the abdominal cavity and started removing the vital organs, kidneys, gall bladder, stomach, intestines and liver. Each organ was inspected, weighed, checked for ruptures, photographed and tissue samples taken.

He next cut the ribs, removed the rib cage and the lungs and heart from the chest cavity. Six ribs on the right side were fractured. There was extensive destruction of the lung tissue and tearing of the intercostals arteries from the aorta. The throat was opened but there was little indication of smoke inhalation. Little blood was found in the chest cavity. The blast had crushed Ray's lungs. He died quickly.

Venables cut the scalp around the head and peeled the skin over the face. A vibrating bone saw cut around the skull, the skull cap popped open and the brain was removed. There was no damage to the brain. The autopsy took several hours with pauses.

The men ordered pizza and ate during a break. Because the room was small, they placed the large pizza box on Ray's body while they ate. It wasn't that the officers were uncaring. They cared about every victim of a crime. There was no other space available without leaving the room and no one wanted to miss anything.

When the autopsy was over, Venables scooped up the organs and placed them in any opening of the body not full. The last organ out was the first back in wherever it fit. The men left and the body was turned over to funeral home employees to sew up and prepare for viewing.

Ray Ryan's day was done.

Chapter 8

MURDER BECOMES PERSONAL

The funeral on Thursday, October 20, 1977 was a brief private affair. About 30 family members and friends attended.

Two uniformed city policemen stood by the entrance with undercover police and FBI agents lingering in the background. One agent posed as a window washer at a gas station across the street taking pictures of people at the scene. A Catholic priest officiated at the 20-minute funeral Mass.

Ernie Dunlevie, Ray's developer partner in Palm Springs, drove Bill Holden to the services. Holden had flown in from Chicago where he was filming "The Omen: Part II." He had talked to Ray the previous week by phone and they had planned a hunting trip that was to take place a few days after Ray's murder.

Martin and Steve drove Holden from the funeral. The next day's newspaper had a photograph of Martin with Holden, leaving one ATF agent angry that local cops got their picture taken with the movie star instead of him. Martin chuckled at that.

The 61-year-old Holden said he first met Ray in 1939 in New York when they were introduced by Lex Thompson, owner of a professional football team, and they met again during World War II in Palm Springs. They had oil ventures together in 1953 with Holden putting up 25 percent, Ray 50 percent and other investors the remaining 25 percent, drilling 13 dry holes. Holden gave up the oil business.

Holden remembered telling Ray, who once had tried to buy RKO Pictures, "I will get out of the oil business if you stop making motion pictures." Holden also told of meeting Ray in Italy in 1958, going to Kenya on safari and buying a hotel they turned into the Mount Kenya Safari Club.

"Ray loved to bet on anything," Holden said. During a visit to Evansville, Holden said he and Ray watched two doves sitting on a tree limb at Ray's house and bet which one would fly away first. Holden said Ray caused him to look in another direction for a second then Ray tossed a stone near his dove causing the bird to flutter and scaring Ray's bird into flying off. Ray always looked for an edge in everything, Holden said with a smile.

Later that day, Steve interviewed the 64-year-old O'Curran at the Ryan house. O'Curran first met Ray around 1950 at the El Mirador Hotel in Palm Springs and thereafter stayed in close touch. Steve learned O'Curran had brushed shoulders with gangsters – Sam Giancana once stayed at his Beverly Hills home – and O'Curran knew John Rosselli and a mobster known as Jimmy "Blue Eyes." Steve dutifully took notes, unaware that Jimmy "Blue Eyes" was Jimmy Alo, a close associate of Meyer Lansky. Steve knew nothing about Rosselli, but had heard of Giancana.

During the interview, Steve got a telephone call from Sgt. James Smith Lane at the police department telling Steve his father had suffered a massive stroke. James Otha Bagbey marked his fifty-sixth birthday in August, and he was in poor health. A few months before, Steve had to take his father to the Veterans Administration Hospital in Marion, Illinois.

Although Steve hadn't been close to his dad for years, he considered his father a bright man who once made good money but had lost his self esteem along the way. After Lane's call, Steve drove to the Marion hospital. His father tried, but couldn't speak when he saw his son. Steve kissed his dad for the first time in his life, unable to recall a time when his father ever held him or gave him a kiss or he had kissed his father. The old man lingered for two weeks before dying.

After the funeral, Steve returned to the Ryan home to continue his investigation. A sympathetic Helen quickly asked Steve "do you think you really should be doing this. Your dad just died." Steve knew he had to tackle the task at hand. "Your husband has been murdered.

I'm okay," he told Helen. She understood how Steve felt. She also had to go on with her life without Ray.

The impact of Ryan's murder on the community, the pressure to solve the killing and the loss of his father consumed Steve. He associated the death of his father with the death of Ray Ryan. As he continued on the case, the image of his father always came to him.

The Ryan case now is personal, and dammit, I want to solve it, Steve thought.

Chapter 9

AN ENIGMA

Steve Bagbey wasn't sure he'd end up liking Ray Ryan.

What he learned at the outset of the investigation into Ray's car-bombing didn't make Ray look too appealing although eventually Steve would tell friends "Ray Ryan was the most fascinating man I never met."

If Steve believed what the Feds claimed, Ray for years had hauled suitcases stuffed with $1 million or more to a Swiss bank then later, whenever he wanted cash for his personal free-wheeling ways or for his business deals, brought hundreds of thousands of dollars back again in suitcases, supposedly "loans" from the bank but actually laundered money – Ray's own and/or organized crime dough.

Ray had hung out with many of the nation's top mobsters. He once was the highest of America's high stakes gamblers, flittering across the world to gamble or on business deals often surrounded with beautiful young women when away from Helen.

Steve knew immediately that he did like Helen Ryan. He had caught only brief glimpses of her at the Ryan home in the early hours after the car bombing as she frequently was called to the phone to talk with friends offering condolences.

Helen was tall and thin, hair streaked with gray pulled back in a bun with strands dangling from both sides and nervously rubbing and clasping her hands and dabbing tears away with a tissue. She looked like a deer in headlights, but Steve was struck by her dazzlingly blue eyes.

When he and federal agents were able to interview Helen the day after the murder, she was more composed, her voice strong and in control. She impressed him as a strong-willed Irish lady handling one of the worst days in her life with dignity, strength and compassion.

Helen reported an unsettling telephone call from a friend two days after Ray's murder. Ingrid Marina Lange of Miami, the 36-year-old girlfriend of Rex "Sexy Rexy" Rand, a long time friend of Ray's, called and said she "had the information ten days too early and now it was two days too late" that Ray was going to be killed.

Ingrid was among wealthy friends in the Miami area that Helen and Ray socialized with in Florida and the Caribbean. The women, sometimes with husbands or boyfriends, traveled to Europe, jetsetters with lots of money and time to enjoy it. How a wealthy socialite knew days in advance that Ray was going to be killed would puzzle Steve and federal agents. AFT agents with the Miami office later interviewed Lange, who said she had met Ray through Rex Rand at the Palm Springs residence of Charles Farrell and that she and Rex had visited Ray in Evansville and at Lake Malone.

Ingrid said Beth Levitz, the wife of the board chairman of a Miami furniture company, told her in early October 1977 that Ray was dead. Ingrid called the Ryan home to express her sympathy. When Ray answered, she realized he was okay and didn't hint of any problems. They had a pleasant talk and she hung up.

In turn, Levitz told agents that Penelope Turtle, once a Bahamas resort manager, had told her Ray was dead. Turtle said she heard about it from someone who told her not to repeat it. She wouldn't tell Levitz who that person was but did tell AFT agents her source was Caroline Mary Harrison, a Londoner who had visited Turtle in Miami. Scotland Yard interviewed Harrison, who first met Ray about 1960 on a trip to Kenya. Harrison denied saying Ray was going to be killed, adding she thought Ray had been dead for years.

But the Miami angle intrigued investigators. Ingrid admitted meeting Charles Delmonico and that she lived in the same apartment complex as Charlie "The Blade" Tourine, Delmonico's father. Other suspects in the car bombing also had homes in the Miami area. Agents wondered if someone in the murder crew or Tourine had "let the cat out of the bag" prematurely about killing Ray but an FBI re-interview of the woman would produce no results.

Helen's information about Lange would be just another tantalizing clue but eventual dead end in the case.

After her talk with the cops, Helen thanked the investigators for their efforts, and Steve was struck by her sincerity. Usually family members are distraught, out of control emotionally, but Helen didn't let it show. When she talked about her husband, Steve felt she really loved the guy and that they were the best of friends who had grown closer the past 10 years after the Feds curtailed Ray's flamboyant lifestyle and flow of money.

It gnawed at Steve why Helen remained with Ray if he was a "player," a gadabout womanizer like Larroca said he was. Steve would learn her marriage brought great joy with the world at their fingertips as Ray's wealth grew, but often left her in tears over rumored flings her husband had with entertainers, stewardesses and other women during his frequent absences from her.

Helen couldn't believe Ray was such a Lothario, and seemed to believe that being surrounded by women was the image Ray needed to portray in public, or the women were shills used to lure wealthy guys into poker and gin rummy games.

Ray and Helen had a strange, lifetime love affair that maybe only they understood. Yet, Steve came to appreciate what she had been through in life, what she had become and considered her a "lady with a capital L."

Both Ray and Helen had hardscrabble beginnings – Helen more so. Born Helen Mary Kelley on March 25, 1909 in Pontiac, Illinois, her father, Mathew, was a shoemaker. Her mother, Anna, was 35 years old when Helen was born and Mathew was 34.

Mathew left home a few years later leaving his wife and four children struggling to survive. Anna moved the family to Milwaukee to find menial jobs and was forced to send Helen to work in a convent for a while to ensure she was well fed and under the watchful eyes of Catholic nuns and priests. Ray grew up in Watertown, Wisconsin in a working class family with several children.

In Milwaukee in the mid-1920s, Helen went out one evening with teenaged friends to a movie. It had been raining and when her group came out of the cinema they huddled under an awning with another group of friends that included Ray Ryan.

The first thing Helen noted as raindrops splattered around them was that Ray, who was five years older, always seemed happy, smiling, kidding around – a state of being. What Ray saw in Helen was a beautiful long-legged woman with clear skin, high cheekbones, dark hair and sparkling blue eyes, Irish through and through, an infectious smile warming anyone around her. While some people might not like Ray, everyone adored Helen.

They enjoyed each other's company and loved to laugh, but they were different in other ways throughout their married life. Ray gallivanted around cities for poker games and horse racing tracks while Helen was a homebody, eager to get back home no matter where she was.

Steve learned that while Ray would toss thousands of dollars into poker pots or on dice tables, Helen, who grew up in a family as poor as church mice, was practical, wanting to save money, waste not want not. Even after they were multi-millionaires, she collected old brooms, dishes, and household items stored in Evansville to furnish a cabin in Kentucky rather than buy new ones they easily could afford.

She dutifully gave to local churches and would spend large sums of cash at times but only after carefully reasoning that the item was worthwhile and useful. She was kind to friends as was Ray. He liked to buy expensive, sometimes hard-to-find, gifts for acquaintances and willingly handed out money for people in need.

Steve felt what you saw was what you got with Helen, but Ray was an enigma, living life on his terms. His world ranged from the down-and-dirty times of gamblers and oilmen of the 1930s and 1940s to the glitter of Palm Springs, Hollywood and Las Vegas of the 1950s and 1960s.

He was a product of a unique period, the growing up of America, when cars and planes replaced the horse and buggy, a time when the rule was that there were no rules, when someone who lived fast, played hard, had brains, daring, a willingness to take chances and a dream could get rich.

He collected an assortment of friends in his travels – important businessmen, scions of wealthy families, owners of sports teams, movie stars, famed boxers and managers, notorious mobsters and run-of-the-mill workers.

But Ray compartmentalized the people he met in life in business and personal dealings into dozens of boxes. He navigated the compartments with ease, never feeling tainted by those he met no matter how unsavory they might be.

Ray could don a different personality – if necessary – to deal with the people in whichever box he was in; a no-bullshit face for tough business negotiations, a mind-consuming focus when gambling, or a jovial, humorous, snappy-thinking chatterbox at dinners and galas.

The other women he was with when Helen was elsewhere were just more of his life's compartments to him. "Helen is my wife. The rest is play time," he once told friends. When Ray came home to Helen, she was there waiting as always.

"There's never been a man in my entire life I love more than him," Helen once told a friend. "The bird may fly away at times but Ray always knows where his nest is." She also knew Ray was bold, daring and fearless in business and life and Helen willed herself to endure it. "Ray isn't happy unless he's walking on the edge," she would say. "If he was younger, he'd be lining up to walk on the moon."

Steve concluded Helen knew what she got into with Ray and always remained devoted to him, warts and all.

After the funeral, Ray's body was cremated. Helen later took the ashes to Africa to spread over the Safari Club so her husband could forever be a part of the land he loved.

The IRS soon settled the tax case for $2.55 million. Ray's estate was valued at $5.5 million in Indiana. Ray personally owned no property. All holdings were through Ryan Oil, which had assets valued at $12 million by an Indiana probate court. Ray had five life insurance policies totaling $535,000 with Helen as the beneficiary. The court ruled Helen was entitled to more than $1 million, Rae Jean nearly $1 million and $180,000 among friends and a charity. Outstanding debts were nearly $300,000 to Larroca's law firm, $90,000 to Barnett, and about $300,000 in administrative fees and travel expenses.

Five months after Ray was killed, city police investigators had spent thousands of hours on the case with no arrest eminent, and Capt. Harold Chaffin decided to assign only one officer on the case. At the recommendations of Sgt. Frank Gulledge and Lt. Martin, Steve became the chief investigator even though there were more veteran cops on the force with years handling vicious crimes.

Martin considered Steve his protégé and knew he was an honest cop, a square guy, an investigator who didn't don blinders and zero in on one suspect and ignore other possibilities. Martin knew the case needed a bulldog and that was Steve Bagbey.

The witness report of an older man with gray hair apparently reading a newspaper in a car parked on the street behind Ray's Lincoln at the bombing scene would stay with Steve for years. Was that man Marshall Caifano, whose intense hatred of Ray demanded that he be around as the murderers set about their work?

Chicago FBI informants had seen Caifano the evening before the bombing at a Melrose Park restaurant with hoods and a day or two after the bombing at Valentino's Restaurant in Chicago with mob figures Joseph Aiuppa, Joseph "Joey the Clown" Lombardo and Charles "Chuckie" English. No informant saw Caifano in Chicago on October 18.

Months after the funeral, Ray's Lombard Avenue neighbor Charles Manion ran into Sommers T. Brown, his old classmate from Notre Dame and IRS attorney who had tracked Ray for years. When Manion and Brown met after the car bombing, Brown told him "hell, I knew everything about Ray. I'll tell you, Charley. If I could change places with Ray Ryan and live the life he lived and know I'm going to get blown up when I'm 73, I'd do it."

Now Steve wondered: *Why did Sommers Brown think that about Ray and who in the hell is this Chicago mobster named Caifano?*

Chapter 10

A BOUNCY THOROUGHBRED

Shortly after 1900, Daniel A. Ryan moved his family to a home at 513 North Montgomery Street in Watertown, Wisconsin, from the small farming community of Emmet located a few miles to the north.

In 1892, the then 28-year-old Daniel married Theresa Gondresick, who had just turned 23. Despite their young ages, both were very popular and a large group of friends showed up for the wedding. Daniel's parents originally were from the Kilkenney area of Ireland. Their families came to America, lived in the East for a while before Daniel's parents arrived in Emmet around 1850 to farm. Born in 1864 near the end of the Civil War, Daniel was the couple's fifth and last child. He had the gift of Irish gab that drew people to him.

Theresa's parents were of German and Polish stock and had lived around Emmet for several years. She had married when she was 18 to a man named Ziebell and had a child named Arthur before her husband died. Arthur was four when his mother remarried.

Daniel and Theresa soon were producing children of their own at about two year intervals. A son born in early 1894 died a month later, but the children who followed lived long lives. George Joseph was born in August 1895, James Eugene (more often referred to as Eugene) in July 1897, Florence Mary in June 1899, and Herbert Jerome in August 1901.

Around that time Daniel moved his family to Watertown because the community was starting to revive. Located halfway along the 200-mile stretch from Milwaukee to the east and the state capital of

Madison to the west, Watertown originally was settled mainly by Irish hunters and trappers and soon prospered with flour mills, sawmills, fertile land for crops and a steady supply of water from Rock River.

A plank road connected the city to Milwaukee shortly after Watertown was chartered as a city in 1853. Two years later waves of German, Bohemian, Welsh, and Irish immigrants came, the railroad arrived and a booming Watertown with 10,000 residents become the state's second largest city with each ethnic group having its own stores, churches and saloons. The Irish had established St. Bernard's Catholic Church in 1845 and the Bohemian/German residents started St. Henry's Catholic Church in 1853.

The nation's first kindergarten started in Watertown in 1856; the city was the first in the state to provide free textbooks to children. City fathers, viewing unlimited future growth, issued nearly $1 million in bonds to build more railroads to the city, but the 1857 nationwide depression soon hit. Cash-strapped bond holders sold the bonds for a fraction of their value and new bondholders demanded full payment and sued the city. The town's population dropped to 5,000.

To avoid raising taxes for bond payments while the issue was battled in courts, the elected mayor and seven aldermen met in secret at the start of each year, approved that year's tax levy then immediately resigned leaving management of the city to appointed officials with no authority to raise taxes, according to W. F. Jannke III in his book "Watertown: A History." This continued until 1889 when the state Supreme Court outlawed bonds not reduced to a settlement the town could live with. After that Watertown began to rebound. A trolley line opened between Watertown and Waukesha near Milwaukee. Automobiles appeared, streets were paved, cigar, shoe and cutlery manufacturing companies opened and motion picture theaters arrived.

Daniel and Theresa's last child was born on January 9, 1904. His name was Raymond John Ryan.

The local newspaper, the Watertown Daily Times, carried a notice of Ray's birth in a daily column of personal and business items: "A boy baby was born to Mr. and Mrs. Dan Ryan yesterday morning. Dan says he is a thoroughbred and a bouncer as well."

The family lived in a comfortable but packed two-story wood structure. Daniel was a dealer in sand and wood from land he owned outside of the city. Arthur, a teenager when Ray was born, was married a few years later and moved a block away. He and Daniel later started a concrete supply business for highway projects.

Ray was the darling of the blue collar family, noted for his wit, smile and ability to get along with – even manipulate – others. He learned early how to use charm to get what he wanted. His childhood days were centered around St. Bernard's Catholic Church. The Rev. Thomas Hennessey, a native of Limerick, Ireland, became St. Bernard's pastor in 1908, and expanded athletic, literary, dramatic, musical and ecclesiastical programs for the parish's young people. A graduate of the University of Notre Dame, he encouraged young men to go to Notre Dame to become priests.

Hennessey turned the church's little chapel into a basketball court. In 1916, James Eugene and Herbert Ryan played on the "Juniors" for boys of high school age while Ray, who was never a gifted athlete, played on the "Kids," a team composed of boys in the seventh and eighth grades. The prized game that year was St. Bernard's Kids team defeating a squad from the public Lincoln School.

Ray had a flair for theatrics that meshed with his lively imagination and desire to be liked. In 1917 at age 13, he had a leading role as Jeremiah in the two-act comedy "A Grain of Salt" during the St. Thomas Day program. He also was an avid reader, and developed a life-long love affair with Africa after reading Edgar Rice Burroughs' books about Tarzan. Years and millions of dollars later, he and actor William Holden would build the Mount Kenya Safari Club in Kenya. As a boy, Ray acquired the nickname Borno although no one is sure why. Borno was a character in another popular jungle book of the time and a state in the African nation of Nigeria. Whatever the reason, Ray was known as Borno in Watertown.

Ray was confirmed at St. Bernard's in June 1918[4] as the city and the nation were swept up in patriotic feelings during World War I. Watertown stopped teaching German at the high school and German

---

4 In 1918, Rev. Hennessey was assigned to St. Mary's church in Austin, Texas. Three years later, he became pastor of Holy Name parish in Henderson, Kentucky across the Ohio River from Evansville, Indiana. Hennessey died in Henderson in 1932. Ten miles away and 45 years later Ray would die in Evansville.

services were dropped at most of the churches. Streets with German names were changed and sauerkraut became "liberty cabbage."

Ray later told friends he signed up with the Wisconsin National Guard when 15 years old although there was no indication his patriotic spirit went any further. His brother George, a telephone lineman, did enter the Army and Herbert the U.S. Navy during the war.

Chapter 11

GAMBLE ON ANYTHING

Ray enrolled in the public Watertown High School, and immediately set out to win friends. He was elected vice president of the freshman class. A fellow student remembered Ray as very handsome and having a way with teachers, charming his way though classes without bothering to study.

He impressed friends with his mathematical ability to total a list of numbers easily in his head. He seemed to have a photographic mind, which is good for a gambler. He could count cards and figure the odds of how cards might fall, a talent that helped make him one of the world's great poker and gin rummy players. Some called him the best gambler ever – a guy who could remember every card and was unafraid to bet big. Yet, some of his gambling victims became convinced Ray's talents included cheating.

When he was a high school sophomore an influenza pandemic swept across America and Ray became deathly ill. He was in agony for weeks, bedridden, losing weight and delirious at times with coughing spells that racked his body. He was sure he was going to die and death frightened him.

He prayed to God, promising that if he lived he would become a Roman Catholic priest. He recovered and always tried to laugh off the promise to God. But his friends knew a life of celibacy as a priest never was in Ray's makeup.

His illness caused him to miss months of school and he returned as a junior in the 1921-22 school year. He was a member of the school's Forum Debating Society that held debates on current topics and mock trials that drew crowds of students, but there is no record of Ray graduating from high school.

He was nearly full height, his closely-cropped hair swept back from his forehead making his Roman nose more prominent. Always well-dressed, he was a good-looking lad who was a favorite with girls but he also discovered more tantalizing things than school as Prohibition began on January 16, 1920, bringing a drastic change to the nation and Watertown.

The city's Hartig Brewery switched from making beer to ice cream yet Watertown had more than its share of bootlegging. Watertown historian Jannke noted an "enterprising team of brothers named Ryan opened an illegal brewery on North Montgomery Street, which lasted for a good many years in the city since the brewery's best customer, according to legend, was the chief of police."

The only Ryans living on North Montgomery Street in 1920 were Daniel's family and the "enterprising" Ryan brothers probably were James Eugene, who was 20, and Herbert, then 18, both of whom went on to operate Watertown taverns for years – Herbert the Shady Nook Tavern on West Division Street, and James Eugene operated Ryan's Tavern on Main Street

The enterprising 16-year-old Ray probably enjoyed any boozy atmosphere where tables could be set aside as a personal training ground for poker, dice and other gambling games. He worked as a shoeshine boy and as a newsboy selling the local newspaper, but found Watertown stifling and pined for the day he could leave, boasting to friends that someday he would be a millionaire.

He was hired as a hotel bellboy, and on the side set up evening poker games for the traveling salesmen. Bitten by the gambling bug, Ray probably sat in on some games.

Gambling flourished in Watertown during the Roaring Twenties and Prohibition. Poker games were everywhere, and punch boards and slot machines brought in by outside racketeers were fixtures in stores, taverns, clubs and lunch rooms.

Watertown native Clemens Stoll said gambling "was just Ray's nature. He'd gamble on anything," including which direction a fly would take off from a pile of horse dung on the street or which bird would fly away first from a tree limb. It was something for the kids to do.

But none of Ray's friends realized there would be a day when he would bet tens of thousands of dollars on football games, play gin rummy for $10 a point, risk $10,000 seeing who could spit closer to a crack in a sidewalk or sit down across the table from Texas billionaire oilman H. L. Hunt, legendary gambler Nicholas Andrea "Nick the Greek" Dandolos, and famed poker champion Johnny Moss.

Ray claimed he attended the University of Notre Dame in the 1920s although Notre Dame archivists found no documentation of him enrolling there. He probably did, only briefly. Decades later, newspapers said Ray gambled away his school money on the train to the university and had to work as a dishwasher to earn enough cash to last one semester, then worked as a waiter and other odd jobs in Detroit and elsewhere before returning home.

His next job was selling Day's Work chewing tobacco and Prince Albert tobacco in a can in Milwaukee where he became known as "cheap tobacco Ryan." He hung out at poker tables in clubs and taverns in Milwaukee and Watertown, honing his skills playing in 50-cent limit poker games.

Watertown residents remembered Ray once was on a losing streak in a poker game and kept tossing IOUs into the pot to cover losing bets, firmly believing his bad luck wouldn't last. By the end of the night, he had won back his losses and much of the other players' money. Another recalled Ray's steely-eyed, expressionless face when playing cards. "Nothing could distract his game. He was in it to win and that was his total focus."

Ray spent a lot of time in Milwaukee and returned often to Watertown, sometimes flat broke and stopping at James Eugene's tavern to borrow money. "The next time Ray would come back with a wad of money," a friend remembered.

Ray was a ballsy kid in the 1920s, ready to take a stab at any idea that might produce money. One friend said Ray always had big dreams "like the time the Mexican ambassador checked into a Milwaukee hotel. Ray was hardly more than a kid, but he walked over to the hotel and tried to talk the ambassador into arranging some mining leases for him – silver I think it was."

But it always would be oil that dominated Ray's heart, mind and dreams.

As one of Ray's friends later would tell a Chicago Sun-Times reporter about Ray: "It isn't rightly fair to call him a gambler. It takes a lot of guts and vision to stake everything you've got going down into the ground for oil. I guess a man who can do that is likely to be a little restless and reckless about everything else too."

Chapter 12

STICK WITH ME, HELEN

It was in Milwaukee a year or so after 1925 that Ray met Helen Mary Kelley. Worldly by Helen's standards, Ray was in his early 20s and pursued the teenaged Helen with determination. She was beautiful and Ray could be clever and overpowering when he wanted to be.

He told Helen of his dream to become rich. "Stick with me and we'll have more money than we can count some day," he said to her. That sounded good to Helen whose family never had money, but she wasn't ready to free-fall into his arms and marriage.

She was the second oldest of the four Kelley children. William was four years older, Elinor three years younger and Bernard Francis nearly six years younger. Her mother, Anna, spent a lifetime at backbreaking jobs to help her family survive. Anna had misgivings about Ray and didn't like Helen seeing him.

The mother was convinced Ray was all bluster, a guy with his head in the clouds, a gambler, a smooth talker and not a good match for her daughter. The thought of the two getting married brought Anna to tears.

Helen's fondness for Ray would take time to develop over a couple of years. Some thought there was a "lover's spat" that caused Ray to leave Milwaukee looking for adventure and to make enough money to prove he was worthy of her. Ray had just celebrated his 25th birthday in early January 1929 and his decision to leave Watertown and Milwaukee may have been more for the adventure angle. But before he left, Ray told Helen the next time he came back would be "for the last time. If you don't marry me, you won't hear from me again."

The next few months epitomized Ray's life – stepping off into the darkness of the unknown and never looking back, confident of his ability to survive and have fun in the process.

Ray and his tobacco-selling partner Frank McLaughlin set out south using money they had saved to get by. They eventually planned to meet up with some Milwaukee friends who were in the oil business in Texas, but first another journey in mind – a trip to Europe.

They ended up around St. Louis in the waning days of January. Ray met an old bum and gave him some coins and the bum in return gave Ray a 3-by-5 inch calendar/diary for 1929 that Ray immediately turned into a journal. He wrote his name on the inside cover, listed his hometown as Watertown, his height at 5-11, weight at 165 and his home telephone number of 133W.

Ray jotted down brief notes each day as the journal's space allowed. He took a sightseeing trip around the city, took in a dime-a-dance club in the afternoon, followed by a visit to a French nightclub on January 30, ending up "drunk as usual." The next three days he had his passport picture taken, bought a phonograph, received a letter from Helen and got a job on a tramp steamer headed for Italy. Two days later he started living on the boat.

Poor people called beachcombers came on board and begged for food. He had a toothache, a problem that plagued him frequently that year and he saw the Mardi Gras parade in St. Louis, which he wrote was "well worth seeing." On February 9, the ship sailed for Galveston. And Frank got seasick by the time the boat reached Louisiana. Two days later Ray wrote the boat "hit Galveston TX this morning, town wide open, visited all shady places." He went to a street dance, then a masquerade ball and got drunk on corn whiskey.

Even at that young age, Ray was an impetuous, headstrong skirt-chaser looking to gamble and, often unintentionally, getting into trouble. In Galveston, he broke two Greeks playing poker, using some of winnings to pay off a note on earlier gambling losses.

The next day he had his fortune told while carousing around the city and also had "a narrow escape. Nigger pulled a razor on me." He cooled off the next few days, staying on board the ship, taking a bucket bath, washing his clothes, playing craps and blackjack and listening to records on his phonograph. He shined brass, polished lamps, scoured the mess room and counted linens.

In late February, the ship set sail for Houston and Galveston and Ray was seasick for the first time and had a fight with the cook. Ray and Frank also listened on the radio to Jack Sharkey defeating Young Stribling in a heavyweight bout in Miami. Sharkey was an up-and-coming boxer vying for the title vacated six months earlier by Gene Tunney, one of Ray's favorite fighters.

On March 1, the tramp steamer Quisconk sailed to Europe.

At the outset, Ray was seasick and the steward caught him sleeping in one of the ship's rooms, but after a few days at sea he took over cleaning the two mess halls for the sailors and passengers. "In the afternoons, there was nothing else to do but lie out on the deck of the ship, soak up the sun and think," Ray wrote in his journal.

Think he did, about how he and Gene Tunney were so alike. Only Ray's view of the world in those days was from the south end of a northbound horse.

He had read newspapers articles about Tunney, a millionaire from his boxing career, and heiress Mary Josephine "Polly" Lauder, the great-niece of Andrew Carnegie, traveling by luxury liner to Europe in 1928 to marry and live in splendor in a resort. Ray was captivated by the articles. He later said "I'll never forget. They went to Europe on a liner. I laid in the sun and said to myself, 'Tunney could go over first class and live in a resort and I had to wash dishes' – well, I made up my mind someday I was going to do the same thing as Tunney."

Ray enjoyed sea life early in the voyage, but soon the days became tiresome, just "water, water water." He had a spat with the steward, was caught fighting with a crew member and ended up scrubbing toilets as punishment.

The boat sailed past Gibraltar, and stopped off at Naples, where everyone went ashore and got drunk. The boat then sailed past the boot of Italy and into the Adriatic Sea where Ray got his first look at the beautiful Yugoslavia coastline – an area he thought was as lovely as the French Riviera. Three decades later, he would buy 70 miles along Yugoslavia's Adriatic seacoast planning to build resorts and bragging he was the only American who owned that much Yugoslavian real estate under the Communist regime of Tito.

After stops at Venice and Trieste, the ship docked at Fiume at the end of April where Ray got drunk and went around the "dirty parts of Fiume" looking for a little fun. He also went to a nearby resort where Tunney once had stayed and "drank and drank."

A few days later the tramp steamer headed back to the United States. The gleam had worn off of Europe for him and the three-week trip back home was the most miserable time of his life. Each day in his diary he simply wrote "monotonous days" and scribbled across one week he added "just like jail."

Ray was desperate to get back to America and Texas – and Helen.

Chapter 13

RAY RETURNS TO HELEN

Thank God, I'm back home raced through Ray's mind when the steamer finally arrived in Miami at the end of April. The excruciatingly boring boat trip through hell was finally over.

He couldn't stand another bucket bath on board. He jumped off the side of the boat and into the bay – glad to be back in American waters again – to get a refreshing cleansing he hadn't had in weeks.

But with an inflated idea of his swimming abilities, he nearly drowned in the bay until hauled back on board by mates. It wouldn't be the only time in his life that he would have to be saved from a watery death.

After nearly drowning, Ray remained on the boat until it eventually docked at Mobile where the crew departed. Everyone was glad to leave the steamer and get paid. Ray's remaining adventure for the year would be on land.

He and Frank headed to Houston, sleeping out at night and getting eaten up by the mosquitoes. They bounced around between Houston, Beaumont and Galveston looking for work, but jobs were tough to find. Ray got Frank a job selling a church magazine while he got a job selling dishes and failed miserably although one week he managed to earn $15. He also worked a couple of days selling magazines.

His luck was better at the poker tables. He cleaned out two guys and ended up with $100 and some jewelry. He met a girl named Rosemary who he said fell for him, but Ray didn't stay around to be with her. He sold his phonograph and hiked the 300 miles from Houston to Dallas.

Years later, Ray talked of those days around Dallas and Fort Worth where he said he was learning about the oil business and buying oil leases, although none of that was detailed in his journal. Often the stories he told years later about himself were based on reality, but he enjoyed embellishing them a bit.

He claimed he and Frank hoarded their money and bought a few leases scattered around where they were staying then. They didn't have money to drill a well, but if a well came in near a lease they had, they sold their lease at a profit. Ray took his money and went to the nearest race track, spending a lot of time at Arlington Downs between Dallas and Fort Worth.

Ray said a friend told him about a place ripe for oil where leases were going for three or four dollars an acre, but the racing season at Arlington still had fifteen days to go and he stayed there playing the horses, and picking up money playing poker and craps. After Arlington's season was over, he headed off to buy the leases only to learn oil had been found and the price per acre now was thirty and forty dollars. "I was just a young punk kid and it took something like that to teach me that the oil business didn't wait for a racing season," he said.

But he had a more pressing problem in Dallas than a racing season or oil leases. Ray was nearly broke. He had sold anything he had worth money by then – the phonograph, records and other stuff. He bordered on being destitute.

It was raging hot in Dallas and Ray and Frank came across a guy with bottles of grape concentrate and Ray paid $50 for all the concentrate and empty bottles the man had. Ray and his buddy set up a stand in a vacant lot, mixed the concentrate with water they could scrounge and started selling grape juice drinks by the cup or quart bottle.

They made a few bucks and Ray even interviewed some men and girls to expand the business. After a week, the business slowed and then came to an abrupt halt when a sheriff drove up and demanded to see a license. Ray and Frank headed down the road carrying as many bottles of grape juice as they could with the bottles getting heavier by the mile. "I'm telling you, anybody wanting to buy grape juice that day could get it cheap," Ray later recalled.

He and Frank started hitchhiking to Oklahoma City and ended up in Perry, Oklahoma, about 60 miles north of Oklahoma City, where they got jobs for a few days working on a farm and living and sleeping in a barn. When they moved on, Ray stole a chicken and fried it to have enough to eat.

They were hired as harvest workers, spending 16 hours a day in the field. The food for the employees was good but the work hard and Ray and Frank took off again.

They met a man named Johnson who was hauling tubular material to oil fields near Gorham, Kansas, in the north central part of the state. Johnson asked if Ray could drive a tandem truck rig. Ray couldn't, but said he could. He would have told Johnson he could fly a plane to get a job. When they reached Kansas, Johnson pointed to two trucks parked side by side and told Ray to back up one to another part of the yard. Not knowing how to back up a tandem vehicle, Ray knocked over the other truck. Johnson gave the guys another job – unloading pipe.

The work also was hard, the food so-so. Workers got meal tickets and whatever they ate during the week was deducted from their pay at the end of the week. At the pay window was a bootlegger with 3.2 beer and bottles of alcohol to spike it and he also ran a crap game on the side. "Between the meal ticket deductions, the spiked beer and the crap game, we thought we'd never get out of the place," Ray said but he got lucky at craps and poker, winning enough money to leave during mid-August.

The bootlegger gave Ray a check – a bad one – to cover his losses to Ray. While waiting around at the bank only to learn the check was worthless, Ray met C. A. Anderson, who went across the Midwest in a candy truck selling "Spell Watch" candy. Inside each box of candy was a letter and customers had to buy enough boxes to get the letters spelling W-A-T-C-H. "Then you got a watch, worth maybe sixty-five cents. Lord, I don't see how they could have been worth more," Ray said. "There was only one 'T' in a gross of boxes."

Anderson was traveling with his daughter, who took a liking to Ray. Anderson was encouraged by Ray's eagerness and ability to sell candy. Ray worked on commission and proved up to the task, being able soon to buy a new pair of shoes. Within a month, he and Anderson were partners, traveling throughout the Midwest. Ray even hired Frank as a salesman.

Ray hadn't seen and had rarely heard from Helen for months and he thought about the pretty Irish lass, but that didn't stop him from taking a shine to several lovely girls he met during his candy salesman travels. One girl, he noted in his journal, "surely is sweet, reminds me of the way Helen was."

Ending up in Kansas City, Missouri in late October with a nice nest-egg, Ray "got a notion" to go to Chicago and wired Helen that he was coming. He rode a train all night to Chicago where he was met in the morning by Helen and that night they were married. "I had known from the day I met her that I would come back for her when I could. She knew it, too," he later said.

On Saturday October 26, 1929, 25-year-old Raymond John Ryan and 20-year-old Helen Mary Kelley were married by Harry Hoyt, a justice of the peace in Waukegan, Illinois, a city between Chicago and Milwaukee.

The wedding night was *a disaster*, at best, although Ray gave no details in his journal. Did Helen regret rushing into marriage? Was her mother still crying? Was Ray too hell-bent for leather on their wedding night for the tender Helen?

Ray only penned a terse note in the journal the next day, saying "plan to separate, have it annulled, folks won't let us." Apparently Ray and Helen were told to suck it up and learn to live together. Ray scurried off to Watertown the next day to play poker and returned to Chicago that evening.

He, Helen and Frank then took off for Tennessee, North Carolina and Georgia on a sales trip. Ray was getting good at selling and was able to buy a new Chevrolet. But the marriage remained testy. Along the trip, Ray wrote that he "caught seven year itch. I'm so fast I expect to scratch it out in three years."

He would need to scratch quickly if he wanted out of the marriage because the nation was heading to hard times. Three days after his wedding was Black Tuesday when panicked investors unloaded sixteen million shares on the stock market. By the end of November, investors had lost $100 million and the Great Depression was underway. Banks failed, businesses closed, and millions of Americans lost their jobs,

It took nearly two decades and a world war for the stock market and the country to recover. But Ray and Helen, despite the rocky beginning, never divorced. And they had to wait a decade or so before they were on the road to having all the money they ever wanted while the rest of the nation struggled.

Chapter 14

CAIFANO'S DEADLY TODDLIN' TOWN

Six months before Ray and Helen Ryan married, Chicago police arrested a small, swarthy, seventeen-year-old Italian kid for auto theft. Chicago punks often stole cars to joy-ride, or to strip down to sell the parts for a few bucks.

The youth grabbed by the police gave the name of Joe Russo, but also he had used others– Frank Robarto, Joseph Rinaldi and George Marini. His real name was Marshall Caifano. He was sentenced to a year in prison on auto theft, and a month later the judge vacated the sentence and placed him on probation. But shock probation was lost on Caifano.

He already had a string of arrests as a juvenile. Years later, he told a prison cellmate that the first person he killed was at a juvenile detention center, smothering a kid with a pillow over some dispute. Mysterious deaths in Chicago jails weren't uncommon in those days and were rarely pursued.

If Caifano did suffocate the youth, it was the first of many murders over the next fifty years that police thought he was involved in directly or having ordered someone else do the heavy work. He never would be charged in any slaying.

His suspected victims would cover the gamut – Barbe, Strauss, Roe, Quattrochi, Drury, Carey, Maritote, Fanning, Gioe, Adler, Touhy, Greenberg, Greenbaum, and others – Italians, Irish, Catholics, Jews, blacks, whites, men, women, rich, poor, guys fairly high up the mob ladder, lowly hangers-on. No one seemed to be exempt.

Born Marcellino Caifano in New York City in July 1911 to Antonetta, then 21-years-old, and Domenico Caifano, who was a few years older, Marshall was the second child. His brother Leonard was two years older and became known as "Fat Lenny" because, fully grown, he tipped the scales at over three hundred pounds. Rocco was born three years after Marshall. The family moved to Chicago and Marshall grew up in The Patch, the city's Italian westside melting pot that over a quarter century produced top leaders of Chicago's organized crime gang known as the Outfit.[5]

Chicago was the second largest city in the United States by 1900 and three-fourths of the 1.7 million residents were immigrants from Germany, Ireland, Poland, Sweden, England and Russia. Overpopulation, poverty, high taxes and natural disasters in Italy produced a flood of immigrants to America after 1870, mostly unskilled laborers, fishermen and peasants from southern Italy.

Thousands settled in The Patch area in Chicago around Polk and Halsted streets. Most immigrants worked hard, went to church, raised families, became part of their community and died unnoticed. Life was hard, poverty rampant. The Italian enclave was surrounded by close-knit neighborhoods of Irish, Jews, blacks, and Poles. Gangs sprang up to protect neighborhood turf and to use coercion, threats, burglaries and thefts to make money.

Boys advanced from stealing silk shirts on clothes lines in wealthier neighborhoods to smashing street peanut machines for the pennies, stealing bicycles, spare tires from cars and eventually the cars themselves. They progressed to hijacking trucks and extorting shop owners and wealthy individuals. Beatings and some killings kept people in line.

A thousand gangs roamed the Chicago streets in the 1920s and only the meanest and wiliest made it to the top. Caifano dropped out of school after the eighth grade and was brought into the notorious 42 Gang by his brother Fat Lenny. The gang name supposedly came from the members reading about "Ali Baba and the 40 Thieves" and thinking they were better.

---

5 Chicago's mob syndicate was first referred to as an "outfit" in the late 1950s by Chicago's newspapers. By the 1960s, the organization became consistently known as "The Outfit."

Small at 5-feet-5-inches and 150 pounds, Marshall Caifano was called "Shoes" or "Heels" – although never to his face – for wearing shoe inserts to appear taller. He boxed as an amateur in the 147-pound weight class under the name of Joe Russo. "Boxing was pretty good for amateurs in those days. I got $30 to $50 for winning. I boxed two years, maybe three," he later said.

Brothers Frank, August and Sam Battaglia and their cousin Paul Battaglia were leaders of the 42 Gang in the 1920s and 1930s along with Leonard Caifano. The members closest to the Caifano brothers were Sam Giancana, Albert "Obbie" Frabotta, Felix "Milwaukee Phil" Alderisio and Charles "Chuck" Nicoletti – all of whom would make a deadly mark on Chicago's crime history. Marshall Caifano, Frabotta, Alderisio and Nicoletti would become known as Chicago's version of "Murder, Inc." and on the street became known as the "Four Horsemen."

Robberies, kidnappings, auto thefts were commonplace, and murders not far behind. By 1930, the 42 Gang was the terror of Chicago's West Side. Teenaged girls were pulled from the streets, dragged into buildings or stables and gang raped.

In 1931, a local court judge dressed in shabby clothes and mingled for a month in the 42 Gang's haunts and became convinced the gang must be destroyed. "If I never do another thing in my life, I'm going to break up the '42' gang," Judge Francis Borrelli said from the bench one day when gang members were brought in on charges. "Most of you are of my race and are a disgrace to the Italian people. I went into your neighborhood, learned everything said about you is true. You're a gang of thieves and I'm going to clean up your district." Despite the judge's efforts, the 42 Gang continued to terrorize Chicago.

In the late 1920s Al Capone, battling for crime supremacy in Chicago against Irish, Italian and other gangs, filled his ranks by recruiting hoods from smaller gangs. Giancana was the first from the 42 Gang elevated by Capone and became a driver for the syndicate's top assassin "Machine Gun" Jack McGurn. Giancana brought into the Outfit other 42 Gang mates like Lenny Caifano.

Marshall Caifano joined the Outfit at age nineteen. He was convicted in 1931 of petty larceny/receiving stolen property and was sentenced to six months in prison. Shortly after being released, he was arrested for robbing a Wisconsin bank and spent more than a year in jail. It would be a half-century before he was convicted of another felony and during that time he rose up the syndicate's ladder with dead bodies littering the rungs.

Caifano was a thug's thug. He never would have the smarts to run the Chicago syndicate. He was closer to a G.E.D. than a PhD when it came to brainpower. But he was useful in taking care of the mob's dirty work with an innate understanding of how to get the message across – a quick punch to the face, a not so subtle threat to bring a store owner or union official to submission, or setting up someone needing to be killed.

Between the 1920s and 1960s, there were 1,000 mob-related killings in Chicago – 546 in the 1920s alone – according to the Chicago Crime Commission. Fewer than a dozen killings resulted in convictions. Caifano, Alderisio, Nicoletti and Frabotta and other crews under their control were suspected in many of those murders.

A retired FBI agent once described Caifano as someone central casting would send over to play a hood in a movie, a man with a rough face, gravelly voice, who emitted a physical power beyond his small stature. He had a square jaw, piercing brown eyes, a widespread nose and a cauliflower ear from taking too many punches as a boxer. Others described him as having the coldest eyes they ever saw, a cruel streak and quickness with his fists or a gun.

Yet some who met Caifano on the golf course or at Chicago clubs considered him a gentleman, a fellow easy to talk to, who liked to laugh, a man with young women always hanging around him. He never was a candidate to be the mob boss, instead handling the rough stuff, collecting the mob's share from gambling operations, straightening out disputes between mob crews, and eliminating trouble makers, talents that later would earn him the Outfit's top role at the mob-controlled Las Vegas casinos.

But those days were far away when Ray and Helen were exchanging wedding vows and Marshall Caifano was back in Chicago after a short stay in jail for auto theft.

Both Ray and Caifano were viewed by outsiders as on the fringes of their worlds. Books would be written about Tony Accardo, Giancana, Frank Nitti, Al Capone and other Chicago gangsters but not about

Caifano. Books would be written about H. L. Hunt, Harry Sinclair, Texas' Bass family and other oilmen but not about Ray.

Yet within their individual circles, Caifano and Ray would become larger-than-life figures, respected or feared by the people around them. It would be more than a decade before authorities and newspapers paid attention to them. By that time both were on the way to making their marks in life.

Neither knew in 1929 that they were on a deadly collision course.

Chapter 15

DAMN FED TURF WAR

Candy salesman. Tobacco salesman. Fifty-cent limit poker games in Milwaukee. That was Ray Ryan's world during the early years of marriage. But none of that interested Steve Bagbey in early 1978 as he plodded along in the murder investigation. He didn't have time to delve that deeply into Ray's background.

In the year after becoming the local chief investigator in the Ryan case, Steve logged 6,000 miles following leads from Chicago and Miami, California to New York. A stack of reports three feet high from the FBI, ATF and police departments in other cities covered his desk.

Being a bulldog investigator had it drawbacks as Steve was finding out.

The city police had hundreds of tips after the car bombing and Steve had to check out ever possibility. He viewed each case – from a phony check to murder – as a defense attorney would.

Those high-priced mouthpieces loved to take cops apart on the stand for not looking for other suspects and he didn't want that to happen in the Ryan case. It meant frustrating months running down suspects who probably wouldn't turn out to be involved, but he had to do that. He wouldn't be able to live with himself otherwise.

Among the tips Steve dealt with were: a recent car bombing in Olney, Illinois appeared to be similar to the one in Evansville; a former Evansville city cop who was in prison heard that a group of Puerto Ricans from Chicago had killed Ray; a local prisoner wrote a letter saying a guy calling himself "Joe Batters" – the nickname for Chicago longtime mob boss Tony Accardo – had been in Evansville; and another convict offered to help find people involved in Ryan's killing and in drug trafficking if let out of jail to do so. "Yeah, sure," thought Steve, stuffing the letters and reports in envelopes and tossing them on top of the growing piles of documents on his desk.

His attention was drawn to Lexington, Kentucky immediately after the bombing when a police officer there, Rex Denver Hall, telephoned Evansville police saying he and his brother ran a private investigation business in Lexington and worked for Ray for a while. Steve spent months building a file on the 34-year-old Hall, who joined the Lexington police force in 1968, rose through the ranks to detective before resigning in December 1977. Hall's private agency provided security guards to companies and parties and bodyguards for visitors.

Steve learned that Hall and two men named Engles, a convicted felon, and Landreth, also a former Lexington cop, were arrested in February, 1978, at an Orlando, Florida motel where police found handguns, a carbine, shotguns, a tear gas launcher, handcuffs, surgical gloves, grenades, a ski mask and other items. Charges later were dismissed because of an illegal search.

Another possible Lexington connection arose when Steve showed photo arrays of possible suspects to witnesses to Evansville's car bombing. He filled out the photo arrays with pictures of city police in street clothes and other cops he had encountered in the investigation. He was shocked when one witness fingered a photo of another Lexington cop in an array.

It took several months of checking and cross-checking before Steve cleared that officer of having anything to do with the Ryan case and concluding the Lexington angle was a dead end. After more weeks, Steve decided the Olney bombing and the Puerto Ricans tips were useless and that "Joe Batters" being in Evansville was a figment of a jail inmate's imagination.

Sgt. Gulledge was curious about Charles O'Curran's frequent visits to Ray and thought it was a possibility that O'Curran was tracking Ray's daily routine to pass on to people wanting to kill him. That concern deepened after Patti Page, the singer who once was married to O'Curran, arrived in Evansville months after the car bombing and was interviewed by Steve, Gulledge and ATF agent Jimmy Canter.

Page had met O'Curran around 1953 or 1954, they married in December 1956 and Ray was the best man at the wedding. She and

O'Curran divorced in Las Vegas in 1973 with Page retaining custody of their two adopted children.

Page said O'Curran demanded alimony and, after legal expenses, received a $60,000 cash settlement. She said O'Curran had gone through the money, was virtually broke, not receiving any more money from his work on Elvis Presley movies and was trying to modify the divorce settlement to get more money from her. O'Curran hadn't worked since 1962 and Page said she was the sole support of the family during their marriage.

Page said she last saw Ray around 1972 in Palm Springs and never felt close to the Ryans because they were Charley's friends. She said O'Curran once told her of visiting Ray in a room at the Waldorf Astoria Hotel in New York and seeing Ray with a suitcase full of money.

Page didn't know if O'Curran had dealings with organized crime, but recalled that during their marriage O'Curran brought a guest to their Beverly Hills home that he later identified as "MoMo," or Sam Giancana. The FBI looked into Page's information but told city police they didn't think O'Curran had a role in Ray's murder. Still, Gulledge wondered about O'Curran.

Steve didn't. He was mad after learning O'Curran had stolen shoes and cameras from the Ryan's home after Ray's funeral. Helen had banished O'Curran, never to talk to him again. Stealing from a dead man was the epitome of lowness to Steve. *You're never sure who your real friends are, Ray,* Steve thought.

At the request of U.S. agencies, authorities in Kenya interviewed M. C. Ruben, who took over in July 1970 as managing director of Ryan Investments Limited, the Nairobi company set up originally by Ray, Bill Holden and Swiss banker Carl Hirschmann to operate the Mount Kenya Safari Club. Ray sold his interests in the club in 1968 but continued to visit the club each year.

Ruben first met Ray around 1959 or 1960 and the friendship strengthened with each of Ray's visits. Even though Ray had no part in decision making at the club after selling it, Ruben said he and other club officials allowed Ray "the courtesy of making suggestions and discussing problems as a sort of occupational therapy" and it gave the new owners an opportunity of "picking his brains" which made Ray happy. "Mr. Ryan loved Kenya and the staff of the club was devoted to him," Ruben said.

Ruben said Ray was a very private person and rarely discussed his personal affairs, although during a 1974 visit Ray briefly talked about the mobsters who tried to extort money from him. "He told me that he refused to pay over any money and, although his life was threatened and he knew the dangers involved, he eventually testified against the men. He was both excited and upset as he related his experiences and stressed the importance of not giving in to organized crime and 'having the balls' to fight back regardless of the consequences," Ruben said. Ray's last visit to the club ended on March 3, 1977, a departure delayed several weeks because Ray had hernia surgery.

Ruben thought about visiting the United States and talked to Ray by phone the day before the car bombing. Ruben thought Ray sounded worried for the first time since he had known him. Ray read him a quotation, which Ruben thought was from Rudyard Kipling, about adversity and success being the same thing. Ray didn't give a clue on why he sounded worried. Ruben assumed it was due to the pressure of the Ray's upcoming tax trial. Ruben said he called Ray's home around midday the following day and was told Ray had just been murdered.

During the early months of the investigation, Steve had read everything he could find about organized crime and devoured the books written by retired Chicago FBI agent William F. Roemer Jr. on Chicago's Outfit, highlighting page after page with a yellow marker as he became familiar with names he hadn't heard of before – Caifano, Aiuppa, Lombardo, Alderisio, Cerone, Alex, Spilotro, Rosselli, Korshak, Eboli.

The Ant, Shoes, Big Tuna, Milwaukee Phil, Greasy Thumb, The Clown became familiar mob nicknames Steve tossed around in conversations with federal agents. He scoured old newspaper clippings passed along by the FBI and past articles in Evansville newspapers to learn more about Ray, his friends, his years in Evansville.

One of the reports Steve received from the ATF said that in November, 1977, an agent interviewed Joseph Charles Calabrese in Los Angeles where he was in a work release program from a federal conviction. Calabrese, when he worked for the Las Vegas Clark County Sheriff's Department intelligence unit, had been assigned to guard Ray during the 1964 extortion trial. Calabrese then quit the sheriff's department to become one of Ray's personal bodyguards.

Calabrese thought Ray was connected to the mob. He left Ray's employment in Kenya around 1968 and flew back to the United States carrying envelopes from Ray to deliver to Frank Costello and Frank Erickson. Calabrese said Ray was "vicious" in business dealings, Marshall Caifano either killed or had Ray killed, and Ray died because "he was getting old and sloppy." Calabrese believed Ray laundered his own and the mob's money.

ATF agents also interviewed Robert H. Kaplan in Los Angeles. Kaplan, who had been Ray's daughter Rae Jean's second husband, said he and Rae Jean went through a "bad divorce" and although living with Rae Jean at times, he moved out when Ray visited her because he and Ray didn't get along. He said four years before Ray was killed, Rae Jean received $3.1 million from a trust Ray set up from oil royalties but had managed to save only $600,000.

Kaplan said he didn't think Ray had any connection with organized crime, but did meet mobsters while gambling and he thought Ray laundered his own cash to avoid taxes, but not organized crime's money. Yeesh, thought Steve, even folks close to Ray couldn't agree on how strong Ray's ties to hoods were and whether he laundered money for them.

But the reports of Ray's close friendships with Frank Costello, Frank Erickson and others syndicate hoods drew Steve's attention. However, the major characters – Costello, Erickson, Sam Giancana, John Rosselli and Tommy Eboli – were dead. In Steve's mind, Costello, Erickson, Eboli and perhaps Rosselli were Ray's "buffer," friends who created a "no-kill zone" to prevent other mob syndicates from murdering Ray after the extortion trial. *When those hoods died, Ray, old buddy, your shield evaporated and you became fair game*, Steve thought.

Steve, Gulledge and other Evansville police knew they needed the cooperation of the FBI and ATF to solve the Ryan case even though federal cooperation was fleeting.

The FBI and ATF bickered, fighting over who would control the investigation. FBI agents complained the ATF claimed it had jurisdiction on a bombing case and wasn't sharing their interviews, impeding the FBI efforts. ATF agents griped that the FBI interviewed sources across the country before they could. One Evansville ATF agent wrote his superiors that "it is the opinion of this writer that the FBI involvement could hinder the bombing investigation of its desired goal, arrest and conviction of the guilty."

Both agencies sent the city police terse summaries of interviews they had conducted. Gulledge finally had enough in early 1978, and called a sit-down meeting with the two agencies. The city considered the investigation a one-way street – they sent all they had to the FBI and ATF and got little in return. City police in other cities felt the same. A Los Angeles detective told Steve that "the FBI eats like an elephant and shits like a canary."

Gulledge believed the ATF was more at fault trying to bolster its standing in Washington and urged all agencies to share all information. The meeting didn't generate results; the FBI and ATF summaries didn't get any more detailed.

Steve saw the turf problem first hand when he traveled with an Indianapolis ATF agent to Miami to interview Charles Delmonico, who along with Caifano had tried to extort money from Ray in 1963. As a courtesy, they stopped off at the local FBI office to say they were in town and why.

The ATF agent wouldn't get out of the car to go with Steve into the FBI office. FBI agents wouldn't go with the ATF agent to interview Delmonico. *Come on guys, we're supposed to be on the same team,* raced through Steve's mind. When they tried to question Delmonico, he told them to leave. Steve returned to Evansville distraught over the rift between the FBI and ATF.

The federal turf war was a pain in the ass.

Steve had the gut feeling that some day he'd be the only one left interested in finding Ray's killers and started scrounging deeper into Ray's early history.

Chapter 16

A CHICAGO RESUME

After the wedding, Ray and Helen settled in Milwaukee where Ray worked as a tobacco salesman during the days and in the evenings roamed the horse betting parlors and poker and dice tables in clubs and hotels in Milwaukee and Chicago.

From what he was learning from federal reports and old newspaper articles, Steve discovered that in this period, Ray's life clicked up to another level, one that followed him the rest of his days.

During these forays Ray had the opportunity to meet Chicago gamblers and racketeers and others who passed through the city from New York, Cleveland, Detroit, Kansas City and elsewhere visiting the hottest spots, checking up on their investments in joints or spending a few days with old friends. In return, Chicago gamblers enjoyed the emporiums in New York or vacationed a few days near a Florida race track.

In the beginning, Ray moved mainly among the lower-level gambling places in Milwaukee, but always looked for ways to move up the ladder. He and Helen lived in apartments, moving to better quarters each time. In 1932, they were at the respectable Sheridan Apartments on 2435 West Wisconsin.

With Ray's attention focused on work and gambling, Helen felt a distant third in his eyes. They didn't have a lot of money, especially when Ray was on a losing streak, and she didn't like staying at home by herself.

Her Irish spirit emerged one evening when she walked downtown to a dress store that used window models to show off the clothing. Ray had talked about stopping and watching the girls during his rounds.

The business owner took one look at Helen and hired her. Later that evening, Ray and his buddies wandered past the store to check out the models and Ray stared in shock when he saw Helen in the store window smiling back at him, twirling around to show off a dress. She wanted to convince Ray that someone in the family needed to have steady work, but Ray quickly ended Helen's modeling career and took her home. Friends admired Helen's spirit, but knew it was a losing cause when it came to Ray's gambling. "Helen was a match for him, but gambling was in Ray's blood and he was good at it," one friend later said.

Ray's days in Milwaukee didn't go unnoticed to authorities. In January 1934, the police raided a bookmaking operation and the 30-year-old Ray was one of fourteen men arrested at a downtown tobacco shop operated by Nick Torti, a former night club manager. Torti handed each gambler $35 dollars for bail. Arrested with Ray were salesmen, a dental laboratory employee, a painter, a retired railroad conductor, a dealer and a process server. A court later fined Ray $5 for being an inmate of a gambling house.

Milwaukee police considered Ray a tin-horn gambler "without any gambling interests in any gambling establishment except as an occasional player." Cops later said he was never ostracized by the local gambling fraternity and was referred to as a "regular fellow" and a "square shooter." He mingled with all levels of society in Milwaukee and Chicago in his evening prowls, building a list of contacts.

Some of them were hoodlums. But Ray's friends would never believe he was a mob associate. "His only association with the mob was when he was playing poker with them," one said. "They were the only guys who had money. He had to have someone rich enough to make it interesting for him to play poker with." Also, to Ray, the gamblers and racketeers were just another compartment of his life.

He also chased oil in the early 1930s, acquiring a lease on 60 acres around Centralia, Illinois, on a tip. "That's how you make money in the oil business," he'd say. "If you're well-liked, you get information – a truck driver, a worker you lent ten dollars to six months ago – anybody can tip you to promising leases."

The field looked good, but Ray owed a Chicago bookie $19,000. He was in Centralia trying to drum up money to drill the wells when the bookie demanded payment. Ray went to a leading oil company in the area to sell one half of the field for $19,000 but wanted the money by 10 a.m. the next day. The oil company official said the legal paperwork to split the lease into two sections would take days and offered to buy the entire lease for $38,000 and pay immediately.

An hour later, the check was delivered to Ray at a hotel. He wired $19,000 to the Chicago bookie then headed to Florida where he lost the rest of the money playing the horses. "I knew I had just sold away a fortune. I knew it. I was disgusted with myself," Ray later said. The Centralia field came in, producing five million barrels of oil.

Rather than being a successful oilman, Ray remained just a gambler and hustler.

He took up golf because deals and money could be made playing a round. He attacked golf with a vengeance, knowing he didn't have to be the best golfer in the world – only better than the guy he was playing against for money.

George Prahl got to see one of Ray's golf hustles, although he didn't realize it at the time. As a 13-year-old caddy at the nine-hole Watertown Country Club in 1936, Prahl and fellow caddy Bill Beckman were working when Ray showed up to play golf with Tom Brooks, whose family ran a Watertown poultry supply business.

Prahl remembered Ray approaching with a beautiful golf bag "full of clubs he didn't know how to use." Ray and Brooks bet on every hole. The first hole was for $5 and Ray took nine strokes and Brooks eleven. The second hole also was for $5 dollars and Ray won again by a stroke or two.

The bet was $10 on the third hole; $25 dollars on the fourth and by the fifth and sixth holes Ray and Brooks were playing for $100 dollars a hole. Ray won each hole by one or two strokes. After the sixth hole, Brooks threw up his hands and walked off in disgust.

Ray had won nearly $250. Caddies usually got 30 cents for lugging golf bags around nine holes plus a dime for a candy bar and a soda. Ray handed both Prahl and Beckman $5 dollars for caddying six holes, big money during the Depression and something a teenager never forgot.

Prahl thought Ray was a wheeler-dealer shrouded in mystery. He didn't realize until years later that he had seen a classic hustle, noting "Ryan was a real con artist."

Ray frequented boxing matches to meet a variety of influential people in Chicago and Milwaukee. High rollers and leading political, business and society figures were captivated by the lucrative world of boxing during the Depression with more than 20,000 people jamming Chicago Stadium some nights.

Ray hung out with noted fighters and managers, becoming friends with some like Barney Ross, who won the lightweight and junior welterweight titles in Chicago in 1935. Ray met former heavyweight champion Jack Dempsey, who retired from the ring in 1928, but fought exhibition bouts across the country including Chicago until 1940. Ray was enthralled with Dempsey and years later promised to make a movie of his life but never did.

Chicago also was the epicenter of two other famed boxers in those days – Billy Conn and Joe Louis. Ray was much closer to the tough Irish fighter Conn, a Pittsburgh native who started boxing professionally in June 1934 at the age of 16 and fought 60 bouts over the next five years. As a welterweight, he took on boxers in higher weight classes for larger purses, defeating former and future world champions and winning the light-heavyweight championship in July 1939.

Louis won the Chicagoland Golden Gloves light heavyweight crown in early 1934 and fought a dozen times that year in Chicago, winning them all and 10 by knockouts. The hottest ticket in the city was to a Louis fight. In September, 1935, Louis fought Max Baer at Yankee Stadium in New York and more than 1,000 people from Chicago boarded special trains and planes to see Louis knock out Baer in four rounds.

Ray was on one of the trains along with well-heeled businessmen, up-scale gamblers, elected state and county officials, congressmen, golf pros and the city's movers and shakers. Ray moved easily among the fight crowd, hanging around after bouts to meet the fighters and their handlers.

Conn started taking on heavyweights, winning all the bouts until he faced the champion Louis in New York's Polo Grounds in June 1941. Although outweighed by Louis by 30 pounds, Conn was securely ahead on points after 12 rounds until he was knocked out by Louis with two seconds remaining in the 13th round.

After retiring from the ring, Louis and Conn became greeters at Las Vegas casinos – Louis at Caesar's Palace and Conn at the Stardust – and by then Ray was one of the high rollers. Conn became Ray's close friend, occasionally visiting Ray and Helen in Evansville. Ray would tease Conn by calling him "a world champion until the last round."

Conn remembered the time Ray was winning big at a casino and tossed the cocktail waitress $10,000 in chips. The woman never came back to Ray's table and Conn was amazed because "Ray would have tipped her even more if she had stayed." But casino waitresses were supposed to pool their tips at the end of each shift, and Ray's waitress simply took the $10,000 and didn't return.

Those days in the Las Vegan casino, however, still were years in the future as Ray and Helen endured their early days of marriage in Milwaukee.

Chapter 17

HUSTLING THROUGH THE SOUTH

Ray and Helen decided to abandon Milwaukee and Chicago around 1936 for Hot Springs, Arkansas and Tyler, Texas.

Ray had had enough of being a salesman. Too boring? Not enough money coming in? It was time to move on and for Ray to prove his ability as a gambler. He had the knack of homing in on the newest gambling hot spot and cashing in.

After plodding through months of reports from federal agencies four decades later, Steve Bagbey eventually suspected that Ray's shift to Hot Springs might have resulted from his frequent visits to mob casinos and gambling joints in Chicago, New York, Florida and other places.

Did Ray's mob friends hope to blend their money with his gambling talents, turning a profit for everyone, Steve wondered.

It was a theory that was tucked away among the federal documents Steve had received. It sounded reasonable to him that was why Ray headed south at that time.

While Tyler was a quiet spot in the mid-1930s, everything went on in Hot Springs.

Folks suffering from rheumatism and arthritis began going to the hotels and bathhouses in Hot Springs in the early 1800s for the healing qualities of the 140-degree natural springs. State geologist David Dale Owen[6] in 1858 found more than half of the population "cripples

---

6 David Dale Owen was the son of English socialist and philanthropist Robert Owen and founder of the Utopian community at New Harmony in Indiana near

going on crutches or sticks and some of them have to be carried in litters to the baths. I believe some remarkable cures have been affected; though the virtues have undoubtedly been attributed in some instances to these hot waters which they do not possess."

While the effects of the hot water may have lured some people, others found more lively things going on there. Since the Civil War, Hot Springs had earned the nicknames of "Sin City" and "Hot Town" more from gambling and prostitution than the thermal hot springs.

The wealthy, famous and notorious came. Jesse and Frank James and Cole Younger stopped by – to rob stagecoaches, although Younger later returned to speak against being an outlaw and Frank James opened a small business. Killings between groups wanting to control gambling in the 1880s forced a citizens committee to run off outsiders and turn clubs over to local owners.

Orator William Jennings Bryan, lawman Bat Masterson, F. W. Woolworth of the five-and-ten cent stores and wealthy Chicago meat packer Philip Armour were among the visitors. Major league baseball teams held spring training there and Rogers Hornsby, Dizzy and Daffy Dean, Babe Ruth and Honus Wagner could be seen on the streets.

Hot Springs was an "open" city where mobsters could unwind without fear of being gunned down. Chicago hoods Al and Ralph Capone and Johnny Torrio came in the 1920s as well as members of the rival Dion O'Banion's mob, staying in different hotels. Meyer Lansky brought his disabled son Buddy to the bathhouses. Also dropping by were Lucky Luciano and Ma Baker's gang.

For a quarter century, Frank Costello spent a week each year in Hot Springs and supplied the racing wire services to clubs where horse race betting during the day blended with poker and dice games in the evenings.

Joining Costello at times were Frank Erickson, the nation's bookmaking king, Gerardo "Jerry" Catena and Joe Adonis from New Jersey's mob and the Fischetti brothers, Murray Humphreys and Jake "Greasy Thumb" Guzik from Chicago's Outfit. Arthur H. Samish, the California lobbyist who ruled over that state's legislature, occasionally

---

Evansville. He was knowledgeable in chemistry and geology and was appointed the first state geologist in Indiana, Kentucky and Arkansas.

slipped into town to see Costello as did Mickey Cohen, a leader in the California mob.

Hubert Cokes was raised in Hot Springs. His father died when he was a child and his mother found what work she could. Cokes dropped out of school after discovering pool halls more to his liking. Cokes left Hot Springs during World War I to hit gambling circles across the country but returned home occasionally, according to Hot Springs historian Orval E. Allbritton.

Cokes was suspected of being the inside man in the 1921 robbery of a Hot Springs gambling joint of $20,000 in cash, diamonds and jewelry. He fled town, but returned a year later and was arrested after a similar robbery of gamblers in Pine Bluff, Arkansas. Charges were dropped for insufficient evidence. Cokes next went to Oklahoma where he shot and killed a man during a gambling argument, but was exonerated in a trial after pleading self defense.

In 1924, he was back in Hot Springs with his wife and a roving eye for the ladies. Police Chief Oscar Sullivan wanted to run him out of town. In April, Cokes followed a woman, who he thought was flirting with him, to a café, not knowing she was there to meet the married Sullivan.

Sullivan burst outside and argued with Cokes, who drew a gun and fired three shots killing the chief. During the subsequent trial, Cokes claimed Sullivan had pulled his gun, although witnesses said the chief's weapon was in its holster. Still, the jury found Cokes innocent and he left the city for good.

Hot Springs drifted during the Depression until 1936 when the state approved spring thoroughbred racing at the nearby Oaklawn track. Oaklawn soon became the country's fifth top race track for mutual handle and attendance and gambling and racing brought a steady flow of visitors, including Ray and Helen.

A carefree Helen, wearing dark glasses and a beaming smile, walked and shopped along Central Avenue. Ray hit the high stakes poker games at the Southern and other upscale clubs where games might go on for days with pots exceeding $100,000.

Decades later FBI reports revealed other tidbits about Ray's time in Hot Springs – Ray won an oil lease from a woman in a poker game (wells drilled on the land produced oil) and another night Ray won $130,000 at the tables.

FBI informants claimed that during the years 1936-1938, when Ray was around Hot Springs and Tyler, an "East Coast gambling syndicate" put up $100,000 in seed money for him to gamble against Texas oilmen, and Ray's success at the tables allowed him to build up a nest egg approaching $200,000, money Ray would use to go after oil.

During this period Ray probably encountered H. L. Hunt, an oilman who had moved his company from Arkansas to Tyler in 1931 to make a fortune in the East Texas oil fields.

Ray and Helen also spent time in Tyler, located 225 miles south of Hot Springs. Known as "The Rose Garden of America" with over half of the nation's rose plants coming from there, Tyler by 1936 had become the "Oil Capital of the World" after the discovery of the great East Texas oil field by C. M. "Dad" Joiner in 1930.

Tyler was a sedate – some say aloof – city 30 miles west of the oil field. The oil boom towns of Longview and Kilgore struggled to provide housing for thousands of workers; crime was rampant and streets were churned to mud from oil field equipment. Tyler's sported brick-paved streets where crime was rare, oil company offices everywhere and a population doubling to 32,000. The city's Sears & Roebuck store was the only one in the nation to show a profit in 1936.

Ray didn't talk much about his early days in Tyler except to say Texas folks didn't like the Irish down there. Still, Ray and Helen bonded with one person in Tyler and that was H. L. Hunt, a friend for life.

Ray and Haroldson Lafayette Hunt, Jr. were kindred spirits. They bonded because of all their similarities, not just their mutual love of gambling.

Both were the youngest in their families (Hunt of eight, Ray of five) and the favorite of their mothers. Ray was born in Wisconsin while Hunt, who was 15 years older than Ray, was born near Vandalia, Illinois, on a farm near Ramsey in February 1889.

Both developed an affinity for cards at a young age, practicing hours and hours trying to figure play possibilities. They had photographic memories, were good at math and today would be considered card counters.

Ray and Hunt had wanderlust as youngsters, Hunt leaving home at 16 and bumming his way across the country – California, Texas and

Arizona – working as a dishwasher and mule team driver and playing poker at camps and saloons. Ray went to Texas, Europe and Kansas.

Ray spent a brief time at Notre Dame while Hunt never attended grade school but, after winning $200 or so from a guy in poker, attended Valparaiso in Indiana for two semesters before a serious case of tonsillitis forced him to drop out.

After his father died in 1911, Hunt took his inheritance and started cotton farming at Lake Village, a small town in southeastern Arkansas, playing poker in Lake Village and nearby Greenville, Mississippi, and during trips to New Orleans. The depression of 1921 caused cotton prices to hit bottom, and Hunt moved 90 miles to a developing oil boom in El Dorado, Arkansas. Hunt did well there and set his eyes on a possible oil boom elsewhere.

Both Ray and Hunt also had eyes for women. Ray's female companions were not lasting except for Helen; Hunt would maintain families, unbeknownst to each other for a while, with three different women in different cities, fathering numerous children with each. Hunt first married Lyda Bunker and started a family at Lake Village.

During trips to Florida as his oil future brightened in El Dorado, Hunt met Frania Tye and started another family with her. He later shipped her off to New York while continuing to provide for them. In the 1940s, Hunt had a third family with Ruth Ray, a secretary at his oil company office in Shreveport, Louisiana, and moved Ruth to Texas.

By that time, Ray and Helen and the Hunts were close. Ray and Helen enjoyed visiting the Hunts, although Helen thought the Hunt's young children were holy terrors. Ray and H. L. loved head-to-head poker and card games and the spirited fun the other provided. Ray Ryan told friends he was the godfather to Ruth's first son, Ray Lee, born in 1943.

But in the mid-1930s oil pickings still were slim in Tyler because of strict daily limits on oil that could be pumped from wells and it may have been Hunt who encouraged Ray to seek oil elsewhere. Ray already loved the euphoric atmosphere that oil booms created and the money that could be made when an oil well came in.

The Ryans returned to the Chicago area in 1938. Ray continued to hit the gambling joints and boxing matches, mingling with noted Chicago-area businessmen and politicians.

Ray's attention was riveted on the June 22, 1938 fight at Yankee Stadium in New York between heavyweight champion Joe Louis and Max Schmeling. The German contender was greeted with garbage tossed by fans in the stands angry over what Germany's leader Adolph Hitler was doing in Europe.

Ray wasn't one of those fans. He saw many of Louis' earlier fights in Chicago but that night he liked Schmeling. Louis quickly knocked out Schmeling, the fans were delirious but Ray lost $25,000. He had bet on the German boxer.

Ray's luck was the same when it came to oil.

He and a partner drilled a dry well in an Illinois county. Six months later a major pool was discovered near where he had drilled. Close but no cigar for Ray.

He still couldn't find a big oil strike but that was about to change.

The first step came at the end of 1938 when the Griffin gusher came in near Evansville, Indiana.

Chapter 18

EVANSVILLE'S OIL BOOM LUCK

No one thought Evansville a place to get rich.

The city was located along the Ohio River near the southwestern tip of Indiana. Kentucky was just across the river and Illinois two dozen miles west.

The downtown was a cluster of 19th century brick Italianates with Victorian ornamentation and a smattering of Art Deco and Modern buildings. Stately century-old homes of business owners and executives were near the riverfront. Elsewhere across the town were clusters of shotgun houses in various factory districts and neat-as-a-pin neighborhoods of modest bungalows, Queen Anne cottages and American Foursquares.

The buildings were a conglomeration of styles and expense, like the people who lived in Evansville.

Evansville was a blue collar town, a place where the old stayed and the talented young moved on to greener pastures after high school.

The area possessed a boom-bust mentality – a promise of good times before things fell apart.

Economic growth was slow until the early 1830s when it was announced Evansville would be the terminus of the planned 460-mile Wabash and Erie Canal connecting Lake Erie using inland streams with the Ohio River.

Merchants, workers and speculators flocked in, followed by German immigrants, craftsmen with a strong work ethic. By the time the canal – with mules and horses pulling barges – was completed in

1853 railroads had been built parallel to the waterway and the obsolete canal was filled in. Evansville went into decline.

The pinnacle of the steamboat in the Civil War era turned the city into a stopping point between Pittsburgh and New Orleans. Steamboats sometimes were lashed together six deep at the city's wharf to meet the need for docking space.

By 1900, Evansville was a world center for furniture manufacturing. A railroad bridge was built across the Ohio River followed by a bridge in 1932 for vehicles.

Then came the Depression where banks closed and jobs disappeared followed by the January 1937 flood, the worst ever along the Ohio River, leaving half of the city under water.

Folks thought things couldn't get worse. And they were right. A boom was looming.

The city was in the southern half of the Illinois Basin – 60,000 square miles of land that stretched from central Illinois to the Tri-State portions of Indiana and Kentucky. Coal mining employed thousands of workers because the basin's oil reserve was puny compared to the billions of barrels of oil underground in states like Texas, Oklahoma and Louisiana.

But the ugly oil duckling of the Illinois Basin suddenly blossomed into a swan because of the Depression, America's 1930s economic hardships and a glut of oil in oil-rich southern states.

Oil originally was bottled as a tonic to treat various aliments until wiser folks refined it into kerosene for lamps and other by-products. In 1901, when the Spindletop well near Beaumont, Texas began pumping thousands of barrels a day, the nation's trains and ships switched from coal to oil. The growth of the automobile industry relied on oil production for gasoline, lubricants and road asphalt.

In December 1930, the massive East Texas field around Kilgore and Longview had been discovered and soon wells were being erected at a rate of one every hour, and millions of barrels of oil pumped. Oilmen bent on hitting pay dirt wasted no time worrying that over-production could diminish the long-term ability to keep oil flowing. Their only concern: making money fast.

So much oil was pumped that the price per barrel plummeted from over $1 to 13 cents by 1931. One promoter strapped for cash sold

40,000 barrels for two cents a barrel while oilfield workers were paying 35 cents for a hot shower and a quarter for a cup of coffee.

To bolster the barrel price, Texas went to prorationing – drastic legal restrictions on how much oil could be pumped from each well in a day. Other states also joined the proration side. While major oil companies could live with producing less if the barrel price eventually increased, independents and wildcatters protested, filed lawsuits and began looking for states with no prorationing.

The welcome mat was out in the Illinois Basin.

By the latter half of the 1930s, oilmen in cowboy hats and boots trekked there, particularly to Evansville, the only large city around. The flow of newcomers became a flood 10 days before Christmas 1938 when a well came in along Wabash River bottomland north of Evansville near the small community of Griffin. There never was an oil find in Indiana like the Griffin "gusher."

At 2,846 feet the deepest ever in the state, the well immediately pumped 1,000 barrels a day with no other well within 25 miles. Griffin residents thought the troubled times of the Depression were over when word of the gusher spread, and they headed to the bottom-lands to see for themselves, yelling "oil…they struck oil" to anyone passing by.

More in hopefulness than irony, they said the well was the biggest thing to hit Griffin in the 13 years since the March 16, 1925 tornado roared through the town, killing more than 50 people and destroying virtually every structure. It was the deadliest tornado in America's history, carving a 219-mile path from the Missouri Ozarks into Indiana and leaving 695 people dead.

The men who drilled the Griffin well found oil euphoric, better than sex for some, an ego trip for others. W. O. Allen Jr., a Tulsa independent oilman, and his partner Ed Ames were among several investors in the well on the 1,600-acre John C. Cooper estate. As the oil shot in the air and covered them black, they headed to the oilmen haven at the McCurdy Hotel in Evansville to crow about their accomplishment.

Ames was congratulated at the hotel. "You sure smell of oil," one man said. "It may smell like oil to you mister, but it smells like perfume to me," Ames responded.

The next day a stream of cars headed to the well site. The Evansville Courier newspaper reported: "Farmers clad in overalls, jumpers and rough shoes clustered here and there talking in low tones; other men in khaki breeches and leather boots laughed boisterously, clapping each other on the back, and a third group, well dressed and with shiny oxfords, stood silently. These last-named men chewed meditatively on cigars, slowing scrutinizing the crowd.

"A wide uneven black line glistened in the bright sunshine. It ran from the base of the derrick about 300 feet southward across an adjoining plowed field. From this trail arose the unmistakable sick-sweet odor of oil."

"If she don't play out and others like her are drilled around here, it'll look like the East Texas field all over again," said one of the crew's drillers as he allowed sightseers to fill small bottles with oil as souvenirs.

The Griffin discovery spread across the Midwest through newspapers. Two days later Ray Ryan reached Evansville; a local newspaper simply noted that Ray Ryan from Chicago was in the city.

Ray believed in striking while the iron was hot and immediately sank money into an offshoot well near the Griffin well, wanting to ride the oil wave expected to surge around the discovery well.

An Evansville newspaper predicted that Ray could be the next guy in the Tri-State to get rich from oil. That wasn't to be. At the outset, Ray became just one of dozens of wildcatters ending up empty handed and with a thinner wallet.

The Griffin "gusher" turned Evansville into a never-before-seen microcosm of characters – grifters, drifters, hustlers, gamblers and card sharks all out for a fast buck. Oilmen with nicknames like Digger," "Dusty," "Buckshot" and "Uncle Billy" showed up. So did men like Sam Garfield, an associate of Detroit's Purple Gang, and veteran gambler Peter Tremont, who was linked to the Chicago mob.

Two of the nation's best hustlers also arrived – Hubert Cokes and Alvin Clarence Thomas. Cokes by then was one of the country's best pool players and gamblers, known as "Daddy Warbucks" because his bald head, prominent ears, six-foot plus frame of more than 200 pounds resembled the character in the comic strip "Li'l Orphan Annie." He also was called "The Giant" because of his determination to be in charge of what was going on around him.

He sent word to Thomas, his friend and frequent traveling companion. Thomas was better known as Titanic Thompson, an almost mythical character, the country's premier hustler who won money at golf, poker, pistol or rifle shooting, card and poker chip pitching, tossing keys into locks or any other scheme he devised like betting he could toss a peanut or walnut on top of a building then switching in a weighted peanut or walnut to win bets. He moved signs listing the distance to a city closer to town then drove by with friends and bet the distance on the sign was wrong.

Thrown into this motley collection of characters was Ray, who was part of all of them – oilman, grifter, hustler, gambler, card shark and more. Competition was fierce. "Ray was like the rest of us. We didn't know much about the oil business, but we were willing to gamble on it," Cokes said years later.

Independent operators and wildcatters faced major oil companies that had thousands of acres under lease and employed scouts, land men, geologists and seismograph crews galore to look for potential oil fields. Hundreds of thousands of dollars were spent on leases and farmers barely surviving in the Depression suddenly had money in the bank. The oil companies couldn't control everything, but another Griffin gusher was like finding a needle in a haystack.

Wildcatters looking for oil liked to say "an ounce of luck outweighs a ton of brains."

Ray believed he had the brains. Now he needed the ounce of luck.

Chapter 19

WHEN OIL WAS KING

F. Harold Van Orman bounded across the marble lobby floor of the McCurdy Hotel with a force unequaled in Evansville.

Although barely 5 ½ feet in height, Harold was an energetic powerful figure with sparkling eyes, dark hair with a trace of white and a sharp tongue when needed. He greeted the uniformed bellboy by name, spoke with the desk clerk and continued his rounds at the hotel, a fiefdom he had ruled since the building opened in 1917.

In 1939 Harold epitomized Evansville's next decade – smart, showy, colorful. The Van Orman family started in the hotel business in Indiana before the turn of the century when Harold's father, Fred, bought hotels in several states including Evansville's St. George Hotel, beginning the country's first hotel chain, according to some.

The St. George later was razed to make way for the McCurdy. Fred, a task-master, started his son off as a dishwasher in the St. George kitchen to learn the business from the ground up after Harold graduated from Harvard in 1908. When Fred died, Harold took over the hotels.

The eight-story McCurdy on First Street was one of the best in the Midwest with 265 rooms nearly all with private baths and hot and cold water. The terrace overlooked the Ohio River and the city's riverfront. The vaulted 26-foot tall lobby gleamed with carved mahogany columns, a coffered wooden ceiling and sparking chandeliers.

The mezzanine, with ornamental iron railings, mahogany handrails and private dining rooms, was billed as the largest in the nation. The hotel featured the Elizabethan and Pompeian dining rooms, and the Coral Room with a cocktail lounge, dining area and a large dance floor. On the top floor was the Rose Room for weekend gatherings.

The hotel was cozy, functional and classy. The chandeliers highlighted a pink glow from the colors of the brown Tennessee marble floor. More than one thousand people went through the lobby daily and Harold Van Orman knew every one of them.

Beneath the hustle and bustle of the McCurdy was a feeling of power, an aura of strength where one had to keep his wits to survive amid the oilmen, speculators, suppliers, workers and riffraff arriving for the oil boom. Operators of the stately Vendome, a half-century old hotel a few blocks away, didn't want people with muddy boots and clothes making a mess of the lobby and rooms. Harold welcomed oilmen of all sorts. He didn't see mud. He saw money.

The McCurdy was alive, and Harold, surrounded by a cast of characters, played a leading role. Stetson hats and cowboy boots were common with oilmen from Texas and Oklahoma. The McCurdy was more Dallas than Evansville.

Oilmen were in constant motion. They didn't live by a clock, but for the moment, the next successful oil well. Oil and life were fleeting things to be drained of their essence and enjoyed before moving on. The men had egos as big as the oil derricks they erected and loved expensive clothes, fancy cars and the ladies.

Harold, one of the nation's best public speakers and toastmasters, could be crude, disarmingly blunt yet leave audiences laughing or crying. At one hotel meeting, his ribald introduction of the president of a major Eastern railroad at a dinner left the president commenting "that's the crudest man I ever heard at a public meeting" and the audience in stitches.

Harold was the interlocutor at local minstrel shows and trooped around the country following circuses. He had been state senator, lieutenant governor and coined a phrase still heard today: "Indiana has the best legislature money can buy."

He married Susie Beeler in 1913, uniting two of Evansville's old-line families. The stormy marriage produced three children. Susie was heralded as the first woman in Indiana to smoke in public.

The couple parted shortly after Susie became the first woman to run for mayor of Evansville and was soundly trounced in a three-candidate race in the 1929 Republican primary. Some thought Harold had sabotaged her campaign. "Suppose she'd been elected she might have started smoking cigars," he quipped.

After the divorce, Harold spent months in pursuit of Harriet Hodgini, a beautiful brunette circus equestrienne of the famous Riding Hodginis. She and Harold married in 1935 and Harriet became a force in the hotel operation during the oil boom.[7]

Helen joined Ray in Evansville in January 1939. They found lodging in an apartment but Ray continued to rent a room in the McCurdy for business and pleasure. Ready to cash in on the oil boom, he acquired a lease on the William Dunn farm a mile from the Griffin well and called on Chicago friends to be investors.

Sam Pian, former manager of the ex-welterweight boxing champ Barney Ross, along with J. L. Smith, a former newspaperman who got into the oil business, and Fred Belmont, owner of the 1933 Grill in Chicago, showed up. Pian was a noted figure in boxing circles because of Ross, a slim Jewish kid who grew up in Chicago and won the light-weight championship in 1933 and the welterweight crown in 1934. Ray had seen many of Ross' fights.

Another investor New Yorker Ernest Eslick, a former show business singer who had come to Evansville to learn the oil business, served as Ray's mentor. Eslick was a talented singer and was noted for his pleasing renditions of "Mother Macree" in his high tenor voice. Ray's well near the Griffin gusher seemed a sure thing until high water from the Wabash River halted drilling in the spring of 1939. After the water receded, it was abandoned. Ray's first attempt was a soggy duster.

He already had other wells underway. Like other oilmen, he traded leases based on tips or won at the poker and dice tables. Once he traded off a lease where oil later was found while his well was dry, and shrugged it off, saying "I was trading around because maybe somebody would get rich. Somebody did. Next time it will be me."

The oil bonanza had passed him by his first year in Evansville. A few wells did produce oil but not enough to be a commercial success. If it wasn't for bad luck, Ray would have had no luck at all in oil.

Oil was survival of the fittest and he was far from being the fittest in the Illinois Basin and it hurt. He watched as others made money,

---

7 Harold's marriage to Harriet ended about a decade later when Harriet left and never returned. A few years later, Harold married Kitty Clark, a strikingly lovely equestrienne and showgirl with the Ringling Brothers-Barnum and Bailey Circus. She remained with Harold until his death in 1958 at the age of 73.

like Annie Stewart, who lived across the river in Kentucky and was known as "Ferryboat Annie" because she once operated a ferry over nearby Green River. She got into oil leasing with a partner in 1938 and had 4,000 acres around wells within a couple of years, money to burn and suitors knocking at her door.

In Crossville, Illinois, the local Lions Club begged residents to rent rooms to oil field workers; thriving restaurants and service stations stayed open around the clock. Thousands of derricks were erected across the Tri-State, some with cattle grazing between them. Wells were in backyards of homes and a small Illinois town adopted a law limiting wells to one per block. Illinois, once 17th in the U.S. in oil production, was third by 1940.

Ray was in his mid-30s, halfway through his life although that wouldn't matter if he had known it. He was fixed only on the present, the next oil or business deal, the next poker table or the next race track in Chicago, New York, Texas or Miami.

A handsome man a couple of inches under six feet weighing about 170 pounds, he had dark hair, a prominent Roman nose, deep-set brown eyes, a quick disarming smile and a face tanned from days in the sun. Being half Irish, his gift of gab made people from fashionably dressed gamblers to drillers and roughnecks wearing plaid shirts, dirty jeans and boots feel at ease around him.

Always wheeling and dealing in oil leases, he put up a flamboyant front to convince others he was a rising star, trying to create a reputation for action, needing people to talk about him, nod or wave as he walked by. If he had to bluff to convince an investor his oil lease was a sure thing, he'd bluff. It was part of the game.

There were oilmen around like Robert S. "Bob" Hays, Edward Burke and Olen Sharp who would become Ray's partners in major oil discoveries over the next ten years. But others avoided him, thinking he was too eager to beat down the cost of leases from poor farmers or leave investors holding the bag while scraping out what money he could for himself.

Decades later after Ray promoted many multi-million dollar deals, an acquaintance noted "if anyone made any money other than Ryan out of such investments it was a mistake." Yet, many folks reaching a handshake agreement on a deal – Ray didn't like wasting time with written contracts – found him true to his word.

Ray concentrated on finding wealthy investors seeking tax breaks through an oil depletion allowance of 27 ½ percent if a well came in or writing off losses for dry holes. Investors often put up the entire drilling cost without Ray spending a dime while Ray got a one-fourth interest in any oil for putting a deal together.

So far all he got out of the ground was water and mud. If it wasn't for his success at poker and dice tables around Evansville and in other cities, he might be back working as a salesman or waiting tables.

Cutting a dashing figure ala Harold Van Orman, Ray prowled the hotel mezzanine and terrace listening politely as oil company executives and women at tables chatted about trips back home to Texas, Louisiana and Oklahoma and gleaning information on what was happening in the oil fields in those states.

The women played bridge or gin rummy for a penny a point with their husbands and friends because poker was considered a back room game for ne'er-do-wells. Bridge wasn't Ray's style because he never liked to rely on a partner for anything.

But, he was interested in learning to play gin rummy, envisioning the money piling up when playing for $5 or $10 a point.

Chapter 20

GRIFTERS, GAMBLERS AND TITANIC

Even months after the Griffin gusher, a wild bunch of men continued to pour into the McCurdy every day. Harold Van Orman liked to be in the lobby when newcomers arrived to check them out.

Most of the resident oilmen were out in the field when an unusual figure entered the hotel one day. Van Orman, who knew a good show when he saw one, could only smile.

The man wore a stylish dark European-cut suit, a fluffy shirt with a silk tie, a cape lined in red and a black top hat. He had a waxed mustache and his hair was slicked back with enough grease to keep a Ford axle spinning for a century.

In a loud fractured French accent, the man identified himself as Count something or other and said he had come to Evansville to make another fortune. Loud enough to turn the heads of men sitting in the lobby, the Count said "I come with two million dollars to invest in oil wells. I vill be in my room waiting for anyone with leases." With a flourish of his cape, he spun and scurried to the elevator.

The Count's arrival sent the newcomers into a flurry of activity for leases to peddle. Soon men lined up at the Count's door to pitch proposals to him, mesmerized by the well-heeled Frenchman who listened patiently but didn't dole out any cash. Frequently he was gone for hours – no one knew where – and when the Count returned the lines formed anew. Even a few veteran oilmen joined the queue.

The excitement went on for three days before someone finally recognized the Count as the practical joker Ray Ryan. Even some of his closest friends hadn't recognized him. He had scoured the city for weeks for the right outfit and theatrical makeup for the spoof and was delighted when he pulled it off.

He loved practical jokes, picking at the foibles of the people around him. Some of his jokes were subtle, others blatant. Ray liked to tell guys who kept drilling dry wells "you couldn't find oil if you came on a sign stuck in the ground with oil written on it and an arrow pointing down." If a gambler couldn't win at the table, Ray offered to play both of their hands so the other man could have a chance.

Sometimes Ray played poker with a gambler called "Mr. Careful" because he always sat with a wall near his back so no one could see his cards. Ray liked to stare at and nod at an imaginary person behind Mr. Careful to see him snap his head around to see if anyone was behind him.

But Ray really preferred more elaborate schemes. If he saw departing oilmen lugging heavy suitcases heading to the elevator to go to the lobby, he'd tell them the elevator was out of service and the bellman sent to get someone to fix it. The men would thank him and head down the stairs, grumbling and banging the suitcases along the railing. Ray would wait until they were out of sight then punch for the elevator and ride to the lobby grinning.

During the days, sometimes weeks, when work in the oil fields was halted due to high water along bottomland creeks and rivers, oilmen gathered at the hotel, backrooms of pool halls and other joints in the city to play poker. Ray usually was there and Hubert Cokes often sat in as did Titanic Thompson.

Titanic was a wannabe oilman when he arrived at the McCurdy at the start of the oil boom in a fancy roadster with two beautiful teenaged girls on his arms, sisters he said. He registered, tipped the bellboy a $100 bill and headed to the elevator with the girls. A couple of oilmen got on the elevator with them. Titanic put his arm around one girl and told the guys she gave the best blowjobs in the city. The men were shocked, the girl giggled.

In his late 40s, Titanic was an affable fellow, tall, slim and moderately well-dressed "though no dude or fashion plate," as one person noted. He was constantly on the lookout for suckers. He once won a fistful of money in the McCurdy lobby by betting that more women than men would walk in during the next hour. Titanic was the only one in the group who knew a women's convention was coming to town that day.

When returning to Evansville one afternoon from an oil lease in Illinois, he passed a man driving a wagon loaded with watermelons. Titanic peeled off several large bills and bought all of the watermelons and had the driver unload and count them. Titanic told the driver to reload the watermelons and drive past the hotel.

He waited with a group of buddies as the wagon finally reached the hotel and told the men he was good at guessing how many watermelons and bet he could come within five of the number of melons on the wagon. The men quickly put several thousands of dollars on the table. After the melons were unloaded and counted, Titanic's "guess" was two off the number on the wagon and he pocketed the money.

No one ever tried to get money back from Titanic. His jackets were tailored to conceal one or two guns in holsters and he was armed most days. Before showing up in Evansville, he already had killed three or four men, usually guys dumb enough to think they could rob him of his gambling winnings.[8]

Titanic had been among the group of gamblers in a three-day marathon poker game in New York in September 1928 when Arnold Rothstein[9] left the table owing more than $300,000 to the other players, including $30,000 to Titanic. Rothstein later thought the game was rigged and refused to pay. George McManus, who had set up the game, pressured Rothstein to come up with the money.

In November, McManus met Rothstein in a room at the Park Central Hotel where Rothstein was shot in the abdomen and died two days later without telling cops who shot him. McManus was tried for murder and acquitted.

Titanic wasn't linked to the shooting but everyone in Evansville knew he wasn't anyone to trifle with.

---

8 One of the victims was a 16-year-old former golf caddy who tried to rob Titanic of money in 1932 in Tyler, Texas. Police found the dead youth wearing a ski mask and with a .38 caliber gun in his possession. No charges were filed and Titanic left Tyler.

9 Rothstein was believed to be the mastermind in fixing the 1919 World Series, the Black Sox scandal, and was an early tutor to Lucky Luciano, Meyer Lansky, Frank Costello, Philip "Dandy Phil" Kastel and Johnny Torrio.

Chapter 21

CHASING MOB CASINOS

Ray plugged away at finding oil. Many turned out to be dry wells although a few, while never big producers, did bring in enough money to keep Ray going.

Occasionally, Ray spent his earnings on expensive jewelry for Helen but, months later, used it as collateral for bank loans to drill more wells.

He disappeared for days at a time in late 1939 and early 1940 and headed for New York to find more lucrative gambling and to mingle with the powerful and rich East Coast people at cocktail parties and nightclubs eager to invest in oil.

One friend gained in the East was Alexis Thompson, who was a teenager when his father, David P. Thompson, once head of Republic Iron and Steel and an official at Chicago's Inland Steel headquarters, died in 1930 leaving Alexis $3.6 million.

Alexis acquired the Philadelphia Eagles professional football team and invested in oil wells with Ray over the next decade drilling numerous wells around Evansville of which about half produced oil. Thompson's wife was the niece of Texas millionaire oilman Harry Sinclair, one of Ray's many gambling acquaintances.

Thompson introduced Ray to the young actor William Holden, who was filming his first major movie in New York. The meeting between Ray and Holden was casual and they wouldn't meet again for several years, but it left an impression. For three decades, few people would be closer to Ray than Bill Holden.

Miami also became a stopover for Ray, who sometimes went with Helen, spending afternoons at the local race track, lounging on the beach or on hotel patios and gambling in the evenings at one of the many casinos. By the late 1930s, Miami was a gambler's haven after Thomas E. Dewey began his prosecutorial rampage against New York racketeers in 1935 and gangsters fled for new bookmaking and gambling territory. Florida became a gathering point.

Before 1900, prostitution was organized crime's chief source of money. That changed with the enactment of the White Slave Act in 1910 prohibiting transportation of women across state lines for prostitution. Illegal liquor traffic was the money maker during Prohibition, and after that it was gambling – slot machines, punchboards, casinos, policy and number rackets.

The Sunshine State grew after World War I, sparked by a road network built during the war. Speculators bought cheap land, drained swamps and developed housing and commercial projects until hurricanes, the Depression and the outbreak of the Mediterranean fruit fly slowed tourism and development to a crawl.

Then around 1936, a refugee from a Chicago crap table operation named Julian "Potatoes" Kaufman turned a tomato packing shed at Hallandale, a tiny farming community halfway between Miami and Fort Lauderdale, into a parlor for small-fry bettors offering horse betting during the day and crap and bingo in the evenings. Soon local gamblers and winter visitors showed up.

So did "Jimmy Blue Eyes" Alo, the sidekick of Meyer Lansky. Alo scouted out new gambling sites for the New York hoods. Lansky and Alo grew up in the same New York gang with Benjamin "Bugsy" Siegel and Charles "Lucky" Luciano.

Kaufman wisely accepted Alo's offer for him and Lansky to be Kaufman's new partners in the Hallandale parlor.

Lansky's vision and innovations over the next few years earned him millions for providing high stakes gamblers in Florida with luxurious surroundings, fine entertainment and good food. Soon there were more than 35 "carpet joints" around Miami. The Farm, the elaborate replacement of the Plantation, the Beach Club and 210 Club were followed in a few years by Greenacres, Colonial Inn, Club Boheme and others. The Gulfstream race track opened in 1939.

Joining Lansky in Florida were hoods from New York, New Jersey, Cleveland, Chicago and Detroit – Frank Costello, Frank Erickson, Siegel, Joe Adonis, Morris "Moe" Sedway, Abner (Longie) Zwillman, Joseph "Doc" Stacher, William Moretti, Morris "Moe" Dalitz, Morris Kleinman, Edward Levinson, Mert Wertheimer, Charles Fischetti and many others.

Ray enjoyed the Florida carpet joints, eager to test his skills. The liveliest action in these brightly lit, noisy casinos usually was at the dice tables where a smiling Ray could shine, nestle among pretty women looking for a good time and swap jokes with other men.

Ray sought out quieter sections of the building for poker games with a small group of serious gamblers. He rubbed elbows with the bookies and casino operators, men he later would describe as only passing acquaintances.

But he had more than passing knowledge of racketeers like Jack Friedlander, the point man for Zwillman and Costello in Florida, and Harry Russell, one of the Chicago mob's main representatives. Friedlander collected cash from casino operators to pay off local police, mayors, councilmen and state officials to reduce raids at mob horse-betting and gambling parlors and to donate to local charities, civic and church groups to buy their silence.

The mob owned Dade, Broward and Palm Beach counties and, many folks believed, the governor's office, too.

During the winter months, hundreds of cabs and limousines carried wealthy visitors from the North to the Miami area's crap and roulette tables. Lansky had to find a way to hide the cash trail of gambling profits, which had been stuffing suitcases with money to distribute to crime dons up north.

Lansky opened numbered accounts at banks in Switzerland and eventually set up mob-backed banks in the islands off the Florida coast, sending the huge flow of cash from gambling through foreign banks so mob bosses could get the money back as "loans."

Federal agents later suspected Ray learned money laundering tactics from watching Lansky's success in Florida – take your cash in suitcases to Swiss banks and get the money back piecemeal as "loans" for your personal pleasure.

What could be easier?

But before he could do that, Ray had to become wealthy.

Chapter 22

WEALTHY BESSIE

The damn thing was going to blow. He was sure.

When it did, he had to be in the middle of the action.

He didn't mind being stuck on some rolling farmland in south-eastern Illinois near the Wabash River those early days of October 1940. The place wasn't important; what he could accomplish was. Other men had failed here; Ray knew he wouldn't.

Eighteen months ago there wasn't a producing oil well in White County; now there were more than 80. The county was the fastest grow-ing for oil drilling in Illinois and Ray wanted to be next to strike it rich.

Oilmen congregating at the McCurdy Hotel in Evansville sus-pected he was onto something big. If he was quiet, Ray was angry and they avoided him; if he was nervous, he had a big deal in the works. This time Ray was fidgety.

He was spending most of his days on the 80-acre tract of Illinois farmland owned by Albert and Bessie Bramlett in Phillips Township 50 miles west of Evansville. The nearest sign of civilization was Calvin – five miles away with a hundred people or so.

The Bramlett property didn't look like much. Sections were cleared for farming; the rest contained clusters of brush and scrawny pine, oak and maple trees. It was in a no-man's land for oil. The nearest success-ful well was several miles away. But that was what wildcatters like Ray thirsted for, finding the next big oil field.

It was a gamble. Thousands of dollars could be wasted drilling outside a proven field, but the bigger the risk, the bigger the reward and that, to Ray, was the fun part.

This time it wasn't as risky as drawing to an inside straight in poker. Ray had an edge.

L. C. Bates and W. L. Lichlyter, owners of the Evansville firm drilling a well on the Bramlett land, came to him a few days earlier with a tip. Three guys who leased the land and started drilling ran out of cash. The lease was about to expire, the hole down to 1,300 feet,

"We need someone to take over," the drillers told Ray. "From the core samples we're getting out, the well looks real promising." With only $15,000 or so needed to complete the drilling, Bates and Lichlyter knew Ray could quickly come up with cash and wanted to be his partners.

Never bashful about making money from someone else's misfortune, Ray stepped in.

He telephoned Cecil Lennan in New Jersey, his partner in a lackluster Kentucky fluorspar mine, and Lennan immediately sent a check for $10,000. Ray borrowed the rest. He had a list of potential investors to call on. "You get money wherever you can – your mother, your brother, your maiden aunt, your friends, your enemies – but you got the money," he liked to say.

He had calculated the odds on the Bramlett deal, judged the pros and cons, thought out different scenarios in his head – things he did a hundred times a day in business or in card games.

Ray thought, planned and plotted. Oilmen considered him a tightly-wound fellow with instinctive shrewdness, ready to jockey for the best position possible then plunge hell bent for leather to accomplish it.

His complicated psyche had many parts – guts, vision, restlessness and sometimes recklessness. His mind never rested. He would appear to be asleep riding in a car only to suddenly blurt out a solution to a deal he was working on or a problem he faced. "Don't sleep on a deal. Make your mind up and do it," he'd say.

This time he was wide awake. No need to downshift his energy and contemplate. He was sure. *The damn thing was going to blow.*

It was about time.

Every day he watched drilling progress on the Bramlett farm – 2,000, 2,400, 2,600 feet. The dark suits he wore for dinners and gambling soirées were replaced by cheaper pants and shirts in the oil field, a Mackinaw jacket on cooler days, knee-length boots and a wide-brimmed brown hat.

Still mingling freely with the oil field workers with chiseled faces and strong backs, he stood out in the crowd. After several days of drilling on the Bramlett well, workers said core samples showed they may be near oil.

Helen started making trips to the well. They had been married for more than a decade and she rarely got involved in Ray's business, but this time she wanted to be there. Helen was a welcome sight anywhere.

She and Ray enjoyed themselves at the Bramlett farm while the drilling continued, talking or playing cards in the doghouse – the boxy wooden building used to store tools or as a place to warm up around a stove when the chill set in.

They were in the middle of a game when the rumbling began. Rushing outside, they saw a worker give a thumbs-up sign. The well was going to blow!

There was a loud whoosh, oil shot through the top of the derrick, black sticky liquid gushed a hundred feet into the sky forming an ebony umbrella that splattered into the dirt around them.

As oil fell like rain, Ray and Helen laughed and yelled with glee, jumping up and down, hugging. They danced and frolicked in the black downpour, spinning over the ground as if they were in the Coral Room.

Ray never was much of a dancer; Helen always was better. Ray stopped moving to watch her. She twirled, slipping on the slick soil and catching herself with her hands. She gathered herself and stood up, her eyes sparkling and a bright, warm, loving smile beaming at Ray.

Oil covered their faces, saturated their clothing. Helen never looked more beautiful dripping with oil, Ray never more handsome. It was one of the happiest times in Helen's life, a moment she never forgot. Never would she be poor again. She and Ray were entering a world both had only dreamed about.

The first well soon turned out 200 barrels of oil a day. The question became how fast Ray could capitalize on the oil field before other wildcatters and big companies set up wells next door. Banks were eager to loan money to anyone finding oil and investors eager to invest.

In partnership with Bates and Lichlyter, Ray created Ryan Oil Company. In two weeks, he had a second well under way that began producing nearly 180 barrels a day. In two more weeks, a third well was started and pumped out close to 300 barrels a day. There was no stopping Ray now. He erected more wells and leased another 30 acres.

In another week, two more wells were drilled, two more the next week, five more in another week and three the following week. Workers hacked paths through the scrawny forests to carve out room for tall wooden platforms for pumps to continue churning out oil even when Little Fox River, a small creek along a corner of the property, flooded during spring and fall rains.

Ray purchased trucks and flatbeds that were quickly hand painted with Ryan Oil Company. He was constantly at the wells watching the process, now decked out in expensive coats and boots and smoking cigars.

At the end of two months, Ray had 15 wells turning out 3,000 barrels of oil a day. Three other wells were the only dry holes in the lot. Every place they drilled it seemed they struck oil. The oil flowed out, the money flowed in.

For the Illinois Basin, the Bramlett wells were productive, but not the biggest. Ray would find far more important oil fields in the next 15 years. But the Bessie Bramlett was his first big well allowing him to kick-start his spiraling rise to wealth.

After less than a year, he sold his interest in the Bramlett leases, raking in $300,000 from the oil production and nearly the same by selling a good portion – but not all – of other leases.

Ray's business philosophy was get into a successful deal; milk it for as much money as possible off the top, then sell while the venture still was valuable. His interest and attention span in projects usually wavered after a while and he had to move on to something else.

He beefed up his oil company, hiring geologists away from other companies by putting money in an escrow to assure workers five years of employment. He bought the latest technical equipment – one of the first wildcatters to buy a gas chromatograph and new oil-finding devices – and went after oil in other states.

Ray was one of the most progressive oilmen around, ready to latch onto the latest ideas to re-pressurize holes to get more oil out. He never thought small. Those who knew him figured there would be no stopping Ray Ryan now – and they were right.

He consolidated ownership of the oil company by buying out his original partners to get absolute control of his destiny. Bates withdrew from the company in March 1941 and Lichlyter the following February.

From then on, ownership of Ryan Oil – the basis of the rest of his massive business deals and fortune – belonged to Ray and Helen. To Ray, that was the way it should be – he and Helen together.

He joined with other investors to develop major oil fields and businesses across the United States and around the world, but at the center, it would be Ray and Helen – together, forever.

Chapter 23

HELPING
START DAVIS OIL

With the Bramlett well, Ray had found a needle in a haystack and he wanted more.

He and Helen could afford to head to Miami more often in the winter when work in the Midwest oil fields slowed. His favorite spot was the Roney Plaza Hotel, one of the hotels where his buddy Frank Erickson had his extensive bookmaking operations in a cabana.

The Plaza, a $2.3 million Miami Beach landmark since 1925, dominated a block along the Atlantic oceanfront with gardens and cabanas. There was much to do during the busy winter season with prize fights, fashion shows, gala parties, musicals, regattas and golf tournaments.

Starting around 1940 and for the next several years, Ray and Helen spent weeks vacationing each winter at the Roney Plaza.

In the evenings, Ray and his friends played cards or Ray prowled his favorite mob-controlled casinos that had sprung up in the Miami area to play poker and roulette or shoot craps.

The days were an idyllic time, lounging in the sun around the pool or on the beach, meeting with wealthy friends from Miami or from up north and catching up over leisurely meals.

Ray was on the beach at the Roney Plaza around 1940 when someone spotted a swimmer in trouble in the water. Ray and another man jumped in and pulled the swimmer out. The guy helping Ray was Jack Davis.

A stocky man with a receding hairline, Davis was near Ray's age. An amicable, successful businessman in New York's garment industry, Davis was an aggressive, dynamic spirit who came to America from Liverpool, England shortly before World War I. He joined the British Navy during the war and took up boxing.

At war's end, he became a buyer in a New York clothing store. In 1921 he set up the Jack Davis Dress Company in Manhattan and married a New York woman. In 1925 they had their first child, a boy named Marvin.

His dress business struggled and after four years he filed bankruptcy then tried again, this time with a firm specializing in cheaper frocks. During the Depression, the Jay-Day Dress Company turned out mass-produced, no-label clothing appealing to a large segment of the public and made Jack Davis wealthy.

Davis was interested in oil and the chance meeting with Ray became a profitable friendship for both. Ray came up with an idea that would lead to Jack Davis and son Marvin eventually creating one of the nation's biggest petroleum conglomerates. Ray's proposal was simple. He provided the money for them to send out landmen in Illinois, Kentucky and Indiana to buy mineral royalty rights for oil from landowners eager to sell for cash.

To insure the landmen didn't waste money on worthless royalties, the landmen got a percentage – called an override – of the oil produced from royalties they bought, ensuring they looked for only the most promising locations. Ray and Davis then could drill on the properties themselves or wait until other oil companies drilled and collect a sizeable percentage of any oil produced. Ray had his own landmen buying royalty rights in more than a dozen southern and western states.

Jack Davis set up Davis Oil around 1941 and began drilling in Ohio and the Illinois Basin then expanded into Texas, Oklahoma and other states. After graduating from New York University after World War II, Marvin Davis spent a year or two in Evansville handling Davis Oil operations there before taking over Davis Oil and moving it to Denver.

Marvin Davis became one of the country's most daring and successful wildcatters with oil and gas holdings reaching the equivalent of 100,000 barrels a day. He became a billionaire, one of the world's richest men, a high stakes gambler, owner of a movie studio, baseball team, hotels, golf courses and a legend in his own right much like Ray would become.

When Marvin Davis died in 2004, a former business partner noted that Marvin "was far, far more entranced by the deal than operating what he acquired, and far, far better at it."

It was a description that also would be applied to Ray.

Chapter 24

SWEET HOME EVANSVILLE

There was just something about Evansville that caused Ray and Helen to make it their permanent home.

The city wasn't as pretty as Tyler, Miami Beach or other cities they had seen but it was a comfortable fit for Helen, a slower pace where friends were always nearby. The only glitch occurred when she was blackballed from joining a prominent women's club because Ray was new oil money. An irate Ray promised that would never happen to her again. It never did.

Evansville was changing and not everyone was glad. Most residents enjoyed simple things and preferred the city the way it had been, not what it was becoming with the oil boom and the impending world war. Theaters showed the latest movies and Hill's Snappy Service's three small downtown diners sold 5-cent hamburgers "fried the way you like them."

Popular attractions included Friday wrestling at the Agoga Tabernacle, moonlight cruises on the river, more than a dozen clubs with dance music with admission fees of a quarter. The most elegant club in the city, the Colonial Garden operated by Wilbert "Witt" Eckstein, charged only 55 cents for admission.

Chicago drew the attention of people in Evansville, including Ray and Helen, even though St. Louis, Louisville and Indianapolis were closer. Evansville's main road was the north-south highway that connected the city with Chicago so it was easier to get to Chicago than the other cities and plenty to do when you got there.

Evansville compared itself to Chicago whenever possible. The McCurdy was promoted as the best hotel south of Chicago. When gambling reignited in Evansville and across the Ohio River in Henderson during the oil boom, folks called the two towns "Little Chicago."

There was something in Evansville for Ray. He could be a big fish in a small pond. Yet, the town offered more.

The city had a history as "a naughty place," as local historian Frank M. Gilbert noted in his 1910 book "History of Evansville and Vanderburgh County." It was "considered all right to race horses or fight chickens or play cards in those days, just so one was not a member of a church." When packet boats left the wharf, card tables were brought out in the main cabin for the men while piano music filled the air in the ladies' cabin.

Store-front horse betting parlors with poker and dice tables opened in the 1920s. The ticker tape national racing wire allowed gamblers to bet on horses at tracks across the United States. A horse track started near Evansville in 1922 in no-man's land, an oddity created when the Ohio River changed course in a flood decades earlier leaving hundreds of acres in Kentucky on the Indiana side of the river.

The race track quickly went bankrupt but James C. Ellis, an oil-man and land owner, took over the track in 1925 and named it Dade Park. The city built a road and railroad track to the track.

Bookmakers operated freely and attempts in the 1930s to rein them in always failed. By 1935, one hundred bookies operated in Evansville, soliciting bets from downtown clerks and salesgirls. Ray had been in Evansville about four months in April 1939 when Mayor William Dress went after gambling again, predicting the gambling crackdown would last "perpetually, everlastingly, forever and longer than that if possible." Forever was a couple of months.

The Trocadero, a deluxe dine-dance-and-drink nightclub, opened in 1939 in "no-man's land." Owners Clarence Wood and Cotton Jones brought in top acts like Duke Ellington and offered dining, craps and card tables on one floor and slots on the other.

Gambling in Evansville would reach its zenith during World War II with bookmaking an estimated $1 million a year business. Ray Ryan often could be seen roaming several of the local bookmaking joints, and even lined up jobs in them for people he met along the way.

A few residents suspected Ray had a financial interest in some of the local gambling operations. Over the years, there would be additional suspicions of Ray's financial involvement in gambling operations in other cities.

Evansville was a starting point for Ray and famed gambling expert John Scarne later noted that in the 1940s, Evansville "had more horse rooms and gambling dives per capita than any other city in America."[10]

It was a place Ray Ryan could love.

---

10 The city's gambling past remains today. The nickname of the University of Evansville's sports team is the Purple Aces and the team mascot is Ace Purple, a riverboat gambler. Indiana's first permit for a floating riverboat casino was Casino Aztar's "City of Evansville." The casino opened in December 1995 and attracted two million people a year. More than $100 million goes through the casino annually. Gambling went legit in Evansville.

Chapter 25

WALKING AROUND MONEY

With Bramlett wells bringing in $1,000 a day during the first half of 1941, Ryan Oil's assets were valued at more than $500,000 and incoming revenue conservatively estimated at around $25,000 a month.

Ray wasn't filthy rich, but on his way.

He remained a wildcatter drilling wells on the edges of proven oil fields always looking for another big strike. Oil was in greater demand as the war in Europe worsened. Germany was tearing through Europe and everyone believed the United States soon would be involved.

In August, Ray sold 12 producing wells at the Bramlett site and two that were being drilled to Trans-Tex Oil Company of Houston, Texas for about $410,000 in cash and oil. The cash figure was about one-third of a million dollars with the balance to be paid on future oil revenue. Ray retained control of the production on the wells in the remaining acres at the Bramlett site along with 16 producing wells he had in other parts of the basin.

He and Helen left the Riverside Avenue address for downstairs accommodations at 24 E. Chandler and less than two years later purchased a large home at 3306 E. Chandler. Winter vacations were spent basking in the sun at the Roney Plaza Hotel in Miami with side trips to the spa at French Lick, Indiana, and Mackinac Island, Michigan.

With a steady supply of cash coming in, Ray needed "walking around" money – at least $10,000 but usually more – jammed in his pocket to convince everyone he was a big time player in business deals and gambling.

He wasn't bashful about flashing money around. Years later and wealthier, he'd pulled even larger chunks of cash, usually dozens of $1,000 bills, from his pockets, cowboy boots and even from a soggy bathing suit after a plunge into the waters around Jamaica. "Walking around" money sometimes got Ray into trouble – nearly fatal trouble.

On December 7, Japan attacked Pearl Harbor and the United States declared war. A few days later, Ray and Helen went to Chicago for a banquet of the Indiana Society, an organization catering mainly to business executives and leaders. They stayed at the elegant Stevens Hotel – a 28-floor, 3,000-room giant built in 1927 for $30 million. Even among the fat cats flocking to the Stevens, Ray was marked as a man with lots of cash in his pockets.

On Wednesday December 10, Ray and Helen arrived in Chicago and went to several nightclubs before returning to the hotel late in the evening. Around 9 a.m. the next morning, there was a knock on the door. When Helen answered the door, two men with drawn guns and displaying what appeared to be badges rushed inside. "We're Secret Service men. You're under arrest," they said before pushing Helen into the bedroom where Ray was sleeping. Helen quickly figured out the men weren't federal agents.

"Wake up, Ray. This is a holdup," she told her husband. Ray peered through nearly closed eyelids and rolled back over. "It's just a gag. Tell them to quit kidding," Ray said. He thought this was a practical joke on him. But it wasn't.

One bandit poked a pistol into Ray's face while the other one rifled through his nearby trousers, taking a wallet containing seven $1,000 bills and $400 in smaller bills. "Where's the forty G's," one of the men asked. Ray said he didn't have that much. The men spent a half hour rummaging through the room looking for more money.

Helen was forced to hand over an expensive diamond ring but managed to hide other jewelry worth thousands of dollars beneath undergarments in a drawer. The men still stole about $500 in rings and watches. They tied up Ray and Helen with Ray's expensive ties and left them in the bathroom. After the robbers left, Helen freed herself and called the house detective.

Ray and Helen never appeared upset by the robbery. The next morning a Chicago newspaper photographer snapped the smiling couple leaving the hotel – Ray in a fashionable, snug-fitting three-piece suit and Helen in an upscale dress and a fur coat. The newspaper noted the Ryans "seem to take the whole thing (robbery) in stride." Ray's age was listed as 35 and Helen's as 25. Ray was 37 at the time and Helen 32, but both looked younger.

The FBI finally caught up with the robbers. In July 1942, agents arrested Taylor Whichard, described as the "Texas Dillinger," in Chicago and Gene Paul Norris in Oklahoma. Whichard had escaped from the Texas state penitentiary at Huntsville in April 1941 after serving four years of a 99-year sentence for armed robberies.

Gene Paul Norris was identified as a notorious gang leader in the southwest. Whichard was sentenced to nine years in jail for robbing the Ryans despite his plea to be given a chance to enter Germany and assassinate Adolph Hitler. Norris received an eight-year sentence and was tied to numerous robberies in four other states.

But the case still wasn't over.

In July 1943, the FBI said that Rodney K. Chambless, sheriff of Madison County, Texas had been arrested for aiding in the escape of prisoners from a Texas jail, including Norris.

The arrest of the sheriff was announced by FBI Director J. Edgar Hoover. Ray had played a part in a major FBI event.

The Stevens Hotel robbery marked Ray's first connection with the FBI.

It wouldn't be the last.

Chapter 26

BELLMAN GIN RUMMY TEACHER

Robert Buente was 17 years old, a member of the Central High School cheerleading team and a bellman at the McCurdy Hotel in 1942. His hotel duties included carrying luggage, escorting guests to their rooms, and fetching laundry, ice, whiskey or other items they wanted. He drew the line at lining up prostitutes for guests. That was the bell captain's chore.

The McCurdy owner Van Orman and his gorgeous circus performer wife lived at the hotel and the wife was "a real shit" to Buente. "She came from nothing and thought she was God Almighty."

Working at the McCurdy in Evansville during the war was a teenager's dream. Anything and everything was possible.

Most oilmen, military officers and guests freely tossed out money for tips. Buente's father was an attorney in town, but the son soon made more money than his dad. Buente once fetched a bottle of whiskey for a guest who started to write a check for $25. Buente said he couldn't take a check. "How about if I make it for $50," the man asked. Buente decided to take a chance because the bottle only cost $6. The check turned out to be good.

The hotel was alive with characters the likes of which Buente had never seen. Sam Garfield, an oilman with ties to the Purple Gang in Detroit, stayed at the hotel, and a couple of other Purple Gang and Chicago racketeers would drop by the city now and then. Garfield once gave Buente a hefty tip to drive his car to Detroit and money to fly back to Evansville.

Titanic Thompson was a different type. Whenever Buente saw him, Titanic was dressed like a typical hayseed, a floppy suit that didn't fit him (mainly because of the guns he carried under his arms), and a fedora that sat too high on his head.

The teenaged Buente figured that was just part of Titanic's act – "hey, I'm just a stupid cowboy ready to be taken for my money." Anyone falling for that soon discovered it was a costly mistake.

Buente was carrying items to a floor of the hotel one day when he saw Titanic practice tossing a key into a door lock – one of Titanic's most renowned hustles. Buente watched in awe as Titanic tossed the key from about two feet from the door and missed the lock. "Hell, that's not like me at all. I never miss this damn thing," Titanic said.

He tossed the key again and missed again. On the third try, the key stuck in the lock. Buente was amazed that Titanic actually could put a key into the lock no matter how many tosses it took and that Titanic spent hours and hours practicing.

Buente also got to see some of the pool games between Titanic and Hubert Cokes, with a big cigar constantly hanging from his mouth, at the Elks Club across the street from the hotel. Hubert and Titanic bet on anything – multi-bank shots, trick shots, bouncing one ball off another and into the pocket. They stuffed the money they won in separate corner pockets. Buente watched the two hustlers plying their trade, wondering how long they had to practice to make those shots. It was a better show than Ringling Brothers.

The pool games at the Elks Club and the poker games on the mezzanine of the McCurdy were magical to Buente. "They pulled all kinds of crap on each other. It was like a bunch of kids really. They had a helluva time all of those guys back in those days. It was fun being part of it."

After the Coral Room closed in the evening, the hotel workers headed to the basement and played craps. Sometimes Buente lost, sometimes he won. After the games, he might head out for a drink. Even wearing his cheerleading outfit after high school ballgames, he could get into any bar or nightclub in Evansville to drink, shoot dice or play cards. No one questioned how old he was. You only had to have money. And Buente did.

Ray took a liking to Buente and asked specifically for the teenager when he needed something. Ray was a spiffy dresser, always neat and well groomed, and Buente often picked up and returned Ray's laundry.

One day Ray called Buente to his room and asked him if he knew how to play gin rummy. Buente did. His family had played gin rummy for years, even though the game wasn't particularly popular around Evansville. Ray wanted to learn gin rummy because many oil executives and businessmen around the McCurdy preferred gin rummy to poker. Ray needed to master gin rummy because at $10 a point he could win a lot more money in a shorter time than he could at poker.

Ray took off his suit coat and he and Buente, in his bellman's outfit, sat on a bed in Ray's room playing gin rummy for an hour or more. Buente explained the game, the strategy involved.

Over a couple of months, they spent hours several days each week playing gin rummy in Ray's room. At the end of one session, Ray handed Buente a $100 bill. After six weeks, Ray was thumping the youth soundly at the game. Buente couldn't believe how quickly Ray learned the game.

Ray finally believed he had learned everything the teenager could teach him and handed Buente another $100 bill. That was special because Ray wasn't known as a big tipper by the McCurdy staff. The teenager and oilman never played gin rummy again.

Immersing himself in gin rummy was typical of Ray. If he wanted to get better at anything, he devoted his full attention to it. Throughout his life when getting ready for high stakes card games Ray practiced and practiced gin rummy or poker with friends for days beforehand, like Titanic Thompson practiced tossing chips into a cup and a key into a door lock.

Ray sharpened his ability to remember the cards he had seen in each hand then deduce what cards the other players had and calculate which cards remained in the deck.

When he got a few years older, Ray exercised and hit a punching bag to build up his strength and endurance before big gin rummy or poker games, much like a prize fighter preparing for a boxing match.

Buente always proudly claimed he taught Ray Ryan how to play gin rummy.

Years later, H. L. Hunt and many other serious gamblers probably wished Buente hadn't been such a good teacher.

Chapter 27

TWO PEAS IN A POD

When World War II was in full swing, Evansville no longer was an isolated, sleepy river city. The city's population increased to 150,000 with 64,000 working at manufacturing war materiel at various plants around town.

In 1942, the federal government transformed 45 acres along Evansville's riverfront into a shipyard building oceangoing Landing Ship Tanks (LST) and other craft for the U. S. Navy. Evansville became the largest inland producer of oceangoing ships during the war, employing 19,000 workers of which a third were women. Dwarfs were used as welders in the smallest sections of ships.

Other city plants assembled 6,242 P-47 Thunderbolt fighter planes, nearly half of the total built during the war, and produced 96 percent of the .45-caliber ammunition used by the military along with land mines, aviation parts, truck cargo bodies, uniforms, tents, stoves, gun stocks, Bailey bridges, incendiary bombs, bayonets and other war materiel. Three-fourths of the city's industrial production went to war contracts.

Over one and a half million servicemen from military camps passed through Evansville. Each week packed trains brought 8,000 to 10,000 soldiers from Camp Breckinridge and Fort Campbell in Kentucky to Henderson and Evansville. The downtown was sidewalk-to-sidewalk with soldiers. Dormitories opened in churches and school gyms. Hotels were at capacity. Women headed to the city looking for a good time with officers at local hotels.

The war years in Evansville were a time of "soldiers, booze and whores," according to old timers. Gambling joints flourished. Lower-ranking soldiers patronized a red light district: rows of shotgun houses along High Street, near the shipyards, Main Street, the L&N train station and the Greyhound bus depot.

The High Street area was called Gear Town because of the intersecting roads First Street, Second Street, Third Avenue and High Street.

Bars and nightclubs like the Club Trocadero, the Dells, Riverview Gardens and Green River Gardens and at the McCurdy, Vendome, Lincoln and Acme hotels did land office business. Henderson had bars and nightclubs. Most of them had card and dice tables in back rooms.

The war years attracted more than soldiers and plant workers.

George "Blackie" Dardeen found easy work in Henderson and Evansville as a dealer at poker and craps tables. He had been a dealer at the Showboat in Terre Haute, Indiana, but moved to Evansville for the more profitable games. He worked at Club Trocadero's dice tables before being hired as a dealer at the Kasey Klub in Henderson.

For two years on his Mondays off, he dealt at a high stakes poker game at Evansville's Grand Hotel. Ray sat in on many of the games and Blackie grew to respect the fearless way Ray played.

"Ray was a nice guy. He had plenty of money. All he did was party," recalled Blackie. "He was a damn good poker player. He was a good gambler." There usually were a half-dozen or so gamblers at the table including Hubert Cokes.

Ray was an immaculate dresser, always in an expensive suit and tie. Cokes and the other players were equally well dressed.

There wasn't a lot of talking at the tables, no kidding around. Each pot had thousands of dollars. No one drank liquor. They had to keep their heads straight for games that sometimes went for 10 hours.

Blackie remembered Ray always walking away with a fuller pocket than when he came in. "Ray just ran over the game. He'd bet so much money people were afraid to call him, tossing down $30,000 to $40,000 on a card sometimes."

Blackie knew Titanic Thompson, too. One night at a Terre Haute gambling joint, Blackie had watched Titanic pull one of his hustles.

Titanic put a cup in the center of a dice table and started trying to toss 20 chips into the cup from several feet away. The first time Titanic managed to put only the last chip in the cup.

A gambler named Pratt from northern Indiana bet $5,000 that Titanic couldn't get five of the 20 chips in the cup. Blackie said Titanic didn't get the fifth chip in until the last toss. Pratt wanted to get his money back and bet $7,000 on Titanic not getting in seven chips. The crowd watched as the last of the 20 chips was the seventh one in the cup. Pratt stormed out minus $12,000.

After Pratt left, Titanic tossed all 20 chips into the cup. Blackie was astonished. *Think of all the hours Titanic had to practice that.*

Blackie remained in Evansville for a couple of years before moving on as a craps dealer in Texas, Tulsa, Miami and eventually Las Vegas in 1948. Blackie saw Ray a couple of times along the way, including two or three times at the Greenacres Casino near Miami. "He just shot craps. He knew all about the gambling."

In 1951, Blackie worked at Benny Binion's Horseshoe Casino in Las Vegas and a few months later was hired at the Flamingo. He occasionally saw Ray at Vegas casinos usually with John Drew, one of the Chicago mob's representatives there. Drew was known as a cheat for rigging dice and card games to fleece rich bettors in Chicago.

Ray ran around with Drew in Vegas and Palm Springs. Some gamblers were convinced Ray wasn't above cheating at cards and hanging out with Drew was more than guilt by association.

To them, it was more like two peas in a pod.

Chapter 28

BUDDY FATS WANDERONE

The two-story Elks Club across from the McCurdy was an imposing structure.

Built in 1909, the brick building had a handsome rounded portico supported by white columns. A dining area was in the walk-in basement with offices, meeting rooms and a pool room on the second level. By the early 1940s, the Elks Club's pool room was the best theater in town.

The stage was pool tables, the acting superb and no intermissions. While Hubert Cokes and Titanic Thompson demanded attention, the arrival of a 30-year-old fat guy enthralled everyone.

Rudolph Walter "Fats" Wanderone, Jr. was 5-feet 10, tipping the scales at more than 280 pounds. It wasn't his chubby features, mop of dark hair and bull-like meandering that drew large crowds but his wizardry with a pool cue and his unceasing chatter. He teased and belittled his opponents while roaming around the pool table with a penguin-like gait.

Wanderone, born around 1913 to Swiss immigrant parents, grew up playing pool in New York City. When his family went to Switzerland for a visit, the kid was tutored by a Swiss pool master. By his late teens, Fats was making a name as a pool player and hustler. He met Titanic in New York one day and they became friends. Fats said Titanic had the hands of an artist, long and agile fingers for sleight-of-hand and card tricks.

Fats saw Titanic win thousands of dollars once by betting suckers he could throw an English walnut atop a skyscraper. Titanic went to a nearby stand and picked out a walnut and tossed it on top of the building. Titanic had filled the walnut with mercury for weight and paid the proprietor $100 to make sure he got the right walnut for the scam.

Fats bounced across the country looking for pool games. He claimed he was the best player around, taking on all comers in America's seedy pool parlors and always played for money because "playing for fun is like shooting it out on a side street with blanks."

Wherever he went, he became that locality's "Fats" – New York Fats, Brooklyn Fats, or just Fats (after the 1961 movie "The Hustler" he was called Minnesota Fats). As a young man, Wanderone met Hubert Cokes around a New York pool table. They met occasionally and sometimes shared a hotel suite in Chicago.

He married Evelyn Inez in 1941 after a whirlwind courtship and moved into Evelyn's home in Dowell, Illinois. By then, Cokes and Titanic were in Evansville for the oil boom.

Around 1943, Fats began to make the 100-mile trip from Dowell to Evansville several times a year to play pool with Cokes and Titanic. When the word went out that Fats was in town, folks hustled to the Elks Club to watch.

Ray played pool with them sometimes and developed a close bond with Fats. In his book "The Bank Shot and other Great Robberies" published in 1966, Fats recounted his meetings with Ray over the Elks Club pool tables. "Ryan is what I really call a five-star general because he is the only millionaire I ever knew who lived like a millionaire. He never moaned and groaned like the rest of the multis on account he knew the cash was just for spending and not for caressing.

"Ray Ryan loved to play pool, only he wasn't anything near a top player but he was as fearless as any man I ever knew. He would risk a zillion on one more roll and if he happened to bust out he would just laugh and start all over again. He did it many times."

Fats said Ray liked to shoot pool with him "because he said I offered the most tremendous odds he ever heard of, even better than the oil fields, and even Daddy Warbucks said the same thing. Me and Daddy Warbucks played most games even but when me and Ray Ryan went to the table for a straight pool proposition I had one pocket, only one pocket and Raymond had six. I was actually playing One Pocket to his straight pool, only I always won the cash because I hardly let Ray get to the table."

Even when Fats wasn't around, Ray stopped by the Elks Club to play Cokes, who also gave Ray the six pockets while he ran his balls into one pocket. Ray's success at the pool tables was the same with Cokes, who once used a mop handle as his pool cue to give Ray an advantage. Cokes won and a janitor waited to clean the floor after the two finished their game.

It was Ray's never-give-up attitude and lack of concern at tossing money on the table in hopes of getting good enough to beat the best that impressed Fats and Cokes.

Chapter 29

HOBNOBBING WITH TOPPINGS

He belonged "to that almost forgotten phase of pros-
perous America which spawned the free-wheeling likes of
Diamond Jim Brady . . . people have seized upon Ray Ryan
as the guy to perpetuate a lost legend and take up where those
glittery old-timers left off. For in him they've come up with a
live, fun-loving guy who kindles the imagination . . . a fel-
low who is the swash-buckling sort who fits such a picture."
– Los Angeles Examiner in 1952

"Ray didn't become Ray Ryan until after he had money," a long-time friend summed up Ray's life once to Steve Bagbey.

Ray was never a plodder who got bogged down in routine. He was memorable for his infectious personality, twinkling eyes and mischievous smile, with an active mind always planning, dreaming and plotting.

Ray's youthful confidence that he would strike it rich didn't become a reality until the oil started flowing and when it did, he went after life with gusto.

Oil and gambling dominated but Ray also had a love affair with horses. First he loved riding horses – an enthusiasm from his early days in Wisconsin that spread to the ornate saddles, elaborate cowboy outfits and striking horses he rode in the Palm Springs Desert Circus parade decades later.

Perhaps even more than riding horses, Ray loved betting on them. He always showed up at race tracks during his Florida vacations. With some success in the Illinois Basin oilfields in the early 1940s, Ray and Helen had time to visit Churchill Downs in Louisville, Kentucky, where they had box seats. He bought Helen a thoroughbred aptly named "Gusher" that won a seven-furlong race at Churchill in October 1943.

Helen missed the race because, after 14 years of marriage, she was seven months pregnant. Despite the pending birth of their child, Ray had left Helen at home in September to head off to the East Coast.

Helen had to live with that. She understood Ray's brain raced like a whirlwind and there always were "things" he felt he needed to do. Things this time meant gambling and hanging out with the rich.

New York City didn't glow anymore in 1943 because of World War II. Broadway's Great White Way's bright lights were a glimmer of the pre-war days. Few cars were on the streets, the once sparkling store windows were a gloomy gray. Street and traffic lights were covered with hoods.

The nation's largest city didn't have a blackout, but a dim-out. It had taken months for the U.S. Army to bring New York's glare down to an acceptable wartime level to prevent city lights from silhouetting tankers and ships along the coast to marauding German U-boats. Signs were covered to prevent being seen overhead by enemy bombers. Baseball games were played in the afternoons and ended a half-hour after sunset.

The dim-out remained in effect in the fall of 1943 despite little fear of enemy attack. The Allies had landed at Salerno; British and American planes were bombing Berlin for the eightieth time. Still, shoes, gasoline, clothing and food were rationed, streets dark, but inside nightclubs, restaurants and hotels the world was bright – if you had money.

On Saturday September 18, John Reid "Jack" Topping, a woman companion and Ray walked slowly along streets warmed by the 60-degree weather to a 26th floor suite at the Hotel New Yorker, the city's largest with 2,500 rooms. Ray had invited Topping to the suite for a night of gambling.

One table was for chemin de fer, a popular variation of baccarat and a favorite of Topping. Chemin de fer is French for railroad, and Topping later concluded he was "railroaded" in the card game. No one ever knew if Ray had been the railroad engineer.

The 22-year-old Jack was a member of New York's socially prominent Topping family, whose fortune came from metals – steel and tin. Jack was the youngest of the three Topping brothers. Daniel Reid Topping was owner of the Brooklyn Dodgers professional football team at the time, and Henry J. "Bob" Topping, Jr. was a noted sportsman and investor.

Dan was married to Sonja Henie, the Norwegian World and Olympic ice skating champion who went on to make films in Hollywood. Dan's first marriage was to an heiress and the second to little-known actress Arline Judge, which lasted three years until 1940 when Dan married Henie. A few years later, Judge married Bob Topping for a year before he divorced her to marry movie star Lana Turner.

The Toppings had money to burn at a time when most Americans just made ends meet. Their grandfathers were Daniel G. Reid and John Alexander Topping and Reid's daughter, Rhea, married into the Topping family. Reid, known as the nation's "tin plate king," once was president of the American Tin Plate Company.

When he died in 1925, he left an estate of $4 million to his daughter and trusts of $250,000 each to his three grandsons. J. A. Topping, head of tin plate and iron and steel companies, died in 1935 at the height of the Depression, leaving a sizeable estate.

Dan and Bob caught the public eye in the early 1940s, but Jack was a familiar figure around New York nightclubs.

Jack and Ray had dined at El Morocco before heading to the hotel with their pretty brunette companion, Ruth Waldo, 21, a public relations counselor and typist. She had formerly worked as secretary for the mayor of Columbus, Ohio, and now lived in a downtown hotel with Choo-Choo Johnson, a model-actress and showgirl.

Jack had $500 in his pocket when they reached the suite crowded with high rollers in expensive suits, booze freely flowing, and several good-looking women to keep the men amused. Jack and Ray took seats at the chemin de fer table. Ruth sat next to Jack and for the next four hours, Jack had a lot of luck even with poor cards and kept raking in pots.

He was about $3,000 ahead when Ruth said she wanted to go home. Jack left with her, promising to return. They walked to her hotel, stopping to look at displays in store windows. At one store, they went inside and Jack bought Ruth a $3,000 fur coat.

When he returned to the suite after midnight, Jack needed cash to get back into the game. Jack later said Ray was "sleeping" when he returned. Jack needed money, after buying the coat for Ruth, so he took $2,000 Ray had left on the table, wrote a check to Ray for the $2,000, and resumed playing.

Jack's luck took a turn for the worse over the next few hours even with better hands than he had earlier. He went through the $2,000 and started writing checks to cover his mounting losses. By morning, he had written eight checks totaling $12,000 before calling it quits, leaving the suite with only $5 in his pocket and a feeling that he had just been cheated in a crooked game.

He went to the authorities and in the first week in October, the police arrested Aaron "Arky" Schwartz for setting up the hotel gambling game. In February, 1944, the case was heard in the city's downtown Traffic Court. Newspapers identified Jack Topping as the brother-in-law of Sonja Henie, the star attraction in the city.

Jack testified in the trial, but the magistrate dismissed the charge against Schwartz, saying there wasn't enough evidence to connect the checks to Schwartz. The magistrate chided Topping for having a bad memory on some of the details in the case and Schwartz' attorney called Topping a "welsher."

The trial was over, but the case wasn't closed to the New York District Attorney's office.

Investigators delved into the checks Topping had written, including the one to Ray. The DA's office sent inquiries to the Chicago Crime Commission asking for information about Ryan. Mike F. Glynn, the New York DA's chief investigator, swapped letters with Virgil W. Peterson, operating director of the Chicago commission.

Peterson passed along what little the Milwaukee police knew – "cheap tobacco Ryan," a salesman in Milwaukee in the early 1930s with an arrest at a bookmaking parlor. He sent Glynn a copy of Jack's check to Ray that had been deposited at Old National Bank in Evansville and processed through the First National Bank in Chicago. Nothing in the letters indicated that the gambling involving Topping was rigged or that Ray was involved. The New York

DA office just wanted to know more about Ray as part of its investigation.

Jack's check was made out to "Ray 'Lover' Ryan." There was no explanation why Jack used the term "Lover." Perhaps, Jack simply was acknowledging that Ray's wife was due to deliver a baby soon or that Ray was absent from the table the night of the game for another reason.

The women hanging around card games knew the score. After several hours of intense gambling, the men needed a break and often picked a girl and headed to a bedroom. The girls knew that big winners handed over wads of $100 bills, jewelry or even a fur coat at the end of the night, things they never could afford in their day jobs.

Topping's complaint triggered an investigation of Sam Jacobs, president of the Rex Trading Corporation where Jack's checks were cashed. Jacobs was a loan shark who charged up to 365 percent interest (one percent for each day) on loans to gamblers in New York's midtown, theatrical and nightclub circles.

He eventually was sentenced to a year in jail and fined $10,000 for conducting an unlicensed, usurious loan agency, one of the stiffest sentences ever for a New York loan shark. Jacobs wept at the sentencing and a year later was arrested for bookmaking at the Jamaica race track in Queens.

Whether that evening at the Hotel New Yorker lingered in Ray's mind isn't known. He soon had something else to think about. On December 8, 1943, less than three months after the card game, Helen Ryan gave birth to a girl, Rae Jean, at St. Mary's Hospital in Evansville.

Rae Jean was the apple of Ray's eye, and Helen devoted her life to their only child.

Chapter 30

TESTING PRO FOOTBALL

In 1944, Ray sought an active role in a new venture – professional sports.

Gambling on college and professional football games brought him in contact with coaches and assistants across the country. He knew some of them well enough to telephone them to get their thoughts about individual players and teams. He wagered tens of thousands dollars on college football games each week, always keeping track of game results, and checking out surprising losses.

Once a heavily-favored team he had bet on failed to cover the spread due to a missed extra point at the end of the game. Ray called the team's coach the next day and asked what happened. The coach said the team was so far ahead that he put in a kicker who never had gotten into a game. The kid's kick hit the team's center square in the butt with the football, he said.

Ray laughed about the story, thanked the coach and hung up, not worrying about losing the bet. The story of why he lost the bet was too funny.

Gambling on teams was fun and usually profitable, but Ray's desire to own a pro football team had grown after being around his friend Alexis Thompson, the owner of the Philadelphia Eagles.

Ray wasn't looking for a long-term involvement with team ownership. That wasn't his style. What attracted him was the challenge. He would break new ground, be able to match wits with other potential owners and go where few had been before. How Ray loved that scenario. And even if the whole idea fell apart, Ray believed he'd find a way to make money out of it.

The National Football League had been around for decades but attendance fell during the war. Talks were under way to start a new professional football league, an idea promoted by Arch Ward, the sports editor of the Chicago Tribune. Ward already had helped create the baseball All-Star game, was involved in Golden Gloves boxing and the annual All-Star football game between top college athletes and the reigning NFL championship team.

The Allies were gaining ground in the war and, most likely, the fighting wouldn't last much longer. Ward knew it would take two or three years to get a new pro league going and by that time plenty of young talent would be back home ready to play and thousands of veterans ready to watch them.

Ward lined up people of wealth to start teams in major cities – an assortment dubbed "men of millionaire incomes." The group met in St. Louis two days before D-Day, June 6, 1944, the Allied invasion of Europe at Normandy. Ray joined with Eleanor Gehrig, the widow of the great New York Yankees first baseman Lou Gehrig, in seeking the prized New York franchise. No league could survive unless New York was represented.

"I am happy to be associated with a sports venture in New York," said Mrs. Gehrig. "Mr. Ryan and I have one ambition in this enterprise – to win a championship for New York every season."

Ray knew several of the potential owners since most were serious gamblers, oilmen, Hollywood actors or Chicago area people.

James Breuil, president of Frontier Oil Company, represented the city of Buffalo. Gene Tunney sought the Baltimore franchise. John Keeshin, a trucking executive, wanted the Chicago team. Anthony J. "Tony" Morabito, a lumber executive, represented San Francisco.

Actor Don Ameche headed a group of movie personalities – that eventually included Bob Hope, Bing Crosby, Pat O'Brien and Louis B. Mayer – for a team in Los Angeles. Arthur B. "Mickey" McBride was there for a franchise in Cleveland, home of his Yellow and Zone taxi cab companies.

McBride was involved in a national racing wire service that soon would draw the attention of Congress and get him into hot water. He had been in trouble even as a kid. As a six-year-old growing up in Chicago, McBride hawked newspapers on street corners and illegally sold streetcar transfers on the side. When the streetcar company brought McBride into court, he was defended by Clarence Darrow, who portrayed McBride to the jury as a "poor newsboy." McBride was found not guilty.

The St. Louis meeting went well on setting up the All-American Football Conference (AFC). Ray had done his homework prior to the meeting. Eager to one-up the next guy as usual, Ray surprised everyone by announcing he had already signed four top players for the New York team – All-American quarterback Glenn Dobbs from Tulsa University, end Jack Russell of Baylor, lineman Martin Ruby from Texas A&M and halfback Bill Daley from the University of Minnesota. Ray set his eyes on playing in Yankee Stadium.

Ward announced the league formation in September 1944 with a goal of eight to 10 teams and a starting date of 1946. Competition was fierce in New York. Two NFL teams already were there – the New York Giants and the Brooklyn Dodgers. The Giants were solid, but the Dodgers had serious problems. The Dodgers, bought by Dan Topping in 1934, played at Ebbets Field, the home of the pro baseball Brooklyn Dodgers, owned by Branch Rickey.

Topping's Dodgers had modest success at first, but in the 1942 and 1943 seasons would win only five of 21 games. In addition, Rickey forced Topping to change the football team's name to the Tigers in 1944 (the team lost all 10 games that year) and then set out to prohibit Topping from using Ebbets Field. Topping had to merge with a Boston team in 1945 (winning only three of 10 games) and played only one game that year in New York

Topping's patience with the NFL was wearing thin. He was a Marine captain assigned to the South Pacific during much of the war and left the day-to-day running of the Dodgers to others.

When he returned home for good he purchased the New York Yankees baseball team and Yankee Stadium for $2.8 million in January 1945 with Larry S. MacPhail, former president of the Brooklyn Dodgers baseball team. Topping began building his own baseball dynasty, now had his own stadium for professional football and wanted a team not in the NFL.

After a meeting of AFC potential owners in December 1944, the Chicago Tribune reported that Ray had sold the New York franchise to Gene Tunney, who had dropped his plan for a team in Baltimore. Ray had sold out "at a profit" along with the contracts of the players he already had signed. Another report said Ray "gracefully" backed out at the request of Arch Ward who feared Ray's gambling reputation would give the league a bad name.

With Ray gone, Mrs. Gehrig soon withdrew as part owner of a New York team but was named to an executive position as the conference's secretary. Tunney, who was serving in the military, soon withdrew as a potential owner because of his military obligation. The ownership of a New York team was in limbo.

There was speculation that Ray was just making a quick buck or serving as a stalking horse to control the New York franchise until Dan Topping decided what he was going to do.

The month after Ray bailed out Topping finalized the deal for Yankee Stadium and the baseball team. Topping quickly dropped out of the NFL and in December 1945 announced he was transferring his football team to the new All-American league. Some reports indicated that Ray managed to get a small financial interest in the Yankees for his efforts.

The All-American conference opened in 1946 with eight teams, four each in two divisions. Topping's Yankees team won the Eastern Division the first two years, but lost in the championship games to the Cleveland Browns. Future football superstars Otto Graham, Marion Motley, Dante Lavelli, Lou Saban, Lou Groza, Ara Parseghian and Alex Agase played for the Browns, coached by Paul Brown. Cleveland won 51 of 58 games in the four seasons of the AFC's existence and the league championship each year.

The 1948 Browns were the first professional football team to go undefeated (14 games) in a season.

Mickey McBride, owner of the Browns, also contributed a bit of pro football history. His team carried five non-roster players to use in case of injuries and he paid them from his taxi company revenues. From then on, non-roster players were known as the taxi squad.

The new league's attendance far exceeded the NFL but escalating player salaries proved too much for the owners. By 1950 the league folded and Cleveland, the San Francisco Forty-Niners and the Baltimore Colts were merged into the NFL. Cleveland would dominate the NFL in the 1950s.

After his first foray into pro sports, Ray never again sought to own a professional team, but went on to other things – hitting high gear as the 1940s drew to a close and it would take twenty years before his foot left the pedal.

His wealth grew each day, and he wanted more.

Chapter 31

HERE, THERE, EVERYWHERE

In January 1946 when Rae Jean was two years old, Ray and Helen purchased a fashionable two-story home at 600 Lombard Avenue in Evansville, putting the house in Helen's name; they would live there the rest of their lives.

The Ryans often traveled across the country and world, but Helen rejected moving from Evansville. Rae Jean lived in the city until she graduated from Memorial High School in 1961.

Ray stayed closer to Evansville searching for oil and in June 1948 an oil well came in on the Berry lease in Gibson County north of Evansville. Veteran oilman Olen Sharp, who never hit a big strike before, had leased 400 acres owned by the Berry heirs and Ray took a one-fourth share, Aurora Gasoline Company another quarter and speculators from Carmi, Illinois, the remaining quarter.

They created the Ryan and Sharp Oil Company and within a year drilled 22 wells bringing in more than a half-million barrels in a year, 10 percent of the oil production in Indiana.

With money from the Berry wells, Ray stepped up his hunt for oil elsewhere and by the end of the 1940s his holdings of royalties, leases and wells stretched across Indiana, Illinois, Kentucky, Texas, Oklahoma, Colorado, Mississippi, North Dakota, Utah, California, Wyoming, Alabama, Arkansas, Georgia, Florida, Idaho, Louisiana, Pennsylvania and New Mexico and in Canada and Mexico.

"The amount of royalties he owned around the country was unbelievable," one of Ray's geologists said. "We were always getting calls wanting to lease his royalties." Ray had a knack for investing and always got more than one-eighth interest on any oil found on his holdings.

He had become the full-fledged "multi" that Minnesota Fats would call him. In two more years, Ray's richest oil strike would be in Texas.

In a decade, he had gone from trading leases at the McCurdy Hotel to being a multi-millionaire. Many other business ventures followed – some spectacular, others mundane – but always highlighted by Ray's determination to find the next big bonanza, an unending focus on increasing his fortune. He had hustled all his life. By the end of the 1940s, he was ready to enjoy it.

Until then, he had gone virtually unnoticed by the news media. But noted newspaper columnist Damon Runyon, a gambler himself and owner of a winter home on an island near Miami, heard about Ray's gambling sprees in New York and Miami. In a national column published in September 1945, Runyon wrote that Nick the Greek Dandolos and before him Pittsburgh Phil (George E. Smith) connoted gambling's high rollers for years but now Ray "plays the highest gin rummy of any man since the game was invented."

Within months of honing the strategy of gin rummy with the aid of the McCurdy bellman, Ray put what he learned to use, especially during his and Helen's more frequent trips to Florida.

Over dinners, at parties and while lounging along the beachfront, they met an assortment of business executives and socialites from Miami and New York. Many of the men were willing to play head-to-head games of gin rummy with Ray. Nothing could keep Ray from playing.

Benny Davis, the writer of the song "Margie," was on hand one day when Ray, who was a poor but daring swimmer, ventured so far out in the surf at Miami Beach that lifeguards had to go fetch him. Davis was impressed with how little nearly drowning in the ocean affected Ray. "He is a cool hand," Davis said. "As soon as he had ungargled the salt water he played a gentleman gin rummy at $10 a point and blitzed his opponent six times running."

Equally impressed with Ray was Evansville newspaper reporter Ed Klinger, who tracked Ray's business dealings and life. Klinger wrote that to Ray "all life is a gamble and he enjoys life. He's quiet, soft-spoken but has a budding vitality that lies just beneath the surface that you sense as soon as you talk to him. He doesn't like to have noisy people around him. Mr. Ryan likes to be where things are going on. He likes action. If he can't find any he makes some. He's intensely loyal to friends and associates, and frequently shows it by gifts that are either expensive or hard to come by."

Two events took place in Evansville in 1948 that had a bearing on the Ray Ryan story.

One was Ray hiring William J. Gorman as general manager of Ryan Oil. Ray prided himself on being able to look into a prospective worker's eyes and tell if he was honest and Gorman was that.

A quiet, unassuming, intelligent person, he was born in Kentucky, grew up in Evansville, graduated from the University of Kentucky, and, after serving overseas in the war, worked at an Evansville accounting firm that had Ryan Oil as a client.

About 30 years old when hired by Ray, Gorman was what Ray wasn't – a stickler for details, ready to take complicated situations and find solutions. Ray was a broad brush stroke guy, eager to spend millions of dollars on deals then wanting to move on to another one after several months when he became bored or needed a challenge.

Gorman was left making chicken salad out of the chickenshit ideas Ray sometimes came up with. He was Ray's sounding board, trusted advisor, often at his side in important negotiations and the guy who mopped up after him.

The other event in 1948 was the birth of James Stephen Bagbey on September 13 at Deaconess Hospital to James Otha and Anna Marie Bagbey. The father worked at a local plant manufacturing radio and later television cabinets. The mother was a housewife.

Their son, Steve Bagbey, never met and knew little of Ray Ryan for nearly 30 years, yet Ray's eventual murder would haunt Steve for the next three decades.

Chapter 32

ALWAYS UNDER CHICAGO'S SHADOW

To understand the people around Ray – and even Ray himself – one had to understand the Chicago of the first half of the 20th century. What happened in Chicago during that period never stayed in Chicago. It just spread across the country from Miami to Los Angeles and places in between.

No matter where Ray went, Chicago cast a shadow over him. Many of his friends and business associates came from Chicago. So did deadly enemies who would crush the life out of him in a split second decades later.

Steve Bagbey's attention was more clearly focused on the Chicago connection about a year after Ray's car bombing from a report passed on to him by Evansville FBI agents Richard J. Eisgruber and Gary R. Perkins around the end of July 1978. Chicago FBI agents had leaned on their mob insiders who offered educated guesses on who killed Ray Ryan. Few mob crews could have pulled off such a sophisticated hit.

Eisgruber laid out the facts in one report: the killing was a professional organized crime type hit; Ryan was believed a friend and confident of La Costa Nostra (LCN) figures Frank Costello, Sam Giancana and John Rosselli.

"All sorts of theories have emanated during the course of this investigation as to the reason for Ryan's murder; however, the most logical and most probable lead being pursued is that of a revenge murder on the part of Marshall Caifano, LCN member, Chicago, Illinois, and Charles James Delmonico, LCN member, Miami, Florida, and son of Tampa, Florida LCN member Charlie "The Blade" Tourine," for Ryan's testimony against mobsters Caifano and Delmonico in the 1964 extortion trial, the FBI report said.

Then Eisgruber got to the crux of the matter.

Citing Chicago FBI "highly placed" informants, he said the name at the top of the list for pulling off the car bombing was Francis John Schweihs, also known as "The German" and "The Nut." Frankie Schweihs was one of the Chicago mob's top enforcers and hit men and was suspected in the 1976 murder of John Rosselli in Florida along with a dozen or more mob killings, including a guy in Chicago named Richard Cain.

Schweihs, Rosselli, Cain — Steve Bagbey eventually would find out all three were linked in some way to Ray Ryan. It was a small world after all.

The 46-year-old burly, bushy-headed, craggy-faced Schweihs was an electronics expert, a top commercial burglar and a man known for "his especially quick and violent temper" who climbed up the mob's hierarchy after serving as bodyguard for Felix "Milwaukee Phil" Alderisio.

Schweihs had a home in the Miami area since the summer of 1975, an apartment in Chicago and another home in nearby Indiana. He was very close to Joseph "Joey the Clown" Lombardo, then a Chicago Outfit leader.

Agents said Schweihs was with "the table," meaning he could do hits for any Chicago street crew. One of Schweihs' associates, Ron DeAngeles of Chicago, born in the mid-1930s, was an electronics expert capable of wiring a bomb and was known as "The Wizard."

Another informant said Schweihs may have used the services of Anthony "Tony the Ant" Spilotro, the Outfit's top representative in Las Vegas, or Joseph H. Hansen, who grew up with Spilotro in Chicago, in the Ryan murder. Hansen resembled a suspect in one of the Evansville police artist drawings from descriptions given by people around the Olympia Health Spa at the time of the car bombing.

Eisgruber's report also said a San Francisco informant claimed a "LCN contract had been issued and was outstanding for Ryan's murder but the "contract was delayed for several years due to the fact that

Caifano was on parole and he wanted to be personally involved in the hit and the contract was not carried out until his parole expired."

Chicago FBI agents John J. O'Rourke and Robert C. Pecoraro fleshed out details about older Schweihs associates including Anthony Panzica, an explosives expert highly capable of utilizing a remote controlled electronic.

Much of the information came from a source listed by the code name "Achilles." Code names were rarely used in FBI reports and only to signify a super-secret informant of utmost importance.

The code name was blacked out in FBI reports to state or local police departments, but not in the report to Bagbey. The report identified "Achilles" as Aladena James "Jimmy the Weasel" Fratianno, famed mob leader and hitman turned federal informant who was under federal protection and being debriefed at a correction center in San Diego.

For all of Schweihs' toughness, federal agents believed that Schweihs might become an informant if facing years in prison, but convincing him to go against the Outfit would take delicate handling. FBI reports also mentioned Alva Johnson Rodgers, who had frequent run-ins with the law and was a close associate of Caifano after sharing a cell with him at the Atlanta federal penitentiary, also was talking to the Feds.

The report said a Chicago FBI supervisor "feels this case [Ryan's murder] has great significance and deserves priority treatment" and the bureau "should continue to give it high priority."

Another FBI report said Ray was intensely disliked by many people and had enemies throughout the world.

Ray had played around with organized crime figures from across the country and Steve thought that was a quid pro quo – *you scratch my back, I'll scratch yours.* Ray probably steered high stakes gamblers to mob-operated gambling joints and invested in oil deals with hoods, but that to Ray was just part of doing business and making some money.

Ray was slow on paying his gambling debts sometimes while paying his monthly bills to local oil supply companies on time, no questions asked. Yet a daughter, whose late father had done business with Ray, hated him for ripping off her dad. Ray also had tons of friends and was liked by nearly everyone he met.

Ray: love him or hate him, Steve thought as he learned there were reasons why some people hated Ray Ryan.

Steve now concentrated on Chicago. What he found was a history lesson.

While Mayor Fiorello LaGuardia and Thomas E. Dewey once battled New York's crime families, no one seriously cracked down on gangsters in Chicago. Those who tried died unpleasantly.

The Chicago mob ruled and expanded its influence westward, concentrating the attention of the nation's hoods on Hollywood's movie industry, helping create the California crime syndicate and turning a road in Las Vegas into today's Strip laden with hotels and casinos they controlled. New York mobs made inroads in those areas, but it was Chicago that made everything work and mesh together.

Chicago originally was a natural passage for thousands of immigrants and products; the city was the world's largest grain port by the 1840s and the center of America's meat packing industry after the Civil War.

A fire in the cow barn of Patrick and Catherine O'Leary on October 8, 1871, fanned by 30-mile-an-hour winds, swept over 17,000 buildings, destroyed the central business district and magnificent hotels, killed 300 people and left 100,000 homeless. Havoc reigned for a decade until the city was reborn.

After "The Great Fire" came the birth of organized crime in the city.

Michael Cassius McDonald, a tavern and gambling house operator, united gamblers and politicians against anti-vice groups and in 1873 elected a favorable mayor.

So many vice districts with saloons, brothels and gambling joints sprang up that a directory was published in the 1870s to help visitors find places like Little Cheyenne, Satan's Mile, Whiskey Row and the Levee. Mickey Finn, operator of Whiskey Row taverns, became infamous for a drink that left patrons unconscious and minus their valuables when they awoke.

McDonald blended together gamblers, swindlers, con men, bordello owners, thieves, elected politicians and cops and it was difficult to tell them apart. The crooks made the money; the politicians and cops were paid off to let vice freely operate. This scenario was repeated for decades in Chicago; only the names and faces changed.

By the early 1900s, Democrats John "Bathhouse" Coughlin and Michael "Hinky Dink" Kenna, sons of Irish immigrants, ruled over the Levee. The Everleigh Club, the most elegant whorehouse with a worldwide reputation, was operated by two sisters, Minna and Ada Lester, who claimed they grew up in Evansville, the daughters of a preacher.

Vice in Chicago expanded when William "Big Bill" Thompson was elected mayor in 1915 and James "Big Jim" Colosimo was the top underworld figure controlling sex parlors with hundreds of girls, many caught up in White Slave traffic.

When small-time Black Hand thugs attempted to extort money from him, he brought in his nephew Johnny Torrio from New York's Five Points Gang. Torrio rubbed out the Chicago extortionists and set out to expand Colosimo's empire. Torrio saw Prohibition as a way to make millions of dollars providing illegal alcohol but Colosimo was satisfied with the way things were. The rift between the two was settled on May 11, 1921 when Colosimo was gunned down at his café.

Torrio brought in his cousin Alphonse Capone as a bodyguard and set up gambling and liquor joints in the city and surrounding towns. He proposed creating separate areas around Chicago for existing Polish, Jewish and Italian gangs to share the wealth, but the other gangs only wanted more territory and the simplest way to achieve that was to kill the other guys. When Torrio left as mob leader in 1925 after an attempt on his life, Al Capone took over and warfare between the gangs began in earnest.

Capone recruited members from the smaller gangs like the Circus Café Gang headquartered on West North Avenue and the 42 Gang in the Patch. Jack "Machine Gun" McGurn, a Circus Café mainstay, became part of Capone's empire in 1923 followed by Anthony "Tony" Accardo. Sam Giancana from the 42 Gang joined Capone in 1928, bringing along Leonard "Fat Lenny" Caifano.

Together they elevated other 42 Gang members including Sam "Mad Dog" DeStefano, Felix "Milwaukee Phil" Alderisio, Sam "Teets" Battaglia, Charles Nicoletti, Lenny's brother Marshall Caifano,

William Daddano, Charles "Chuck" English and Albert "Obbie" Frabotta.

Gang wars reached a crescendo and top leaders from some gangs were killed. Of the 1,000 mob-related killings in Chicago from the 1920s through the 1960s – 546 in the 1920s alone – less than a dozen resulted in convictions.

After an attempt on his life, Capone orchestrated the February 14, 1929 machine-gun killings of seven rival gang members by hoods dressed as cops at the S.M.C. Cartage company warehouse. The St. Valentine Day's massacre effectively ended gangland murders for a while. Two years later Capone stopped being a force in the Outfit after he was convicted of tax charges and sentenced to 11 years in prison.

The Outfit's leadership in 1932 fell to Frank "The Enforcer" Nitti, a Sicilian immigrant once a barber in the Italian neighborhood known as The Patch.

Under Nitti's tenure, Chicago went Hollywood thanks to a couple of low-ranking hoods.

Hollywood had captured the imagination of the public, Chicago racketeers and a kid who shined shoes in Watertown, Wisconsin, all dazzled by the names in lights, money, handsome men, beautiful women, life in the fast lane. The infant movie industry was ripe for mob exploitation.

From one-reel nickelodeons movies in the early 1900s, Hollywood went to feature-length silent films and on to the first "talkie" in 1927. The Oscars were awarded in 1929 and soon the Marx Brothers, Shirley Temple, Jean Harlow, Mae West and Mickey Mouse became household names.

The Depression sent Chicago's prostitution operations into a tail-spin and William Morris "Willie" Bioff, a native of Russia and a pimp in Chicago's Levee district, needed to come up with cash by 1932. He was trying to organize Chicago's kosher butchers when he met George Browne, business agent for the Chicago stagehands' Local 2 of the International Alliance of Theatrical Stage Employes (IATSE) who was trying to organize chicken dealers on the side. The local stage union was in disarray. Of 400 union members, 250 were unemployed and Bioff and Browne set up a soup kitchen where unemployed stage-hands ate for free.

Bioff and Browne, short men with wire-rimmed glasses and fleshy faces, demanded Barney Balaban, owner of Chicago's Balaban and Katz theaters, restore a pay cut taken from IATSE members' salaries in 1929. When Balaban refused, Bioff and Browne convinced Balaban to pay $20,000 to the soup kitchen instead then blew the money on roulette at a casino owned by Nick Circella, who knew Browne and Bioff had hit upon something big and passed the word along.

At a sit-down meeting with Nitti, underboss Paul "The Waiter" Ricca, Charles "Cherry Nose" Gioe, Phil D'Andrea, and Louis "Little New York" Campagna, Bioff and Browne detailed their scheme. If one theater owner would pay $20,000, the Outfit knew Hollywood movie studios would pay millions to keep unions in check and eliminate strikes. Gangsters from other cities jumped on the bandwagon. Corruption was rampant in Los Angeles and expanding Chicago's influence to the West Coast was inviting and easy.

Syndicate thugs help elect Browne the union's international president at the 1934 IATSE convention in Louisville, Kentucky. He immediately started recruiting movie industry workers and the union grew to represent 120,000.

He headed to California with Bioff as the union's international representative. John Rosselli and Jack Dragna, sent earlier to California by New York and Chicago mobs, kept track of them and Circella went along as a day-to-day watchdog.

Born Franco Sacco in Italy in 1905, John Rosselli started as a street hood in Boston, moved to New York City after someone who informed on him to the cops was murdered and soon ended up in Chicago where he became a driver and bodyguard for Al Capone.

While hoods around him were thuggish, Rosselli was handsome, suave and trusted. Because of health problems, he was dispatched to the warm climate of California to take care of the Outfit's gambling, bookmaking and loan sharking chores and to mingle with the Hollywood elite. He blended in well and eagerly assisted in the movie extortion operation.

Faced with kickbacks or union strikes, studio executives like Joseph Schenck at Twentieth Century-Fox and his brother, Nicholas, head of a conglomerate that included Metro-Goldwyn-Mayer, Loew's theaters and several other studios, fell in line. Over six years the extortions brought in more than $1 million from four major studios while Bioff and Browne lined their pockets with under-the-table deals and siphoned off cash from a union strike fund.

Chicago and East Coast hoodlums made appearances at the best restaurants and nightclubs in Los Angeles, mingling with movie stars and starlets. Rosselli married actress June Lang in 1940 and after the divorce nuzzled with other actresses including Marilyn Monroe. Abner "Longie" Zwillman found comfort with Jean Harlow.

Rosselli and other racketeers became producers, assistant producers or consultants in the movie industry. Bioff bought 80 acres in the San Fernando Valley near the estates of movie stars, wore tailored suits and filled his home with rare books, oriental vases and bodyguards. His union card was made of gold. Circella and Browne opened a nightclub.

The good times ended around 1938 when "Progressive" members of the IATSE union rallied to get the mobsters out. The Screen Actors Guild rose up amid fears that Browne wanted to bring actors into his union. The rumblings attracted the attention of California state officials, newspapers and finally the Internal Revenue Service and federal investigators.

The syndicates' Hollywood shenanigans collapsed like a house of cards. Joseph Schenck was convicted of perjury and tax fraud in 1940. He rolled over on Bioff and Browne for only four months in jail, returned to producing movies and later received a full pardon from President Harry Truman.

Browne and Bioff were charged with violating federal anti-racketeering statutes.[11] Nick Circella was indicted by a grand jury in September 1941, went into hiding with his girlfriend Estelle Carey and wasn't found by FBI agents until December. By that time, Browne and Bioff had been convicted and given eight and ten years. Four months later, Circella pleaded guilty to extortion and got eight years.

Bioff and Browne decided to help the Feds for reduced sentences and in the spring of 1943, a federal grand jury indicted Nitti, Ricca, Gioe, Campagna, Rosselli, D'Andrea, Francis "Frank Diamond" Maritote, who married Al Capone's sister, and IATSE business agent

---

11 Bioff resigned his union post in 1939 after returning to Chicago to serve a six-month sentence on a 1922 pandering conviction. Browne was ousted as the IATSE president in 1941.

Louis Kaufman. Afraid of being confined to a cell, Nitti shot himself in the head near his home less than five hours after indictments were handed down. The first two shots passed through his fedora before he killed himself with the third, according to published reports.

On New Year's Eve 1943, the remaining seven defendants were convicted, and most were sentenced to 10 years in jail.[12] Bioff and Browne left prison at the end of 1944. Knowing he was a marked man, Bioff left for Arizona to start a new life under the name of William Nelson (his wife's maiden name). But Bioff couldn't – or wouldn't – hide forever.

With Nitti dead and Ricca in prison, Tony Accardo took over the Outfit and ruled for more than two decades in tandem with Ricca after he was released from jail.

Accardo wanted to find Bioff and cops later concluded it was the rising street hood Marshall Caifano who would answer Accardo's nagging question of where was Willie.

And Bioff wouldn't like the answer.

---

12 The top mobsters were mysteriously released from prison three years later prompting a Congressional investigation that went nowhere.

Chapter 33

LIFE IN THE PATCH

Anthony "Tony" Montana was born in 1933 in the heart of the Patch and the 42 Gang. The youngest of twelve in a family desperately trying to make ends meet, Montana quickly learned around his home that "the first one up on the morning was the best dressed for the day."

The only cars those days in the Patch's heart along Taylor Street belonged to the wise guys and the area's city council alderman. Electric street cars carried passengers along cobblestone streets. At Halsted Street there were small mom-and-pop food stores, chicken stores, grocery stores. Peddlers with handcarts or stalls were everywhere. Farmers brought their products to sell along Randolph Street.

Montana went with his father to pick up food goods for stores that couldn't get to the market. Then they went through the alleys selling items they picked up for themselves, calling out to housewives what they had to sell. Two pounds of potatoes went for 25 cents. Anything left over at day's end was given away to the poor.

Montana, who later moved to Las Vegas and planned to produce a film about the 42 Gang, remembered that the Patch "was romantic then. It was slow moving, everybody got along." If the 42 Gang was in the neighborhood, "they would say 'if you see something happen, you don't see it'."

Neighborhood gangs were a necessity. The Italians arriving in the Patch usually spoke only Italian. "All the police officers and politicians spoke English because they were Irish. They used to torture these Italians. When they went to work they were beat up. This is how the 42 Gang started. They started a group to beat up on the Irish who were beating up on them.

"These were kids. Kids don't have brains. They started when they were 12 or younger. They did a little bit of everything. The big thing was they raped a lot of broads. They had crazy guys in there. They graduated in crime. They started stealing cars, chopping them. They started the extortion, getting so much money from these people on Market Street."

Montana hung around street bosses Jimmy "Monk" Allegretti, Joseph "Joey Caesar" Devarco and top hoods like Ross Prio, Charley and Joe Fischetti, Willie Messino and Rocky "The Parrot" Potenzo. Fat Lenny Caifano took a liking to Montana. Lenny was a big tough guy who once got so mad he overturned a pool table going after a man. His bodyguard was Anthony Eldorado, who was nicknamed Tony Pineapple because he'd use a bomb to blow up anything the bosses wanted.

Montana said Lenny laughed a lot, had a kind word for most folks and rode a green Indian motorcycle along Taylor Street popping wheelies. Lenny was one of the classiest men Montana ever met and might have become the mob boss if he hadn't been killed at a young age.

As a teenager, Montana served as a lookout at one of Lenny's gambling joints. Montana lingered outside a candy shop across the street from a warehouse where the gambling took place. If cops drove around the block twice indicating a raid may be in the works, Montana rushed into the candy shop and called the warehouse to alert the guys to get ready to destroy gambling material.

After getting a driver's license when he reached 16, Montana drove Lenny's Ford several days each week picking up gamblers and taking them to designated gambling sites, usually basements in people's homes that Lenny rented for the night.

Montana earned $35 to $40 a night, big bucks for a Patch kid. If a player was winning when Montana arrived to pick him up, he was told to come back in a couple of hours. "They didn't want the guy to get out of there. If he went broke, they'd give him more money and put him on the juice (loaned money with excessive interest). If a guy won that I picked up, he'd tip me." A few years later, Montana began working as a bartender in mob whorehouses in downtown Chicago.

He got to see Marshall Caifano and his crew up-close – killers in the Chicago mob's version of "Murder, Inc."

Felix "Milwaukee Phil" Alderisio was someone to be avoided. "He didn't say hello or goodbye. He didn't talk. He listened. If you looked into his eyes you saw tombstones," Montana said. Charley Nicoletti was a smart, polished fellow. At the age of 15, Nicoletti killed his father who was beating up on his mother. "After a guy kills his father everything else comes easy."

Obbie Frabotta was a quiet, not too bright fellow. "You never got boo out of him. Obbie was dumb. Nicoletti was the smarter of the guys, maybe a coin toss with Marshall. Milwaukee definitely wasn't smart. You have to understand, people who kill people aren't too fucking smart."

While others saw Marshall Caifano as a vicious evil-eyed killer, Montana saw a different side of him among fellow mobsters. "Marshall was smooth and soft. He was a mannerly person, smiling all the time." Much of the time, he was happy, even jovial, laughing a lot. But everyone in the Patch knew not to mess with Caifano even in his lighter moments.

"By talking with him, you knew he was tough. He had a Bogart-type voice – deep. He got his point across. He was well mannered, well dressed, well feared. He was jolly but everyone knew he was dangerous. Your reputation preceded you in those days."

No one gave Marshall any crap, Montana said. He recalled a night when a well known female entertainer at Chez Paree, one of the mob's main nightclubs, insulted Marshall after the place closed. Caifano grabbed the girl and ordered her to "suck my dick." She immediately did. "Nobody in the joint looked at them or said boo. He didn't give a fuck. Everybody knew he was mad. If she had been a man, she would have been dead. Oh yeah, she sucked his dick."

Caifano married a neighborhood girl, but always had good looking young women on his arm when he went out in the evenings. "Look at the girls he got, cocktail waitresses; you get that kind of girl. You marry an Italian girl to have your kids and after that you're fucking around."

Montana was in Las Vegas during the 1950s before making the town his permanent home in 1970. During his early Vegas days, Montana saw Ray Ryan perhaps ten times.

"I never sat down and talked with him. He was always gambling with a couple of broads next to him, shills. Shills were the girls who would start the games with the high rollers. You'd think they were playing but they were not playing and the high roller would come in and sit next to them. He was a womanizer like everyone else. He went to Vegas for two things – women and gambling."

Chapter 34

CAIFANO'S CHICAGO RESUME

The Chicago Crime Commission didn't notice Marshall Caifano until the late 1940s when he was mauling his way up the syndicate's ladder – a syndicate hatchet man, playboy hoodlum, a guy who set up killings if he didn't do them himself.

Few of the details of Caifano's extensive and heavy-handed background filtered down to Steve Bagbey in the FBI and ATF reports that arrived at his desk. Most of what he learned about Caifano's history, Steve had to discover on his own through books and newspaper articles or from people familiar with Chicago's crime history.

Caifano escaped early detection in the murder of 41-year-old Frank Quattrochi, a Prohibition era gangster gunned down in front of a tavern in early 1946. A hat band of a gray fedora found near the shooting had the initials "M.C." and police thought the shooter was Al Capone's youngest brother Mathew. A couple of years later they figured the "M.C." tag probably stood for Marshall Caifano.

It was Caifano's suspected link to the Hollywood extortion case that eventually raised eyebrows. When Ricca, Rosselli and others were heading toward a federal court trial, the Outfit sent messages to Bioff, Browne and Circella to keep their mouths shut.

Circella's girlfriend Estelle Carey lived in a five-room, third-floor apartment near Lake Michigan. A beautiful blond, Carey was a former "26 girl" (a dice game where for a few coins a patron could try to win a free drink) before becoming a hostess at Circella's Colony Club, luring rich gamblers to high stakes tables and keeping them happy. Also, she may have kept Caifano happy with nighttime liaisons.

Police and firefighters arriving at Carey's apartment in early February 1942 found a brutal scene and Carey dead. She had been tortured, stabbed with an ice pick, throat slit, beaten with a blackjack or brass knuckles, teeth knocked out, nose broken and the flesh burned off her body after her housecoat was set afire. Most felt her murder was a warning to Circella to keep quiet. Browne's wife also had received phone calls warning that her husband wasn't to talk. Circella kept quiet, but Browne and Bioff, angry about women being threatened, decided to tell all.

Caifano and other hoods were questioned in Carey's murder and released but police suspected Caifano had a hand in her death.

Meanwhile Caifano had another woman on his mind – Susan Darlene, who came to Chicago from Kentucky. Caifano had divorced his first wife, Lena, who bore him children and remained in the background. He and Darlene married on July 20, 1946. She was a stunning blond with bewitching sex appeal and about 25 years old, a decade younger than Marshall. Even after they later divorced, Caifano frequently came back to Darlene and became irate if other men dated her.

The FBI and ATF began sending Steve Bagbey dribs and drabs about Marshall Caifano in 1978, but not the detailed accounts that Steve wanted. There were mug shots of Caifano, a rap sheet of his extensive contacts with police, often when he was picked up on "general principle" to see if they could shake anything out of him after a killing, burglary or theft in Chicago.

There were names – but no backgrounds in the skimpy FBI reports – of people who might have committed murders for or with Caifano. From the limited information, Steve knew Caifano was a bad dude.

Steve also knew he'd have to flesh out the details from old Chicago newspaper accounts and retired cops.

He learned out that Caifano had a crew of a dozen or so collecting money from syndicate gambling operations on Chicago's North and West sides. Sometimes Caifano went along for collections but usually left those chores up to Alderisio and Nicoletti along with Leonard Patrick and David Yaras, who had gambling operations on the side.

They met at restaurants or offices to count the money before passing it upstream in the Outfit hierarchy. If there were union problems or trouble with a business owner, Caifano would show up with goons to settle things. He also had his own bookmaking operations and interests in several legitimate businesses.

Caifano spent many evenings at Rush Street nightclubs meeting with friends or catching the latest act with a girl on his arm while his bodyguard or driver waited outside. Afternoons at the driving range or golf course saw him improving his game.

Many Chicago hoods took up golf because Al Capone fell in love with the game in the 1920s and played daily. Those around him followed suit to be close to Capone. Hoods down the pecking order also took up golf to be around their individual bosses. So many Outfit members played they occasionally held their own golf outings. Caifano was one of the better players.

Caifano's rising status was due to Giancana, who by 1943 was back in Chicago after serving about four years in the federal prison in Terre Haute, Indiana, for alcohol law violations.

In Terre Haute, Giancana learned of the money that could be made in the policy wheels in Chicago's black neighborhoods from the bragging of Edward Jones, a wealthy black policy operator who was incarcerated for tax evasion. Giancana made a mental note to take over the policy racket once he got out.

For years the Chicago bosses had ignored the policy game in black neighborhoods and hadn't made a serious attempt to take over the national racing wire business. Giancana wanted to change that.

The policy or numbers wheel was brought to Chicago by a riverboat gambler named King during the 1893 World Fair. People bet pennies, nickels, dimes, quarters or dollars to play and the game was popular in Chicago's poor black neighborhoods. There were dozen of policy operators, who spun wheels two or three times a day and selected 10 numbers. Bettors had picked three numbers and if their numbers came up on a 10-cent bet, they won $10. The chance of winning was around 8,000 to one. More complicated versions allowed bettors to win bigger cash pots.

Policy operators grew rich as the coins added up to millions of dollars a year. Giancana and Fat Lenny Caifano tried to push out black policy operators. After Jones returned to Chicago from prison, he was kidnapped and held for ransom in May 1946.

Theodore Roe, another prominent black policy wheel operator, negotiated the ransom and delivered the $100,000 to free Jones, who fled to Mexico. The Outfit tired to muscle out Roe, but Roe refused to leave and surrounded himself with bodyguards.

Leaving the policy racket alone for a while, Giancana moved into distributing jukebox, pinball and vending machines, recruiting David Yaras, Leonard Patrick and others to oversee different parts of the city.

And the syndicate went after the lucrative racing wire business.

That part of the Outfit's story also would have Marshall Caifano's fingerprints all over it.

Chapter 35

CHICAGO KILLING FIELD

Shortly after 1900 John Payne, a former Western Union employee in Cincinnati, devised a way to encode the results of thoroughbred races to send to bookmakers in cities.

Monte Tennes, one of Chicago's top gamblers, signed up for service in Illinois in 1907 and soon forced Payne out. Tennes established the General News Bureau race wire and expanded into California, Texas, East Coast, and Midwest. Tennes sold his race wire in 1927 to Moses Louis Annenberg, who had amassed a fortune in the newspaper and dry cleaning businesses.

Annenberg's East Prussia family had settled in Chicago in the same Irish neighborhood that produced two other men destined to play roles in future race wires – James M. Ragen Sr. and Arthur B. "Mickey" McBride, the same Mickey McBride once defended when a newspaper boy by Clarence Darrow and later bought a pro football team in Cleveland.

Steve Bagbey mulled over this part of his background investigation on the Outfit because one FBI report he received included an informant saying that Ray Ryan apparently had met Annenberg in Chicago, perhaps in the early 1930s, and became a friend. That was only a brief mention in the report. But Steve knew that Ray's friendship with owners of a national racing wire service didn't stop at Annenberg. There also was Mickey McBride and probably others.

Annenberg took over half interest in Tennes' racing wire and hired Ragen to run it. Chicago gambler John J. "Jack" Lynch owned 40 percent of the racing wire. Annenberg bought out 20 racing wire competitors and in less than a decade dominated the country.

Annenberg eventually tried to squeeze Lynch out of the business by creating the Nationwide News Service racing wire and drastically cutting prices. But Lynch took his woes to Frank Nitti, who ordered Annenberg to settle up with Lynch or be killed. Annenberg reportedly paid nearly $1 million in 1936 to placate Lynch.[13]

Annenberg closed Nationwide in 1939 because the Internal Revenue Service was after him for back taxes and penalties on his various businesses.

Five days later, the Continental Press race wire sprang up under Ragen, "Mickey" McBride and McBride's brother-in-law Tom Kelly. Tony Accardo tried to take over Continental, but Ragen wouldn't budge. The Chicago syndicate then started its own racing wire, the Trans-American Publishing and News Service, but Ragen held strong against the Outfit pressure.

Accardo opted for the traditional Chicago-style solution to eliminate competition.

They decided to kill Ragen.

Ragen publicly proclaimed that Accardo, Guzik and Murray "The Camel" Humphreys were after him and presented the State's Attorney office a list of Chicago syndicate bookie and gambling joints operating in the open without fear of police interference. He claimed the racketeers controlled street cops, top police brass, judges, prosecutors, mayors and other elected officials.

On June 24, 1946, Ragen waited at a traffic light on State Street with his car windows down when a beat-up old Ford truck with a tarpaulin covering the bed pulled up on his right. Two men pulled aside the tarpaulin and fired shotgun blasts into Ragen's car and sped off. It took two months for Ragen to die in a Chicago hospital. There were allegations someone sneaked into the hospital and poisoned Ragen with mercury at a time when Ragen appeared to be recovering nicely.

The Chicago coroner said death was due to lingering gunshot wounds, although the autopsy uncovered traces of mercury in Ragen's system. Police said a shotgun that was recovered also was used to kill three Chicago hoods in the past three years.

---

13   Lynch was worth an estimated $10 million at one time. But he doled out some of his money to friends and lost even more gambling. By the time he died in 1945, he left an estate of only $25,000.

With Ragen dead, McBride and Kelly owned the Continental racing wire, but the Outfit ran it from the background and the mob's Trans-American wire service quietly went out of business. But Ragen's murder would have a domino effect leading to an even more notable slaying in a few years and the name of Marshall Caifano surfaced in both killings.

The next victim would be the most notable of all – a police officer dedicated to putting mobsters behind bars. But in Chicago such cops were rare and seldom lived long.

William J. Drury was a 22-year-old string bean, over six feet tall and weighing 130 pounds, when he joined the Chicago police force in 1924. Drury was committed to arresting criminals. Drury and his partner John I. Howe ran down thieves, burglars, robbers and gangsters in Chicago's Loop. Newspapers soon called them the "Watchdogs of the Loop." But some of their police superiors were in the mob's pocket and the officers were transferred to uniform in 1930 after arresting two of Al Capone's hoods.

Drury, Howe and other officers including Drury's next partner Thomas Connelly were assigned to State's Attorney Thomas Courtney's office in December 1932 in another effort to control them. Heading the unit was Captain Daniel Gilbert, the chief investigator. To Drury, Gilbert was a fox guarding the henhouse and over the next six years Drury saw how pervasive the mob's influence was, especially where Gilbert was involved.

Drury continued to arrest top Outfit hoods only to see charges dropped or convictions not processed. Still a darling of reporters, he was promoted to sergeant in 1933 and lieutenant in 1938 and headed detectives protecting Chicago's 1933 World's Fair. In 1943 he was named acting captain in the Town Hall district, the north side cesspool filled with gang gambling and bookmaking, and continued the arrest of mobsters. A few months later, Drury, Connelly and other cops were fired.

After a two-year court fight, Drury and Connelly were back on the job in September 1946 and given 30 unsolved murder cases including the Ragen case. Within a few months, they found witnesses who identified William Block, Lenny Patrick and David Yaras as Ragen's killers.

The FBI said Yaras and Patrick were part of Marshall Caifano's crew and called them syndicate torpedoes. The three men eventually were indicted but charges were quickly dropped after two witnesses recanted their identifications. A grand jury was called to investigate Drury and Connelly and when they refused to sign a waiver of immunity to testify, they were fired for the final time.

For three years, Drury and Connelly became personal crusaders against organized crime, writing articles, assisting authors on a book about Chicago's underworld and detailing mob activity in Chicago and Miami to reporters. When the Kefauver hearings got under way in 1950, Drury fed the senators information about the Outfit prior to an upcoming Kefauver committee hearing in Chicago.

The timing was important because Gilbert was running on the Democratic ticket for Cook County Sheriff against Republican John E. Babb. Gilbert already had been cited by Kefauver as the "world's richest cop" for having more than $300,000 in assets on a cop's salary. Gilbert said the money came from stock and grain speculation and betting on baseball and football games.

Drury joined with Marvin Bas, a 45-year-old attorney working on Babb's campaign, to dig up dirt on the syndicate's gambling operations. On Monday September 25, 1950, Drury met with Kefauver's chief investigator to discuss Drury's planned testimony at the upcoming Chicago congressional hearing. Drury also claimed he would prove that Yaras, Patrick and Block had killed Ragen.

After the meeting, Drury drove home. When he backed his new Cadillac into a detached alley garage, four men rushed the car. Shotgun blasts shattered the windshield, slugs ripped into Drury's chest, face and right arm. An hour later his wife found her 48-year-old, mortally-wounded husband in the garage. The Loop was without a watchdog.

A couple of hours later, Marvin Bas finished dinner at a restaurant near Rush Street and headed to his car when he spotted two men following him and started running. The men caught up with Bas, fired a fatal bullet into his head then jumped into a car and drove off.

Police officials and the mayor said crime in Chicago wasn't as bad as the slayings might suggest. Kefauver said the murders "show the savagery of Chicago's gangland." Chicago mob bosses headed to Mexico "on vacation." Police investigated an informant's claim that

Drury's killer was a little-known New York gangster and that the go-between was Sam DeStefano, a loan shark and killer who had been in the 42 Gang with Caifano. No one was charged in the murders although there was suspicion that Caifano had a hand in them.

Gilbert had a lousy record as the state attorney's office chief investigator, although the Outfit didn't think so. During Gilbert's 18 years in that office, there were 1,038 unsolved murders in Chicago, including 188 gang and rackets murders of gamblers, hijackers, noted and run-of-the-mill hoods and even a prominent Republican politician who was taking on the mob.

The slayings had one positive result. In the November 7 election, Babb defeated Gilbert for sheriff while Republican Everett Dirksen won the Illinois U. S. Senate race, a victory some heralded as steps to end mob rule in Chicago.

But in the Windy City, a new broom doesn't always sweep clean. Killings continued and it would take several more murders before Marshall Caifano felt the heat in Chicago and needed a remote place to hang out.

And that place would be where Ray Ryan was hanging out by then.

Chapter 36

PARTNERING WITH ODDSMAKER

By the end of World War II, Ray was a vibrant, youthful-looking forty-one year old with an engaging smile, money and desire, exuding confidence. The next 15 years would be his best of times, when money was no object, life was lived to the fullest and his most memorable escapades occurred. The last 15 years of his life would be the worst of times.

He was everywhere, it seemed – in Evansville watching over his oil company's operations and visiting Helen and daughter Rae Jean; going on junkets to casinos in Europe; rubbing elbows with friends, oilmen, bookies and gamblers in Chicago, Dallas and Miami. He started making trips to California and soon would head to a little known spot in the Mohave Desert called Las Vegas.

He set aside Saturdays in the fall to bet on college and professional football. "On Saturday, Ray would be busy as a bird dog betting on every team in the United States," said Frank Bogert, once manager at the Palm Springs' El Mirador hotel. "He'd talk to some bookie on the phone and say I'll put up $1,000 on this team, $1,000 on that team. He worked all day betting on football games."

Ray lost many bets, but never talked about them. People only heard about the ones he won. Although he took his time to pay off his losses, he expected to get his winnings immediately. Once winning a $10,000 bet against a dilatory St. Louis bookie, Ray hired an airplane and sent someone from Evansville to St. Louis to collect immediately.

Ray liked to bet on anything, just for the hell of it. As one old friend later recalled "we used to spit at a crack in the sidewalk for

$10,000. I suppose over the years it evened out. But Ryan seemed to hit the middle every time. Ray's got an awful lot behind him, but none of it is equal to his luck. Don't ever bet against Ray Ryan. He's got the magic touch."

While Ray usually stayed at the Roney Plaza Hotel in Miami, he purchased an interest in the recently opened Sea View Hotel in Bal Harbour about 15 miles north of Miami around 1948 and started enjoying the sun and wealthy friends there.

Like other Miami Beach hotels, the Sea View was home to a flourishing gambling business. Ray would claim he was unaware of bookmaking at a hotel cabana. But a state investigator learned a year later that a St. Louis bookie and mob captain occupied the hotel's ocean-side Cabana No. 1 in the winter for bookmaking. Ray Ryan was among the people the bookie frequently called.

Many racketeers had winter headquarters in the Miami area. Frank Erickson hung out at the Wofford Hotel and held gambling concessions in several hotels including the Roney Plaza where he and Ray met frequently, usually over a meal or a friendly game of cards. Erickson would be the link connecting Ray with other mob guys and associates.

Martin "Marty" Guilfoyle, a veteran Chicago bootlegger, gambler and bookmaker, also operated in Florida. A few years after the war, Ray was introduced to a guy named Jimmy Snyder at Guilfoyle's Miami gambling joint. Ray and Jimmie hit it off from the start.

"He liked my style and I liked his," Jimmy said in his 1975 autobiography "Jimmy the Greek: By Himself." Jimmy said Ray was "a tall, handsome guy with an upbeat personality. Everything was always happy with Ryan, whether he was flush or busted. He looked like a movie star, with straight brown hair brushed back flat on his head." At that time, Jimmy was making a nationwide name for himself as an oddsmaker on sports.

Jimmy and Ray each had talents the other man needed.

Ray was a heavy bettor and wanted Jimmy's knowledge about horses and sports teams. Jimmy liked to gamble on games, but had to hide his bets. His oddsmaking business would suffer if people knew which teams he actually bet on. Ray became Jimmy's partner placing bets for both of them. Jimmy occasionally came up with $100,000 to bet on a big game while Ray bet $150,000 on each of six or seven

172

games. Usually Ray would put up the money and Jimmy got one-third of the winnings.

"I have known a lot of guys who have bet money in my time, but I have never – *ever* – known of a higher roller than Ryan. He was, and remains, an unforgettable character in my experience," Jimmy wrote. Harold Salvey, one of the original owners of a Florida racing wire syndicate, had urged Jimmy to stay away from Ray telling Jimmy "he'll screw you sooner or later." But Jimmy and Ray never had any conflict. "Salvey had been right on so many things, but his opinion on Ryan was never confirmed," Jimmy said.

Born Demetrios Georgos Synodinos in 1918, Jimmy grew up in Steubenville, Ohio, a rough-and-tumble steelworker town where his father ran a butcher shop. While called the "City of Churches," Steubenville also was wide open during Prohibition with gambling and prostitution.

Jimmy hung out with school chum Dino Crocetti, the son of an Italian immigrant barber. As teenagers in 1936, the two hustled work at cigar stores, billiard parlors and poolrooms offering gambling. Jimmy parked cars at the Half Moon Nite Club and was a dealer at the craps table. Dino was a card dealer at the Rex Cigar Store.

Jimmy became a student of gambling, studied the horses and college sports and devised systems to figure winners. Within a few years he was a gifted oddsmaker known as Jimmy "The Greek" Snyder, projecting odds from sports to presidential candidates. By the mid-1950s, he would be the country's top oddsmaker and on national television predicting pro football games.

Dino Crocetti abandoned his job as a dealer to take up singing. He changed his stage name a couple of times before deciding on Dean Martin. Jimmy and Dean became close friends with Ray, who spent hundreds of thousands of dollars to advance the careers of both.

A year after meeting Ray, Jimmy attended the North-South college football all-star game at Bal Harbour. At a hotel, he spied a beautiful brunette and learned she was Joan Specht from Evansville where her family owned the Hercules Body Works. Joan attended Saint Mary's of the Woods College in Terre Haute, Indiana, and Jimmy began courting her.[14]

---

14 Jimmy married Joan in 1953, remaining together until Jimmy's death in 1996. They had six children, three of whom died in infancy from cystic fibrosis.

When visiting Evansville to see Joan, Jimmy stayed with Ray, who squired him around to parties and dinners.

Some people found Jimmy a gregarious, funny man. Others thought him an overweight blowhard. Jimmy invested in oil deals with Ray but only got a dozen dry holes.

But the budding friendship between Ray and Jimmy would pay dividends in a few years.

Chapter 37

THE MOB MOVES TO VEGAS

The Florida mob casinos around the end of World War II in Broward and Dade counties – the Greenacres, Club Boheme, Island Club, Club Collins, Colonial Inn, Club 86 and Farm Casino – were still going strong with bookmaking at major hotels.

But the public was stirred up, tired of the increasing publicity of payoffs to local and state officials and police. Grand juries went after the wide-open gambling. A 1944 Broward County grand jury reported numerous nationally known criminals were there; gambling abounded with police aid and with little effort to curb the hoods.

Organized crime even managed to take over the S and G Syndicate, which had supplied the racing wire service to Florida bookie parlors since 1939, netting $8 million a year minus payoffs to cops and elected officials. Under pressure from Jack Friedlander, S and G officials accepted Harry Russell, a Chicago bookmaker from the Capone days, as part owner.

Meyer Lansky had opened cash cow casinos in Cuba in 1940s that lasted until Fidel Castro took over the country in 1959. Ray Ryan was among those Americans taking flights to Lansky's and other mob casinos in Cuba. But casinos in Cuba were too far away for most of the nation's big time gamblers.

With their Florida gambling empire seemingly slipping away from them because of public outrage, the hoods looked for a location to draw high rollers from Texas and California more frequently.

That turned out to be Las Vegas, Nevada.

Early visitors called a spot that blossomed with water and greenery in the desert Las Vegas, Spanish for "fertile plain." Surveyor John Charles Fremont led an expedition to the West in 1844 and put Las Vegas on the map – literally, by listing the town on 20,000 copies of a map of that area he produced. Las Vegas soon became a stopover for people heading west, and prospectors on the way to the California gold fields. The town was established in 1905 and its main pastime was gambling.

The Nevada legislature in 1931, seeking ways out of the Depression, legalized gambling and prostitution, reduced the waiting time for divorces and began allowing quickie marriages. Construction of the massive Boulder (later named Hoover) Dam 30 miles southeast of Las Vegas brought many of the 5,000 workers on weekends to Las Vegas for women, alcohol and gambling.

While Texas was inundated with oil in the early 1930s, Las Vegas was flooded with roulette wheels, poker tables and whores.

Hoodlums came in the late 1930s and early 1940s to strong-arm their way into the casinos along Fremont Street. Arriving in California around 1936 was Benjamin "Bugsy" Siegel, part of New York's infamous "Murder, Inc." group of killers, fleeing grand jury investigations back East.

Strikingly handsome, Siegel floated among Hollywood's elite and expanded the mob's West Coast gambling and racing wire enterprises. With John Rosselli as one of his partners, Siegel muscled into dog and horse tracks and narcotics trafficking from Mexico. He brought along Allen Smiley, Moe Sedway and Morris Rosen to run the racing wire operation along with Gus Greenbaum, who had gambling operations in Arizona.

Siegel passed through Las Vegas often and saw the need for a more elegant place away from the aging downtown Fremont Street casinos. He envisioned a fabulous casino/hotel amid the sands along U.S. Highway 91 south of town.

The casino originally was the brainchild of Billy Wilkerson, publisher of the "Hollywood Reporter," who ran out of money. Siegel moved to build the Flamingo, the nickname of Siegel's girlfriend Virginia Hill.

Phil Kastel brought in suitcases of money from the East Coast syndicates for construction. Siegel demanded the best – expensive carpets and fixtures, European woods, swimming pools, tennis courts, a riding stable – and the project soon fell behind schedule, costs skyrocketing to $6 million. Eastern mobsters thought Siegel and Hill were stashing millions of their dollars in numbered Swiss bank accounts.

The Flamingo's opening on December 26, 1946, months before the hotel was ready, was a disaster even with a star-studded array of George Jessel, Jimmy Durante and the Xavier Cugat orchestra. Bad weather prevented Siegel from flying in his Hollywood friends and the casino lost tons of money each day. Siegel closed the Flamingo in January and reopened it in March when the hotel was ready. There was a slight profit by May, but not enough.

On June 8, 1947 while Hill was on a trip to Europe, Siegel was murdered by a sniper at the bungalow they shared at 810 North Linden Drive in Hollywood. One bullet passed through the jacket of Allen Smiley, who was sitting on the couch next to Siegel. Even as police hurried to the scene, Greenbaum, Sedway and Rosen walked into the Flamingo 250 miles away and said the casino was under new management.

Federal and Chicago investigators came to believe that Marshall Caifano was involved in setting up the mob crew to kill Siegel, bringing in a sharpshooter to get the job done. It wasn't the last time that Caifano thought of using a rifle to kill someone.

Over the next decade after Siegel's murder, organized crime built more casinos – Thunderbird, Desert Inn, Sahara, Riviera, Dunes, Tropicana and Stardust – and the mob and Las Vegas were wed in their own quickie marriage.

Soon Ray Ryan and Marshall Caifano would meet in Las Vegas and that would not be a quick or happy get-together.

Chapter 38

CHEATING BOOKIES

Steve Bagbey's interest picked up when he started digging into information about Ray Ryan's activities in California and Nevada.

All the other stuff that happened before – Chicago, Miami, New York City, Florida and elsewhere – was vital for background, but what Ray did in California and Nevada could lead to finding someone to arrest in the car bombing, Steve reasoned.

Ray Ryan already had headed west in the late 1940s to Los Angeles, Hollywood, Las Vegas and Palm Springs, which was halfway between Las Vegas and LA. In Los Angeles, he rented a suite at the Beverly-Wilshire Hotel for extended periods. Old and newly acquired friends stopped by. Card-playing went on all hours of the day and he was betting heavy on horse racing. No one could miss him.

Allen Smiley, always looking for the next rich "sucker" to take for a bundle, had heard of Ray's heavy betting and asked about him. Smiley once chaperoned a wealthy oilman to the New Orleans area Beverly Club owned by Frank Costello and Philip "Dandy Phil" Kastel, then to a Las Vegas casino and then to a gambling den in the Midwest. In the process, the oilman "lost a small fortune" of $100,000 or more in each place.

Smiley thought Ray might be his next victim.

Tommy Guinan, whose sister was Prohibition-era actress and New York nightclub hostess Texas Guinan, knew Ray spent up to $125,000 a day on bets, but warned Smiley to stay away from him. Ray liked to place large bets at post time and often made a killing when he could get a bet down.

No one knew Ray had come up with elaborate schemes to know the race winners, hoping an unsuspecting bookie might be willing to accept his bets after post time. One scam was him sequestering in the shower in his hotel suite while his friends, gamblers and bookies, waited in the living room to go to the track. Meanwhile, Ray sneaked in a phone call to a spotter at the track to find out the first race winner.

When he left the bedroom, Ray apologized for making the guys miss the first race, adding he really had a favorite horse he wanted to bet on. Usually one of the waiting bookies – convinced Ray had no idea who actually won – accepted his bet on the race. Ray picked up thousands of dollars in the process.

Another scam involved his frequent lunches with bookies. They'd meet before the races and never were out of each other's sight before heading to lunch.

As the waiter passed out the menus, inside Ray's menu was a piece of paper listing the winners of the first two or three races. Ray scanned the menu not looking at the food items but memorizing the note. He earlier had slipped the waiter $500 to pass the note to him.

During lunch, the men talked calmly about a lot of things. Eventually Ray casually mentioned that he'd like to place bets on the early races at the track. Some bookies never suspected anything, believing Ray couldn't know which horses won because he was with them the entire time. Bookies who took the bets of $10,000 or more on each race soon discovered lunch was a costly affair.

That wasn't cheating to Ray. It was just being smart enough to get the edge on the next guy, something they were trying to do to him.

He managed to pull off the charade numerous times early on but later most bookies shied away from taking his bets after post time no matter if they had been hanging around with Ray the entire day. He never bet huge bundles of cash on the scams because he considered it a practical joke rather than a money-making idea. He loved to amuse his friends later with stories about putting one over on a bookie.

His enormous personal appeal also brought him into contact with movie stars, studio executives and producers in Los Angeles and Palm Springs. Hollywood folk flocked to Palm Springs to get away from prying eyes and the hub-bub of the sprawling LA. The pace in Palm Springs was slower, the weather milder, and no one cared what anyone – straight or gay – did behind the walls and iron gates of the mansions.

Ray relished the company of movie stars and executive moguls, cementing friendships with Johnny Rosselli and other hoods, and drawing wealthy businessmen into his sphere in the relaxing atmosphere of Palm Springs and Los Angeles dinners and galas. Ray collected hundreds of photographs of him with his new friends and movie stars.

One of Ray's closest pals was actor Bruce Cabot, who was the same age. Cabot had more than 60 films under his belt by the time they met. He had a leading role in the 1933 movie "King Kong" but he never attained stardom.

Ray found Cabot entertaining, always amusing with wonderful stories about Hollywood and Cabot's own varied background. Cabot was close friends with Hollywood superstar John Wayne, a man Ray admired and wanted to be around. If Ray's young daughter, Rae Jean, was around, Cabot loved to entertain her.

As Ray's friend, Cabot never had to worry about money. They sunned at hotel pools, cut up at parties and meals and attended fancy events in Hollywood and Palm Springs. In the actor's declining years, Ray paid for all of Cabot's doctor and hospital bills and eventually the cost of Cabot's funeral at his home in Carlsbad, New Mexico, in 1972.

Another of Ray's acquaintances was Phil Regan, a well-known tenor who had appeared in two dozen motion pictures in the 1930s and 1940s. Regan had just starred in the role of Lucky Ryan in the 1946 movie "Sweetheart of Sigma Chi" when they met. Born in 1906, Regan grew up in a cold-water flat in Brooklyn, the son of Irish immigrants. He later joined the New York City police department, and at a party given by a vaudeville producer, he went to a piano and sang. A radio executive hired him and his career as the "singing cop" in radio and movies began.

Through Regan, Ray would meet young Chicago businessman Ralph E. Stolkin, a multimillionaire, and their partnership would lead to striking big oil in West Texas, backing a Dean Martin/Jerry Lewis movie and going head-to-head with Howard Hughes for ownership of a major Hollywood studio.

Chapter 39

STOLKIN AND KOOLISH

Ray Ryan spent more time in Evansville in 1948 to devote attention to expanding his oil company's empire and ensure the oil find in Gibson County was moving forward.

Daughter Rae Jean was just past the toddler stage and getting ready to go to the first grade. Ray had a still camera and a movie camera to take pictures of her and to film her learning to ride a horse.

He maintained contact with his friends across the country and the world by telephone. Ray liked keeping up with his buddies by phone, ending the conversations when he desired.

Ray occasionally took Helen and Rae Jean to Palm Springs. He made solo trips for extended periods, tending the oil business or gambling. With the amount of money rolling in from his oil wells then, it was likely Ray made one of his periodic trips to Switzerland with a suitcase full of cash to hide away in his favorite bank.

But his eyes were on Texas.

What soon would be his greatest oil discovery brought him together with an odd group – an oilman who started from scratch, a handsome man attracted to women and Chicago characters with dubious reputations. Ray didn't shy away from them because all of those descriptions fitted him, too.

Ray and Robert Simpson "Bob" Hays, born in Emporia, Kansas in 1898, met in the early days of Evansville's 1940s oil boom. Hays had left school at the age of 14 to work on an oil field pumping crew then as a cable rig tool dresser, roughneck, and oil supply house worker.

A 6-3, 160-pound balding guy with a keen business sense, Hays was likeable, knew his way about oil fields and had several successful wells around Evansville. He left during World War II to serve as an Engineering Corps officer, but kept in contact with Ray.

Ray also met Edward Burke, an oil investor, in Evansville. Burke asked Ray to find a job for his son, Edward G. "Buzz" Burke Jr., who was in Miami after getting out of the military and on his way to becoming a playboy.

Then, with the impetus from singer Phil Regan, along came Ralph Stolkin and his father-in-law Abe Koolish. The son of a Chicago optometrist, Stolkin attended Illinois universities and in 1942 married Ruth Louise Koolish, the daughter of Abraham Leonard Koolish.

Koolish started K & S Company in 1915, a Chicago mail order operation selling cameras, novelties and jewelry. He expanded into distributing punchboards, where for a few cents a person might win a cheap watch or other merchandise. There were few lucky winners and hundreds of complaints to the Better Business Bureau.

Koolish also ran a life insurance company offering coverage for an entire family at $1 a month premiums, but the small print allowed the company to reject two-thirds of all claims and pay out $10 or less in benefits for most remaining ones. The Federal Trade Commission ordered him to cease false and misleading claims, a squabble that dragged on for years while Koolish made a fortune.

Son-in-law Stolkin borrowed money from a relative and started Monarch Sales in 1946, a mail order business distributing Reynolds ballpoint pens and table- sized radios. Monarch Sales moved 20,000 radios a month and after two years, he sold the company, netting more than $1 million in profit. He also was in the punchboard business with Koolish, earning Stolkin the title of Punchboard King.

By 1948, the 30-year-old Stolkin had amassed a tidy little fortune of more than $3 million and was ready to go on to other things – namely Hollywood and oil. He knew Phil Regan and asked for intro-ductions to heads of film studios and people prominent in the movie industry. Stolkin also learned that Regan knew Ray Ryan and wanted to meet him to invest in oil. In January 1949 at the Beverly Wilshire Hotel in Los Angeles, Regan introduced Stolkin to Ray, who had just formed the Ryan, Hays and Burke Oil Company and leased a site on the R. B. Brown property in West Texas.

Ray first refused to bring Stolkin into the deal. But Ray warmed to the idea when he learned Regan would get a share of Stolkin's profits. Regan had urged Stolkin to put up all the money to drill the well and Ray offered Stolkin a half interest if he did. That was the arrangement Ray preferred – getting his share of a well without using his own money for drilling.

Stolkin had dabbled in oil before and knew there were more dry holes than producing ones. He opted for only a one-fourth interest and gave Ray $50,000. Fearing the well might be a failure, Stolkin sold a quarter of his interest to Koolish and 10 percent to another individual. Regan handed over $4,000 for one-eighth.

Now all they had to do was wait and see if the R. B. Brown lease located in some God-forsaken place in Texas called Scurry County would be worth a plug nickel.

Chapter 40

WEST TEXAS OIL MILLIONS

How Ray first heard about Scurry County isn't known.

Perhaps it came from Bob Hays through his Texas connections or from Ray's own people who had sources everywhere seeking leads for promising oil fields and scouring newspapers for news of the latest oil finds.

He already had 300 producing wells in the Evansville area and dozens more in 14 other states. But most experts didn't think abundant oil existed in Scurry County, although one geologist was convinced there was a giant oil field. His opinion was ignored by his own company.

If there was a massive oil pocket there, Ray wanted to be among the early birds. Playing second fiddle wasn't his style.

Scurry County is 200 miles west of Dallas/Fort Worth. Snyder, the county seat, was a cattle and cotton town of under 4,000 people. The county's first successful oil well was drilled in 1923, but over a quarter century only 4.6 million barrels were pumped, a trifling amount by Texas standards.

Most major oil companies let oil leases in Scurry County expire around World War II because of drilling costs and the slim chance of finding anything.

Few people realized Scurry County was sitting on a sea of black gold resulting from a geological oddity created more than 250,000,000 years ago. At that time the land of the present West Texas and Eastern New Mexico was covered by a bluish shallow sea filled with marine organisms.

As the waters receded, a giant horseshoe atoll was created in the lowland area. As the mountains and hills eroded, the atoll became a subsurface accumulation of fossiliferous limestone as much as 3,000 feet thick. The important Canyon Reef of the atoll angled diagonally from northeast to southwest across today's Scurry County.

Marine plants, spore-bearing land plants and amphibians settled to the sea's bottom. Billions of dead coral-like marine creatures endlessly piled on. The decaying organic material turned into oil over millions of years and the reef eventually was covered by 6,000 feet of silt. The formation had giant spaces between the rock crystals where oil formed in the huge pockets.

The first hint of what laid beneath Scurry County came in the summer of 1948 when Sun and Humble Oil hit a low spot on the Canyon Reef several miles north of Snyder. While the well showed promise, there was doubt about massive oil reserves. Then in November 1948 Magnolia Petroleum brought in a well at the reef's southeast edge. Seventeen days later Standard Oil's well came in 12 miles away, north of Snyder, producing more than 500 barrels of oil a day. Six weeks later in early January Lion Oil hit oil west of Snyder producing nearly 700 barrels a day.

Ray was the first wildcatter in and began drilling at the R.B. Brown No. 1 property six miles northwest of Snyder and three miles south of the known North Snyder reef field.

The land didn't look like much – an undulating series of small ridges interspersed with a few farm houses. The "creeks" mostly were ruts of dirt that overflowed during heavy rains. There was no sign of what laid below the surface.

Drilling started on March 6, 1949 and when completed around April 25 at a depth of 6,640 feet, word leaked out about what was found. The Dallas Morning News newspaper on April 20 cited unconfirmed reports of a major reef field "that would top the list in West Texas." The newspaper said Ray may have found a reef that ran 10 to 12 miles north-south and possibly two or more miles in length, adding "such a reef, if proven, presents staggering possibilities."

A follow up article soon proclaimed that "Scurry County, already the scene of feverish oil development, had burst wide open" and Ray's well was producing 30 to 40 barrels an hour with estimates it could reach 90 barrels of oil hourly on completion.

Ray, Hays and Burke had a three-fourths interest in the R. B. Brown No. 1 but sold a one-fourth interest to Sunray Oil of Tulsa to take over the well's drilling and pumping operations with Ray and his partners retaining a half interest. The remaining one-fourth interest was owned by "Chicago men," the newspaper reported. Ray and Sunray quickly began drilling the Brown No. 2 offset well 1,320 feet south of their first well and suddenly Scurry County had an oil boom.

A court document filed later by Ray's friend singer Regan said the ultimate gross recovery of oil in just the one-fourth interest involving Stolkin was worth $22.4 million. Ray, Hays and Burke turned down an offer of $17.5 million for their R. B. Brown half interest after their third well came in.

Scurry County quickly became the nation's most talked about oil boom since East Texas 19 years earlier. Thousands of people poured in overnight seeking high-paying jobs and Snyder's population tripled to over 12,000 within a year. Two thousand trailers for housing were hauled in.

Home owners rented out beds on an eight-hour basis to men from three round-the-clock shifts. Oil field workers packed into tents and earning $60 to $90 a week soon had new cars parked outside. Some workers had to sleep under lampposts near the town square. A community hydrant provided drinking water and a couple of outhouses served people sleeping outdoors. "You could read a newspaper at night on the square from the well gas flares," one resident said.

Bootleggers brought in pints of whisky from other counties. Snyder's one marshal kept busy running drunks into the one-cell jail. Once guys sobered up, they were pushed out for the next shift of drunks. Oil men bought and sold oil leases on café tables or in the lobby of the town's dingy Manhattan Hotel.

Maps listing owners of county properties were obsolete every two weeks. One farmer sold $100,000 worth of royalties and a week later was out picking his own cotton because everyone else was working in the oil fields. The local bank suddenly had $15 million in deposits.

Scurry County oil production soared to 5.3 million barrels in 1949, exceeding in one year the amount of oil pumped in the previous

25 years. The output hit 38.8 million barrels the next year and 49.5 million barrels in 1951. Life magazine heralded Scurry County in a December 1950 article headlined "West Texas Taps a Big New Oil Pool."

Hollywood actors invested in Scurry County oil. Bing Crosby and Bob Hope had two 1,000 barrels-a-day wells by October 1949 and were drilling two more with Texas partners. Hope flew into Snyder in August 1949. "How did you folks know I was coming," he joked after getting off the plane and being swarmed by autograph hounds. "I'm certainly happy at the kind of liquid we have located. California can have its orange juice." Don Ameche, Randolph Scott and Gene Autry backed wells in West Texas, too.

Ray drilled wells as fast as possible around Scurry County – some were dry holes but he had a dozen or so successful wells in 1949 and 1950, each producing 1,200 or more barrels a day.

He had time to visit and gamble with his close buddy H. L. Hunt, who moved to Dallas around the time Ray and Helen left Tyler around 1938. Ray often talked on the phone with H. L. Hunt. Both men were too busy to have many sit down meetings although Ray visited Hunt in Dallas when he could. Hunt was a teetotaler and Ray liked his bourbon.

When Ray was in Dallas, Hunt needled him by sending someone to buy only a half pint of liquor to have on hand. "That tight old SOB," Ray jokingly lamented to friends. "He's got more money than God and he knows I drink and like good bourbon."

Ray scooted off to Chicago in August 1949 to attend the All-Star college football game that was backed by Chicago journalist Arch Ward. Ward was pleased as Ray beamed and told about his great oil find in Texas.

Ray and other oilmen met at the Adolphus Hotel in Dallas for high stakes gambling. One of the men saw a Texas oilman turn over $250,000 in $1,000 bills to Ray one night either for a gambling debt or a business deal, no one knew which.

There were parties – poker, girls and booze – where oilmen rewarded a favorite party girl by ordering expensive jewelry, clothing or a robin's-egg blue Cadillac convertible delivered to the hotel.

Ray knew all the top oilmen in Texas like Hunt, Glenn McCarthy and Clint Murchison. He gambled with, but didn't particularly like,

Henry F. Sinclair, the founder of Sinclair Oil who was a less than skillful gambler, and the men of the oil-rich Bass family. Sinclair originally followed in the footsteps of his pharmacist father after the family moved to Kansas, and then started dealing in oil leases. His oil holdings in Oklahoma made him a millionaire before he was 30 and he established Sinclair Oil.

But he was snared in the Teapot Dome scandal in the 1920s when Secretary of the Interior Albert B. Fall was accused of leasing tracts of government oil land to private companies in exchange for bribes. Investigators claimed that Sinclair gave Fall more than $230,000 in Liberty bonds and $36,000 in cash for a lease in Wyoming. Fall was convicted of bribery and sentenced to a year in jail. Sinclair was found innocent of fraud but was sentenced to six months for jury tampering and not cooperating with a Congressional investigation.

As Ray's Scurry County oil production grew, he returned occasionally to Evansville to be with Helen and Rae Jean, or made trips to Las Vegas, Palm Springs and elsewhere. Sometimes he headed to New York's Stork Club or the Mocambo nightclub in West Hollywood, tossing around hundred dollar bills for the band to play his favorite tunes.

In West Texas, he spent evenings in the growing city of Midland, 50 miles west of Scurry County, opening an office there. Within a year, 215 oil companies had offices in Midland.

Ray and Buzz Burke dined at Midland's Petroleum Club and fine restaurants. They stood out, dressed in expensive suits, always laughing and having a good time, envied by others. Pretty women hung around them, especially Burke who suddenly had a personal fortune of more than $2 million thanks to oil. Less than a decade later, he would marry a former Miss Universe with a ceremony at the Chicago law office of Sidney Korshak.

The gambling boom also hit Midland. Bookies with nicknames like Sailor, Egghead and Strawberry led a fast-paced business taking bets from oilmen. Gambling parties were held at the homes of bookies and oil company executives, bashes starting in the evenings and lasting until early morning. Top chefs prepared the meals and herds of pretty girls provided entertainment during breaks.

Ray, Hays and Burke opened an office in the state capital of San Antonio as Ray, Stolkin and Koolish drilled a successful well in the Mud Flats Field near Corpus Christi.[15]

Ray's other investors in the fall of 1949 included mobsters Frank Costello, Frank Erickson and Erickson's brother L. J. Erickson, who poured over $20,000 into wells in Schleicher County near San Angelo and another in Oklahoma. The oil deal with Costello and the Erickson brothers later would cement federal investigators' belief that Ray was linked to organized crime, allegations he never could shake.

Adding to that was a little-noticed raid at the start of 1950 at the Miami Sea View Hotel, where Ray was part owner. Cops found a large bookmaking operation with wagers totaling $100,000 a day.

The raid and the oil deals with organized crime figures soon became a costly headache for Ray.

And it made it harder for the Feds and, years later, even for Steve Bagbey not to believe that Ray might be mobbed-up.

---

15 Entertainer Phil Regan filed a lawsuit in 1950 in federal court in Chicago seeking the 8 percent of Stolkin's profits that he was due from the Scurry County and Mud Flats oil fields. Regan eventually got a settlement of $100,000. Regan continued his friendship with Ray for two more decades, often showing up at Palm Springs parties. In 1973, Regan was convicted of trying to bribe a California county supervisor with $6,000 for a favorable vote on a controversial rezoning of a condominium project and served a year in jail. Regan died in 1996.

Chapter 41

ONCE A CHEAT...
ALWAYS

As an investigator, Steve Bagbey needed to know why someone was murdered. He was positive Ray's testimony against two hoods trying to extort money from him was a prime reason. *But was there more?*

A murder in Evansville usually was a spur of the moment thing, like an argument that turns violent. Yet, Steve knew some killings resulted from long-time grievances that festered for weeks or years – a series of events that culminated in the final act of murder. *That's like lining up a row of dominos then toppling one to watch domino after domino fall into another,* Steve thought.

The longer he reread federal reports and his own notes, the more Steve realized Ray's car bombing could be explained by the toppling domino theory even if it took several years or decades before one domino hit the next one.

He believed the first domino leading to Ray's death originated in 1949.

A living legend in that year, Nicholas Andrea Dandolos claimed that $500 million passed through his fingers during his years of gambling. Nick the Greek won and lost hundreds of thousands of dollars at a time without blinking an eye. "The next best thing to playing and winning is playing and losing. The main thing is the play," Nick said.

He had gone bust 73 times in life, won $1 million on the horses before he was twenty, broke one of the roulette banks at Monte Carlo in 1919 and was arrested for passing a $100 worthless check a decade later – a gambler roller-coaster ride.[16]

Born into the family of a wealthy rug merchant in Crete, Nick grew up in the Turkish city of Smyrna, was educated at a Greek Evangelical College and spoke Greek, Turkish, French and English. He arrived in America at 18 years old with $150 in his pocket and took up betting the horses and winning.

In his heyday, Nick dined with Al Capone, consistently beat Arnold Rothstein at cards, and could gamble for days, surviving on orange juice, sandwiches and cigars. His most famous marathon poker game was in 1949 in a Las Vegas downtown casino against legendary gambler Johnny Moss. The two played half a dozen variations of poker over several months. At the end, Nick was tapped out and, legend has it, Moss had won $2 million. Weary and without money, Nick nodded to Moss and spoke a memorable line in poker: "Mr. Moss, I have to let you go."

Nick and Ray faced off in their own series of poker games a few months later. Their encounter attracted no publicity and less attention because Ray Ryan, at least at that point, wasn't as famous as Johnny Moss.

But what happened between the two did become part of a major novel and movie and caused many people to regard Ray Ryan as a cheat when it came to cards, an onus that stayed with Ray the rest of his life.

"Once a cheat, always…in some people's eyes," Steve mused.

Besides the Flamingo, the only major casino along Highway 91 was the Thunderbird which opened in 1948. The Flamingo was mob-controlled and the Thunderbird soon would be.

In the fall of 1949, Ray and Nick squared off at the Flamingo playing 15 or 16 times several days a week from 1 p.m. to 6 p.m.

Most games were poolside within view of adjacent hotel rooms but they sometimes played in other areas of the Flamingo. Ante was $1,500 and only black chips worth $500 each were used for betting. Nick and Ray played low-ball, or Canadian poker, where the lowest hand – not the highest hand – won.

---

16 Nick always paid his gambling debts no matter how large they were, and was nearly penniless when he died of a heart attack on Christmas Day in 1966 at the age of 80.

When they sat down across from each other, word quickly spread and 50 or more people gathered to watch. Benny Binion stopped by from his downtown casino some days. Allen Smiley came as well as John Drew and other curious people.

A 22-year-old, blue-eyed blond with an eye-catching figure also showed up frequently. Born in Coral Gables, Florida, Dorothy Jean Biegger was known as Jeanne. As a beautiful teenager she had modeled for a catalog company, followed by photos on magazine covers and a Dr. Pepper calendar.

On New Year's Eve 1948, Jeanne joined the entourage of the Orange Bowl Queen for a night at Miami's Beachcomber Club where she saw a charming singer performing with his comic sidekick. It was love at first sight for Jeanne. Only later did she find out he was married and had four children. In August 1949, the singer got a divorce and on September 1, Jeanne married the handsome crooner, Dean Martin.

Jeanne was in Las Vegas because Dean and Jerry Lewis had opened at the Flamingo that September. Jeanne spent some of her honeymoon watching Ray and Nick play cards, mesmerized at what unfolded before her eyes. Others watching were equally mesmerized at Ray's luck as he raked in pots. Nick won some hands, but lost far more. Ray left little doubt that he was the best player around. Ray's friend John Drew probably secretly smiled at Ray's "luck."

Stories about how much Nick lost ranged from $100,000 to over $250,000. James Harakas, described as a Detroit underworld figure who was an executive of a California electronics firm, later testified in federal court that he made four deliveries totaling $323,000 of Nick's losses to Ray's Flamingo hotel room. Harakas didn't know where Nick got the money, Ray never gave a receipt and Nick never asked for one. Harakas didn't know if Nick paid Ray more money.

Everything seemed settled. When the Desert Inn opened the next year, Ray and Nick were among numerous gamblers and celebrities sitting in on card games amid the fanfare. But in 1951, Nick was told he had been cheated by Ray.

A man named Steve Pappas confessed he helped Ray by rigging electronic devices to let Ray know Nick's hole cards. Pappas said someone in one of the hotel rooms behind Nick's seat used binoculars to see his cards and passed that information on to Ray using a concealed radio receiver emitting electronic impulses that could be felt on a leg or arm.

At Binion's newly-opened Las Vegas Horseshoe Club in 1951, Nick confronted Ray and accused him of cheating. Harakas said Ray didn't deny rigging the game but contended all he got out of it was $135,000. Ray was willing to repay that much to Nick, adding "I don't want anyone to know about this because of the embarrassment," according to Harakas.

Nick eventually claimed he lost $550,000 in the crooked game and never got any money back. Ray's memory was fuzzy and he said if he won anything it was closer to $15,000.

But the story of Nick being victimized in a rigged game had its own life and was passed around Hollywood, Las Vegas and the world of gamblers.

Ian Fleming, a former journalist, banker and stock broker who worked for British intelligence during World War II, had heard the story. After the war, Fleming wrote spy novels and the main character was British secret agent OO7 James Bond. Fleming liked the tale of the rigged card game so much that he used it as the basis of the memorable card game in his book, "Goldfinger," published in 1959. The book was adapted for a movie in 1964.

In the book, Bond was asked by a man named Simmons to find out how Goldfinger consistently won large sums of cash from him playing two-handed Canasta at a Miami Beach hotel poolside table. Bond discovers a beautiful girl named Jill Masterson lounging on a hotel room balcony overlooking the pool using binoculars to see the cards in Simmons' hand. She passed the information to Goldfinger through a radio device that resembled a hearing aid.

Whether Ray really did cheat Nick didn't matter because the story followed Ray forever. He would be considered a card cheat using electronic devices and peeking schemes to win. He claimed he didn't cheat, but in the world of high stakes gamblers perception was reality.

FBI reports about the 1950s and 1960s that were turned over to Steve Bagbey were dotted with informants saying Ray cheated at poker and gin rummy. Federal agents and California police reported hearing that Ray and Drew were planning rigged dice or card games at the Palm Springs' El Mirador hotel to win a large sum of money from wealthy actors and individuals. The FBI never verified if rigged games took place.

After Ray's murder, Benny Binion summed up Ray's status among gamblers to federal agents: "Ray was well liked in Las Vegas although he was known as a cheater in gambling. Ryan always paid his debts and did not owe me money at the time of his death." For Binion, that was a ringing endorsement.

But Nick the Greek wasn't willing to drop his feelings about Ray. Nick never forgave Ray for cheating. He wanted his pound of flesh and it took more than a decade to get the wheels in motion.

Nick eventually took his plea to the Chicago mob, a move that became a major step – *the first domino* to Steve Bagbey – leading to Ray Ryan being murdered.

Chapter 42

BOAT RIDE WITH HUNT

H. L. Hunt liked to say he won $15 million over the years gambling, but if he declared those winnings he would have to pay $11 million in back taxes, according to author Harry Hurt III in his book "Texas Rich" about the multi-millionaire oilman. So high stakes gamblers never gave a complete list of their winnings. One reason for Hunt was the taxes he'd have to pay; the other reason was that he gambled so much he couldn't keep a record of his winnings and losses even if he wanted to. Even in oil and business dealings, Hunt often keep notes on scraps of paper stuck in various pockets on what he had agreed to, leaving it to the folks around him to try and piece together exactly what Hunt's agreement had been.

While Hunt won millions gambling, his luck didn't extend to Ray, who jokingly called Hunt his "pigeon" when it came to cards and betting on football games. Hunt didn't seem to mind losing to Ray because he kept coming back for more and to enjoy Ray's company. It was only money. Hunt had tons of it.

Like Nick the Greek, Hunt enjoyed the play as much as winning but Ray enjoyed winning more.

Both yearned for a big head-to-head game of gin rummy. Hunt was an excellent poker player but thought he was good enough to take on Ray at gin rummy. Hunt would have his chance on a boat trip from New York to Europe, a legendary gin rummy game – a classic battle of fat cats – that would be retold over and over. Both had been too busy to find the time to get together before then. Many versions exist about how the trip came about and what happened.

One Hunt biographer said the trip was on the French liner Liberté in 1954. The FBI later was told the trip was in 1950. The Liberté was the talk of New York in 1950, the most elegant passenger liner around. Built by Germany in 1928 as the Europa, the ship was a troop carrier in World War II in the Baltic Sea. Set afire by Allied bombers, the boat was captured by the Americans in 1945, given to France as war reparations and renamed Liberté.

The French spent $19.5 million to turn the Liberté into the finest and fifth-largest passenger ship with a capacity of 1,500 passengers. French artists transformed rooms with rich tapestries, wall murals, exotic woods, decorative panels and paintings. There was a swimming pool, steam rooms, bars, a library with 5,000 specially bound volumes, a hospital, boulevard-like promenades, exotic plants and flowers, 30,000 bottles of wine, 6,500 bottles of champagne and whiskeys and superb French food. The Liberté's maiden six-day voyage from New York to France occurred in September 1950.

Most likely, Ray and Hunt sailed on one of the ship's first voyages. By the time the Liberté docked in Europe, Hunt had lost $248,000, $345,000 or $600,000 according to various accounts later. Hunt never said what transpired on the trip. Hunt always said Ray was "an honorable person."

More than a decade later, Paul Rothermel[17], who was Hunt's security chief and executive assistant, told FBI agents he knew that Hunt lost over $6 million to Ray during the trip. When Hunt wired his Dallas office to send the money, members of Hunt's staff were so concerned that they flew to Europe and brought him back. The $6 million figure continued to show up in FBI reports over the years but no one knew for sure how much Hunt lost because he overstated gambling losses and low-balled winnings to keep the Internal Revenue Service off his back.

---

17 Rothermel resigned from Hunt's operations in 1969 following an investigation into alleged mismanagement and siphoning off of millions of dollars from H.L.H. Products, a food division subsidiary of Hunt's vast empire. Rothermel was given federal immunity in the case while two other H.L.H. Products employees were convicted of using the mails to defraud. Two of Hunt's sons, Nelson Bunker Hunt and W. Herbert Hunt, were charged with hiring private detectives to wiretap phones of the products firm's officials, but they were found innocent in a trial. Rothermel also figured in a later squabble following H. L. Hunt's death in 1974 over his encouraging Hunt to write a new will in 1971 and leaving a substantial portion of his estate to his wife Ruth.

Hunt got another chance to overstate losses after Ray and Jimmy the Greek Snyder got through with him. Ray had introduced Jimmie to Hunt in a phone call in 1949 as Ray and Jimmie were pooling their talents – Ray's money and Jimmy's oddsmaking expertise – during the college football season.

Ray proposed he and Hunt bet head-to-head on college football and told Jimmy "I'll put up the money, Greek, and you've got a third of it. You just give me the teams to bet." The first weekend, Ray lost $100,000, but told Jimmy not to worry. "I've got a lot of money and I believe in you," he said to Jimmy.

Jimmy knew about Southeastern Conference teams while Hunt favored Southwestern Conference teams. Ray and Hunt decided that each would pick three games from their respective conferences, betting $50,000 on each game. The winners each week were based on the spread of individual games from Chicago bookie Leo Shaffer. He had been a bootlegger and muscle man for the Capone mob during Prohibition, served a jail term for trying to force a Chicago area restaurant owner to sell Capone's booze even though the restaurant served only soft drinks. Shaffer eventually became one of Chicago's major bookmakers, simply known as "Bookie."

At the end of each football weekend, if Hunt lost he sent a check to Ray and if Ray lost, he paid Hunt. Jimmy said Ray seldom lost. He had an edge. He knew that each week Hunt jotted his upcoming picks on a notepad at his desk with stars marking his favorite bets.

Ray worked out a deal with a secretary in Hunt's office. Each Friday, Jimmy called the secretary, who looked on Hunt's desk to see which teams he planned to bet on Saturday.

To thwart Hunt's chances of winning some games, Jimmy had Ray place $20,000 bets with Shaffer on teams Hunt favored in order to reduce the spread by a point or more and increasing Ray's chances of winning. If Hunt picked a team Jimmy thought was right, Ray also bet $50,000 on that game and collected from the bookie even if Hunt won that game in their head-to-head competition. After two seasons, Ray and Jimmy had won $600,000.

Ray and Hunt abandoned their weekly football contest in 1951 when Senator Estes Kefauver's congressional committee hearings sent the country's bookmakers scrambling for cover. Ray and Hunt continued to wager separately, heavily and more carefully over the next six years, often with Shaffer. But their favorite bookie's days were growing short and so were the high stakes gambling days of Ray and Hunt.

Lyda Bunker Hunt died in 1955 and Hunt married Ruth Ray in November 1957.[18] His gambling brought his new wife to tears. A few years later, the federal government was after both men because of a major bookmaking investigation in Terre Haute, Indiana that involved Shaffer.

By early 1958, Hunt called in his outstanding bets and never gambled again. Ray's high stakes gambling days also were numbered.

Later federal investigators suspected that the long friendship between Ray Ryan and H. L. Hunt included a more nefarious side – that the two occasionally had financed big-time bookmaking operations and crooked gambling games to fleece high rollers and movie folks.

But the Feds never were able to crack the bond between Ray and Hunt.

---

18 Hunt set up substantial trusts for the women and children of his second and third families. Ray and Helen were the trustees for the trust set up for Ruth Ray from oil and gas properties worth in the range of $1 million. Ray and Helen often visited H.L. and Ruth in Dallas. Ray liked to call H. L.'s Dallas mansion "Hunt's Medicare Bunny Club."

Chapter 43

ALWAYS A DEAL

There wasn't a business deal Ray wouldn't consider – his own or someone else's – no matter how harebrained it appeared. His greatest flurry of deals came with money he earned from oil wells. Publicly he said his oil production was 5,000 barrels a day but an oil partner put it at more than 10,000 barrels a day.

That mattered little to Ray because money was for having fun.

Dean Martin and Jerry Lewis were becoming one of the hottest acts around, earning $15,000 a week for their stint at the Flamingo in 1949. Their first movie "My Friend Irma" released in October 1949 received rave reviews. Ray met Dean and Jerry in Palm Springs around that time and the three hit it off.

Ray would be closer to Dean perhaps, in part, because Dean was an old Steubenville, Ohio mate of Jimmy the Greek Snyder.

Despite their growing popularity, Dean and Jerry didn't make a lot of money for themselves. Too many people took cuts from their income before anything dwindled down to them. The Paramount contract with Hal Wallace Productions allowed the team to make one independent movie a year.

The entertainers told Ray they wanted to start their own movie company but didn't have the money. Ray agreed to put up the cash for them to start York Pictures. In the spring of 1950, he assembled a group that included Ralph Stolkin to create Screen Associates, Inc. to underwrite and profit from independent movies made by Dean and Jerry. Stolkin was getting his chance to be a mover and shaker in Hollywood.

York Pictures and Screen Associates agreed to make a total of seven films. The first one, "At War with the Army," opened in 1951 and drew good crowds but Martin and Lewis still were unhappy with their cut. They balked at making more films with Screen Associates, which filed a lawsuit seeking $10 million in damages. Two years later, Martin and Lewis agreed to pay over $800,000 to get out of the contract.

Despite the dispute, Dean remained Ray's friend because Ray already had moved on to something else – luxurious flying machines.

Glenn Odekirk, a 1927 engineering graduate of Oregon State University, had come up with the idea originally. He met Howard Hughes on one of Hughes' movie sets a few years after leaving college and would be with Hughes for more than 15 years serving as the millionaire's Man Friday when it came to airplanes.

Howard Robard Hughes, Jr. had inherited controlling interest in Hughes Tool Company at age 18 upon the death of his father, a Texas oil wildcatter who patented a rotary drill that revolutionized the oil drilling industry. The young Hughes bought out his relatives, took over as sole owner of the company, married a Houston socialite and moved to Hollywood to make movies. In 1930, Hughes spent $3.8 million on "Hell's Angels," a film about World War I pilots, and one of the pilots used in the movie was Odekirk.

While a financial failure, the movie stirred Hughes' interest in aviation. He formed Hughes Aircraft Company in 1932 and started building the world's most advanced planes. Odekirk was hired to improvise alterations and serve as co-pilot or flight engineer on Hughes' record-setting flights. They garnered records for flying at 352 miles per hour; flying coast-to-coast in a record 7 hours, 28 minutes; and flying around the world in three days and 19 hours, in the process breaking Charles Lindbergh's record time flying from New York to Paris.

During World War II, Hughes set out to build a plywood cargo plane capable of transporting 750 troops or 35 tons of materiel across the ocean and Odekirk designed and built the craft known as the "Spruce Goose" that was completed after the war.

When Hughes turned his attention to buying controlling interest in RKO Pictures in 1948, Odekirk set out on his own, spending the next two years remodeling a World War II surplus Catalina PBY into a luxury flying machine unequaled by any plane of its time. Odekirk and Dave Swedlow, head of a plastic company, purchased a PBY for $12,000 and revamped it into "an aerial luxury yacht . . . with all the comforts of home."They incorporated their operation as the Southern California Aviation Corp.

The plane had the latest navigation and radio instruments, a radio speaker and phone system, sleeping compartments with five beds, air-conditioning vents, stainless steel and chrome kitchen appliances, a freezer, a furnace and hot and cold running water. The 104-foot long, 15-foot wide wing could be used for a sun deck at destinations. On board were 12-foot skiffs with masts, sails, outboard motors, walkie-talkies and fishing equipment. The price tag was $200,000.

Odekirk had met Ray earlier and broached the idea of turning out luxury planes. Ray jumped at the proposal, pumping cash into the project, taking over as the corporation's president. Ray acquired 22 surplus PBYs from a Canadian company and opened a plant at the Ontario, California airport, hiring over 70 workers. By late 1950 the first of a planned score of modified PBY Catalinas flew out.

Ray shuttled potential oil investors across the country on one of the planes, making sure a large card table was handy. If guests wanted to play poker or gin rummy for money on the flight, the pilot reduced the plane's speed to make the trip longer. If they weren't interested in gambling, the pilot flew at normal speed. Ray also was working on a major oil deal in the Middle East at the time and flew in one of the converted PBYs, attracting attention wherever he went. Ray sold his personal flying boat to Egypt's King Farouk in 1952 for $265,000.

Southern California Aircraft operated for about 12 years with Bill Gorman overseeing the business at the outset and Frank Hayden, Ray's West Coast business manager, taking over later.

Expanding into maintenance and repair of commercial, private and U. S. military airplanes, Southern California Aircraft employed 600 to 1,000 workers by late 1950s.

After one partner used company funds to build himself a home, Ray bought out everyone by 1958 and turned the corporation into a holding company, waiting for the day he could use the company for another venture – and make a profit in the process.

After all, money was for spending, not caressing.

Chapter 44

IRAQI OIL BITTER PILL

In the early 1950s, Ray got mired in international intrigue and Hollywood trickery.

For once, he was in over his head – battling big oil companies overseas, the intricate mind of Howard Hughes at home and losing millions of dollars along the way.

Ray probably got tangled in the Middle East oil venture because of Joseph Edward Davies, the best known native son from Ray's hometown of Watertown, Wisconsin.

Born in 1876, Davies became a lawyer active in Democratic politics and was appointed to several federal posts by President Woodrow Wilson. After losing a U. S. Senate race in 1918, Davies joined a law firm in Washington, D.C.

He supported Franklin Roosevelt for president and was appointed ambassador to Russia in 1937 then was named ambassador to Belgium and Minister to Luxembourg before World War II. In 1941, he wrote the book "Mission to Moscow," seeking American support for Russia's plight in the war. The book was made into a movie in 1943, but by then, Davies was viewed as a naïve promoter of pro-Soviet propaganda.

After the war, Davies joined the Washington law firm of Davies, Richberg, Tydings, Beebe & Landa and one of his daughters had married Millard E. Tydings, an attorney and U. S. Senator from Maryland. America was becoming more dependent on foreign oil and Davies understood the Middle East and knew Ray Ryan.

American and European companies had a stranglehold on Middle East oil production, dominating in Saudi Arabia and Iran. The trouble spot was Iraq which was under the control of the Iraq Petroleum Company owned by British, American, Dutch and French companies.

Oil flowed smoothly from Saudi Arabia and Iran but Iraq was in turmoil. The Iraqis used an oil refinery in Haifa, Israel and oil production often was shut down as Israel fought to establish its nation. Foreign owners also paid Iraq less of a share for its oil than other Arab nations, Iraq's national treasury was on the verge of bankruptcy and the Parliament talked of nationalizing oil production.

In the fall of 1950, Frances William Rickett approached Ray about taking over a major oil field in the Zubair region in the southeastern corner of Iraq. Rickett was a mysterious character, a wealthy Englishman who had attempted to corner vast pockets of oil production in Ethiopia and Mexico in the 1930s. He saw a possible oil gold mine in Iraq but needed Americans with money and clout to step in.

Ray teamed with Sherman Hunt, the brother of H. L. Hunt, and proposed bringing in rigs extracting 400,000 barrels a day from the Zubair field. But that required Iraqi Premier Nuri canceling the portion of the Iraq Petroleum agreement for the Zubair area.

In January and March 1951, Ray and Sherman Hunt flew to Baghdad accompanied by geologists and attorneys to talk with Iraqi leaders. Bill Gorman went along to look after Ray's interests. They hired Millard E. Tydings as their attorney to try to influence top Iraqi officials and officials at the U.S. and British embassies. During the Middle East trips, Ray met the Shah of Iran and played poker with Egyptian King Farouk at a French Rivera casino.

Iraq Petroleum's British, American, Dutch and French oil companies refused to allow outsiders to muscle in on their oil fiefdom. The ensuing battle stirred up a hornet's nest of diplomatic protests bordering on an international incident. Washington officials said Ray caused "discomfort" among the cartel nations.

Iraq Petroleum was forced to open talks to increase Iraq's future oil royalties and Nuri kept the door slightly open for Ray's proposal if negotiations fell through.

During the 1951 Memorial Day weekend, Ray rented plush suites at the Blackstone and Ambassador East hotels in Chicago to await further developments. None came and millions of dollars were at stake. Ray told reporters he only was in Chicago to see the Ezzard Charles-Joe Maxim fight, adding "it was a lousy fight." Oilman James

Breuil and Edward Barrett, one of Ray's friends from his Chicago days and by then Illinois Secretary of State, accompanied Ray to the fight.

Around Memorial Day, Iraq Petroleum agreed to increase royalty payments to Iraq. Ray accepted defeat with style. "You get into something like that and you're likely to get your head chopped off," he said. He cut his losses and moved on, but it was a bitter pill to swallow.

In the summer of 1952, Ray and actor Bruce Cabot traveled to Watertown for ceremonies honoring Davies. Both Ray and Davies funded scholarships for local high school graduates to attend the University of Wisconsin. Ray paid for a $34,000 bust of Davies that was unveiled at the event.

When Ray rose to speak, he was tongue-tied. "Maybe I can't talk, but I can read and I'm going to read this," Ray said and started reading the words on the plaque, but managed a few words, then broke off reading the rest only as "etc. etc."

Then more at ease, he told the audience about growing up in Watertown and about his family. After the luncheon, he met with the editor of the local newspaper and proposed setting up scholarships for newsboys because he once was one.

Overall, Ray was excited by the trip and visiting home again. As he and Cabot flew out of Watertown, Cabot told him "I wish I were as big a hit in my hometown as you were in yours."

Years into the murder investigation, the idea germinated in Steve Bagbey's mind that if the Central Intelligence Agency really did talk to Ray, it may have started when Ray was involved in the Iraq oil deal. *Ray's buddy Ambassador Joseph Davies may have initiated getting the C.I.A. and Ray together,* Steve thought.

In his frequent visits to the Middle East, Ray came into contact with many national leaders, perhaps gathering information that the C.I.A. wanted.

Steve believed the Middle East was often in turmoil and the U.S. needed the latest details of what was happening there. Also Ray seemed to have a highly developed patriotic spirit and would be easy to cultivate, especially if the C.I.A. tossed some money his way.

The Evansville FBI agents denied that Ryan was a C.I.A. contact. Still, Steve wondered about the possibility.

Chapter 45

OUTSMARTED BY HOWARD HUGHES

With the Martin and Lewis film whetting their Hollywood appetites and the hopes of Screen Associates slipping away, Ralph Stolkin and Ray in 1952 were hot on the trail of RKO Pictures which was floundering thanks to Howard Hughes.

Hughes gained control of the old Radio-Keith-Orpheum Corporation by acquiring 24 percent of the stock in 1948 for $9 million. Under a Justice Department order, Hughes split the company into RKO Pictures and RKO Theatres, keeping control of RKO Pictures and putting RKO Theatres into a trusteeship for several years before selling it.

Hughes' heavy-handed micro-management style tore RKO Pictures apart. Prominent producers and directors abandoned the studio over various disputes. Hughes eliminated three-fourths of the studio's 2,500 workers. Production was shut down for months as Hughes fretted over possible Communist influence in the movie industry. A legal dispute with the Screen Actors Guild further compounded RKO's problems. The studio was losing millions of dollars a year.

A crippled RKO appealed to Stolkin and Ray, who put together a team that included Buzz Burke, Abe Koolish and Sherrill C. Corwin, operator of palatial Los Angeles movie theaters. They hired as their attorney Sidney Korshak, a Chicago native who earned a law degree at DePaul University in 1930 and began representing members of Capone's mobs.

Korshak was turning his attention west to Los Angeles and Las Vegas casinos hoping to shine before the Hollywood crowd. He put no money into the RKO deal but expected to be the labor consultant for Ray and Stolkin.

Irked by RKO's financial problems and the Screen Actors Guild wrangling, Hughes agreed to sell the studio. On September 23, 1952, Ray and his partners signed on to buy over one million RKO shares from Hughes for $7.3 million with about $1.3 million to be paid immediately and the remaining $6 million in two years.

Stolkin was happy, saying "I felt the time was ripe. The movie business has been in a lull. Our group believes that the business hasn't even begun to scratch the surface of its future potential and that we can help it prosper and develop." He said the best management and talent would be hired and film production resumed. Everyone expected Hughes would spend more time with his aviation interests.

Stolkin was elected RKO board president and Burke, Koolish and Corwin board directors along with Bill Gorman, who ran Ray's massive Evansville-based oil company and was selected to represent Ray on the RKO board.

Gorman hadn't seen the RKO agreement until late in the negotiations, and was surprised to discover it didn't include the contracts of several of Hollywood's most prominent stars – particularly Jane Russell, who Hughes had under personal contract – sure box office attractions to bring millions of people into theaters.

Gorman thought the RKO deal was lousy and urged Ray to back out. But Ray, being Ray, had moved on and was deep into his next project of getting a group together to buy and restore the old Mirador Hotel in Palm Springs.

Three weeks after the RKO purchase, the Wall Street Journal ran two lengthy articles about the new owners that put Ray, Stolkin and Koolish on a slippery slope to unravel the deal. The articles on October 16 and 17, 1952 noted it "seemed questionable whether any of the new management could be as colorful" as Hughes, but the new owners "deserve to be much better known than they are."

The newspaper termed Korshak as a "sort of catalytic agent" and noted Korshak's name came up before the Kefauver committee as the attorney who organized an early parole for Charles "Cherry Nose" Gioe after the Browne-Bioff movie industry extortion.

The Journal's first report concentrated on Stolkin and Koolish, outlining their backgrounds as distributors of punchboards, Koolish's misleading claims of his mail order business and his questionable life insurance business, all contributing to his net worth of $4.3 million.

On the second day, the Journal concentrated on Ray, and it wasn't pleasant.

The reporter noted Ray looked much younger than 48 years old, had the build of a football tackle and was the top man in a series of oil ventures in many states, a high stakes gambler and horse bettor. "I would like to have the money that Ray loses," Stolkin admiringly told the reporter.

Ray wore a checkered sports jacket, tan gabardine slacks, a mono-grammed shirt and brown alligator loafers for the interview. On one wrist was a heavy gold link bracelet with his name inscribed on a gold plate and on the other an identical bracelet with a wristwatch.

The Journal delved into New York mobster Frank Costello admitting before the Kefauver committee in March 1951 his acquaintance with an oilman named Ryan. Ray told the Journal he was the man Costello referred to. Costello said he invested in an Oklahoma oil deal with Ray at the behest of bookmaker and friend Frank Erickson. He described Ray as "just an acquaintance but I have known for a long, long time – maybe 15 years" and that he probably met Ray with Erickson in Miami years ago at a race track.

While admitting to the Journal that he knew Costello, Ray said his investment in the oil deal with Costello was inadvertent. Ray said oil-man Jim Breuil offered him an interest in the well, which he took, and Costello and Erickson didn't secure an interest in the lease from him. But Breuil told the newspaper the lease that ended up in Costello's hands moved through Ray. It was reported that Costello had invested $41,000 in the oil deal and got back $92,000.

The Journal didn't mention another oil deal in Texas Ray had with Costello and Erickson that turned out to be a dry hole, but did report the Kefauver committee testimony of George Patton, a former Dade County, Florida, sheriff deputy who was one of the many cops, sheriffs and elected officials being paid off by gamblers like Jack Friedlander.

Patton recalled a raid in the spring of 1950 at a bookmaking operation at the Miami Beach Sea View Hotel, where Ray was part owner. Patton said he stumbled into a big bookmaking operation at the Sea View while checking other nearby hotels for slot machines. The cops found sheets for bets of up to $1,000 and arrested several people. They let a hysterical woman worker walk away only to learn she had been carrying $27,000 in betting receipts.

Patton said the bookie operation brought in between $50,000 to $100,000 a day in bets and he was later told the Sea View bookmaking operation was "Harry Russell's place." The Journal reported Ray said "in most positive terms that he has never engaged in any form of professional gambling."

The article failed to mention the part of Patton's Kefauver committee testimony about oilman Harry Sinclair losing $800,000 in two nights of gambling at the mob-run Golden Shores Club in Dade County. Patton said Friedlander, one of the Golden Shores operators, opened some nights only for special high stakes gamblers coming to Miami, handing three cops $1,000 each to make sure the club wasn't raided that night.

Patton said on one special night "a big well-known gambler named Ryan had steered" Harry Sinclair to the Golden Shores where Sinclair lost $800,000 over two nights of gambling and eventually paid $500,000 to settle the debt. The Kefauver committee didn't ask Patton for more details.

Several years later, informants told FBI agents that the Ryan in the Sinclair case was Ray Ryan, who got $100,000 for steering Sinclair to the tables – one-eighth of Sinclair's losses, the typical royalty percentage when oil is found on someone's land – and headed off to Iraq.

Singer Phil Regan told the FBI he hosted a party at a Miami hotel where Ray and Sinclair first met in the late 1940s. After the party, Ray and Sinclair got into a craps game in which Ray took Sinclair for $400,000. Regan wasn't at the game but said another oil company president had admitted helping Sinclair pay off the debt.

The Wall Street Journal articles proved devastating to the new RKO owners – punchboard kings, questionable insurance and sales mail schemes, links to major mob figures, big time gamblers. Hollywood wasn't comfortable with that group running a major studio.

Bending to the mounting pressure, Stolkin, Koolish and Gorman resigned from the RKO board the following week. Grant resigned a month later while Burke and Corwin held on a little longer. At the end of 1952, Ray and his partners turned their stock holdings back to Hughes and kissed goodbye to the $1.25 million they had given him. Ray had lost over a quarter million dollars. Gorman was right. The RKO proposal was a lousy deal.

It was a couple of years before Ray's group realized they had been suckered. Hughes' people had thoroughly checked out the backgrounds of Stolkin, Koolish and Ray before selling RKO.

Hughes had waited a few days before leaking the backgrounds of the new buyers to the Wall Street Journal. Hughes got what he wanted out of the deal – $1 million more to his vast fortune and continued ownership of RKO.[19]

The RKO disaster did have some benefits for Ray.

Before, he was a moneyed oilman with Texas connections moving around the Palm Springs and Los Angeles scene. Now he was known by Hollywood columnists. The more they were around Ray, the more they liked him and the more they wrote about him.

During the rest of the 1950s, Hedda Hopper, Nate Gross, Sheila Graham, Earl Wilson, Joan Winchell, Jim Murray and other syndicated columnists followed Ray's movements, reporting on his flamboyancy, friendliness and willingness to spend money in buckets.

His life provided great fodder to fill up column space for the next 15 years. Columnists called him a zillionaire, oilionaire, the poor man's Howard Hughes; they wrote about his extravagant parties, exotic trips and his gambling exploits.

He loved the attention.

Ray was becoming Ray Ryan.

---

19 Hughes making $1 million while RKO was losing money by the truckload didn't sit well with stockholders in 1952. Lawsuits were abundant. By the end of 1954, Hughes paid nearly $24 million to buy out other stockholders and become sole owner of the studio. Six months later, he sold RKO and netted an overall profit of about $9 million. His days at RKO were over. Hughes turned his eyes toward owning Las Vegas casinos.

Chapter 46

CAIFANO TAKES OVER VEGAS

Marshall also was becoming Marshall Caifano in Chicago in the early 1950s. High roller deals like Iraqi oil and RKO weren't on his mind. He was concerned about more mundane things – revenge.

Caifano was rising in the Outfit hierarchy. He had Fio "Fifi" Buccieri and Felix "Milwaukee Phil" Alderisio as his drivers and enforcers, shuttling him to the restaurants and bookmaking spots, waiting outside pitching coins against a wall while Caifano conducted syndicate business or enjoyed a meal.

He was called on to handle important chores for the mob. The Outfit was renewing efforts to take over the policy rackets in black neighborhoods. Black operators were murdered and others gave up without a struggle, their businesses taken over with the mob bringing in their own black lieutenants or white associates to run the games. The main west side policy operator was James "Big Jim" Martin, who was wounded by shotgun blasts in his Cadillac in 1950 and encouraged to get out of the business.

Sam Giancana and Leonard "Fat Lenny" Caifano leaned on the recalcitrant Theodore Roe, the most important south side holdout. Chicago was the country's only large city where blacks still controlled policy games and Roe had to go. Giancana tried to shake him down for money in 1945, but was brushed off. A year later, Roe fled through the streets with bullets whistling around his head as men tried to kidnap him.

By 1950, Roe's main operations netted him $1 million a year on which he paid federal taxes. On June, 18 1951, he was driving home after leaving the Arlington Park race track and dropping off a friend at home when four men in a car cut him off. Two men flashed badges, saying they were the state's attorney police, but they didn't look like cops.

Roe later told police a heavyset man pulled him out of his car, roughly grabbed his coat lapels and cursed him. Roe said someone fired at him from the car, he pulled a gun and gunshots echoed on the street. Roe's bullet struck the heavyset man in the head and he exchanged gunfire with the other men until one ran off and the other two sped away. Roe thought he might have shot one of the other two guys in the leg.

Lying dead on the street with a bullet wound to the temple was the 42-year-old Leonard Caifano. Cops thought the shooting was a kidnapping gone wrong, but the word on the street was that it was an attempt by Fat Lenny to scare Roe. A sheriff's department special deputy star, which had been handed out for years by Cook County sheriffs, was found at the scene. Lenny had gotten his star two years earlier after the sheriff was told he carried a lot of money.

Investigators believed Lenny's brother Marshall and Giancana had been with Lenny. Marshall was found a few days later at his apartment but said he had been at a boxing match in Milwaukee when his brother was killed. Caifano spent time representing the Outfit in Milwaukee where Frank Balistrieri was being groomed to take over. Balistrieri ran sports betting and vending machine businesses and had an interest in a Milwaukee boxing club along with Caifano.

The police hauled Caifano to the state's attorney office where Caifano denied any involvement in the shooting. He also had to drop his pants to show he didn't have any bullet wounds. He was questioned for hours before being released.

Caifano told cops he had worked as a clerk at a now-closed book-making joint even though his apartment had fancy drapes and expensive furniture. Roe wouldn't identify Marshall as one of the men who stopped him.

The state's attorney accused Roe of murder and pursued charges on the policy rackets. Eventually everything was dropped. Marshall Caifano wanted revenge for his brother's death, but was counseled by older hoods to pick the right place and time. He went about his syndicate chores of collecting Outfit gambling money but knew Roe had to pay for killing Lenny.

On August 4, 1952, fourteen months after Lenny's death, the 55-year-old Roe left his apartment and headed to his car. Two men waited in a car behind a billboard in a nearby vacant lot passing around a half-gallon jug of beer.

When they saw Roe, they grabbed 12-gauge shotguns, got out and fired five shots, two striking Roe in his chest and a third his head. The city's policy king, the man who held out against the mob, was dead as the killers drove away.

Five thousand people came to view his body. Another 2,000 attended the church service amid more than 100 floral baskets. Thousands lined the sidewalks along the hearse's route. The undertaker said Roe's funeral was larger than the one in 1946 for black boxer Jack Johnson. Within a few years, Roe's south side policy games came under the Outfit's thumb. Big Jim Martin's west side area went to Giancana, Sam Battaglia, Caifano, Leonard Patrick and William Block.

Now Caifano's name had been linked to the murders of Roe, Drury, Ragen, Estelle Carey, Quattrochi and others. He had to get out of town until the heat died down. He took his share of money from an auto business insurance scam and headed to Las Vegas, buying land and checking on mob casinos. Arthur Pete Brady, the Desert Inn pit boss, was the Chicago mob's contact man in Vegas, keeping prying state gambling agents from seeing visiting hoods. Caifano dined privately with John Drew and others at tables in casino kitchens.

Darlene Caifano joined her husband in Las Vegas in the summer of 1953 and became friends with Pete Brady's wife. A few months later, Denise Brady was arrested for shoplifting in Beverly Hills and Darlene hustled back to Chicago to avoid being charged.

If Caifano hadn't known about Ray Ryan before arriving in Las Vegas, he quickly learned about him. Ray drew attention by his heavy betting at the tables and the gorgeous women around him.

John Drew, who kept in touch with Ray by phone or met him in Las Vegas or Palm Springs, filled in Caifano about Ray. Drew always looked for ways to set up crooked games to cheat high rollers, and investigators suspected Ray was in cahoots with Drew on such games.

That idea was sparked by a 1953 letter from Dallas police to the Chicago Crime Commission that detailed an August 1951 meeting in the Adolphus Hotel in Dallas. Informants told police that John Drew and hoodlums from Chicago, New York and Texas talked about gambling and bookmaking operations.

At one of the meetings, someone called to say that Ray Ryan was in town and the gangsters discussed rigging a hotel room with one-way mirrors to see players' hands in a gin rummy game where $50,000 or more could change hands each game. They talked of using a device emitting low electric shocks to tell their partners at the table which cards to toss or when to lay down their hand.

The report never indicated that Ray had attended any of the meetings of the gangsters. But Ray's name had been tossed around at the meeting in the Adolphus Hotel and came up in subsequent reports. That was enough for investigators to continue to believe Ray was directly or indirectly involved in such scams.

Years later Maurice Friedman, an investor-developer, told authorities that he lost $25,000 playing in a crooked peephole game at the Adolphus Hotel in the early 1950s. Friedman also helped set up a more elaborate peephole scam 15 years later at the Hollywood's Friars Club where prominent actors and businessmen were cheated out of hundreds of thousands of dollars.

The FBI reported Edwin "Pete" Gebhard, an electronics expert from Miami, was involved in the crooked games at both the Friars Club and the Adolphus Hotel. Agents said Gebhard was described as a close friend of Ray and theorized the two rigged card games at times.

H. L. Hunt's name showed up in the Friars Club scam because Gebhard had called Ray and Hunt during the planning stage. Investigators never learned why Gebhard needed to talk to Hunt and Ray. But they always wondered.

Chapter 47

RAY RYAN AS A LURE

Caifano may have seen Ray at Las Vegas casinos but never met him in the early 1950s. Yet Caifano always looked for ways to make a quick buck and a wealthy oilman seemed an easy mark.

The idea of extorting money from Ray first occurred to Caifano in 1953 when it came time to get rid of Louis "Russian Louie" Strauss.

Strauss, a gambler, blackmailer and card cheat always in need of money to cover his losses, had something on Horseshoe Club owner Bennie Binion that could result in Binion's license being revoked. Strauss wanted money to keep quiet. Binion appealed for help to Jack Dragna, the head of the Los Angeles syndicate. Dragna's solution was to kill Strauss.

After nothing happened in a year, the job was given to Aladena "Jimmy the Weasel" Fratianno, a versatile mob enforcer and murderer. Joining Fratianno in the venture were "Milwaukee Phil" Alderisio and Caifano, a friend of Strauss. Because the syndicates prohibited any murders in Nevada, Strauss had to be killed elsewhere.

As the murder plot unfolded in April 1953, Caifano introduced Fratianno to Strauss in Las Vegas. Fratianno later claimed he was the one who told Strauss that Ray Ryan owed him $300,000 or so and he wanted Strauss, who knew Ray, to go with him to Palm Springs and be the go-between to encourage Ray to pay up.

Strauss, at the urging of Caifano, agreed to accompany Fratianno and Caifano to Palm Springs because he would make money and Ray seemed easy pickings.

Caifano bailed out of the trip at the last moment, sending Alderisio to go with Fratianno and Strauss. Fratianno and Adlerisio convinced

Struass they had to stop at a house in another California city before going after Ray. At that house a group of men waited and Strauss was garroted to death when he walked in.

Fratianno and Alderisio quickly returned to Las Vegas to set up alibis and the other men disposed of the body. Strauss' murder made no waves in newspapers and the full story of Strauss' killing wouldn't be told for another 25 years after Fratianno turned federal informer. Caifano, Alderisio and Frabotta were brought in for questioning but investigators ended up empty-handed.

It wouldn't be the last time that Caifano used the name of Ray Ryan to set up someone to be killed. The next time would be two decades later in Chicago.

Although Las Vegas supposedly was a cooling off period, Caifano frequently returned to Chicago and people ended up dead. He was there in August 1954 when two old-line hoods sentenced during the Browne-Bioff Hollywood extortion case – Charles "Cherry Nose" Gioe, 53, and Francis "Frank Diamond" Maritote, 61 – were slain within a three-day period.

After his release from prison, Gioe demanded a return to his former status in the Outfit. He tried to muscle in on unions and may have talked to congressional investigators looking into labor rackets to avoid being deported to Sicily. On August 18, Gioe was gunned down as he sat in his car on a Chicago street.

Three days later, shotgun blasts killed Maritote as he got out of a car, in which his 2-year-old son was sitting. Pistol shots completed the task, the same shooting pattern as Gioe's murder. Maritote had talked too freely to reporters after Gioe was gunned down. Caifano was suspected in the killings, but that was all.

Back in Las Vegas, Caifano had his name legally changed to John Michael Marshall on March 29, 1955 in a Nevada court. From then on he would be known around Las Vegas as Johnny Marshall, a man seeking a new life in a town where gangsters with nefarious backgrounds rose to a level of respectability.

A few months later at the Riviera hotel/casino operated by Gus Greenbaum, Caifano noticed a fat-jowled fellow from the past. Greenbaum said the man was William Nelson from Phoenix who he hired as the casino's entertainment director.

But Caifano knew better. He never forgot the face of an enemy. He recognized Nelson as Willie Bioff, the guy whose testimony in the movie extortion case sent Ricci, Rosselli and others to prison.

After testifying, Bioff had moved to Phoenix, changed his name and even became a friend of Arizona Senator Barry Goldwater. He enjoyed the good life before and was willing to run the risk of being found to continue to make money.

Caifano told Greenbaum to get rid of Bioff but Greenbaum balked. Caifano dutifully passed the word to Chicago – he had found Willie.

Bioff realized Caifano had recognized him. He put his home up for sale and planned to move to a safer place with his wife. He was too late. On November 4, 1955 as Bioff started his pickup truck at home, a powerful bomb exploded and blew him to bits. A seven-carat diamond ring he wore couldn't be found. No one would be arrested in Bioff's murder.

The Outfit closed the book on Willie Bioff and Caifano's star in Las Vegas grew brighter.

Chapter 48

PALM SPRINGS BECKONS

After taking a financial beating in the Iraq and the RKO failures, Ray didn't hunker down and lick his wounds. He wasn't the hunkering type. He needed a deal in a place where he – not foreign governments or Hollywood's inner circle – could be in control.

He found it in Palm Springs.

It would take Steve Bagbey years to piece together the life Ray enjoyed in the Palm Springs area. But little he uncovered changed the impression he already had about Ray.

The city was Ray's home away from home, a winter playground in the doldrums, ready to rebound, just waiting for someone to take charge. He planned to make his mark with El Mirador Hotel, the city's beacon that had fallen into disrepair.

He put together a group to acquire El Mirador and ponied up most of the cash for the acquisition. Many of the other 16 stockholders in National Hotel Enterprises already lolled away the winters in Palm Springs or knew Ray from Chicago, Florida or California.

The group president was E. Roy Fitzgerald, president of National City Lines that took over public transportation in numerous cities. Ray was among those who encouraged officials in a couple of cities to approve Fitzgerald taking over the local bus operations. Some claimed Ray's "fee" for helping Fitzgerald with the Los Angeles franchise was in the $1 million range.

Other stockholders in the hotel acquisition included Fitzgerald's three brothers; John L. Nelson, former director of the Edgewater

Beach Hotel in Chicago; E. C. Houghton, president of Los Angeles Transit Lines; William Reichel from Oakland; Eddie Barrett, the Illinois politician; and Evansville oilman Olen Sharp.

El Mirador's pink Byzantine tower had dominated Palm Springs since 1928. Prescott Thresher Stevens built the 165-room hotel for around $750,000 on desert land north of the town. He started in Colorado as a cattleman, became a Hollywood real estate investor then moved to Palm Springs in 1913 because his wife suffered from tuberculosis. Palm Springs had only one paved road at the time. Electricity and telephone service didn't arrive until 1927.

The Coachella Valley was inhabited for more than 350 years by a band of Cahuilla Indians called the Agua Caliente ("hot water") because of the valley's bubbling hot springs. Pioneers searching for a route to Colorado came in 1823. A stagecoach stop was established before the Civil War; the railroad came in 1876. A general store, a hotel with a bath house and other businesses were built at the eastern base of the 10,850-foot San Jacinto Mountain, California's second highest mountain range. A drought nearly erased the small community and by the time it was over in 1905, most settlers had left.

Nellie Coffman and her family arrived in 1909 and established the Desert Inn hotel, a sanitarium and a tent city for people with health ailments. Writers and photographers came to relish the scenic beauty and long horseback rides across the desert. Word spread about Palm Springs and Hollywood stars and wealthy Los Angeles businessmen came on vacation or quick weekend getaways.

Stevens opened the El Mirador on January 1, 1928. The tower bell was imported from a church in Amalfi, Italy and there was a swimming pool and tea gardens. The hotel attracted Mary Pickford, Douglas Fairbanks, Lillian Gish, George Raft, Charles Laughton, Victor McLaglen, Jeanette MacDonald, Al Jolson and Jimmy Durante in the early years.

The collapse of the stock market a year after the opening left Stevens with financial problems. After he died in 1932, the El Mirador was taken over by Los Angeles attorney Warren Pinney.

Palm Springs survived the 1930s by offering get-away activities. Trav Rogers opened a dude ranch and a nightspot known as "The Mink and Manure Club." Actors Charles Farrell and Ralph Bellamy built the prestigious Racquet Club. Detroit hoodlum Al Wertheimer ran the Dunes Club gambling joint in the Cathedral City community south of Palm Springs.

Bob Hope came to Palm Springs in the late 1930s to live and he and his wife Dolores could stroll down the main street of Palm Canyon Drive without being disturbed. No one asked for autographs in Palm Springs except on checks.

There were more than 30 horseback riding clubs during the Depression. Hotels went up, a polo club opened. The Desert Circus, an event usually held in April marking the end of winter, started in 1936. Balls and dances were abundant during the Desert Circus.

To promote the El Mirador, publicist Frank Bogert churned out photographs and publicity releases about famous guests from Edgar Bergen, the Barrymores, Charles Chaplin and Greta Garbo to Amos and Andy, Marlene Dietrich, Walt Disney, Bing Crosby, Rudy Vallee and Shirley Temple.

Aquatic stars Buster Crabbe and Johnny Weissmuller, both of whom would play the role of Tarzan in motion pictures, and Duke Kahanamoku of Hawaii held diving and swimming exhibitions. The city was incorporated in 1938 with a population of 5,300 that climbed to more than 8,000 during the winter season.

During World War II, the surrounding desert was used to train General George Patton's tank corps. The government bought the El Mirador for $420,000 and turned it into the 1,500-bed Torney General Hospital for invalid military personnel.

Hotels and apartments filled with relatives of the soldiers; the Chi Chi, Doll House and other clubs offered exciting nightlife. The hospital was declared surplus after the war and Ray and his group purchased the 21-acre property and started extensive remodeling of the hotel.

During most of 1952, Ray's crews installed an Olympic-sized swimming pool, colorful cabanas, patios, a rock waterfall, dining rooms and shops. Olive, grapefruit, orange, lime, tamarisk, palm and eucalyptus trees lined the walks. Dining rooms were the South Pacific Room, the Kiva Room, Starlight Patio and Palm Terrace.

Separate two- and three-bed cottages were built and Ray moved into one of them. Eventually Cottage 52 became his Palm Springs home where he entertained the nation's top gamblers, oilmen buddies, movie stars and business and Hollywood executives.

Ray became the El Mirador's executive vice president overseeing hotel operations. Helen and Rae Jean came to Palm Springs on occasion. Helen was there in March for a party honoring Bing Crosby and his son Lindsay, who were leaving for a trip to Europe. Bing sang, Jack Benny played the violin, Phil Harris and Alice Faye entertained the guests.

After more than $2 million in renovations, the sparkling El Mirador opened just before Christmas 1952. On hand, in addition to the Hollywood set, were the nation's top industrialists, bankers, oilmen and Charles Farrell, the mayor.

So was Arthur Samish, the 300-pound high stakes gambler, lobbyist, and political power broker who controlled California's state legislature more effectively than the elected politicians. An even larger crowd of 1,200 showed up for the even grander New Year Eve's bash.

Ray and Helen said Palm Springs, not Florida, now would be their winter home. "I just love this country and this town of Palm Springs," Ray said. After El Mirador opened, a group approached Ray about acquiring the San Francisco 49ers football team. He turned them down to devote his energies to the hotel and Palm Springs.

The El Mirador sparked Palm Springs' greatest decade of opulence and fun. Nearly every Hollywood star came to visit, and many built homes there. Presidents, presidential wannabes, kings, European princes and princesses, counts and countesses stopped by.

Always the promoter, Ray kept hotel guests guessing and intrigued. Bellhops periodically walked through the lobby paging such actors as Clark Gable or Cary Grant, even though they weren't in Palm Springs, just to leave people abuzz that they might catch a glimpse of a movie star.

Ray bought into the Palm Springs Villager, the town's long-running monthly magazine, and articles and photographs featuring Ray and El Mirador's guests and events appeared with regularity.[20]

Ray's stays in Palm Springs began to last longer and Helen's visits became less frequent. He ate breakfast at the El Mirador and frequently was joined by singer Eddie Cantor, who had a home nearby.

---

20 Ray sold the Villager to the Palm Springs Life magazine in 1959.

Ray joined in the frequent early morning and/or evening horseback rides into the desert and mountains.

Those were idyllic days for Ray that had little variety. He sunned at the pool watching pretty girls and chatted with buddies before having lunch. He could be seen through out the day in the El Mirador playing cards or board games with friends and guests. More high stakes games usually were reserved for his cottage in the evenings. Dinners normally were elaborate affairs with a host of friends at a Palm Springs restaurant or at the hotel with Ray picking up the tab.

Ray frequently was on the telephone discussing business and oil deals or simply finding out what his old mates were doing. Long time acquaintances passed through the town and many stayed at the El Mirador – Frank Erickson, John Rosselli, Texas oilmen and many others. Ray always was eager to see and be with them.

Ray was the epitome of the Palm Springs welcome wagon.

Saturdays were devoted to betting on horses and sports events, sometimes $100,000 or more on games. He'd load up buses and take friends to major football games in California. One oilman remembered a game that Ray had bet $250,000 on.

When it became certain Ray would lose the bet, the oilman watched as Ray sat expressionless, chewing gum and showing no emotion at losing that much money. The oilman was amazed at Ray's seemingly nonchalant attitude.

Ray hosted dinners, balls and galas at the El Mirador. In January 1953 when Jimmy Demaret won the Palm Springs Invitational golf tournament defeating Ben Hogan, Ray treated visitors to a lavish party. Bob Hope, Bing Crosby and Dean Martin did comedy routines and another comic predicted Ray would have to knock down one of the nearby mountains to handle the guests coming to the El Mirador in another year.

In April, 1953, Ray was the High Sheriff at the annual Desert Circus, an honored position for the accompanying balls, galas, dinners and a parade. Donning costly cowboy attire, he was surrounded by beautiful Palm Springs women who served as his deputies and circulated around the city welcoming visitors and raising donations for local charities. Movie star Bonita Granville, the wife of oil millionaire Jack Wrather, was the Desert Circus Queen that year.

The highlight of the Circus was the colorful costumes of the Beaux Arts Ball, a splendid display of dining and amusing entertainment held on Friday before the parade.

Ray made plans to make next year's Desert Circus bigger and better when he again would be High Sheriff.

Chapter 49

PARTY HEARTY

Ray never stopped looking for oil in numerous states, Canada and Mexico between the fun times in Palm Springs.

Sam Garfield, someone Ray had probably met in Evansville, worked as a landman for Ray in Wyoming and Colorado.

Garfield grew up in Detroit and one of his schoolmates was Moe Dalitz, a member of Cleveland's Mayfield Road gang during Prohibition. The gang operated casinos in Covington and Newport, Kentucky and later controlled a major Las Vegas casino.

Garfield, who was friendly with leaders of Detroit's Jewish Purple Gang, worked for Mammoth Petroleum and Refining Company, taking over the company in 1934 when the owner was gunned down by a former employee. Garfield knew many racketeers, including Meyer Lansky and New Jersey gangster Gerardo V. Catena.

Garfield, attorney Allen K. Swann and two other men were run out of Evansville after Sheriff Frank McDonald raided Garfield's Gar-Dan Drilling Company and found a bookmaking operation in 1951. McDonald claimed the raid broke up the nerve center of a nationwide gambling syndicate that had moved into the city after the Kefauver hearings when bookmakers were forced to move to smaller cities to operate.

Garfield moved to Denver and scouted oil fields for Ray and other oilmen but that didn't last long. Garfield, Swann and another man got swept up in the biggest stock swindle of the decade. The scam bilked the public of millions of dollars by inflating the prices of certain stocks then selling them through high-pressure boiler room operations. Garfield turned government informant to avoid jail time and disappeared from public view.

Ray wasn't involved in the stock scam but did get caught in another hustle. In 1941, he had met tennis player Bobby Riggs, who came to Evansville with Don Budge to play in a series of exhibition matches sponsored by Ray's friend Alexis Thompson, the pro football team owner.

Riggs also was a golf hustler. At the Greenbrier Country Club in White Sulphur Springs, West Virginia, in 1953, Riggs played high stakes golf with a group that included Ray, New York Yankees owner Dan Topping and Jose Dorelis, a Bulgarian perfume-maker. Ray was a mediocre golfer but played with enthusiasm and recklessness. He had a miserable week on the golf course. The worse he played, the more he bet on the next hole and the more he lost. At the end of the week, Ray owed the other men around $500,000.

Riggs wasn't impressed with Ray's golf, but he liked that Ray didn't squawk at losing that much money. The next day Ray invited everyone to his hotel suite where he opened a suitcase filled with $1,000 bills and paid off his losses. "He paid us off without flinching, with a smile. He was a great high roller," Riggs told friends and a magazine writer.

"Boys, if I win tomorrow, I want to be paid in the same way," Ray said. The next weekend, Ray won $180,000 from Riggs playing gin rummy, about what he had lost to Riggs at golf.

The West Virginia junket was typical of Ray's getaway trips from Palm Springs for fun and gambling. But he always returned to Palm Springs to be surrounded by amusing dinner companions that might include Dean Martin, Frank Sinatra, Clark Gable and Bing Crosby.

When Dean's son Ricci was born in 1953, Ray was named the baby's godfather. Also hanging around Ray was Charles O'Curran, whose 1952 marriage to movie star Betty Hutton ended in divorce three years later. Ray decided to play a role in finding O'Curran another wife.

Ray spent nearly all of his time during the early 1950s in Palm Springs. "He was around the hotel all the time. He probably was the nicest guy who ever lived. He had a great personality, everybody loved him and he was popular as hell all over town," said Frank Bogert, who had been around the El Mirador for years and eventually took over hotel management in 1954.

Bogert added that "Ray was in every party, everything, every place. He put on parties in the South Pacific room at the El Mirador, a Hawaiian party, all sorts of big events. He never did anything halfway. Whenever he did it, he got the best, the best decorations, the best of everything.

"Everybody could go to his parties. Anytime there was a party he put on everybody went. They knew it was going to be good. He probably was the richest guy in town; at least he spent money like it."

Chapter 50

THE REY OF PALM SPRINGS

In the year after the El Mirador opening with Helen rarely around, Ray found companionship among young women.

In Ray's earlier days in Palm Springs, one was a pretty singer in her early 20s who performed in Las Vegas and various California clubs. "Ray was shacking up with her for quite a while," Frank Bogert recalled years later.

Many girlfriends followed but no one knew the extent of their relationships with Ray. He certainly had more than a passing interest in some of them.

"Ray had a lot of singers as girlfriends. Funny thing, he was partial to singers," Bogert said. Some other girls who showed up at parties with Ray weren't known to other guests and Ray introduced them as his "niece."

An El Mirador employee later told the FBI that Ray knew a madam in Los Angeles who supplied up to 20 girls to mingle and entertain guests at Ray's parties. Several friends believed Ray just wanted young women around him for show, to flash around at parties like he flashed $100 and $1,000 bills at meals and gambling tables.

There always were plenty of women around. One was Ginny Simms, a fun-loving cut-up with a winning smile. The Texas-born Virginia Simms was in her late thirties and between marriages in 1951.

A featured singer with the Kay Kyser orchestra in the 1930s, she later appeared in movies with Kyser, Fibber McGee and Molly and Edgar Bergen and Charlie McCarthy and recorded hit songs. She had been married to millionaire architect Hyatt R. Dehn, who started the Hyatt hotel chain. In 1961 her marriage to Donald W. Eastvold brought Ray and Eastvold together for business deals.

But another singer much closer to Ray was Roberta Linn, Lawrence Welk's lovely Champagne Lady for a couple of years. Performing on Welk's tours and shows and on her own Los Angeles television show left her stressed out, ill and in the hospital. She and Welk parted ways around 1953.

Linn was what Ray liked in a female – pretty, talented and young. She was asked to sing at a cancer fundraiser in Palm Springs when headliner Dinah Shore got sick. After the dinner, a handsome man in a tuxedo approached her to invite her to a party that evening at the El Mirador. Linn was 18 at the time, naive and the man, Ray, was more than 25 years older.

Linn in her book "Not Now Lord, I've Got Too Much to Do" said her protective mother wouldn't let her go to the party, but the next morning Ray was at their motel door dressed in jeans and cowboy boots to invite her to go horseback riding. He was driving a Ford Thunderbird with two large steer horns on the hood. After charming Linn's mother and getting her permission, Ray took Linn to a downtown store to get a western outfit.

"He was a dear, dear friend and I guess I loved him," Linn wrote. "I was really smitten with him. I guess he was my first great love. I had a real crush on him. He was a guy who was Catholic, married and had a very strange life." Linn said she wouldn't date anyone else for the next six years, waiting for Ray to return to Palm Springs so she could visit him there. Ray was a lot of fun and a great guy to Linn.

She went nearly everywhere with Ray – long horseback rides of up to 15 miles to Bermuda Dunes or Indian Wells for breakfast, moonlight and morning rides with the Desert Riders group. On one midnight ride, she heard two riders in the dark with English accents and in the morning light found she had been riding with David Niven and Cary Grant.

Linn and Ray also had jaunts to the Santa Monica pier to enjoy the beach, even sticking their heads through cutout openings of large poster paintings of people in old-time swimming outfits to pose for a photo.

When Ray traveled, he often called Linn for long talks and for her to sing his favorite song, "Melancholy Baby" to him when he was all over the world. Whenever Ray returned to Palm Springs, Linn met him at the El Mirador where she mingled with movie stars and entertainers and enjoyed lavish parties.

Ray also took Linn on trips out of the country. One was a trip to Germany and another to Cuba, where they stayed at the Intercontinental Hotel and Linn was around executives and men from Chicago, New York and Florida – guys she later learned were mob people. During that stay, she and Ray drove down the coast to visit Ernest Hemingway at his home.

They also went to New Orleans and other places while Ray worked on business deals and played high stakes gin rummy games. Ray believed Linn was good luck for him and Linn, who didn't know much about gin rummy, sometimes sat at Ray's side as thousands of dollars crossed the table.

Ray also helped put together Linn's first show in Las Vegas in 1955. He had Charlie O'Curran stage her act and O'Curran got Nelson Riddle to do her music and Edith Head her gowns. Linn's performance received top reviews.

Ray once dropped by to see Linn when she was performing at the Copacabana nightclub in New York. He got tickets for "My Fair Lady" starring Julie Andrews on Broadway and sent Linn to a famous designer store to pick out a special dress for the evening. At the show, Ray fell asleep in the first row and began snoring.

Another time, she went to the Waldorf Astoria where Ray and H. L. Hunt had rented the top floor. They ordered caviar for her because she had never had it, and she watched television while Ray and Hunt gambled. A day or so later, the three went by limousine to Yankee Stadium and watched Don Larsen pitch a perfect game in the World Series.

During those years, Ray also kept his attention on Palm Springs. He made plans to make the 1954 Desert Circus in Palm Springs the most extravagant ever, warming up the entertainment season a month before the Circus with a St. Patrick's Day gala featuring colleens in fetching green dresses, an Irish tenor and an overflow crowd that included former ambassador Joseph E. Davies, Frank Sinatra and

Metropolitan Opera star Lily Pons. Ray and Roy Fitzgerald danced Irish jigs with "leprechauns" – midgets dressed in Irish costumes.

The queen of the Desert Circus was Phil Harris' wife Alice Faye. The event's parade had camels, colorful floats, twenty marching bands, mounted police officers and horsemen from riding clubs decked out in ornate cowboy outfits. Desi Arnaz along with a bevy of women rode in a stagecoach; Eddie Cantor rode on the back of a three-wheel motorcycle and Parade Marshal Walt Disney in another stagecoach.

Sitting atop his horse Nugget on a $15,000 silver saddle made for him in Seattle, Ray wore the finest of cowboy outfits with hand-tooled trimmings and silver ponchos. He received the largest ovation as he rode past the 25,000 spectators along the route.

That year's star-studded Beaux Arts and Circus balls were even more outstanding.

The Circus Ball was a dazzling production. Ray and Faye, both in cowboy outfits, made a grand entrance punctuated by blanks fired from Ray's guns. Phil Harris, Ginny Simms, Desi Arnaz, Gordon MacRae and Faye entertained with songs. When MacRae began a soft shoe dance, Arnaz, Harris and Ray drew laughter by pretending to walk out of the hall.

The theme of Friday's Beaux Arts costume ball was "A Night in Spain." Ray moved the ball from the Tennis Club to his El Mirador. He had worked weeks planning the event before making a short trip to Miami then jumping into his private plane and returning to Palm Springs for a pre-ball cocktail party in his bungalow.

Guests spent the day of the ball at the outdoor pool, drinking and laughing. Many passed the time playing gin rummy.

Ball queen Lily Pons wore an original gown by Jacques Fath, the French designer who had created gowns for Rita Hayworth, Ava Gardner and Greta Garbo. Ray was the king in regal robes and a crown borrowed from Mike Romanoff, a zany Los Angeles and Palm Springs restaurateur who claimed he was a descendent of White Russian nobility.

Ray and Pons sat on thrones between two "Nubian" slaves, tall bare-chested black men wearing turbans. The men waved long poles with huge ostrich feathers to circulate the air in the warm room because someone had forgotten to turn on the air conditioners.

The Queen's ladies in waiting wore flowing dresses. Guests were clad in matador and other Spanish outfits or in Roman attire as Cleopatra, Marc Anthony or goddesses. Entering the room, they bowed and curtsied before the king and queen amid the colorful balloons and Spanish shawls. "I think this is the most successful party Palm Springs ever had. These things usually lay an egg," one woman party-goer said.

The Dean Martins, Lucille Ball, Desi Arnaz, Kay Williams Spreckels and society's elite were among the 600 guests who danced to the music of Eddie La Baron's orchestra. Ray laughed merrily throughout the proceedings. His only complaint was the long time it took to judge the best costumes. "That crown hurt my head so much we had to pick somebody in a hurry," he joked.

That year's Desert Circus events were lauded as the finest ever, a tribute to Ray's determination to have the best. He also made sure Roberta Linn would be the queen of the 1955 Desert Circus.

Ray was the king, the "rey," of Palm Springs in some people's eyes.

But there were others who considered Ray Ryan a pompous showman desiring to be a big fish in a town filled with much better known glitterati. In some later books about Palm Springs, Ray barely earned a footnote.

Not everybody loved this Raymond.

Chapter 51

FEDS WATCH
RAY'S FRIENDS

Other eyes also were watching another side of Palm Springs.

Not far from the rich and powerful, the glamour and the pizazz, California authorities found a growing tumor of organized crime. Florida was driving away racketeers and many migrated to Las Vegas and California.

California Governor Earl Warren established a Commission on Organized Crime that issued a disturbing 1953 report saying the state was a haven for mobsters with Los Angeles and Palm Springs the "favorite rendezvous of many."

New York, New Jersey and Chicago mobsters visited or lived in walled-in estates around Palm Springs including former Capone attorney Abraham Teitelbaum; Joseph "Doc" Stacher, with ties to Las Vegas and Reno casinos; and gangsters Abe "Longy" Zwillman, Meyer Lansky, Allen Smiley, Ed Levinson and Gerald Catena.

The report chastised an apathetic public for "social acceptance of murderers, blackmailers, pimps, dope dealers and gamblers" living in luxury and masquerading as respectable citizens. An earlier Riverside County grand jury also reported the sheriff for Palm Springs failed to enforce laws against gamblers, inviting the invasion of organized crime with the attendant corruption.

Despite the furor, attitudes in Palm Springs didn't change. An ex-president, movie stars and mobsters could be found at different tables in the same restaurant. No one pried as long as everyone was a good neighbor. The city would be the gift that kept on giving to hoodlums.

Not surprisingly, a California state report in 1978 – 25 years later – found 45 Mafia leaders in Palm Springs including 32 from Chicago like Tony Accardo, Joey "The Doves" Aiuppa, Frank "The Horse" Buccieri, James "The Turk" Torello, Vincent Dominic Caci and Jerome Zarowitz.

Ray would admit to meeting some of them, but claimed he was unaware of their backgrounds. Yet, Ray's name continued to show up in police investigations and reports collected over the years that eventually were passed on to Evansville police and ended up on Steve Bagbey's desk.

California police and FBI dug into the backgrounds of people in Palm Springs in the mid-1950s as did investigators in Chicago, Dallas, Houston, Las Vegas and New Orleans. Ray's name appeared in early confidential police reports, usually as a sidebar to other people the cops were tracking.

Officials in Chicago, Nevada and Texas swapped information about Ray's long-time friend from Chicago, John Frank Drew, who was applying for a gaming license in Nevada, and noted numerous calls between Drew and Ray.

Virgil W. Peterson, Chicago Crime Commission director, received information that Drew and associates, including Ray, were "trying to lay a trap for some of the big movie stars and, in particular, Jack Benny from whom they hope to take a lot of money in a crooked gambling deal."

Drew and Johnny Moss, one of the country's top gamblers, were spotted at high stakes card games with Ray and some of Ray's buddies at El Mirador cottages, fueling speculation that some of the games may have been crooked.

Los Angeles police also hinted that Ray, Allen Smiley and others were involved in a "shakedown" of a nephew of Tom May, an executive of the May Company department stores. The nephew lost a large sum of money gambling in games with Ray and others and May, who didn't want the publicity, allegedly paid off $250,000 to settle the debt to Ray.

In another report, Houston police had hauled in Philip "Dandy Phil" Kastel, who along with Frank Costello once controlled slot machine distribution in Louisiana, dating from the mid-1930s, and operated the Beverly Club near New Orleans with Meyer Lansky and Carlos Marcello.

The Houston cops photographed documents in Kastel's possession, tracked his phone calls, including some to Ray, and released Kastel without any charges. Kastel said he was in Houston looking after "oil interests," but, in fact, was trying to collect a $600,000 debt from an oilman's recent widow.

The Chicago Crime Commission also watched Ray's longtime friend Edward J. Barrett, feeling Barrett was too close to members of the Outfit. It was noted that Barrett was named vice president of the El Mirador in early 1953 after he lost a close race for a third term as Illinois Secretary of State in the Republican landslide.

The most logical answer for Barrett being named to the El Mirador post was that Barrett needed a job and Ray, wanting to be close to an old friend, simply provided him one at the hotel.[21]

Association with hoodlums like Costello, Erickson, Kastel and Drew followed Ray through life. Folks who didn't know Ray, and a few who did, sometimes referred to Ray as "the Mafia guy," but never to Ray's face.

The possibility of a Mafia connection was a reaction of many folks that Ray never could shake.

---

21 Barrett was convicted in 1973 for tax evasion, bribery and mail fraud for receiving $180,000 in kickbacks while Cook County Clerk. He was sentenced to three years in jail, filed an unsuccessful appeal taking two years, but avoided prison because he was gravely ill and was paroled by the U.S. Parole Board. He died in April 1977.

Chapter 52

MONEY ISN'T FOR CARESSING

"Money is like manure. If you spread it around, it does a lot of good.
But if you pile it up on one place, it stinks like hell."
Clint Murchison Sr., Texas oilman

Ray Ryan would spread around money when it came to helping needy individuals and children. He occasionally donated to established charities but preferred helping individuals, peeling off $500, $1,000 or more for anyone with a hard luck story.

Remembering his days as a newspaper boy, he often tipped newsboys $10 for a paper, precipitating a mad rush the next day by carriers to find him first.

Frank Bogert was in his office one day talking to a woman while Ray waited within earshot in an adjoining room. The conversation got around to the woman's daughter who was a gifted piano player but the family couldn't afford a piano. After the woman left, Ray told Bogert "go buy her a grand piano and don't tell her where the money came from." To Bogert, that was typical Ray. "He was always trying to help somebody do something."

Marshall "Mickey" Finn also found Ray's generous side. Finn joined the Los Angeles police force after World War II, following in the footsteps of his Irish father and grandfathers.

Finn, an athletic 6-foot-3, was assigned to an impoverished crime-ridden area of downtown Los Angeles and formed a neighborhood club for Latino and Asian kids. He took them to Santa Monica for a barbeque and swimming and set up a Sea Scout Troop that met in an abandoned jail cell rigged with hammocks and seagoing gear. Actress Ann Sheridan helped finance summer camps and served as a hostess.

Finn came to Palm Springs to promote his club and participate in Desert Circus festivities, riding a burro in one parade, serving as under sheriff in another and eagerly joining in the parties. He wanted to establish a 160-acre Boys Ranch in the San Jacinto Mountains where children could go in the summer to ride horses, swim and enjoy some time away from the Los Angeles ghettos.

Ray put up the bulk of the cash, recruited other backers and chartered the Mickey Finn Boy's Ranch in May 1954 with Ray as president. Finn turned in his badge and devoted his energy to running the ranch.[22]

Ray seemed to have a lot of ready cash in those days. When he appeared to be running short, he disappeared for a day or so and returned flashing plenty of money. Friends speculated he had a stash somewhere.

Bogert was used to Ray's pockets being filled with "walking around" money. They were visiting Chicago once when Ray gave Bogert $70,000 in $1,000 bills to take back to someone in Los Angeles. Bogert assumed Ray was paying off a gambling debt, but he wasn't sure and didn't ask.

Bogert was scared to death with that much money in his possession and told Ray he might be robbed driving back to Palm Springs. "Don't worry," Ray said, "no one would ever think you had any money." On the way to Palm Springs, Bogert stopped off at a hotel for the night and fell asleep with the package containing $70,000 next to his head on the pillow.

He went to Palm Springs before heading to Los Angeles to hand over Ray's money. Bogert's father recently had died in his isolated mountain cabin several miles away and a friend asked Bogert if his father left any money.

As a joke, Bogert pulled out Ray's package and told the friend he just found all that money buried near his father's home. Two weeks later Bogert returned to the cabin and the entire yard had been dug up and holes were everywhere.

---

22 The camp lasted a few years before it was closed for lack of donations. By then, Ray was having problems with the law and spending less time around Palm Springs.

Thieves were noticing that Ray carried a lot of money. The Los Angeles Sheriff's Department learned that two thugs had heard that Ray carried $75,000 to $100,000 and planned to rob and murder him on one of his trips to Los Angeles or Las Vegas. The detectives told Ray the robbery never took place because he was with Bogert at the time. Ray started a rumor that he no longer carried large sums of cash but actually continued to do so.

Police also started keeping track of Ray's visitors. The FBI and California police learned Frank Erickson had visited him at the El Mirador in 1955. Ray said Erickson was "a paying guest." Both had been seen playing cards in Las Vegas with casino owner Gus Greenbaum and high stakes gamblers.

Another of Ray's visitors at the El Mirador was Anthony "Tony" Pinelli, a Chicago hood considered the Outfit's gambling boss in Lake County, Indiana. Pinelli had moved to Los Angeles around 1945 and got into real estate acquisition while keeping his hand in Chicago area gambling operations. He remained tight with the syndicate's leaders from Al Capone to Tony Accardo and Sam Giancana.

Pinelli was spotted greeting Accardo and two other hoods in 1953 when they arrived in Los Angeles on the way to mob-controlled casinos in Las Vegas. LA cops quickly sent Accardo on his way and Las Vegas police dogged Accardo until he returned to Chicago. The widely publicized visit highlighted organized crime's influence in Las Vegas and contributed to a future Nevada crackdown on gangsters.

Meanwhile, Ray was hanging out with Clark Gable in Palm Springs. Gable visited the city when not at his Las Angeles home or making a movie on location. He was looking for a place to live in Palm Springs.

Gable was in his early 50s and had a messy divorce in 1952 from his fourth wife, Lady Sylvia Ashley, a Londoner and former chorus girl who grew wealthy through divorces from an English lord, a baron and actor Douglas Fairbanks Sr.

Clark and Sylvia were married in 1949 and stayed together 17 months. The next years were spent fighting in court. She hated hunting, a sport Clark loved. She accompanied him on the set of his movie "Across the Wide Missouri" and detested the lack of comfort.

Single again, Clark went horseback riding with Ray several days a week dressed simply in jeans and a shirt while Ray wore a stylish cowboy outfit. They'd sit for hours, talking, drinking and swapping stories.

Clark had returned from making the movie "Mogambo" in Kenya. Released in 1953, the film turned out to be an unexpected success.

Clark regaled Ray about the beauty of Kenya, the vast plains and climate – a place close to Ray's heart since reading the Tarzan books as a boy. Ava Gardner and Grace Kelly starred in the movie. Clark went on a safari with Kelly, who kept up with the group through the bush, smiling and never complaining about the heat, bug bites or scratches. Clark admired that in a woman.

Among the women seeking Clark's attention was his long-time friend and occasional lover Kay Williams Sprinkels, a blue-eyed, athletic blond who was fun to be around. Raised on a Pennsylvania farm, Katherine Williams gained success as a New York model and moved to Hollywood in the 1940s. She appeared in more than a dozen small roles but had little interest in being a star. One of her three marriages was to millionaire sugar heir Adolph Spreckels II who claimed in his divorce that Kay was intimate with Clark during the marriage, an allegation she denied.

The Palm Springs crowd loved Kay for her beauty, intelligence and off-the-wall wit. She wanted to be a part of everything Clark enjoyed, including horseback riding, and begged Ray to take her along when he and Clark rode into the desert or to the mountains.

Ray was reluctant to bring her along but finally relented. The three had an enjoyable ride. Kay never complained, but Ray remembered she ended up "with blisters on her butt." In 1955, Kay and Clark secretly took off for Minden, Arizona, for a quiet wedding attended by a few friends.

Ray enjoyed being a matchmaker.

Chapter 53

FUN, FUN, FUN

Ray savored his role as a practical joker.

He occasionally ambled up to the guests at the El Mirador cottages and told them the hotel was cutting off the water supply the next day for repairs and to fill up pots, containers and bathtubs with water. He would go back to make sure the guests filled up containers in anticipation of a water cutoff that never was planned or done.

Another time after Frank Bogert and his wife returned from a trip to Ireland, Bogert's wife received a telephone call supposedly from New York. The caller said the Irish Sweepstakes ticket the Bogerts had purchased had been drawn and they would get $1 million by turning in the ticket.

Bogert returned home from work to find his wife tearing up the house looking for the ticket. She talked of buying a new house, sending the kids on trips. There was so much they could do with $1 million. She had turned the house upside down and couldn't find the ticket.

Bogert knew they never bought a sweepstakes ticket in Ireland. It was all a gag and Bogert quickly figured out who the culprit was. A laughing Ray admitted calling up Bogert's house and impersonating someone from the sweepstakes office.

Ray was a sucker for anyone with a deal.

One man came up with the idea of making paper out of the plentiful banana trees growing in Central and South American. Ray sank a bundle of money into that project only to find out it didn't work.

Another guy had a scheme to turn red volcanic rock from Mexico into lightweight aggregate for cement pumps. Ray put up thousands of dollars to ship a load of the rock to San Diego. The cement pump makers tested the rock and said the material wouldn't work because it had holes that filled with water. Ray also invested in a uranium operation in Utah that reportedly had limited success.

Still, Ray had to keep his money in circulation.

Entertainer Danny Thomas told a columnist about a high stakes gin rummy game in Palm Springs one day when Ray got a telephone call from Texas oilman Clint Murchison. "Is that right, Clint? My end of the deal will be only a half a million dollars? Okay, I'll send the money over this afternoon," Ray said.

When Ray returned to the gin rummy game, Thomas asked what kind of deal cost a half million dollars. "How the hell should I know," Ray said. "You guys know how that Murchison mumbles."

Ray toyed with buying boats to turn into gambling ships between Los Angeles and Mexico and establishing a race track near Palm Springs, two more ideas that went nowhere.

He also drilled near Palm Springs figuring he'd either strike oil or at least water which was needed in that area. Ray didn't get oil or water. "Anybody could sell Ray anything," a friend later said. "He loved to make a deal. I don't think half the time he gave a damn whether it was a good deal or not."

Ray did better putting on a show. In April 1954, President Dwight Eisenhower came to Palm Springs for a week of golf and entertainment with the El Mirador as the centerpiece. When the entourage of staffers and Secret Service agents arrived, over 2,000 leading California Republicans and visitors flocked to Palm Springs. Crowds lined the streets as the motorcade headed to the home of a Los Angeles bakery tycoon, Eisenhower's host.

Ike's staff and the accompanying news reporters stayed at the El Mirador. Ray convinced national columnist Walter Winchell to show up, sending a plane to pick him up in Las Vegas and later taking him to Los Angeles for a scheduled engagement.

Ray, Ed Houghton and other hotel stockholders held a party for California Governor Goodwin Knight, who wore an elegant western outfit to the event. One guest needled Ray, telling him "you're in danger of losing your reputation as being the number one western dresser around these parts. Just look at the suit the Governor is wearing."

"I loaned it to him," Ray shot back. And Ray had.

Ray seldom was far from Palm Springs during those years. It was a wonderful life of horseback rides, lounging around the pool, a plethora of friends and girlfriends, partying, late night gambling at the cottage and popping off to Las Vegas on a whim with friends for a night at the tables.

Ray kept up with his hectic pace with power naps in the afternoon. He had the ability to curl up on a sofa and sleep for an hour or two, awakening refreshed and ready for action late into the night.

Bogert sometimes went with Ray on the trips to Las Vegas. Bogert quickly lost what money he had in his pocket at the dice tables while Ray played high stakes card and dice games for hours.

"I had gamblers like Jake Freeman in Las Vegas tell me Ray was the best card player in the world. Ray could remember every card played. How do you do that in poker, I don't know, but Ray knew the odds. Ray also liked to play hearts in Vegas. Gamblers there seemed to like to play hearts for a gambling game," Bogert said.

Once, Ray was at dinner at a Las Vegas hotel when stopped by Johnny Meyer, the publicity man for Howard Hughes. Meyer asked Ray for $5,000, saying he had a "real pigeon" he was going to play in a gin rummy game.

A short time later, Ray's dinner was interrupted again when Bruce Cabot came rushing up also wanting money for a gin rummy game. "I got a sucker lined up for gin. It's like finding money," Cabot said. Ray fished cash from his pocket and gave it to Cabot.

After dinner, Ray went to the card room to see how his friends were doing. He found Meyer playing Cabot at gin. Ray had ended up financing both of them.

Stories circulated about Ray's own winnings at Las Vegas. One tale was that Ray won $300,000 at craps and before leaving offered casino officials to flip a coin double or nothing. They turned down the opportunity.

Although he enjoyed the attention, Ray downplayed the stories of winning a bundle of money gambling.

"Never have I heard of myself losing a bet," Ray said. "My oil business is the big thing. A man couldn't get by very long gambling because you just don't win over the long haul and I don't care who the man is. Some of the stories I hear about myself are fantastic. I wish some of them were true."

Still, his friends thought most stories were true.

Ray spent many long evenings at the El Mirador drinking, partying and playing cards. Then early in the morning, Bogert and other riders often went horseback riding with him. One morning Ray had partied the night before and had only one hour of sleep before climbing on a horse for a long ride in the mountains. Bogert saw Ray sleeping on the horse during most of the ride.

Bogert also saw the usually quick-witted Ray fumble when speaking before a group, especially after a few drinks. At the Desert Riders club meetings, members introduced guests accompanying them. Ray took Roberta Linn to one session but when he rose to introduce her he couldn't remember her name and ended up identifying her as "Robert E. Lee."

At another meeting, members were expected to tell a joke or two. Bogert gave Ray two jokes to tell. "Ray had a couple of drinks and when he stood to speak he got the two jokes mixed up. When he tried to tell one of them and came to the punch line Ray said 'hell, I got the wrong punch line' and sat down."

The two once went to Hawaii on a horseback riding excursion. "When we got there, Ray said 'let's go to Singapore', I told him we came over to ride and everyone is expecting us. Ray always wanted to go someplace else from where he was."

In December 1955, Ray gathered up Helen and Rae Jean and headed to Europe for a Christmas vacation. They visited Spain before going to St. Mortiz, Switzerland to ski. At Toledo, Spain they went to the bull fights.

At Spanish festivals, once the fighting bulls are brought into their stalls, smaller bulls with blunted horns are released in the arena for spectators to try their hand at bullfighting techniques. Ray took a cape and waved it at one of the little bulls.

After a few reluctant passes by the bull, Ray grabbed the animal with his hands and wrestled it to the ground like an American rodeo bulldogger. Someone said the bull he faced was a small one. "I don't know about that. When I was in the arena with him, he certainly looked big," Ray said later.

At St. Moritz, Ray broke his leg skiing and was hauled down the mountain by rescuers. Nate Gross, the Chicago American newspaper columnist, penned a version of what had happened. Ray claimed a European nobleman bet he wouldn't ski off the 9,800-foot Piz Nair Mountain. Although a skiing novice, Ray hit the slope, crashed into a tree and broke his right leg. His only complaint was that the nobleman refused to pay off the bet, Gross said.

It was more than a month before Ray could return to Palm Springs, hobbling around with a cast on his leg. He couldn't stand being slowed down and he wasn't going to miss one of the most elaborate galas he ever planned – a birthday party for the beloved Millie Considine, the wife of international reporter and columnist Bob Considine.

Ray and Charlie O'Curran had worked on the party for weeks and Ray wasn't going to let a broken leg slow him down. When his doctor refused to remove the cast, Ray called in a local veterinarian who sawed it off. Ray grabbed a cane and limped away.

Millie loved everything western and Ray and Charlie were determined to give her a western show. They invited her friends in Hollywood and Palm Springs for an overnight stay in Las Vegas in what would be proclaimed "the party of the year."

Ray hired two DC-6 airplanes to pick up 150 guests for the trip to Las Vegas in late February 1956. There was a Bloody Mary-Dramamine cocktail party at Los Angeles and a chuck wagon-style brunch at the El Mirador. Entertainers strummed guitars and sang. Everyone was dressed in western outfits; Ray's colorful outfit was embroidered with blue cacti, brilliant sunsets and coyotes.

At the Las Vegas airport, the guests were greeted by 100 dancing, war-whooping Paiute Indians sending smoke signals into the air, three bands and 200 men on Arabian horses circling the plane firing blanks from their guns, all hired by Ray. More than 1,000 Las Vegas residents were there to greet Millie.

Although the temperature was in the 30s, the visitors boarded horse-drawn stagecoaches, hay wagons and buggies and headed to the Sands Hotel and Casino. Ray, waving his cane, hopped onto a wagon with singer Ginny Simms and several other pretty cowgirls as the two-mile long caravan rattled past frozen puddles to the Sands.

The dinner of cocktails and filet mignon in the Venetian room for Millie Considine included a 10-piece band and a show by Peggy Lee. Sophie Tucker, Roberta Linn and other celebrities tabled-hopped.

People were "branded" by a rubber stamp with an MC in honor of Millie, who won the drawing for a prize heifer. The group laughed, talked and danced the night away, some slipping away to the casino's dice and card tables.

The event cost Ray at least $50,000. But he hit the casino tables and won some of the trip's cost back. He had rooms for those guests who had to catch a little sleep before hopping on one of Ray's leased planes to get back home early. The rest followed later in the second plane with Ginny Simms and Roberta Linn singing on the flight home.

Ray never mentioned his troublesome leg injury the entire time. Even more importantly, Ray's reputation as a party host was intact.

A month later, Ray took care of fellow Watertown native Joseph E. Davies, who probably encouraged Ray's ill-fated attempt to lease the Iraqi oilfield but also helped Ray to meet Yugoslavian President Tito, leading to Ray's purchase land along the Adriatic seacoast.

Davies recently had been divorced from his wife of 20 years, Marjorie Post Close Hutton Davies, one of the nation's 10 richest women. At 79, Davies no longer was the vibrant person of the past. He was thinner, weak, with nagging health problems and sunken eyes.

Ray invited Davies to the El Mirador to recuperate, relax and get his head straight. Davies mainly stayed out of sight. Ray did his best to make his old friend feel better during his two-week visit.

In three more years, Davies would be dead.

Smiling Ray and Helen at Churchill Downs race track in Louisville in early 1940s. Photo: Evansville Courier and Press

An Evansville police officer looks over the remains of Ray's Lincoln Continental after the October 18, 1977 deadly car bombing.

The necklace Ray wore the day he was killed.

Steve Bagbey, the city police chief investigator in the
Ryan murder, posed with only a few of the
massive number of documents he collected in the case.
Photo: Evansville Courier and Press.

Ray Ryan over the years

Ray in high school, upper left

Ray in his 30s, upper right

Ray in his 60s, right

Helen strolls along the main street of Hot Springs, Arkansas in 1936.

Helen enjoying the winter season in Miami in 1940.

When Ray hit his first big Bessie Bramlett oil well in 1940, he soon had enough money to start his own oil company in Evansville and the beginning of a vast fortune.

Ray and Helen settled on a final home in Evansville at 600 Lombard Avenue in 1946.

Ray and Helen during their early years at home in Evansville.

Helen kept a photo of her mother, Anna, over the fireplace at home.

Ray, Helen and Rae Jean on the beach in Florida in the mid-1940s.

Helen enjoying a day at the pool in Miami around 1941.

One of the earliest times that Ray started hanging out with movie stars probably was in the early 1930s when the movie "The Irish in Us" was released starring Pat O'Brien, right in top photo, and Olivia de Havilland, left in the above photo.

Ray was the center of attention during a show featuring ventriloquist Edgar Bergen in Palm Springs.

Ray Ryan, center, with Bill Holden, left, and John Wayne during a break in the filming of the 1959 movie "The Horse Soldiers" starring Wayne and Holden.

Ray collected numerous autographed photographs of his friends to display in his hotels.

Ray and Helen, right, hosted a party at the El Mirador for Bing Crosby and his son Lindsay, left, who were going on a trip to Europe on the Queen Elizabeth.

Ray Ryan, right, with his long time friend actor Bruce Cabot.

Ray and Helen, center, with Olen Sharp and his wife Mazie at a St. Patrick's Day event at the El Mirador in the early 1950s. Ryan and Sharp set up an oil company following the discovery of a large oil field in Gibson County, Indiana in 1948.
Photo provided by Bette Kay Sharp.

Ray's Lake Malone Inn in Western Kentucky

Ray, seated left, and Phil Harris, right, work with friends on a Desert Circus event in mid-1950s.

Ray, right, with Kirk Douglas, center, and friends at German beer party at the El Mirador.

Dancing Indians greet Ray and Millie Considine as they exit a plane in Las Vegas as part of a lavish party Ray staged for Millie's birthday. Photo: Palm Springs Historical Society

Charles O'Curran, Helen Ryan, Patti Page and Ray Ryan pose during the wedding reception for Page and O'Curran in Palm Springs.

Native performers during a show for guests at the Mount Kenya Safari Club

Carl Hirschmann, left, and Bill Holden at the Mount Kenya Safari Club.
Holden and Hirschmann were part owners in the club.

Helen Ryan, center, with writer Robert Ruark, and Rae Jean Ryan, left, and Rae Jean's friend Nancy Kollker at the Mount Kenya Safari Club.

Helen Ryan with actor Jimmy Stewart at the Mount Kenya Safari Club.

Marshall Caifano aka Johnny Marshall

Charles Delmonico

The Hoods

Frank "The German" Schweihs

Joey "The Clown" Lombardo
during his prime mobster years

Joey "The Clown" Lombardo
when arrested in 2006

271

DEPOSITED IN THE

OLD

NATIONAL BANK
IN EVANSVILLE

NOTICE TO DEPOSITORS

In receiving items for deposit or collection, this Bank acts only as depositor's collecting agent, and assumes no responsibility beyond the exercise of due care. All items are credited subject to final payment in cash or solvent credits. This Bank will not be liable for default or negligence of its duly selected correspondents nor for losses in transit, and each correspondent so selected shall not be liable except for its own negligence. This Bank or its correspondents may send items, directly or indirectly, to any bank including the payor, and accept its draft or credit as conditional payment in lieu of cash; it may charge back any item at any time before final payment, whether returned or not, also any item drawn on this Bank not paid at close of business on day deposited.

It is further agreed that the said items are deposited subject to the provisions of The Indiana Financial Institutions Act and especially subject to the order of the Members of The Department of Financial Institutions respecting withdrawals.

PLEASE ENDORSE ALL CHECKS AND DRAFTS, LISTING THEM SEPARATELY BELOW.

	DOLLARS	CENTS
Currency		
Silver		
Total cash		
Checks		
Frank Costello 1-45 210	3,691.	67
National City Bank of New York,	3,691	67
Frank Erickson, 1-320 260	2,768	74
L.J.Erickson, 1-229 260	922	92
Ray Ryan 85-543 653	3,593.	23
" " "	25,000	00
Total $	39,668	23

FOR CREDIT OF
RYAN OIL COMPANY

October 4
EVANSVILLE, IND. ____ 19 49

DEPOSITED IN THE
OLD NATIONAL BANK
IN EVANSVILLE, IND.

By   RYAN OIL COMPANY

September 16   194 9

NOTICE TO DEPOSITORS

IN RECEIVING ITEMS FOR DEPOSIT OR COLLECTION, THIS BANK ACTS ONLY AS DEPOSITOR'S COLLECTING AGENT...

Allierose B. Galt	5798.13
30-4	11,596.26
Frank Costello 1-45 210	2,666.57
L.J.Erickson 1-229 260	666.66
Frank Erickson 1-320 260	2,000.00
National City Bank of New York	2,666.67
Central Pipe Line Co. 73-80 421	48.36
" " " "	191.65
" " " "	158.16

Total $19,994.43

Bank deposits showed Frank Costello and Frank Erickson invested in a few of Ray's oil deals.

Artist drawing of man witnesses saw at the car bombing scene

FBI surmised that man in the drawing may have been Joey Hansen

Chapter 54

AT THE PINNACLE

By 1956, Palm Springs had become more of a year-round palace of leisure than just a winter time haven for the wealthy. Located in the eastern foothills of the San Jacinto Mountains, the city had mild winters and 350 days of sun.

Cathedral City was to the south and stretched out to the east were the small communities of Rancho Mirage, Palm Desert, La Quinta, Desert Hot Springs, Indian Wells and Indio with large residential estates of the wealthy and famous.

Jack Benny and Mary Livingston, George Burns and Gracie Allen, Mary Pickford and Buddy Rogers, Debbie Reynolds and Eddie Fisher, Phil Harris and Alice Faye, Desi Arnaz and Lucille Ball, Dinah Shore and George Montgomery, Bob Hope, Bing Crosby, Lily Pons, Eddie Cantor, Jeanette MacDonald and Gene Raymond had homes around Palm Springs or were frequent visitors there.

Fabulous parties were held at the El Mirador, Thunderbird, Blue Skies Trailer Park, Racquet Club, Tennis Club, Shadow Mountain Club, Beachcomber, Chi Chi, Palm House, Doll House and Howard Manor.

Chi Chi was the hottest of the hot spots for several years. Irwin Schuman bought out his partner in a downtown café and in 1941 opened the Chi Chi Grill Cocktail Lounge, expanding it into the largest nightclub west of the Mississippi River and bringing in Sophie Tucker, Rudy Vallee, Tony Martin, Duke Ellington, Xavier Cugat, Louis Prima and Louis Armstrong to entertain.

By the mid-1950s, Palm Springs was in its heyday. People ogled Anita Ekberg in her bikini at poolside. Frank Sinatra brought in guests for night-long parties. There were elite golf courses, tennis competitions, winter polo matches, rodeos, regattas at nearby Salton Sea, sports car rallies, theater productions, numerous festivals, swimming pools (one for every 12 people in the village), dances, charity balls, horseback riding, croquet, hunting, fishing and other activities to pass the time.

There was always something to do in Palm Springs.

Another attraction was the availibility of cheap land. When the government divvied up the land before there was a Palm Springs more than half was given to the Indians. Shortly after his arrival in Palm Springs, Ray began purchasing land and developing thousands of acres with shopping malls and housing. After a while, the joke was that Ray owned nearly as much land around Palm Springs as the Indians.

He took off in the summer of 1956 to Europe with Bill Holden and Barney Hinkle, who was his partner in one of the local developments. Holden and Ray wanted to go to Russia but couldn't get visas after refusing to use a Russian tourist agency for the trip. Instead they visited Sweden and Germany, fished the fjords in Norway and sampled the best beers in Copenhagen. Holden left in June to return to the United States. Hinkle and Ray continued on to Switzerland and Ray stopped off in Rome before returning to America.

On his return, Ray geared up for the wedding of Charlie O'Curran and Patti Page. O'Curran's divorce from Betty Hutton was final in 1955 and he soon became engaged to Page. He was in his early 40s and Patti 13 years younger.

Born Clara Ann Fowler in Claremore, Oklahoma in 1927, she picked up the name Page after being hired to sing at 18 on a Tulsa radio station on a show sponsored by the Page Milk Company.

By the mid-1950s, the blond Patti Page was the hottest young singer in the country. She had recorded 22 songs with four reaching No. 1 including "The Tennessee Waltz" and "(How Much is That) Doggie in the Window." She was the country's "singing rage," and her beauty and voice dominated television screens across the nation.

Some friends said Ray pumped money into helping Charlie catch Patti. Charlie was debonair with dark hair and mustache, a lithe body from years of dancing, but never had much money. Ray helped Charlie with cash and advice.

With the marriage scheduled a few days after Christmas 1956, Ray had the local police chief arrest Charlie as a joke and put him in jail. Charlie was deathly afraid of bugs and wouldn't sit down on the jail mattress. Patti begged Ray to end the charade and get Charlie out of jail. Ray did.

Patti and Charlie were married at the Las Vegas home of Wilbur Clark. Ray was the best man and the young wife of Illinois politician Edward Barrett was Patti's matron of honor. The couple and their guests returned to the El Mirador for Ray's lavish reception attended by Danny Thomas, Frankie Laine and a host of movie studio executives and friends. After the reception, Patti and Charlie rode off in a new copper-colored Thunderbird Ray purchased as a wedding gift.

The newlyweds returned to Los Angeles where Charlie was to start work as a choreographer on an Elvis Presley movie. Charlie would work on five Presley films over the next five years, but after that his Hollywood career skidded to a halt while Patti's career continued to blossom. Ray tried to stay close to Patti, popping up with friends a couple of years later when she recorded "I Cry Myself to Sleep" at a New York studio.

The year 1957 was one of Ray's busiest at the El Mirador and Palm Springs. Frank Bogert left to take over management of the new hotel Desi Arnaz was building in Indian Wells. Running the El Mirador was becoming a headache for Bogert.

"There were 17 stockholders and every one of the goddamn guys was there. Every one of them thought they were my boss. They'd come and complain and want to do things that were all wrong and I finally went to Roy Fitzgerald and said 'I'm leaving. I can't put up with 17 bosses'." Bogert ran Arnaz's hotel for a couple of years before it was leased to two men from Texas, and he never worked at the El Mirador again.

Ray also was having trouble with his fellow El Mirador stockholders. He felt the El Mirador was too sedate and wanted to liven up the place, but ran into roadblocks from other stockholders. He started thinking about buying everyone out.

Ray concentrated on his role as the High Sheriff for the 1957 Desert Circus, the 21st annual event that had the theme "We've Come of Age." Robert Wagner and Natalie Wood were the King and Queen and actor Randolph Scott the grand marshal.

The Desert Circus' three-hour parade down Palm Canyon Drive was the biggest ever with elephants, hundreds of horse-mounted police patrols and riders, bands and floats – including one that featured Liberace and his brother George. More than 2,500 people participated in the parade including Ray on his silver saddle riding a golden palomino horse.

Temperatures during the week were in the high 80s, warmer than usual, and the young girls and women who were Ray's "deputies" strolled around the city in bathing suits. Ray posed for poolside publicity shots with two girls in revealing outfits helping him with his cowboy boots.

Helen worried about the photographs of Ray surrounded by women and the rumors regarding his girlfriends.

Bogert liked Helen and once when she came to Palm Springs for a visit, she talked with him about the stories of Ray's philandering. "Those people are always telling me about the girlfriends Ray has," Helen told Bogert. "Nobody could have that many girls. I don't believe any of it." Helen thought the stories were lies.

Bogert didn't set her straight. He liked Helen but he liked Ray more.

Another long time friend of Ray's in Palm Springs also knew Helen very well. "Ray didn't make her life very pleasant for a long time," the friend said. "I talked to her about that after Ray died. She had a really good attitude about that. She said 'look, what was I going to do? If I got mad at him and wanted a divorce, he'd come crying back to me.' She was in a situation she couldn't change. On the girlfriend thing, I think Ray may have had one he was quiet serious with for a while but I think a lot of the rest was for show."

Helen didn't sit and brood over what Ray was doing in Palm Springs. She was happy back in Evansville, taking care of Rae Jean and enjoying her own set of friends. In the mid-1950s, Helen met Lydia Herron, a well-known ice skater in Germany who had married an American and moved to nearby Clay, Kentucky.

When ice skating was offered at Evansville's new stadium, Herron was hired as the first instructor. Helen called Herron and said she wanted to be her first student. The first night they met "we skated and skated and skated," Herron recalled. The two became close friends and also enjoyed water skiing and playing golf.

Other Evansville friends liked being at parties Helen held at her home. "We always felt welcome there. We just had so much fun," one frequent guest said. "Helen was beautiful," another woman said, remembering the first time she saw Helen at an Evansville downtown clothing store back in the 1940s. "There was this girl with long black hair, sapphire blue eyes and beautiful figure. She was gorgeous, a typical Irish beauty. We became like sisters. I loved Helen. We did a lot of things together, regular home-style fun." Helen didn't miss Palm Springs.

In May, Roy Fitzgerald fell ill, returned to his suite at Chicago's Sheraton-Blackstone Hotel and entered St. Luke's Hospital. A month later, he was dead at the age of 63.

Ray took over as El Mirador president and pumped up the entertainment with big bands. He started a Bavarian Beer Festival complete with authentic Bavarian costumes, free-flowing beer and a German band. The country's top Bavarian dance experts gave free polka and Rhinelander dance lessons. Ray, in a Tyrolean hat, raised toasts to fellow drinkers.

He also hired an unknown singer, Ronnie Deauville, to perform at the El Mirador. Confined to a wheelchair, Deauville had done occasional vocal spots with the Tommy Dorsey, Ray Anthony and Glen Gray orchestras before a health problem forced him to be confined to an iron lung for several months. After getting better, Deauville wanted to return to performing.

Ray was lauded for hiring the singer, which led to Deauville getting performing dates across the nation. Ray was at the pinnacle of his success.

But, as the end of 1957 approached, things would never be the same.

Chapter 55

FEDS' MOB WAKE-UP CALL

Ray was respected and adored in Palm Springs in 1957 but, because of the company he kept, he started attracting the attention of federal agencies.

The Feds didn't initially focus on Ray. In their pursuit of gangsters, agents realized that Ray was a peripheral figure. He was seen with Mafia types frequently enough that federal law enforcement did eventually put him under the microscope.

After Ray's murder 20 years later, investigators would come to believe that events occurring across the country in 1957 played small roles in leading to Ray's death.

For decades, the FBI refused to recognize the existence of the "Mafia" organized crime; after World War II, agents spent their energy chasing real and perceived Communists in America.

But even FBI Director J. Edgar Hoover couldn't ignore the organized crime syndicates after 1957.

The public was outraged over mob violence and greed. Federal agencies were left red-faced when they failed to contain the threat. Hoover was forced to crack down on the "Mafia" with intensity over the next two decades and pass laws that would break organized crime's grip on cities.

One event in 1957 that adversely affected Ray was Tony Accardo stepping down as the Chicago Outfit's boss and turning over day-to-day operations to Sam Giancana. Giancana in charge of Chicago wouldn't prove good for Ray Ryan.

Accardo was in his early fifties and had ruled for more than a decade with Paul "The Waiter" Ricci. During that time, Chicago gained significant control of several Las Vegas casinos and skimmed casino money.

In Chicago, Accardo had backed Richard J. Daley for mayor in 1955, convinced that Daley wouldn't be a threat. He was right. Daley replaced officials who had anti-mob attitudes and closed down the detective intelligence unit known as Scotland Yard which kept track of local hoodlums.

But, Accardo knew it was time to move out of the limelight. One of his oldest and most trusted friends Jake "Greasy Thumb" Guzik, the Jewish gangster and the mob's financial wizard, had keeled over dead of a heart attack in February 1956 in a restaurant.

Giancana was growing too strong and speculation was if Accardo didn't step aside, he might suffer a common Chicago disease – acute "lead" poisoning.

Accardo "retired" to a home in Palm Springs.

Frank Bogert, who squired around prospective home buyers looking at properties, drove Accardo around the area. During the tour, Bogert pointed out where Thompson grape vines grew, noting each time "there're some Thompson vines." Bogert didn't realize Accardo had no idea what he was talking about until Accardo looked at him and said "that Thompson guy must be a millionaire."

Another 1957 event put additional pressure on the federal government to admit that organized crime existed and that its control of Las Vegas couldn't be denied.

A taxi stopped in front of the large apartment building at 115 Central Park West in New York City just before 11 p.m. on May 2, 1957.

Philip Kennedy, a 30-year-old former semi-pro baseball player who managed a modeling agency, stepped out first to allow a well-dressed 66-year-old man to climb out. Kennedy bid good night to his older friend, who lived in a penthouse apartment.

Kennedy didn't notice a black Cadillac pull up and a younger heavy-set man, about six feet tall and wearing a dark suit, walk past him and the doorman. The heavy-set man caught up with the older man in the lobby, said something softly to him, then pulled out a

.32-caliber gun from his pocket and shot him in the head. The gunman ran past the doorman, jumped into the Cadillac and disappeared.

Frank Costello, heralded by Kefauver's committee as the nation's "No. 1 racketeer," lay bleeding on a leather couch in the lobby. Kennedy and the doorman helped Costello into the taxi and rushed him to Roosevelt Hospital.

But Costello's wound was superficial. The bullet struck near the left ear, furrowed under the scalp and emerged near the right ear. It was a lousy attempt to kill the "Prime Minister of the Underworld."

Police believed that Vito Genovese had Costello shot in an attempt to regain leadership from Costello of the family that Genovese had ruled before fleeing to Italy to avoid a murder charge.

Vincent "The Chin" Gigante, an up-and-coming street thug, was later tried in the attempted murder of Costello but found innocent.

The biggest news from the shooting turned out to be a crumpled piece of paper police found in Costello's pocket at the hospital. On the paper was:

"Gross casino wins as of 4-27-57, $651,284

Casino wins less markers $434,695

Slot wins $62,844, Markers $153,745.

Mike $150 a week, Jake $100 a week, L. $30,000, H. $9,000."

Within a month, police decoded the note's secrets which would shake Las Vegas to its core. The note writers were Lou Leader, a Chicago gambler and auto dealer who managed the recently opened Tropicana casino in Las Vegas, and Michael Tannic, a casino employee.

The note listed the first 24 days of revenue for the new Tropicana casino where Costello, Kastel, Meyer Lansky and Carlos Marcello had hidden ownership. The mob power in Las Vegas couldn't be ignored any more.

Embarrassed Nevada officials were forced to crack down and in three years would create a Black Book banning hoods from owning or even entering a casino.

Other 1957 events would spell even more trouble for syndicates nationwide and forever change the face of organized crime.

On October 25, 55-year-old Albert Anastasia, the man who headed the infamous Murder, Inc., crew that killed over 60 people, was gunned down in New York's Park Sheraton Hotel barber shop.

First Costello, now Anastasia. It was a throwback to the 1930s when numerous well-known gangsters frequently were shot or murdered. Mob bosses knew the public and federal government wouldn't put up with another decade of wanton killing. They had to sit down and iron things out.

The national sit-down occurred on November 14, at the home of Joseph Barbara, once a hitman for the Buffalo crime family, in the isolated upstate New York village of Apalachin, population 400. On November 13 over 60 well-dressed men with gold watches, diamond belt buckles and expensive cars showed up in Apalachin, sticking out like sore thumbs.

That same day federal narcotics agent Joseph Amato was testifying before the McClellan Committee in Washington, D.C. about Mafia influence in the garbage collection industry. "We believe there does exist in the United States today a society specifically, loosely organized, for the purpose of smuggling narcotics and committing other crimes," Amato told the committee.

While he spoke, the "loosely organized" Mafia was gathering 220 miles to the north.

Sergeant Edgar Croswell, a steely-eyed, 42-year-old New York state trooper, wondered what was going on when the Cadillacs and Lincolns rolled into Apalachin and called for police reinforcements.

As the hoods gathered at Barbara's home the next day, Croswell and other officers started checking license plates of parked vehicles. Panic set in and a dozen hoods stumbled through the woods trying to get away. Others stayed, tossing aside any identification. "It looked like a meeting of George Rafts," Croswell later said.

Most of New York's and New Jersey's top gangsters were there – Joseph Bonano, Russell Buffalino, Paul Castellano, Gerardo Catena, Carlo Gambino, Vito Genovese, Antonio Magaddino and Joseph Profaci – along with mob leaders from other states and various union representatives. They listed their occupations as undertaker, butcher and nightclub, restaurant, drapery, concrete, vending, and dress factory business owners. More than $300,000 in cash was found on them.

Sam Giancana was not arrested, escaping through the woods and ruining a $1,200 suit in the process. When he got back to Chicago, an angry Giancana blared that the Apalachin fiasco never would have occurred if they had met in Chicago.

The Apalachin convention blazed across the front pages of newspapers. FBI Director J. Edgar Hoover no longer could ignore organized crime.

On November 27, 1957, Hoover issued a directive to field offices creating the Top Hoodlum Program and ordering agents to go after leading gangsters in their areas.

Most federal agencies weren't ready to jump into the battle immediately but one department was and because of that Ray Ryan ended up in the pages of Life magazine, spent months in Europe and made his mark in Africa.

Chapter 56

TERRE HAUTE SENDS RAY PACKING

On November 29, two days after Hoover's directive, eight men bundled in heavy coats and hats stamped their feet and dug their hands into pockets to stay warm in the near freezing weather along Wabash Avenue in downtown Terre Haute, Indiana. One occasionally walked the few feet to the intersection with Seventh Street to see who might be nearby.

Wabash and Seventh was the town's center. U.S. 40 ran east-west along Seventh and U.S. 41 north-south along Wabash. In the 1930s, Terre Haute proudly proclaimed the intersection as the "Crossroads of America." On that day in 1957, Terre Haute's crossroad intersection was the center of something sinister.

Terre Haute was a wild town with gambling and prostitution, yet a place where people turned out for a downtown parade honoring a grand champion steer raised by a local 4-H girl. Election fraud during World War I sent most of the city administration to jail.

During Prohibition, there reportedly were "at least 3,000 speakeasies, blind pigs, moon (shine) joints and old-fashioned farm houses where home brew is available." Houses of prostitution and gambling joints openly existed for decades and in 1955, magazines had nicknamed Terre Haute "Sin City."

The eight men enduring the cold on Wabash Avenue were special agents of the U.S. Treasury Department's Internal Revenue Service. They had watched the three-story building at 671 ½ Wabash for two weeks, starting just after the news of the meeting in Apalachin, and saw six to eight men go in each day and spend 12 hours there.

Armed with a search warrant, the agents waited in the cold for a way to get inside the building and up the stairs quickly. Shortly after noon Jules Horwick opened the first floor door to go outside. Special Agent Glen Johnson tapped him on the shoulder, took his keys and agents rushed up two flights of stars, through three locked doors to rooms where telephones rang incessantly.

Six men in the front room were answering eight phones. A ticker tape machine was clattering nearby. Wastebaskets were filled with betting slips; betting odds charts were scattered across the table. A corner table held food, liquor and other refreshments. The place was so busy the bookies couldn't go out for lunch.

Federal prosecutors estimated that during the 10 weeks the business operated the bookmakers handled more than $3 million dollars in bets on professional and college football, baseball's World Series, hockey and horse races.

Under the tax law, the federal government should have gotten more than $300,000 in taxes from the betting. The bookies logged more than $1.3 million in bets on the busy Thanksgiving weekend and $1 million plus for college football games scheduled in December and year-end bowl games.

Arrested were two Chicago men – Horwick, 56, and Leo Shaffer, 59, the man known as "Bookie" and the favorite bookie of H. L. Hunt and Ray Ryan. Also arrested were a former sheriff from Indianapolis, gamblers from Indianapolis, Las Vegas and Miami Beach and E. M. Wyatt, 60, of Terre Haute.

Wyatt was the only one in the room who had taken out a federal gambling stamp. The stamp was on a wall, but he had never paid taxes on the betting income. Congress approved the federal Gambling Tax and Stamp Act in 1951 requiring bookmakers to take out a $50 occupational stamp and pay 10 percent tax monthly on the bookmaking gross revenue.

After the law went into effect, Shaffer and Horwick moved their Chicago bookmaking business to Canada until they were ordered to leave the country in 1956. They then moved their base to Terre Haute.

U.S. District Attorney Don A. Tabbert had the task of sifting through the thousands of documents to make sense of the massive

Terre Haute bookmaking operation and to try and get silk-suited, well-known bettors before a scheduled August 1958 grand jury in Indianapolis.

The array of bettors was impressive – Zeppo Marx, the youngest of the Marx Brothers; bridge experts Tobias Stone and John Crawford; a New York Park Avenue physician; oilmen from Oklahoma and Texas; jewelers; investment and real estate brokers; business executives; a church trustee; beer and liquor distributors; an ice cream manufacturer; a filling station owner; auto dealers; dress manufacturers and retailers; a department store president; and an attorney.

The two biggest bettors, logging in thousands of dollars in bets each, were Ray and Hunt, and Tabbert desperately wanted both of them before the grand jury. Tabbert's determination smacked of more than just an eager federal prosecutor going after two big-name high rollers.

Were Ray and Hunt the financial backers behind the bookmaking operation? Terre Haute was just 100 miles north of Ray's home in Evansville. Shaffer was Ray's and Hunt's favorite bookie. Getting Ray and Hunt before a grand jury might turn up evidence to that effect.

Years later, Tabbert said IRS agents were interested when Ray's name came up in the Terre Haute case because "they knew we had somebody who was not just considered an oilman in 1957, but someone who had nefarious connections."

If Ray was worried about the Terre Haute raid, he didn't show it. In Palm Springs, he purchased a Christmas gift that year for himself – a 1958 Lincoln Continental convertible, receiving a gold ignition key from the dealer.

He also was promoting the upcoming annual Desert Circus, which would be a salute to Texas with Ray's friend, Texas oilman Glenn McCarthy, to be the grand marshal and High Sheriff.

Ray hired a DC-3 plane and lined up a star-studded list of entertainers to fly to five Texas cities to promote the Circus. Song writers Sammy Cahn and Jimmy Van Heusen, Phil Harris, Roberta Linn, Frank Sinatra, Dean Martin, baseball figure Leo Durocher and Mike Romanoff were among those making the trip that was a rollicking adventure of characters, booze and laughter.

Cahn and Van Heusen, who had just received an Oscar for "All the Way," wrote a song to salute Texas entitled "It's 1,200 miles from Palm Springs to Texas." Martin cut records to distribute to Texas dignitaries. Ray's name was listed on the label as one of the song writers. "All I actually contributed to the tune was the distance from Palm Springs to Texas, and I had to look that up on a road map," Ray said. Fans and local officials greeted the Palm Springs folks in Austin, San Antonio, Houston, Fort Worth and Dallas.

But Ray knew his time in Palm Springs was running thin with Tabbert preparing for the grand jury in Indiana.

In the summer of 1958, Ray politely bowed out as president of the El Mirador, citing other business duties, and Ed Houghton took over.

Ray also knew he didn't want to be a witness in the upcoming bookmaking grand jury or in the trial planned for 1959. More than 160 people were called for the grand jury, but at least 40 would refuse to testify. John Drew was among those taking the Fifth Amendment. Sam Garfield also was among the witnesses but offered nothing.

Tabbert discovered Hunt and Ray were slippery as eels. He went after both men aggressively using all federal government resources available. Of the hundreds of names in the bookies' black book, Hunt and Ray were the highest of high stakes gamblers.

Ray and Hunt knew too many embarrassing questions could be asked if they showed up. Hunt's attorneys fought the subpoena until his doctor submitted a report saying Hunt couldn't appear because he was recovering from a throat operation.

Ray didn't offer a doctor's excuse. He simply took off for Europe, staying at the best hotels, mansions of wealthy friends or at luxury villas and yachts that he rented.

Ray was in Belgium as Tabbert worked to get that government's cooperation to serve the subpoena. As Tabbert closed in, Ray took off for Switzerland and Tabbert had to start the process all over again in a different country. Ray's constant moves throughout Europe wasted months of work by Tabbert. The prosecutor finally ran out of time and was forced to abandon his efforts to get Ray.

When in Switzerland, Ray was near Carl Hirschmann, who was president of the Commercial Credit Bank of Zurich. U.S. tax agents later claimed that millions of Ray's – and possibly organized crime's – dollars found their way to that Swiss bank.

In September 1958, Life magazine published a four-page article about the Terre Haute raid under the headline "The Big, Big Bettors Hide, Hide and Hide." Life said the raid bagged "a major U.S. gambling center and had made the biggest haul of big-name gamblers and customers ever cornered in the U.S." Bettors came from 43 U.S. states, Cuba and Canada. There were photographs of arrested bookies hiding their faces under handkerchiefs, coats or newspapers made into masks, and celebrities who testified before the grand jury – bridge experts Stone and Crawford and Zeppo Marx.

The magazine also published pictures of the two main bettors who didn't show up – Ray and Hunt. Ray was "reputedly one of the country's biggest bettors, he probably bet directly through Terre Haute" and Hunt "reportedly has bet enormous sums a week on football games," the magazine reported.

Ray also was absent when the bookies' trial opened in the summer of 1959.[23] He remained on another "extended vacation" to Europe.

Don Tabbert didn't know it, but because of him, Ray headed into a business deal for which he would be best remembered.

---

23 The eight men indicted by the grand jury in 1958 went on trial in federal court in Terre Haute in June 1959. After a six-week jury trial before Judge Cale J. Holder, the men were found guilty of conspiracy, federal excise tax evasion and failure to register as a gambling syndicate. All were sentenced to five-year prison terms although the sentences of two men were suspended because of their ages. A total of 133 people testified in the trial, including 53 alleged bettors. Nine bettors or bookies took the Fifth Amendment and wouldn't testify.

Chapter 57

HEAVEN ON EARTH

Ray spent months enjoying the gambling casinos, scenic and probably female pleasures of Europe, staying with wealthy friends and slipping from country to country when needed to avoid being subpoenaed by the U.S. federal prosecutor.

Still unsure of the next step in the Terre Haute bookmaking case and getting bored, Ray called William Holden to meet him and go hunting. They got together in Rome, mulled over hunting possibilities and, almost on a whim, decided to go to Africa.

This was the first time Ray had been to Africa, but he had heard about the country from Clark Gable and from reading the Tarzan books as a child. Neither Holden nor Ray had been on a safari or knew much about hunting, but both were fearless and looking for a new adventure. Joining them on the trip to Africa was Carl Hirschmann.

The three flew to Nairobi in January 1959. Again, Ray's timing was impeccable, arriving as unrest in Kenya had calmed.

Between 1952 and 1956, Kenya was in the throes of the Mau-Mau revolt, an uprising by the Kikuyu tribe determined to exterminate Europeans and cease being a British colony. In six years, British troops killed more than 11,000 rebels who in turn had killed 200 Europeans and 2,000 Africans supporting the British.

By 1959, Kenya's situation had settled and the government hoped to attract foreigners to invest in the emerging nation.

Ray, Holden and Hirschmann headed to central Africa's golden plains where safari seasons were mid-December through March and mid-June through October. They hired two professional hunters, Terry Mathews and Tony Archer, and an assortment of gun bearers, skinners, scouts, cooks, drivers and camp workers.

The land was a hunter's paradise with buffalos, leopards, elephants, antelopes, zebras, gazelles, giraffes, hippopotami, impalas, elands, rhinoceroses and over 200 species of wild birds.

They bounced along rutted trails, enjoying the lush landscape, brilliant sunsets, wide open spaces dotted with occasional villages. They joked and laughed and, after tents were set up and meals cooked in the evenings, drank and relaxed.

After a few days, the group had traveled more than 70 miles from Nairobi and the hunters had found animals worthy of being stuffed as trophies including a massive buffalo that the group had killed.

While stalking another herd, the telescopic sight on Ray's rifle worked loose as he was shooting and recoiled, making a deep gash on his forehead.

Mathews and Archer patched Ray up the best they could, but had to find a doctor, the nearest one being 50 miles away in the village of Nanyuki. The doctor there treated Ray and because Ray needed a few more days of rest, the group drove a few miles east, a swift climb up another 650 feet in altitude, to the Hotel Mawingo located at 7,000 feet above sea level with an enchanted view of nearby Mount Kenya.

At 17,058 feet, Mount Kenya, the highest in Kenya and second highest in Africa, dominated the central highlands. Formed millions of years ago by a series of volcanic eruptions, the mountain was covered with glaciers, even though it is located along the equator.

As Ray, Holden and Hirschmann sat in the hotel lobby, Robert Ruark and a friend who had been elephant hunting up north showed up. Ruark was a nationally known columnist, magazine writer and author who covered the Mau-Mau revolt and wrote about hunting in Africa. Holden and Ray were in need of a shave and a haircut and they and Ruark were suffering from gout.

Ray's banged-up head still hurt and he complained to the others about the hotel service. Ruark, in a column written a few weeks later, said they talked about the view of the finest scenery in the world but a hotel without "action," no girls or music. "I'm a Palm Springs kid myself," Ray said. ""There you got action and scenery. But I am kind of all shook up by this Africa."

Ruark told the men that the hotel owner, Jack Block, might sell the place. "Why don't you buy the joint and provide the action," Ruark said, writing in his column that Ray, Holden and Hirschmann "like a Greek chorus" shouted "let's buy it."

Lucinda de Laroque, later in writing the book "Paradise Found: The Story of the Mount Kenya Safari Club," had a different version of what happened that day. De Laroque said Ray badgered Mathews at dinner for the name of the owner. "Call him up and tell him I want to buy the place," Ray said.

Bill Holden had another version. Holden said he and Ruark harassed Ray for griping about the service and hotel conditions and told Ray he should put his money where his mouth was. Ray suddenly got quiet and Holden knew what that meant. Ray was pissed. He didn't like being badgered by friends when he had the cash to do whatever he wanted. That's when Ray made up his mind to buy the hotel and make something of it, Holden said.

Ray later said "as soon as I saw the place I knew I had to do something about it. I speculated out loud about how wonderful it was for me to be here in Africa, away from all that Hollywood atmosphere."

Ray said he'd pay 25,000 English pounds for the property, but Mathews, one of the hunters, recommended 30,000. Mathews reached Block's wife by phone in Nairobi, who called back later saying: "Jack said double it." Ray was jubilant, never believing Block actually would sell. Block had paid 25,000 pounds for the hotel more than a decade ago and added another 45,000 in improvements.

The next day Mathews, Ray, Holden and Hirschmann drove to Nairobi, met Block and reached a compromise of 52,000 pounds. Everyone was happy. Now Ray had to dig into his pockets to give the hotel an elegance to match the view of Mount Kenya.

Being near the heart of the Mau-Mau terror reign, few visitors ventured into that part of Kenya and it was only in the last few years that business had picked up.

The first European settler to the area had been Colonel Eric Percy-Smith, a retired British army officer who served in India. In the early 1930s, he reached Nanyuki and came upon the clearing along the Mount Kenya foothills. He wired his find to Myra Wheeler, a San Francisco woman he had met in India, and she joined him with her daughter Hannah.

Percy staked out 700 acres and built a grass-thatched cottage for them to live in. He became a big game hunter and trapper, catching exotic animals to sell to zoos across the world. Percy made trips to Europe selling exotic animals and on one trip, he got into a fight at a bar with a French sailor and died from a blow to the head, leaving Myra despondent and not knowing what to do.

She soon encountered Rhoda Lewisohn, the wife of a wealthy New York City financier. Rhoda had gone to Africa to visit a friend and met a Frenchman named Gabriel Prud'homme on a safari and fell in love. Rhoda divorced her husband, ending up with a sizeable settlement, and married Gabriel in Paris. He was a pilot and they flew across Kenya looking for a place for a new home.

The property they chose was the land where Myra and Percy once lived. Myra eventually agreed to sell if Gabriel flew to France and took the cremated ashes of her late husband to Africa. Gabriel did and flew Myra over the land where she scattered the ashes over the ground Percy loved.

In January 1938, Rhoda took over 5,390 acres of land and formed the Mawingu Limited company. She and Gabriel built a mansion along the slope of a hill not far from Percy's original hut between the Nanyuki River and slopes covered with bamboo and juniper. She called the home Mawingu, which was Swahili for the cotton-ball clouds that skirt the mountain slopes.

One wing had eight bedrooms on the first floor and upstairs living quarters with a breathtaking view of Mount Kenya. Throughout the house were thick imported carpets, rooms filled with priceless furniture, the best imported bookcases, fabrics, gilt mirrors and a grand piano in the drawing room. Bathrooms had mother-of-pearl lavatory seats. Tiger pelts and panther skins were tossed along wooden floors. The grounds included a rose garden and ornate fishponds.

Although Rhoda and Gabriel were in love, Gabriel was a playboy at heart, frequently bedding other women he invited to the house whether Rhoda was around or not. When war broke out in 1939, they went to France. After France fell to the Germans, Gabriel joined the Free French Air Force while Rhoda returned to live in California. They divorced a couple of years later and Rhonda never returned to

Kenya. Gabriel returned to the Kenya home at times, but died in 1947 in an air crash in Khartoum.

Block purchased the house after it had been uninhabited for a year, enlarged the dining room, added a wing to bring the number of bedrooms to 25 and opened the Mawingo Hotel. During the Mau-Mau uprising, he tried to sell the hotel for an army base but drew no interest. Even after the uprising was over, the hotel fared only a little better and Block was eager to sell.

Ray and Holden first thought of using the place to entertain Hollywood and Palm Springs friends. But Hirschmann, who knew hotel operations, saw the possibility of turning it into a magnificent resort for the wealthy wanting to experience Africa at its best.

Again, the timing was right for Ray. Commercial jet service was starting to grow, providing quicker and quieter air travel across the world. Pan American inaugurated the New York-London jet service in October 1958 and Boeing turned out 707 passenger planes at a record pace. The first jet service within the United States started in December 1958 and soon airplanes were flying to Europe, Africa, East Asia, South America and Australia.

Ray proudly claimed the safari club was "just two meals" and 20 hours away from America.

Chapter 58

SAFARI CLUB GLITTER

After Ray wired Helen to join him in Kenya, she arrived and was appalled at the ramshackle state of the hotel. She knew fixing it up would be expensive, and that changing Ray's mind would be impossible. Besides, she was enthralled with the snow-capped Mount Kenya and endless view of pastures, streams, forests and thatched-roof cottages of the villages.

Holden and Hirschmann asked their wives to come. Soon Ardis joined Holden and Rita Hirschmann her husband. Holden was enjoying time away from Hollywood, living in Switzerland, Hong Kong and Kenya while making movies outside the United States. A few years later, Holden had a studio built at the club and in 1962 filmed the movie "The Lion" there.

Ray pumped in most of the money to turn the hotel into a resort for the rich. He owned 80 percent and Holden and Hirschmann 10 percent each in the club. Ray set out to turn the Mawingo Hotel into a dream – a lot of it accomplished with his own hands. Ray kept Jack Mills as hotel manager and left signed blank checks for him to use when he was away.

Workers ripped out walls, lowered ceilings and constructed new wings. A heated outdoor swimming pool was installed, the dining area expanded again, orchid walks created, a horse stable and trails carved out of the forest. Flower and grass seeds and trees were imported from Europe, Australia, North America and Central America. Apple, orange, lemon and grapefruit trees were planted.

Ray manned a bulldozer to erect dams for lakes. He rode horses each day across the land checking on work progress and handing out dollar bills to workers. He bought watches in Nairobi to give away to workers. Holden gave away bicycles.

Ray expanded a bird sanctuary and shipped in exotic species of birds – black swans from Australia, cranes, eagles, flamingos, snow geese, Tibetan and Egyptian geese, herons, peacocks, parrots, sunbirds – and hired gun bearers to protect them from leopards and other preying animals.

After several months, the hotel was taking final shape.

Ray's love of the Kenyan countryside flowed in a letter he wrote to a Palm Springs friend in 1959. He told of a huge stretch of the Tana River running through millions of acres of undeveloped land and that he was negotiating with the Kenyan government for 500,000 acres.

"I can irrigate this entire area from the Tana River and it will be every bit as rich as the Nile," Ray wrote. "This river has been overflowing for thousands of years and it has topsoil like you get in Wisconsin only instead of being three or four feet deep, it is thousands of feet deep. You can raise sugar cane and realize 8/900 dollars an acre profit per year. We will have to build our own barges, set up our sugar refineries and processing plants, build cities for the natives to live in and then make it possible that we get into Mombassa where we have world markets."

To Ray, it was place to "set your roots and make untold of millions. I also have been very busy on our club which is heaven on Earth. It is situated on the foothills of Mount Kenya, on the equator, where we have elephants, rhinos, buffalo, waterbuck and all the smaller game right on our doorsteps. The temperature is between 80 and 90 in the daytime and at night you need a blanket. Every one of our rooms and suites has a fireplace and it is heavenly to sit in front of the wood-burning fire and when looking right and see snow covered Mount Kenya and to the left a warm fireplace with a good Scotch in your hand or a bottle of Schlitz beer."

Ray signed off with "Safarily yours."

"What Kenya needs is more white men with money," Ray told friends. "If I had to start all over again this is the country I'd come to. Boy, for peanuts, you could take some of all that (Tana River) water that is going to waste and make a Garden of Eden."

Hirschmann brought in top chefs from Europe and assembled a kitchen team of international repute to prepare eight-course meals. A large vegetable garden was planted. Ray purchased thousands of nearby acres and brought in 10,000 head of cattle. Large freezers were imported to store game killed by guests.

Visitors woke up to the sterling view of the mountain and tea from sterling silver pots. A nine-hole golf course and a bowling green, a game Holden liked, were carved out of the land. Ray even talked of building an ice hockey rink where the equator would be the center line, but never did.

Cottages were built around the club, each with sunken baths, fireplaces and telephones. The club offered massages, the best liquor and entertainment. Ray established Ryan Investments and within the year, opened offices in Nairobi and Palm Springs to sign up visitors.

He knew guests wanted to hear tom-toms for a true African experience and had a village of several hundred huts built near the club. Natives were brought in to live and to play tom-tom drums each evening. Instructions on how and when to beat the tom-toms were written in Swahili and posted on bulletin boards.

He brought in members of the Chuka tribe, who dressed in white feathers and grass skirts and performed their gyrating victory dances for guests. He erected a school and clinic for the village natives and club workers.

To attract sportsmen, he built a small airfield to take guests on fishing expeditions along the coast or at African lakes. Visitors arriving at Nairobi were brought the 140 miles to the safari club in a comfortable Rolls Royce bedecked in zebra skin upholstery and a well-stocked bar. He purchased the Kenyan business Zimmerman's Taxidermies so animals shot by guests could be stuffed and he invested in several other Kenyan companies.

Within a year, Ray spent more than $1 million and didn't blink an eye. "So it costs money. So what," he said. "If it costs another $1 million, what does it matter? Whatever it costs to get the job done properly that is the way it's going to be. Here you have Heaven on Earth. And what do Americans know about it? All that the Americans know about Kenya is Mau-Mau, Mau-Mau, Mau-Mau."

Ray said Kenyans should tell the world about "the weather, your beautiful countryside, and the way you can go about in a shirt during the day and need a fire and blankets at night."

He spread the word, trumpeting the scenic beauty of the club in newspaper and magazine articles over the next two years. The Palm Springs office signed up Hollywood folk to visit the club that included Ava Gardener, Frank Sinatra, Stewart Granger, Bob Hope, Bing Crosby, Jimmy Stewart, David Niven, director David Lean, Sidney Poitier, Steve McQueen and Charlie Chaplin.

Holden and Ray swapped stories and drinks at the club with Ernest Hemingway. Greek millionaires Stavros Niarchos and Aristotle Onassis, the Aga Khan, royalty from Europe and political leaders like Haile Selassie and Willie Brandt came. One of Ray's favorites was Adnan Khashoggi, the billionaire arms dealer who Ray called "my little Arab friend."

Ray led guests on tours through the kitchen and grabbed a megaphone to warn swimmers in the pool to watch out for elephants lurking nearby, although no elephants were around. "I like things to be fun, fun, fun," he said.

He roamed the club with a backgammon board looking for a guest or club worker willing to play. His personal hotel suite had a table for poker, blackjack and other card games. Often he rested during the evenings, smoking a cigar or a pipe, having a drink or walking along the edge of a lake.

Holden used a spyglass at his cottage to look into the club bar area and make sure the shelves were stocked with liquor. He and a local man sometimes staged mock fights before startled guests, who broke into applause and laughter when they learned it all was a joke. He hid snakes and spiders in peanut cans and pots to watch the guests' reactions.

De Laroque's book said when their wives weren't around, Ray and Holden brought in other women and "alternated the fairer sex like jewelry, dropping one gem at the airstrip for the outward bound flight to Nairobi and collecting another pearl on the incoming service."

Among international celebrities and well-known Americans named as the club's charter members were Winston Churchill, Prince Bernhard of the Netherlands, Walt Disney, Jack Dempsey, Lily Pons, U.S. Senator Lyndon Johnson, General Curtis LeMay, U.S. Senator Everett Dirksen, H. L. Hunt, Joan Crawford, Frank Sinatra, Conrad Hilton, Norman Vincent Peale, Ivy Baker Priest, William Randolph Hearst Jr. and California's Pat Brown.

However, Ray's old gambling buddy Frank Erickson added other charter members – Gerardo (Jerry) Catena, Thomas (Tommy Ryan) Eboli and Pasquale Eboli. That troika of mobsters ran the Genovese family in New York while boss Vito Genovese was in jail.

Erickson's signing of membership cards for his old mob friends would lead to the federal government breathing down Ray Ryan's neck in a few years.

The safari club would be Ray's hideaway for four to six months each year for the rest of his life. He'd spend months in Palm Springs, but Africa was his love. He always wanted to be part of that land.

And he was – in the end – when Helen spread his ashes over the area.

Chapter 59

RAY BACK, CAIFANO OUT

The Terre Haute gambling investigation was history by the end of 1959 and Ray returned to Palm Springs on a more regular basis.

Between the Terre Haute grand jury and later trial, Ray made trips to other parts of the world and returned to America at times, but that tip-toeing around no longer was necessary. Ray now could divide his time between Kenya and Palm Springs without a worry.

The Safari Club was starting to flourish and he had more money than he could ever spend, even for him. Some of the money Ray made at the club was funneled through Hirschmann's Swiss bank, a move that wouldn't go unnoticed by the Feds.

While Ray wriggled out of trouble, Marshall Caifano was getting into it.

As Sam Giancana took control of the Chicago syndicate, Caifano's role in Las Vegas expanded as the mob's "outside" guy there. His role was to keep everyone in line while the "inside" folks skimmed and distributed millions of dollars from casino revenues for behind-the-scene mob bosses across the country.

Caifano was better suited for the tough guy role than that of a financial wizard with a green eyeshade and an adding machine. He wasn't suave like Johnny Rosselli, who could mingle with ease and be liked. Caifano preferred being a hoodlum playboy chasing after chorus girls and waitresses, many of whom grew tired or fearful of his demands and tried to avoid him.

He shuttled between Las Vegas and Chicago to take care of Outfit business there. His flame burned bright, but it wasn't eternal. He was his own worst enemy. His brashness and love of power would send him into a downward spiral from which he never recovered.

Tony Accardo never liked Caifano, but Giancana, probably with the backing of East Coast hoods, had no problem elevating his former 42 Gang member Caifano to a top post in Vegas. FBI agents believed Caifano's wife Darlene was part of the reason.

Caifano's 11-year marriage to Darlene fell apart in August 1957 and they separated. Former Chicago FBI agent William F. Roemer, Jr., in his book "Roemer: Men Against the Mob" said agents learned that while Caifano was in Las Vegas, Darlene spent Fridays with Giancana for dinner and an overnight stay at a hotel. Hoping to drive a wedge between Caifano and Giancana, agents told Caifano of Darlene's liaisons. Roemer said Caifano wasn't angry, telling an agent "Sam's got the hots for Darlene. That's great."

But a Chicago Crime Commission memorandum reported Caifano was incensed that Giancana was "playing around with Darlene" while she was still his wife. Caifano wanted to beat up Giancana, mob boss or not, but was persuaded not to after "a meeting of some of the big mobsters to iron out the mess." Caifano couldn't alienate Giancana and lose his power in Vegas, but Giancana apparently was encouraged to leave Darlene alone.

East Coast and Chicago organized crime's influence in Las Vegas was no secret after the public scrutiny of the Kefauver committee hearings. Las Vegas Police Chief Alexander "A. H." Kennedy laid out his concerns to Chicago's crime commission director Virgil Peterson as early as 1953.

Kennedy said the casinos along the Strip, in the jurisdiction of the sheriff's department and not Kennedy's office, were controlled by the mob and served as headquarters for gangsters from across the country. The Sands, Desert Inn and Thunderbird casinos were the most important of those operations with the Sahara and others not far behind.

The Thunderbird was secretly owned by Frank Costello, Meyer and Jake Lansky and Joe Adonis. Lt. Governor Clifford Jones and members of the state tax commission, which approved permits of casinos and their operators, were part owners or extremely close to people in mob-controlled casinos. Governor Charles H. Russell was elected by gambling interests, Kennedy said. To him, the underworld held full sway without fear of arrest.

Las Vegas was in the grip of mobsters and even Congress was getting the message.

Arkansas Senator John L. McClellan's Select Committee on Improper Activities in the Labor of Management Field had hammered at the Teamsters and other unions in 1957 and mid-1958 then subpoenaed Chicago hoods in a probe of the syndicate's infiltration of restaurant and other unions.

Top Outfit leaders called before the committee refused to testify – Tony Accardo, Ross Prio, Joseph Aiuppa, Jackie Cerone, Joseph Divarco, Sam Battaglia and even Caifano were subpoenaed. The Senate voted contempt charges against them but nothing serious resulted. The committee then went after Teamsters President James Hoffa.

Back in Las Vegas a few months later, the Outfit's own attention focused on Gus Greenbaum, who managed the Flamingo and later the Riviera. Greenbaum was an alcoholic and drug addict, ran up sizeable gambling debts and couldn't be trusted any more. Caifano told him to pack it in, give up any ownership interest and go away. Greenbaum refused.

In early December 1958, Greenbaum and his wife were brutally murdered in their Phoenix home, their throats slashed by a nine-inch butcher knife left in a plastic bag. The wife's hands were tied behind her back, Greenbaum was in his pajamas and his three-carat ring was missing.

Surprisingly, the Nevada Tax Commission chief investigator said there was no connection between the murders and gambling activities in Las Vegas, leaving the case up to Phoenix police. No one was ever convicted in the murders.

However, the Greenbaum murders fueled the fire again about hoodlums in Las Vegas. By early 1959, Caifano was pulled back to Chicago and the Nevada state legislature talked about cracking down on gangsters.

In February 1959, Caifano faced trouble on the home front. His wife Darlene filed for divorce charging Caifano had been abusive. Denise Brady, Darlene's Las Vegas friend, testified about the abusiveness.

A few days after the divorce was final, Caifano married blond model Marye Evelyn Evenson, who he met the previous year. She had been dating a mild-mannered low-ranking bookmaker, but Caifano sent a couple of goons to discourage the man from seeing her again.

The 34-year-old Marye and Caifano were married in March with Alderisio, Frabotta, Sam Battaglia and Lenny Patrick pelting the couple with rice as they left the church. Caifano continued to party with buddies at Rush Street restaurants, nightclubs and strip joints, having fun and being visible. A regular hangout was the Trade Winds restaurant.

Caifano along with Battaglia, Frabotta and Alderisio owned Twin Food Products and the mention of their names was enough to convince restaurants and other business owners to buy from them. Caifano had his own Chicago bookmaking operations run by underlings with federal gaming licenses and was used by Giancana at times to strong arm officials of union locals or businesses.

When someone needed to be eliminated, Caifano seemed to be the one to call.

In December 1959 just 23 days after being released following 25 years in prison, Roger Touhy was gunned down on the steps of his sister's Chicago home and his bodyguard Walter Miller wounded by two or three men who suddenly appeared behind them in the darkness. Miller, an ex-cop, managed to fire off a couple of shots at the gunmen.

Touhy, one of the syndicate's most hated targets, died a short time later at a hospital at age 61. He had battled the Capone outfit during Prohibition and was sent to prison in 1934 for the kidnapping of John (Jake the Barber) Factor, a crime Touhy said he never committed. Touhy claimed the Chicago police department was part of the frame-up to send him to jail so Capone could take over unions Touhy controlled.

Touhy was the symbol of resistance to Capone and his murder smacked of revenge. Robert Wiedrich in the Chicago Tribune wrote that "alive and out of prison Touhy was proof that a man could thumb his nose at the latter day successors to the old Capone gang – and live. Dead, Touhy would be dramatic proof that the crime syndicate never forgives an enemy."

Cops questioned Caifano, who said he had been at home when Touhy was shot. Miller couldn't identify the assailants and no one was convicted in the murder.

In early January, William "The Saint" Skally was found in a car in a parking lot, killed by a bullet wound to the top of his head. Skally was a bootlegger and counterfeiter who reportedly was a stool pigeon for federal agents who broke up a large counterfeiting ring in 1959.

Later in January, Arthur Adler, recently ousted owner of the Trade Winds restaurant, was reported missing. Adler's wife claimed Caifano, Frabotta and Alderisio, frequent patrons of the Trade Winds, were involved in her husband's disappearance. Cops believed Adler was the front man for Caifano in the restaurant until November.

Adler had been called before a federal grand jury investigating the syndicate moving into Rush Street businesses, but claimed he knew nothing about the mob. His nude body was found two months later in a sewer by two city inspectors checking on complaints of poor flow. The coroner's office thought Adler died of fright. Caifano, Frabotta, Alderisio and Joseph "Little Caesar" DiVarco couldn't be found for the coroner's inquest. No one was convicted in Adler's slaying.

While Chicago continued on its deadly course, Nevada was taking action. The state legislature enacted the 1959 Gaming Control Act that set up a new five-member Nevada Gaming Commission to issue licenses, collect gaming taxes and oversee the gaming board's investigative and enforcement duties.

In 1960, the gaming commission issued a "Black Book" of undesirables to be banned from casinos. Caifano was among the first 11 people listed in the Black Book along with Giancana.

Caifano rebelled at being told he couldn't hang around the casinos and his pals. He decided to make a stand against the Black Book.

That would cement his downfall in Las Vegas.

Chapter 60

MR. PALM SPRINGS

While life was good – even grand – in Palm Springs, Ray's attention drifted to a section of Western Kentucky about an hour's drive from Evansville when he hit a big oil field at Duke's Ridge in the latter part of 1959.

It would be his last major oil find. Duke's Ridge was very productive, not up to the scale of Scurry County, Texas, but big enough. The wells were around Muhlenberg County in Kentucky and Ray liked the down-to-earth people there.

While always ready to hop about America and the world, mixing with movie stars and fellow gamblers, Ray later would find peace and contentment in this isolated area of Kentucky.

That, however, would take several more years of being hounded by hoodlums and the federal government. All of that would end the high-flying style he so loved and eventually his life, which he loved even more.

The initial success at Duke's Ridge excited Ray. He and Helen jumped into his Cadillac convertible in Evansville and headed to Texas to celebrate. "I'll buy you some jewelry," he told her. Along the way, Ray's car went off the road and into a ditch filled with water. He hopped out as the water slowly filled the passenger seat where Helen was sitting.

"Get me out of here," she pleaded. "I will in a moment," Ray said. He opened the trunk, grabbed a camera and took photos of the car in the ditch – for insurance reasons perhaps – while Helen sat in the vehicle fuming, getting soaked and needing help.

Ray was a notoriously bad driver. He drove like he lived – fast and unwilling to follow rules.

Once a state policeman stopped Ray for speeding and an attorney riding with Ray shouted "thank God you stopped us. I thought the son-of-a-bitch was going to kill us." Ray and the attorney joked with the trooper who let them off without a ticket.

Ernie Dunlevie, Ray's Palm Springs development partner, also remembered riding with Ray on a trip to Colorado, white-knuckling it most of the way because "Ray always was on the wrong side of the road going around mountain curves."

Dunlevie first met Ray in the early 1950s during a morning horse-back ride around Palm Springs. He was impressed with Ray. "He was a great promoter. He promoted parades down Palm Canyon Drive to go to the canyon and barbeque with a lot of friends. He was great with numbers. He could remember cards and he had a pretty good memory on other things too."

Later Dunlevie's wife met Ray when they went to dinner at a Palm Springs restaurant. "When the bill came, Ray grabbed it and reached into his pocket and pulled out a roll of bills. My wife later said she didn't know that much money existed," Dunlevie said.

Ray usually carried around $60,000 to $70,000 in $1,000 or smaller bills and Dunlevie also saw Ray with suitcases full of money. "Sometimes we wondered where he got them," he said.

Ray was back in Palm Springs for the 1959-1960 winter season eager to promote the Mt. Kenya Safari Club. Helen remained in Evansville with her aging mother, Anna, who would die in February 1960.

Ray attended his first Bachelors Ball in Los Angeles. He asked Los Angeles columnist Joan Winchell to have a costume made to his measurements "and make sure it's sensational. Money is no object." Winchell had a designer make a spectacular African chieftain outfit with ruby red shoes and ostrich-plumed crown.

To promote the Safari Club, Ray planned a series of balls at his favorite gambling places across the world – Palm Springs, Paris, London, Monte Carlo, Jamaica, Hong Kong and Tokyo.

Once after visiting Hong Kong when Holden was there filming the movie "The World of Susie Wong," Ray told of a street of shops that specialized in aphrodisiacs. "I tried several of them. But you know the best aphrodisiac is a good-looking young woman," Ray said with a smile.

The Palm Springs' Safari Ball was held in March. Columnist Earl Wilson described Ray as an "oilionaire" who was among some of his best friends like Clark Gable, Desi Arnaz, Lucille Ball, Phil Harris, Alice Faye, John Carroll, Jane Russell and Bob Hope. Ray had an elephant tethered at El Mirador's entrance and wore a tuxedo tie and cummerbund that appeared to be leopard skin. "Look, he shoots his own ties," Jane Russell quipped.

Money was no object on other projects, too. Ray embarked on a flurry of developments that had people calling him "Mr. Palm Springs." An early project was a 32-acre shopping center in Palm Springs with a market, drug store and the city's biggest bowling alley.

In late 1960, he spent $1.4 million to buy out the other stockhold ers in the El Mirador, renaming it Ray Ryan's El Mirador. He spent $100,000 to update the hotel, the $100-a-day cottages and auditorium, and added more guest rooms on a four-acre tract.

Convinced the hotel would remain a "going-Jessie," a term he used for a good thing, Ray brought in big bands, the first being the popular Eddy Howard 15-piece group, into the hotel's new Silver Palm Room. Guests included European royalty and society elite wearing silver mink stoles or hair dyed silver. At a 1960 Christmas party, guests were to suggest gifts suitable for the "man who has everything." Bing Crosby gave Ray a box of penicillin pills, amid laughter from people in the room.

The Palm Springs Times noted that Ray "moved in a minimum of time and a maximum of money to restore the glamorous days of the old El Mirador bringing a new kind of flair to the once staid old village. His myriad enterprises and his flamboyant promotion of them have added a chapter to Palm Springs history that would be difficult to equal on any scale."

Ray met visiting governors, presidents and politicians like the Kennedys, Ted and Robert, the nation's top golfers and sports figures.

One was George Low Jr., a professional golfer, one of the nation's best putters and a golf hustler who often visited Ray in Palm Springs. Low was among the numerous hangers-on that Ray liked to have around.

A handsome, witty fellow, Low was unabashed in living in luxury on someone else's dime. "The only time I pick up a check is to hand it to somebody," he liked to say. He gave putting instruction to Ray and Bing Crosby, and won bets on putting greens by punching the ball in with his foot while the others used putters.

He went across the country staying with friends with money, once saying "I spent $50,000 a year of my friends' money." Ray knew he was just one of Low's stopovers. "There's always another Ray Ryan down the road for George," said Ray, who liked to introduce the golfer to friends as "George Low, America's guest."

Ray also treated others. For one Rose Bowl game, he hired buses and took a large group of friends to Pasadena, starting with a champagne breakfast and plentiful liquor on the buses. He gave each guest a portable radio to listen to other bowl games on the way. He also treated himself, handing over a check for $1,000 to Dodgers owner Walter O'Malley in early 1961 to buy the first season box seats sold at Chavez Ravine, the team's new home that opened in 1962. And he once purchased 100 suits costing $250 each from Sy Devore, Hollywood's haut couturier for male movie stars, the largest single sale Devore ever had.

Around Palm Springs, Ray usually dressed in one of his richly embroidered, colorful cowboy outfits. He passed out cards and coins with "Howdy Pardner" printed on them to guests and visitors.

He played the cowboy angle to the hilt and enjoyed every minute of it.

Chapter 61

LET'S MAKE A DEAL

One of Ray's biggest business deals came when he and Ernie Dunlevie acquired 2,000 acres for luxury homes at Bermuda Dunes, located about 20 miles east of Palm Springs.

Ray turned his old Southern Aviation Corporation from the PBY luxury airplane days into the Desert Bermuda Properties, getting a tax write-off for the substantial debt that had built up in Southern Aviation over the years.

He and Dunlevie spent $500,000 installing 11 miles of streets at Bermuda Dunes, 14 miles of water mains and a large fresh water lake fed by a 75-foot waterfall. They moved forward on a hotel, airport and golf course.

Dunlevie originally had another partner named Terry Ray, who Dunlevie described as a "screaming alcoholic." Terry once told bankers back East, during a telephone call, to go to hell. Dunlevie wanted to buy Terry Ray out and Ray Ryan agreed to become Dunlevie's partner.

Wanting to end the partnership, Dunlevie discovered Terry Ray had taken off to Mexico. Dunlevie said Ray Ryan stuck "a fist full of money, $10,000 in my pocket" to go to Mexico and find the guy.

Dunlevie found Terry Ray in Mexico and flew in an attorney to prepare documents.

"We developed a contract with a Mexican stenographer who didn't speak English by cutting words out of a magazine and pasting them on the paper. Anyway, we finalized the deal. That's how Ray Ryan and I became partners," Dunlevie said.

He and Ray simply shook hands to complete their agreement.

"I don't believe in contracts. I just shake hands on a business deal," Ray liked to say. "Anybody who buys anything from me can always sell it at a profit – back to me."

One of the first movie stars to sign up for a Bermuda Dunes home just off the golf course was Clark Gable. Dunlevie and Ray cut Gable a deal for a lower land price because he was a big catch. Everyone wanted to be able to say they lived in the same neighborhood as Clark Gable. Unfortunately, Gable died a short time after his home was built.

A second subdivision of 180 home sites, Jamaica Sands Estates, followed with phenomenal success. The first section sold out within five months with $1.2 million in sales. Ray acquired a large tract of land near Indio that he sold to developers for homes.

Ray's most intriguing project was at Salton Sea, California's largest lake. Located an hour's drive southeast of Palm Springs, the Salton Sea was a national oddity. The lake was created in 1905 when a rampaging Colorado River swept over a canal being built to bring water south of Yuma, Arizona and cascaded into what was known as the Salton Sink. It took two years to close the canal breech. By then a fresh water lake of 400 square miles covered the sink basin with no outlet.

Over the years, the growing number of farms dumped tons of salty pesticide- and fertilizer-contaminated soil into the basin. Salton Sea was 230 feet below sea level and saltier than the Atlantic or Pacific oceans. It was described as a mistake of man and nature. With no outlet, everything flowed down into the lake including sewage waste from Mexican cities to the south. The sea filled – sometimes flooded during massive rains – despite being in an area where only two inches of rain fell during the year and temperatures reached 120 degrees.

But Salton Sea was great for speedboat racing on the calm waters. The lake was well stocked with fish and campers and fishermen started coming. An earlier promoter developed homes and a yacht club at Salton City along the western side of the lake.

Ray opted for the lake's northern tip closer to Palm Springs, where he had often gone horseback riding and relished the desert vistas and the striking reddish brown color of the Chocolate Mountains. He believed the area would be "California's Riviera."

Ray and Trav Rogers began construction of the North Shore Yacht Club around 1958. The project was first class. Before any home sites were sold, Ray spent over $1 million putting up a clubhouse, a 400-boat marina, a 50-unit hotel, sewage systems and 22 miles of streets and roads. He spent a small fortune digging for water before installing 27 miles of water lines including a segment to bring in drinking water from the town of Mecca nine miles away. He required anyone buying lots to promise that they would build there. He wouldn't sell to speculators.

Ray staged parties in Palm Springs to promote Salton Sea. On the first anniversary of the development, Ray held a "Texas Millionaire Party" and turned the club into a miniature Las Vegas for make-believe gambling. Boat racing speed king Donald Campbell was a guest.

The Yacht Club and marina became popular. The Beach Boys went there; Jerry Lewis and the Marx Brothers docked boats at the marina. There were boat races and dances. The area became a lively, swinging place with golf courses and a state park nearby.

Ray also started a North Shore Beach housing development with Don Eastvold. On paper, it looked like a blend of talents – Ray's money and promotion talents and Eastvold's experience in land development in the state of Washington where he had been a state senator and the Attorney General.

Eastvold came on board around 1961 for a one-fourth interest. Within two years, they had plotted and sold 1,000 lots and added more. Eastvold and his new wife, singer Ginny Simms, promoted the development. But Ray soon wanted out and in 1962 sold the Yacht Club to Trav Rogers and other investors.

Fifteen years after the North Shore project was completed, heavy rains in adjacent valleys brought torrents of flood water into Salton Sea, destroying the marina, club and other shore facilities. The swinging era was over and Salton Sea never recovered.

Ray also was working on a major resort area of 240 acres along the Jamaican coastline at Montego Bay with Carl Hirschmann and Cincinnati, Ohio, developer Kenneth Hammond. By 1961, they reportedly had spent $3.5 million installing canals and a basin for 500 yachts. Another $35 million was projected for two hotels with a total of 600 rooms, 75 apartments and larger residences, a yacht club, marina, docks, recreation and convention facilities and a shopping center. But little was built because much of the property consisted of wetlands.

Mixed in with his gambling and developing, Ray frequently spent hours telephoning friends across the country. The quality he liked best in some friends was distance.

One Evansville oil company supplier cooled his heels nearly an hour one day while Ray was on the phone. When he hung up, Ray apologized, saying "I was on the telephone with my old friend Bill Holden. He's in his cups and I couldn't hang up on him. I had to get him settled down."

In the spring of 1961, Ray was back in Evansville for daughter Rae Jean's graduation from high school, holding a party for her friends at his Lombard Avenue home. He knew few of her classmates and walked around shaking hands with the boys calling them each "son." Rae Jean's graduation present was a new convertible.

Some of Rae Jean's schoolmates had never seen her father. A few years earlier, Ray was in Evansville working in the yard when a group of Rae Jean's friends came over. They thought the man in the yard was a new gardener Helen had hired.

Ray, Helen, Rae Jean and her close friend and classmate Nancy Kollker took off for two months at the Safari Club before the girls were to enter Indiana University. The girls rode in a Jeep across the African bush at 45 miles an hour as natives in the back dropped lasso loops on poles to snare an ostrich, giraffe and an antelope. They posed on the back of a rhino and around huge elephant tusks with columnist and author Robert Ruark, who was visiting there.

Before the trip, Ray was offered a chance for another deal – to buy into a Lake Tahoe casino. Frank Sinatra and Dean Martin had approached him about acquiring the Cal-Neva Lodge, a gambling operation on the California-Nevada state line.

Ray considered the proposal until he checked and discovered the hidden partner in the deal was Chicago mob boss Sam Giancana. Ray said he wasn't interested. He wanted nothing to do with Giancana, who occasionally stayed at the El Mirador. Shortly after trying to encourage Sinatra and Martin to stay out of the Cal-Neva deal, Ray was at the El Mirador when someone told him Giancana wanted to talk to him. "Fuck Giancana," Ray said, remaining seated.

Sinatra, Martin and others did become owners of the Cal-Neva. A few months later Martin realized Giancana's involvement and sold his three percent interest, probably at the urging of Ray. The Cal-Neva deal turned out to be a losing proposition for Sinatra.

But Ray's troubles with Giancana and his underlings were just beginning.

Chapter 62

NICK THE GREEK
WANTS REVENGE

Fifteen years after the poker games at the Las Vegas Flamingo, Nick Dandolos still steamed about losing to Ray Ryan in what he believed was a crooked game.

Being cheated ate at Nick. No one did that to him. Hell, he was Nick the Greek, not some yokel from the sticks. Everybody knew him, and he knew everybody. He didn't want to be the butt of jokes about being snookered by some oilman. He busted guys like him dozens of times at card tables. No one could make a fool of him.

Ian Fleming's book "Goldfinger" was published in 1959, more than a year before, and was popular. In one chapter, Goldfinger played cards at a Miami hotel and wore an electronic device while a hidden spotter with binoculars told him the cards his opponent held. It was Nick and Ray at the Flamingo in 1949 all over again – a rigged game.

Everyone around Nick knew Fleming had used the Flamingo story as the basis for that part of the book. Unfortunately, Nick didn't have James Bond on hand to rat out the cheat.

More embarrassing was talk of an upcoming movie based on Fleming's book. Dandolos couldn't live with that. It was he who walked out of a poker game with $500,000, beat a roulette wheel at Monte Carlo and liked to brag that he had $500 million pass through his hands at gambling tables during his life.

But by 1961, the six-foot Dandolos – a cultivated man with a caustic wit and a talent for conversational counter-punching – was a shadow of his former self. Nearly 80 years old, he was in failing health, virtually broke and headed toward playing at $5 limit poker tables in Los Angles for any action.

Nick went to syndicate folks he knew in Chicago and Las Vegas for help to get money he desperately needed from Ray.

Marshall Caifano was willing to come to Nick's aid, not because he was a Good Samaritan but because he needed money, too. Being in Nevada's Black Book of undesirables was strangling Caifano. Now banned from Vegas casinos, his power was on the downhill slide along with his cash flow.

When the Black Book list came out on June 13, 1960, casino owners weren't sure how far the state might go to enforce the ban. It didn't take long to find out.

Five days later, Caifano stopped into the El Rancho Vegas and the staff summarily tossed an angry Caifano, cursing and threatening, from the place. An irate Caifano didn't like being snubbed. He was too important a syndicate figure for such treatment.

A few hours later a fire broke out in a backstage dressing room and within minutes the flames consumed the casino, lobby and theater restaurant where Betty Grable had performed that evening. Owner Beldon Katelman said the damage was $1 million, but nearly $500,000 in cash was saved along with safety deposit boxes left by guests.

Authorities thought the fire was deliberately set, but eventually had to rule it accidental without positive proof of arson. The word on the street was that Caifano torched the place or had it torched.

Caifano retreated to Chicago, but in October was back in Las Vegas, spending several days at numerous Las Vegas mob casinos where he was greeted by executives.

The Gaming Control Commission chairman and a phalanx of aides stormed into the city and plowed through the casinos that catered to Caifano, confiscating cards and dice to embarrass the operators.

He was found at the Desert Inn lounge and ordered out, leaving after owners pleaded with him that their gambling licenses would be in jeopardy. He decided to file a lawsuit challenging the Black Book and seeking $150,000 in damages claiming he was denied his constitutional due process.

His was the first challenge to the state's belated efforts to ban gangsters from casinos. Hoodlums with extensive criminal backgrounds owned casinos or worked in them, and were regarded by the state as legitimate businessmen, but not Caifano.

He again returned to Chicago and went back to his old tricks. A string of mob murders occurred and Caifano was a suspect in a couple of them. In one killing, he was brought in for questioning with Charles Delmonico and both were released without being charged.

The cops still considered Caifano one of the 19 leaders in the Outfit. He continued to have front row seats at the Villa Venice nightclub to see the performance of Frank Sinatra and the "Rat Pack." Caifano partied at nightclubs and chased bunnies at Chicago's Playboy Club.

But below the surface, his star was fading. His marriage to his third wife, Marye, fell apart in late 1960 and they divorced. Caifano went to live at the residence of Darlene, his second wife, for a while. Still known as the Rush Street "rover boy" and a "playboy hoodlum" in the newspapers and crime commission reports, Caifano began dating Sudi Thomas, a 21-year-old hostess at the Gaslight Club where Sudi's dimensions were listed as 36-23-36. He and Sudi married in June 1961, moved into a home in Oak Park and shortly afterward to a more expensive dwelling in a better area.

Helping Caifano find the home was Lewis C. Barbe, an insurance company owner who met Caifano four years earlier while playing cards at a north side private residence. "We got to be great friends," said Barbe who got to rub elbows with Giancana, Alderisio, Frabotta, Ross Prio, Sam Battaglia and James "The Monk" Allegretti.

Barbe also insured hoods' nightclubs and restaurants, homes, vehicles and valuables, but quickly found some didn't pay full monthly premiums, forcing him to spend thousands of his own dollars to make up the difference. Next he was sucked into mob fraud, filing false claims of property supposedly stolen in burglaries and hijackings or destroyed in fires.

Caifano's lawsuit in Las Vegas proceeded through the court system, keeping his name in the news and he was becoming a continuing embarrassment to the Outfit. He watched as Alderisio, once his driver, and Frabotta rose in the syndicate's hierarchy while his control over Chicago gambling enterprises was parceled out to other hoods.

But, the Outfit was in turmoil. The Chicago FBI made extensive use of wiretaps on mob hangouts and phones. The information couldn't be used in court, but it gave the agents an inside look at what was going on. To hassle the mob, the agents frequently doled out juicy tidbits of info to selected reporters.

Congress, at the urging of U.S. Attorney Robert F. Kennedy, enacted several laws in 1961 to halt interstate distribution of race wire information for sports betting and take on gambling enterprises. Within a year, many race wire operations were closed. Robert Kennedy quickly became a hated enemy.

Even in Evansville, few bookies remained open. It was tougher getting big bets down because bookies lost the opportunity to lay off bets elsewhere. Federal agents also attacked gambling, prostitution, labor racketeering, and hoodlum infiltration into legitimate businesses, especially in Chicago. It was getting more difficult to earn a dishonest buck.

Caifano needed money and the quickest way was extortion – threaten rich guys and pocket the dough.

Nick the Greek's plea for help gave the Outfit an idea how to extort cash from Ray Ryan. Alderisio had been indicted in 1962 for trying to extort a vice president of a Colorado bank in Miami by threatening to harm the man's daughter. Alderisio eventually walked on that charge.

Alderisio was less lucky in a shakedown of Robert Sunshine, a disbarred attorney and confessed swindler. Sunshine had received $65,150 in 1961 from Ruby Kolod, part owner of the Desert Inn, and William "Ice Pick" Alderman, supervisor at the Fremont casino, in an oil well deal where the well already had been capped. When the subterfuge was discovered, Alderisio threatened Sunshine and his family if the money wasn't repaid. The case eventually went to trial.

Caifano worked on his Ray Ryan caper for months and investigators later believed he got approval from Giancana to proceed. Ray was a major player at Las Vegas casinos, betting hundreds of thousands of dollars in one night at the tables, and no one harmed a "whale" like Ray without a mob boss agreeing to handle any complaints from casino owners.

Charles Delmonico was brought in to help Caifano. Known as Charles White, Chuck White or Chuckie White on the street, Delmonico was a trusted hood and someone Ray didn't know. Delmonico lived in Florida, but was a soldier in the Outfit. At 5-foot

7 and 175 pounds, he had a mean streak and a record. He was expelled from Cuba in 1959 for narcotics trafficking and convicted in the mid-1950s on gambling charges in New York and Pennsylvania.

Born Charles James Tourine Jr. in New Jersey in 1927, he legally changed his name in 1953 to Charles Delmonico. His father, Charles "The Blade" Tourine Sr., was a high ranking East Coast hood with a long history of doing the bidding of Meyer Lansky in gambling casinos in Florida and Cuba, dipping into drug trafficking on his own and earning his nickname for being handy with a knife.

No one knew how much money Ray had, although news accounts hinted his fortune might be as high as $100 million. Caifano just knew Ray had plenty of cash.

Caifano boasted to friends that soon he would have more money than he would know what to do with.

Little wonder that Caifano had Ray in his sights.

Chapter 63

SHAKEDOWN

Joseph Glaston was Ray's publicity man at the El Mirador and his wife was Ray's secretary at the hotel. At 9:30 a.m. on April 30, 1963, Glaston's wife took a call from a man wanting to speak to Ray.

The man identified himself as Johnny Marshall and said he was at the Indian Wells Country Club. Glaston's wife, as she usually did with first-time callers she never heard of, said Ray was out although he actually was in the office. She wrote down Marshall's telephone number at the country club.

Ray didn't recognize the name and didn't return the call, thinking the man was just a panhandler. Ray hated those guys.

He had spent months at the Mt. Kenya Safari Club in early 1962. On his recent flight from London he had met Mavis Schickell, a shapely British Airways stewardess who agreed to accompany Ray to Palm Springs for five days.

Johnny Marshall, nee Marshall Caifano, called back at 2:30 p.m. Glaston's wife asked if he knew Ray. "Yes, from California and Las Vegas," Caifano answered. "Are you a gambler?" she asked. "Well, sort of," said Caifano chuckling. She mentioned a gambler in Las Vegas who Ray was acquainted with and Marshall said he knew him.

After saying she'd have Ray call back, she made reservations for Ray and Schickell to fly to Las Vegas later in the day and stay at the Desert Inn. She passed the message to Ray.

He called John Drew at the Stardust Hotel in Las Vegas to ask who was Johnny Marshall. Drew said Caifano was a mob guy, but that he was "okay." Caifano called again at 4:15 p.m. and was told to come to the El Mirador to meet Ray at the barber shop.

Ray was waiting outside the barber shop when a car with two men arrived. Ever suspicious, Ray had told the El Mirador bell captain Joe Johnston "I'm not sure what's going to happen. I don't know these two guys. If I get into the car with them, I want you to follow me." Johnston said he would follow with Miss Schickell, who Ray didn't want in the car with the two men.

Ray said he had to go to the airport to catch a flight to Las Vegas, and the men said they would drive him. He got into the rear seat next to Caifano with Delmonico at the wheel. As they drove off, Ray looked back and saw Johnston and Miss Schickell get into a car and follow.

"You owe Nick the Greek $15,000 and we think you clipped him out of it," Caifano told Ray as they drove to the airport. "I don't own him anything," Ray countered. Caifano and Delmonico wanted much more than that from Ray, but had decided that Nick would get only $15,000.

Caifano warned Ray "you better take our protection – give us the fifteen grand you won a week ago at a crap game in Vegas. We'll protect you from the mob. They're going to kidnap you. We can handle it for you."

"You're silly," Ray said, not impressed with the sordid shakedown attempt. Delmonico suddenly swung his arm around and struck a heavy blow to Ray's chest. "That's just to show you we mean business," Delmonico warned.

The blow startled Ray but only made him angry. No one hit him. Ray became madder and madder the more he thought about what Delmonico did.

When they reached the airport, Caifano and Delmonico asked where Ray was staying in Las Vegas and he said the Desert Inn. The thugs let Ray out and drove away. Johnston and Mavis Schickell pulled up behind them. They saw Ray was upset but okay. Johnston left and Ray and Mavis boarded the plane.

In Las Vegas, Ray and the pretty blonde were met at the airport by Lonnie Joe Chadwick, a gambler and long-time friend of Ray's. Ray asked Chadwick to reach Drew and straighten out the shakedown matter. Drew, in Reno by then, called Ray and told him there was nothing he could do.

"I'm not going to stand for any shakedown started by Nick the Greek," Ray said "I'm not going to give them any money that I worked all my life for. I'm not going to give it up."

Ray's lips hardened, his fists clenched. He wasn't going to put up with that kind of crap from anyone.

Chapter 64

NO RIDE IN THE DESERT

After Ray left for Las Vegas, Caifano, Delmonico and Allen Smiley, who hadn't been with the other two earlier, chartered a plane and flew to Las Vegas.

Joining them on the flight was Sandra Crosby, former Vegas showgirl and estranged wife of Bing Crosby's son Philip. Sandra Crosby later said none of the men talked about Ray during the trip or at dinner that evening in Las Vegas.

Later that night, Caifano called Ray at the Desert Inn and said he'd be at Ray's room at noon the next day, May 1. Ray said he'd leave the door unlocked.

Ray spent the morning in the casino. If Ray was nervous about the meeting with Caifano, he didn't show it. He headed to his room as noon approached and saw Delmonico and Nick in the hallway. He spoke to them, really greeting Nick, who was a long-time acquaintance, and not the asshole Delmonico, who Ray despised. Neither man answered Ray.

Caifano was waiting in the room. When Ray walked in, the steely-eyed, rough talking Caifano was in Ray's face demanding money. It was Caifano's no-bullshit mode that he had used time and again when threatening people. A shiver went down Ray's spine. *This guy is a mean S.O.B.*, Ray thought.

"The combine, the syndicate, has kept you from being kidnapped in the past. From now on you will have to pay $60,000-a-year protection money. You're one of the people we're going to put in line. I know you know a lot of important people including (U.S. Attorney General) Bobby Kennedy, but we'll take care of that too," Caifano said.

Ray was taken aback, but tried not to show it. He believed Caifano was a loner trying to shake him down and that some of the top-level mob guys he knew eventually could rein in Caifano.

"Let's bring Nick the Greek into the room to talk about this," Ray said. Caifano waived off that suggestion, saying he thought the room might have a concealed tape recorder.

Ray pushed the issue, saying "listen since I met you, I've written some letters and I put your names in it. If anything happens to me you'll burn."

Caifano wasn't worried about that. "All right, so we'll burn. Somebody else will get you," Caifano snapped back. "Let's not talk here. Let's go some other place. We need to go for a little ride." Caifano aimed him toward the door.

Ray had to think fast. There was no reasoning with this guy and, one thing for sure: he wasn't going for a ride in the desert. "I wasn't to go out (be killed) in a car," Ray thought – an omen to the way he actually would die.

Outside the room, Ray, Caifano, Delmonico and Nick started walking down the hallway. Ray's eyes scanned the corridor as he thought about what to do. He might have spotted "Milwaukee Phil" Alderisio lurking in the background.

As they approached a side hall, Delmonico said they could use a side door to get out. Ray's mind raced a mile a second. He knew he had to get away. *What the hell am I going to do?*, he thought.

Just then a bellboy pushing a rolling luggage rack approached. Ray ducked to the opposite side of the rack and raced toward the lobby. His sudden move surprised Delmonico and Caifano.

Ray sprinted for the lobby, shouting over his shoulder "shoot me in the back. That's the way you do business." He heard someone behind him yell "where are the other fellows?" Ray kept running.

He ran into the casino lobby and hot-footed it to the cashier's cage where two security guards were standing. "Call the FBI," Ray shouted to the security guards, who stared blankly at him.

Ray told them he just ran from two guys trying to shake him down. The security guards didn't move. Ray realized these guys were useless.

"I'll take care of that myself," a frustrated Ray said, walking away and looking back to see if Caifano and Delmonico were behind him. He didn't see them.

Ray hustled around the casino, always staying in the open among the people milling about. He found Alderisio and told him he was going to call the Feds. Still fuming over being struck by Delmonico, Ray talked to Alderisio to give the syndicate a heads-up about how he was treated.

"Look Ray, you've got a good reputation. Don't spoil it by talking to the FBI. Don't be a stool pigeon. You know a lot of people. You can get this straightened out," Alderisio told him. "I don't have it straightened out yet," Ray shot back.

Ray grabbed a casino phone and dialed Moe Dalitz, the mob-linked Desert Inn behind-the-scenes owner. Dalitz assured Ray that Caifano was considered a low-ranking hood now. That helped Ray make up his mind.

He figured he was right from the beginning – Caifano was running this extortion on his own without orders from Chicago. That meant the Outfit wouldn't strike back if he went to the cops, Ray concluded.

Shortly before 1 p.m., FBI resident agent M. B. Parker got the call from Ray and immediately headed over to the Desert Inn. Parker called the Clark County Sheriff's Department and a detective joined him. Ray told them what had happened.

Police located and arrested Caifano and Delmonico and found more than $20,000 in Caifano's pockets.

The news of the arrest of the hoods and their attempt to shake down and kidnap Ray Ryan quickly spread to Palm Springs. Ernie Dunlevie heard it on the radio and thought Ray must be frightened and in need of a friend. Dunlevie hopped into his airplane and flew to Las Vegas.

At the Desert Inn, he asked the desk to call Ray's room. The phone rang and rang but no one answered. That really worried Dunlevie. He asked hotel employees where Ray was. One worker remembered seeing him in one of the back rooms.

Dunlevie hurried to the rear of the casino and there was Ray sitting calmly at a table playing baccarat. Only a couple of hours after someone wanted to take him for a ride in the desert, Ray's first thought after getting away was to gamble.

These things roll off his back, Dunlevie thought.

Chapter 65

KEEPING RAY ALIVE

A Chicago newspaper reporter heard about the extortion attempt and reached Ray by phone.

Ray told the reporter that Caifano and Delmonico "told me I was only one of a lot of guys that were going to be 'protected' if they paid off – here in Palm Springs and some other spots. I was just one of them."

Asked if he had received other shakedown attempts, Ray said "yes – there's no use telling you where – but I didn't pay off and I never will."

A knowledgeable Chicago columnist, who frequently included inside information on the mob, wrote that Caifano's actual demand was $500,000 immediately plus $60,000 a year. *"Now, that sounds like the Caifano I know,* Steve Bagbey thought when he later learned of what the columnist had written. *"$60,000 a year from Ray would be chump change to Marshall."*

Caifano was an overbearing pain-in-the-ass in Vegas, a lifetime hood who needed to go to jail, and the FBI was eager to prosecute him. Agents debriefed Ray to get details of the extortion, making notes, asking questions, getting answers and asking more questions. Agents were sent to Palm Springs to interview people there. The Feds asked that sheriff deputies guard Ray because Caifano, Delmonico and Smiley soon would post bail and be on the streets.

The agents knew the key to the case was keeping Ray alive. The FBI couldn't follow Ray around the clock – or throughout the world – and recommended he hire his own bodyguards and disappear while agents built a case to present to federal prosecutors.

Ray quickly applied for a license to carry a concealed weapon and hired bodyguards including an ex-boxer and a former local cop. Additional bodyguards were hired in upcoming months, all tough-looking men who could be counted on in an emergency.

Joseph Charles Calabrese, a lieutenant with the Clark County Sheriff's office, was assigned to guard Ray during the investigation and eventual trial. After the trial, Calabrese quit the department and became one of Ray's regular bodyguards, following him to Kenya, Evansville and elsewhere. For more than three years, Calabrese stayed close to Ray.

Ray felt the safest places for him were Palm Springs, the Safari Club, Europe and Evansville. Later, he sometimes drove his Continental convertible around Evansville, jokingly telling friends "they are out to get me." He told that to the owner of an oil field supply company in the city then asked if the man wanted a lift. The owner turned Ray down, later saying he was unsure if it was because the mob was after Ray or Ray's terrible driving.

As Nevada authorities turned the case over to the FBI, Ray cleared up business deals in Palm Springs and headed to Europe, briefly leasing places to stay including a yacht in the Mediterranean. Mostly, he stayed at the Safari Club.

Ray was determined to follow through on seeing Caifano and Delmonico in prison. "Those guys deserve to be in jail and if I can put them in there, I am going to do it," Ray told friends.

Federal prosecutors convened a grand jury in Los Angeles in July 1963 and sealed indictments were issued for the arrests of Caifano, Delmonico and Smiley. Smiley was arrested in Los Angeles and Delmonico in Miami Beach that day. Caifano was arrested with his wife Sudi four days later while waiting for a haircut at a Hollywood salon. The couple had suitcases packed and cops believed they planned to flee the country.

The three men were charged with conspiracy and commission of the federal crime of interstate travel in aid of racketeering. A trial was set tentatively for October in Los Angeles federal court.

In August, an Evansville newspaper printed a story about the October trial and included photos of Caifano and, for the first time, Delmonico.

When John Stinson, executive vice president of First Federal Savings and Loan Association in Evansville, saw the picture of Delmonico, he immediately called the local FBI office and said Delmonico was the guy who had robbed the East Side branch of $22,800 a year earlier.

On October 8, 1962 a well-dressed man who said he represented the Better Business Bureau had walked into the bank and asked for the branch manager. The man then pulled a gun, ordered Stinson to open the vault, stole more than $22,000 in cash then forced Stinson to take a worker's car and drive him four blocks away before letting Stinson out to walk back.

Agents took Stinson and Diana Schraeder, the chief teller, to Los Angeles where they identified Delmonico as the man who robbed them. Police speculated that Delmonico was in Evansville in 1962 checking on Ray's whereabouts for Caifano and when Delmonico found Ray wasn't around, he decided to make the trip worthwhile by robbing the bank.

Chapter 66

THE EXTORTION TRIAL

The extortion trial didn't start until January 7, 1964 and by then Caifano had other legal problems in Chicago.

A week earlier on New Year's Eve, he and six other men were indicted for conspiracy to defraud an insurance company. Lewis Barbe, the Chicago insurance man in bed with the Outfit, was facing charges in another matter and feared for his life. To get out of those charges, Barbe turned informant and detailed a scam where the seven men bought steel wire worth $782, insured it for $48,000 then reported the wire stolen and tried to collect on the insurance. Barbe said Caifano was part of the scam.

Caifano had to put that matter aside to concentrate on the extortion trial.

Ray wasn't around when the trial began in a Los Angeles federal courtroom. Newspapers reported he was under heavy FBI guard at the Beverly Hilton Hotel while the El Mirador publicity man said Ray was on safari in Kenya. Ray had been secreted away for several days as Assistant U. S. Attorney Thomas Sheridan spent hours going over documents, conferring with investigators and outlining to Ray what he would be asked on the stand.

Ray developed a respect for and a friendship with Sheridan, finding him intelligent, concise and knowledgeable.

The 34-year-old Sheridan had spent years in federal anti-trust and criminal divisions and once was a special assistant to Attorney General Robert Kennedy. With Manuel L. Rule, a San Pedro attorney, expected to be named the U.S. Attorney for the California Southern

District, Sheridan planned to leave the office and go into private practice.[24]

Knowing Caifano was dangerous, Sheridan entered the nearly filled courtroom for the extortion trial flanked by four federal agents. Ray showed up to testify on January 16 with several FBI agents at his side.

In a calm, strong voice and flashing an occasional smile, Ray outlined his oil and business background, gambling with Nick the Greek and the extortion attempt. Ray testified that if he won anything from Nick it was only $15,000.

Ray's background as a high stakes gambler was raised by both the prosecution and the defense.

"I've gambled all my life – ever since I could afford to," Ray responded to one question. He said he was "angry, nervous and scared" during the shakedown by Caifano. Was he scared when he ran down the hall to escape the three men? "No, I was thinking. I thought I'd make my stand. If I was going to get it, it would be right now. I wasn't going in that car into the desert."

Defense attorneys hammered at him about hunting in Africa and his gambling.

"Do you frighten easily?" one attorney asked.

"Yes, I do," Ray answered.

"Are you afraid when you're hunting this big game?"

"No."

"Why?"

"An animal can't shoot back," Ray said.

"White hunters are killed by elephants, though," the attorney noted.

"'It's much less dangerous in Africa than it is in Los Angeles," Ray responded.

Another defense attorney went after Ray on his gambling.

"Do you gamble with friends or to make money?"

"I would gamble with anyone if I felt they could afford to lose and I could afford to win," Ray said.

---

24 Several years later Ray hired Sheridan to represent him in Internal Revenue Service and Justice Department cases. By then, Rule was a federal judge who would become a thorn in Ray's side.

"Do you get pleasure out of it?"

"Yes."

"Do you gamble to make money – if you can?"

"I don't want to lose," Ray said.

Sheridan had more than three dozen witnesses, but Drew, Alderisio and Lonnie Chadwick said they wouldn't testify and Sheridan didn't bother with them.

The day Nick the Greek took the stand, his attorney said a $1.5 million lawsuit would be filed against Ray over the rigged Flamingo card game. But in court, Nick testified he never authorized anyone to collect the debt. "I thought Ray would pay me, of course." At the close of the prosecution's case, the judge dismissed the charges against Smiley but not Caifano and Delmonico.

A break in the trial came the last weekend in January and Caifano hopped a plane to Las Vegas with a goal in mind – to be noticed by the authorities. Police picked him up for failing to register as an ex-felon and tossed him in jail, just as Caifano wanted.

On Monday, he was released on a $250 bond and returned to Los Angeles on Tuesday for resumption of the trial. There was a reason for making sure the cops knew where he was on Monday.

On that day, Lewis Barbe appeared at a brief hearing at the Criminal Court Building in downtown Chicago. The judge continued the steel wire fraud and conspiracy case because Caifano was still on trial on Los Angeles. The hearing lasted about a half hour.

The 32-year-old Barbe left the courthouse about 10:20 a.m. and walked a block north to his car. As he turned the ignition, a massive explosion rocked the vehicle. The car's hood shot up over the 45-foot high roof of a business in front of the car and landed 100 yards north of the structure. All the windows in the building were broken. The right door of the car was ripped off, the left door flew open.

Barbe turned sideways, threw his hands in the air and fell onto the pavement, screaming for someone to cut his shoes off because his legs were hurting. The buttons were ripped from his coat, his pants shredded and his hair singed. He told police officers who ran to the car to remove important papers he had in there.

An ambulance rushed Barbe to a hospital where doctors worked for two hours to save his badly mangled leg. Three to six sticks of dynamite had been placed under the frame of the vehicle and Barbe survived because the force of the blast was directed up and to the front of the car rather than toward the passenger compartment.

From his hospital bed the next day, Barbe told a Chicago Tribune reporter that the man behind the bombing was Caifano. "I know where this came from and I know who's responsible. It's Caifano. He did it to me because of what I was going to do to him in court. I don't know who actually carried out the bombing, but I know he engineered it," Barbe said.

He said he had received telephone threats at home and six times in recent weeks hoodlums came up to him on the street or in restaurants and blew whistles in his face as an Outfit warning against informing on the mob. Barbe remained in the hospital for months.[25]

Caifano's attorney argued for a mistrial in the Los Angeles extortion case because of the publicity linking Caifano to the Barbe bombing. The motion was denied and the trial in the Ryan case resumed.

On February 7 the jury took seven ballots to find Caifano and Delmonico guilty.

A week after his Los Angeles conviction, Caifano was back in court in Chicago for another hearing on the steel wire scam. Caifano wore a $200 silk suit with matching silk necktie and shirt and complained that the Chicago winter slush dulled the shine on his polished black elevator shoes.

---

25 Eugene Yocca, an ex-convict and burglar and a former bartender at Rush Street crime syndicate joints, later was arrested in the Barbe case but the charge was dropped because the only witness against him was another ex-convict. Yocca then pleaded guilty to burglary charges and was sentenced to eight years in prison.

Chapter 67

CAIFANO'S OTHER PROBLEMS

Ray received 1,000 telegrams and letters congratulating him for testifying against mobsters.

His spokesman sent out telegrams saying Ray "admits the gambling spirit burns brightly in his heart" but Ray had drilled "more than 1,000 wells in 16 states and later staked millions of dollars on a myriad of business ventures that have generated employment for more than 10,000 persons."

Caifano and Delmonico were sentenced at the end of March in the extortion case with Caifano receiving 10 years and Delmonico five years in prison. Both posted bonds pending an appeal.

A month later, Alderisio, Kolod and Alderman were convicted in Denver on the Sunshine extortion. Alderisio eventually went to jail in 1969 after appeals were exhausted.

In April 1965, Caifano and five other men went on trial in Chicago on the steel wire fraud case. One witness against Caifano had received several telephone bomb threats before the trial and was placed under police protection for a year.

The six defendants were found innocent. Caifano showed no emotion as the verdict was read while the other men jumped to their feet and shouted. A smiling Caifano was happy enough to run down the seven flights of stairs in the courthouse.

After the extortion trial, Delmonico returned to Indiana to face the Evansville bank robbery charges. His famed Washington, D.C. attorney Edward Bennett Williams produced documents of witnesses saying Delmonico was in Florida when the robbery occurred. Williams also showed that Delmonico had passed a number of lie detector and truth serum tests. In 1965, the government dropped the robbery charges against Delmonico.

But the bank official and Evansville FBI agent J. Robert Duvall remained convinced that Delmonico was the robber. Duvall studied the transcripts and polygraph test and believed Delmonico found a way to beat the machine.

Delmonico said he was in the invasion of Okinawa and Duvall knew that was a lie. Duvall was among the Americans who landed on April 1, 1945. Fighting didn't taper off until mid-June. Delmonico didn't get to Okinawa until August. There were other things Duvall knew Delmonico lied about. The FBI agent couldn't believe anything the guy said.

Steve Bagbey had talked often with Duvall about the Ryan case. Duvall was a smart, quiet, veteran investigator who didn't sugarcoat his beliefs or thoughts.

He was positive Delmonico robbed the bank and he hated when agents, attorneys and bosses upstream in the FBI hierarchy let some smooth-talking defense mouthpiece con them into letting a guilty guy go free.

Duvall later would be convinced that the death of a person extremely close to Ray was a murder even though the local coroner ruled the death an accident. But that case didn't fall under federal jurisdiction and there was nothing Duvall could do.

Caifano and Delmonico headed to prison in October 1966 when their appeals in the extortion case were denied and the U.S. Supreme Court refused to review the case.

Caifano's legal problems weren't over. He was back in court in 1967 with four other men on charges of defrauding a Crown Point, Indiana, contractor of $42,500 by providing him with $200,000 in counterfeit stock as collateral for a loan. Caifano pleaded guilty during the trial after prosecutors agreed the sentence would run concurrently with the Ryan case sentence.

Caifano now was a nonentity in the syndicate, stripped of power because, as one informant said, Caifano "was so stupid he can't handle something when he's told how to do it, step by step."

Caifano languished in prison as Giancana decided to step down as the Outfit's boss in the mid-1960s after spending a year in jail for refusing to answer questions, even after being given immunity by a grand jury. Caifano watched as Alderisio and Sam Battaglia rose to the top level of the mob boss for brief stays before going to prison, too.

Most of all, Caifano brooded in jail as Ray Ryan walked around a free man – and alive.

When Caifano was released in 1972, his chances of regaining his former mob status were slim, but his desire for revenge was too great not to succeed.

His rebound would be fueled by his hatred of Ray Ryan.

Chapter 68

EVERYBODY WATCHES RAY

After the extortion trial, Ray tried to resume his normal fast-paced life even while trailed by bulky bodyguards.

He hustled as fast as he could, building, promoting, thinking of new ideas to liven places up, make people happy and hopefully bring in some money. The extortion mess had gone on too long and forced him into a semi-dormant state.

It was time to kick things up another gear. But beneath the hectic surface there was a queasy feeling that Ray was plodding in quicksand.

He staged a White Hunters Ball at the Bermuda Dunes Country Club with a safari-style atmosphere that included a cheetah and other exotic animals.

He had an 18-hole golf course built at the Kenya Safari Club and promoted the Salton Sea Beach development that had brought in $10 million in sales over the past five years. To spark the El Mirador, he hired a belly dancer who was the biggest hit in Palm Springs since sunglasses, according to one columnist.

Daughter Rae Jean, moving to California to attend college after one year at Indiana University, was married in the summer of 1964 in California to William W. Hurst, an IU graduate and law student at the University of Louisville. Ray liked Hurst and when a son was born, they named him Ryan. It was a happy time for Ray.

But things just weren't the same. Dark clouds were starting to dominate Ray's life.

The Safari Club was losing money at the rate of $140,000 a year and there was talk of closing the club using it as a getaway for Ray and Bill Holden.

The El Mirador also wasn't doing as well financially as hoped. But the real problem was the looming presence of the "G."

The Feds had started an investigation of Ray around 1966 although Ray had no idea of that at the time. He was warned by Sam Giancana before the extortion trial that "you think you have trouble with those two guys (Caifano and Delmonico) wait until Uncle Whiskers or "G" (the government) gets ahold of you." Ray never believed Giancana had that much influence. But soon Ray was being hounded by federal and state agencies.

It was a local police agency that first found Ray Ryan worth investigating.

The Los Angeles Sheriff's Department had compiled an extensive secret file on Ray in 1960, collecting a hodge-podge of tips from informants, newspapers articles, credit bureaus' reports and background data dug up by the department's and other agencies' intelligence division.

The document was passed on to the Riverside County Sheriff's Department, the county where Palm Springs is located. They, in turn, gave a copy to the FBI. The FBI wasn't sure why the LA Sheriff's department had put together a file on Ray. More info on Ray was added to the reports in subsequent years.

The local department probably was reacting to the governor's commission that found more and more East Coast and Midwest hoodlums migrating to Los Angeles and Palm Springs. The investigators could have put together Ryan's file because his name came up in the Terre Haute bookmaking probe and he could have links to gambling operations in California.

Much of the information from the LA department would be incorporated into subsequent FBI reports on Ray. There were numerous minor factual errors and a lot of unverified claims by informants but it was clear what investigators were interested in – how Ray got his money and the friends he acquired.

Local authorities interviewed Ray in the presence of Frank Hayden, Ray's West Coast business manager, in late 1960 or early 1961 at the El Mirador.

They asked about John Rosselli (Ray said he met Rosselli years ago in Las Vegas but didn't know what business or social connections Rosselli had); Joseph "Doc" Stacher, the New Jersey hood who ran gambling operations out West (Ray said he met Stacher years ago in Las Vegas but couldn't recognize him now and didn't know Stacher's business interests); and Frank Erickson (Ray said he had known Erickson for years but didn't know Erickson's business connections).

For all of the talk about Ray's sharp mind and memory, he seemed to go into a dense fog when asked for details about his friends.

The local investigators compiled a ton of data about Ray including: Ray's oil company had a net worth of at least $5 million; he was a long-time friend of Frank Costello, Frank Erickson and John Drew; had known Tony Accardo for 15 years; had some connection with Sam Ferer, one of the nation's largest "lay off" bookmakers, and Carlos Marcello, the New Orleans mob boss; and had thought of outfitting a gambling ship between Acapulco and California and starting a quarter horse race track at Palm Springs.

Informants said Ray consistently associated with gambling groups. They noted Ray, John Drew and noted gambler John Moss operated poker and craps games at the El Mirador in 1953. Others said Ray specialized in gin rummy for large stakes and that sometimes Ray insisted on a new deck of cards each hand. "He has some way, either to mark cards during the game or by using marked decks, to cheat his opponents," one report claimed.

Another informant said Ray "is still nothing but a card cheat and a dishonest gambler" using one-way mirrors and electronic devices in rigged games in Palm Springs. Ray, according to the informant's version, used something like a hearing aid or an electronic device attached to his leg to receive impulses letting him know his opponent's cards. It was Goldfinger all over again.

Several of the reports' unnamed informants were heavy gamblers and the local police and FBI apparently didn't seriously consider the possibility that the informants were simply sore losers out to embarrass the guy who beat them.

Instead, the Los Angeles FBI highlighted Ray's mingling with racketeers and the continued claims of him cheating at gambling.

What helped stir that interest was a gathering in Palm Springs in October 1965 that newspapers called "Little Apalachin" when word of the meeting surfaced two years later. Ray was suspected of helping set up the Palm Springs get-together at the home of two Las Vegas showgirls.

At the meeting was Vincent "Jimmy Blue Eyes" Alo and Anthony "Fat Tony" Salerno, members of New York's Genovese family; Miami Beach bookmaker Ruby "Fat Ruby" Lazarus; and Jerome Zarowitz and Elliott Paul Price, who were associated with the $25 million Caesars Palace hotel/casino being built in Las Vegas.

Lazarus had refused to testify before the 1959 grand jury investigating the Terre Haute bookmaking operation. Zarowitz spent more than 1 ½ years in prison in the late 1940s for attempting to bribe two players to fix the 1946 National Football League championship game.

Authorities believed the Palm Springs meeting was to discuss laying off bets on the baseball World Series that was underway, how the ownership of Caesar Palace would be parceled out and setting up a better interstate bookmaking system.

And the FBI seemed to suspect Ray of rigging games even more after agents uncovered a sophisticated system of peepholes, binoculars and electronic equipment in the attic above gin rummy and poker tables at the Beverly Hills Friars Club in 1967.

More than $400,000 had been lost by wealthy businessmen and movie stars at rigged gin rummy games since 1962. In mid-1967, a federal grand jury indicated Johnny Rosselli along with a former part-owner of a Las Vegas hotel, a former casino operator, the owner of a Hollywood film service and a professional gambler. The FBI said spotters in the ceiling used electronic "shock" devices to let their players at the tables know what cards to discard and when to knock and lay down their cards.

Ray's name came up because Edwin Nathaniel "Pete" Gebhard, the Florida electronics expert, had installed the peepholes on the club's third floor.

Agents discovered that while Gebhard was in Los Angeles, he made telephone calls to Ray's El Mirador and the personal business office of Texas oilman H. L. Hunt. Agents suspected the calls could be connected to the Friars Club shenanigans.

The FBI report said Gebhard was an "extremely close associate of Ray Ryan, who in the past, was used by Ryan to operate illegal cheating devices." Agents planned to subpoena Ray for the Friars Club grand jury, but learned he was at the Safari Club and unavailable.

Testimony in the 1968 Friars Club trial showed that an industrialist lost $200,000, a shoe company owner $80,000 and other victims included singer Tony Martin, Zeppo Marx and comedian Phil Silvers, best known as Sgt. Bilko on television.

George Emerson Search, who helped install the peephole system, testified he had installed similar crooked systems since 1962 at the Trinidad Hotel in Palm Springs, the Flamingo and the Variety Club in Las Vegas and private residences.

Rosselli and four other defendants were convicted in December 1968 in the Friars Club case with most receiving four to six years in prison.

While escaping the Friars Club fallout, Ray was less successful against the Justice Department and the IRS, who focused on his mob acquaintances and money salted away in foreign bank accounts, convinced Ray laundered his and organized crime's money overseas.

The FBI had planted electronic eavesdropping devices around mob figures in 1962 and 1963 and had 23 instances where Ray's voice or name was picked up on bugs, but agents never publicly disclosed what they learned. The calls fueled more interest in Ray.

The Feds were ready to attack Ray at his core – the multi's financial empire.

Chapter 69

THE "G" CRACKS DOWN

It was time to gang up on Ray Ryan and federal agencies were eager to do so.

If Ray thought testifying against two gangsters in the extortion trial would earn him points with the Feds, he was mistaken. Everyone wanted a piece of him.

IRS auditors combed through Ray's United States operations trying to track his money but hit a roadblock in obtaining records from his companies in Kenya and the Mount Kenya Safari Club.

The U.S. Justice Department hammered away at getting the membership documents in which Frank Erickson had sponsored 18 members including Gerardo "Jerry" Catena, Thomas "Tommy Ryan" Eboli and Pasquale Eboli. Catena was an underboss in the Genovese family and Thomas Eboli the acting boss.

A federal grand jury in Los Angeles issued subpoenas to Ray, Frank Hayden, manager of Ray's California businesses, and Helen Hansen, Ray's secretary, for the records of Mawingo, Ltd., the Kenyan company operating the club.

Before subpoenas went out, Hansen was in the process of changing Erickson's name as a sponsor on about half of the membership cards in her office because Ray didn't want to embarrass the other original members: statesmen, political leaders and movie stars. At least three of the original cards were destroyed, but Ray's attorney told the Feds a short time later about them and other changes in membership cards by Hansen.

On March 5, 1968, Ray appeared before a grand jury in Los Angeles probing his income tax issue. He invoked the Fifth Amendment to any questions about his corporate and personal income. During that appearance, the LA assistant U.S. Attorney showed up and asked Ray what he knew about Pete Gebhard's gambling activities and rigging of games. Ray also refused to answer those questions.

In December 1968, another grand jury indicted Ray on conspiracy and obstruction of justice charges for destroying Safari Club records.

To deal with the growing legal problems, Ray hired the best attorneys around – Raymond G. Larroca and Herbert J. (Jack) Miller Jr. of the Washington, D.C. law firm of Miller, Cassidy, Larroca and Lewin. Miller was a former assistant attorney general in the Justice Department's criminal division under Attorney General Robert Kennedy until setting up his law firm in 1965. A member of Miller's law firm was Courtney A. Evans, a former FBI agent.

Ray also hired Thomas Sheridan, who had handled Ray's extortion trial for the U.S. Attorney's office, to help handle legal proceedings in California. Sheridan had left the Feds for private practice by then and was in the same law firm as William Simon, a former FBI agent.

The FBI tried to put the squeeze on Ray by asking that Simon be taken off the Bureau's Special Correspondent's List, which provided limited access to FBI documents and expedited responses to questions from people friendly to the Bureau. The agency also wanted to curtail Bureau info reaching Miller and Evans.

Memos bounced around FBI offices in Los Angeles that said Sheridan and Simon had represented a hood, backed by Meyer Lansky, seeking a license for Caesars Palace casino in Las Vegas. The memos added that Simon, Sheridan and Miller represented Ray Ryan and again brought up Ray's connection with Gebhard. The FBI nitpicking over Ray's attorneys had no measurable bearing on his legal problems in California, but showed the Feds' seriousness at causing Ray harm.

Ray's Evansville attorney Wilbur Dassell had died in December 1967 and when he returned to the city, Ray asked his barber to recommend another attorney. The barber suggested George Barnett Sr., who became Ray's attorney and confidant.

Ray soon was up to his ears in court dates in California and legal squabbles involving his oil company in Evansville.

His attorneys sometimes got hearings closed to the public and he had a phalanx of bodyguards and attorneys to shield him through reporters and photographers waiting outside.

After one hearing, Ray grabbed a persistent photographer by the arm hoping to prevent him taking a photo and dragged the photog along saying "let's go to the car. I'm going to help you across the street." The cameraman frantically tried to snap shots with the one hand as a smiling Ray trotted three blocks to his car holding the photographer by the arm.

When Ray reached the car, bodyguards blocked the windows and Ray hid his face behind a briefcase. The photographer did manage to get one usable shot of a smiling, panting Ray.

With the IRS on his heels, Ray bailed out of some of his businesses.

He sold the El Mirador in 1968 to actor John Conte and his wife. Four years later the Contes ran into financial difficulties, filed bankruptcy and were forced to sell the El Mirador still owing Ray more than $600,000. The once-proud El Mirador was turned into the Desert Hospital.

The Safari Club, where Ray already had spent millions, was in turmoil because of a labor dispute between club workers and management. The dispute was resolved with the personal intervention of Kenyan President Jomo Kenyatta.

The club remained open but Hirschmann sold his 10 percent to Ray, who continued to dole out membership plaques like candy to Palm Springs friends. "I don't think there was a person in Palm Springs that didn't end up with one of those plaques," one said. In 1968, Ray sold his interest in the Safari Club although he continued to spend months there each year.

Even more disastrous for Ray's ego, he had to stop high stakes gambling with his money drained by the Feds.

The fun days were gone. For the next three years, he mostly would be found in a courtroom.

In June 1969, the IRS filed a tax lien for $8.9 million in back taxes and penalties for the years from 1958 to 1965, tied up his far-flung U.S. business activities and bank accounts and cleaned out his safety deposit boxes in Evansville. Pending oil production deals and drilling contracts were terminated and Ray faced losing oil and gas leases.

More galling, he had to get the government's permission to visit the Safari Club. The Feds demanded Ray turn over financial records from his Kenyan companies and the Commercial Credit Bank in

Zurich, where Hirschmann remained president. Ray and his attorneys were unwilling to do that.

The IRS sent a letter to the Swiss Federal Tax Administration claiming Ray was "an established major organized crime drive figure" and that $1.9 million in "loans" from the Swiss bank "constituted the return to Ryan in the form of so-called loans having their source from proceeds of organized crime operations deposited in the Commercial Credit Bank by Ryan himself." Ray bristled at claims he was an organized crime associate or laundered mob money.

The IRS was attempting to convince Switzerland, the protector of the secrecy of numbered accounts, to provide information about Ray's transactions. Swiss banks generally cooperated if fraud or other serious crimes were involved, but not for tax evasion.

The IRS sought to link Ray to a criminal organization in hopes of getting the Swiss to hand over documents usable in U. S. courts. The federal government viewed Ray as a good test case to crack the stringent Swiss banking rules.

The legal haggling over Ray went on for years as his attorneys fought all Fed efforts in Swiss courts.[26]

Ray was being squeezed and it hurt.

He couldn't even caress his money now.

---

26 In 1971, the IRS won the approval of the Swiss Federal Supreme Court for Ray's Commercial Credit Bank information, the New York Times reported, noting the "Swiss court called the many objections of Mr. and Mrs. Ryan 'more technical than legal, more imaginary than real'." Thanks to Ray, the U. S. government made a dent in Swiss banking laws.

Chapter 70

TAX CASE CONVICTION

In 1969, the Justice Department's obstruction case over the Safari Club membership cards went before federal U. S. District Judge Manuel L. Real, who before being appointed a federal judge had handled the U.S. Attorney's office's briefs challenging the appeals of Caifano and Delmonico from Ray's extortion case.

Real wasn't in close contact with Ray during the extortion trial and certainly didn't have any warm and fuzzy feelings about him afterward.

Judge Real dismissed a conspiracy charge included in the Safari Club case against Ray in early 1969, but gave him or his attorneys few breaks the rest of the way. Federal appellate courts would be more forgiving.

Ray went on trial that summer in Los Angeles with Helen and Rae Jean in the courtroom. He said he wasn't feeling well but Real accused him of feigning illness. The trial was delayed at one point when Ray felt weak and was rushed to a hospital. His attorneys said Ray had heart problems.

Real rejected Ray's attorneys' efforts to have federal officials testify they knew before Ray was indicted that the Safari Club records had been altered because Ray's attorney, at Ray's request, had told the Feds so.

At the trial conclusion in July, a jury took 45 minutes to convict Ray of altering the Safari Club records and in November, Real sentenced him to three years in prison and fined him $5,000.

"As soon as I found out what I did was wrong (changing the membership cards) I notified my lawyer to go to the Justice Department," Ray told the court at sentencing. "I am not a criminal. I have never been a criminal and have never had a criminal background. The only people I really hurt were my family and my friends. I am truly sorry."

Ray choked with emotion and his eyes filled with tears. Helen and Rae Jean were sobbing in the audience. Ray immediately posted a $50,000 bond in order to appeal.

Less than two years later, an appellate court reversed the jury verdict and ordered Ray acquitted. The higher court said the government knew records were destroyed before the indictment was issued and that Real erred in telling the trial jury that the original grand jury was investigating conspiracy, travel in aid of racketeering, extortion, robbery and perjury when the charge actually filed involved only obstruction.

The Feds then went after Ray in 1972 for failing to file foreign investors' reports for his interest in a Jamaican development company. A federal court tossed out the charge a year later.

Only the tax case remained, but it wouldn't go away.

At the heart of the never-ending IRS investigation was Sommers T. Brown, the agency's chief trial counsel. Brown doggedly followed Ray's background for years, digging up every scrap of information he could. The IRS got a court to grant Ray immunity to testify but his attorneys fought the order.

The IRS said it had developed dates of deposits made to the Swiss bank but not "the original source of these monies which were deposited by Ryan. As of this date, there is no proof that this source is, in fact, LCN (La Costa Nostra) personalities."

That didn't mean the IRS gave up on the idea that Ray laundered mob money.

And Ray's problems weren't limited to dealing with the money laundering issue, but trying to make money while enclosed in the IRS' web of legal restrictions.

He looked for any deal possible even with the IRS watching over his shoulder and was swept into an Arizona land deal that would become the largest swindle in the state, amounting to millions of dollars over several years.

Ray's connection was Capital Management Systems Corporation (CMS), which peddled land for home sites – some of which turned out to be worthless to build on – to military and civilian personnel assigned to posts in the Far East.

Ray's daughter had divorced her first husband and married Robert H. Kaplan, who had grown up in Palm Springs near the Ryan home and first met Rae Jean when he was 10 years old. After having a daughter named Kelley, they divorced, but continued to live together at times.

Kaplan was president of CMS from 1969 through 1971. Ray put up the money to buy stock in the company; Kaplan owned no stock but Rae Jean had a 15 percent interest in the company.

The question was whether Ray put money into Arizona land deals because he was duped by others, had his own devious reasons for being involved or wanted to give Rae Jean and Kaplan something to do.

Land frauds weren't unusual in those days. Abraham Koolish, one of Ray's partners in the ill-fated RKO takeover, and several other men were caught in a mail fraud case in 1963 dealing with land in eastern Oregon. They were charged for mailing literature depicting lakes, mountains and water sports activities on 7,000 acres of desert-like land being sold for $395 an acre while actually valued by local officials at $20 an acre.

The massive Arizona land fraud involved Ned Warren Sr., who came to the state in 1961 virtually penniless and over the next 15 years formed over 100 companies with some selling worthless desert land as vacation home sites.

Warren already had a history of fraud from Chicago to New York and Connecticut. He set up dummy companies, palmed off worthless land and mortgages, skimmed the down payments made by clients, then sold the companies to legitimate buyers or filed bankruptcy.

Numerous other third-party companies, like CMS, were brought in to sell Warren's vast properties and became entangled in the scheme.

Also tied into Ray's and CMS' Arizona land sales was Don Eastvold, Ray's partner in the Salton Sea development[27], and Moksha

---

27 Eastvold and his wife Ginny Simms developed a resort on Lake Pelican near Breezy Point, Minnesota, that ended in bankruptcy. Merwyn Bogue, who was the comic Ish Kabbible and cornet player with the Kay Kyser band, developed the resort's entertainment program. Bogue also was associated with Ray and Eastvold in their North Shore development. Eastvold and Simms had a real estate development on the Baja Peninsular near Tijuana, Mexico, that newspapers in 1975 said turned out to be one of the largest swindles in that country.

Wendell Smith, a former assistant attorney general under Eastvold in the state of Washington.

CMS also sold land for home sites in the state of Washington with Smith's Wendell-West Co. Some of that land was unsuitable to build on. Ray and Smith earlier had worked together on a planned major development south of Palm Springs on land Smith bought from Ray.

The Wenatchee (Washington) World newspaper, investigating land deals in Washington and Arizona, reported most of CMS' initial Arizona sales people came from Bernie Cornfeld's former Swiss-based Investors Overseas Services that sold $2 billion in mutual funds overseas before collapsing in the early 1970s.

Smith met Cornfeld and top lieutenant Elmore "Mo" Cotton through Ray. Smith's people helped get CMS started with Warren as a land sales broker. Cotton became CMS president followed by Kaplan.

CMS sold land to American servicemen in the Orient for three different Warren developments, including supposedly rolling land that actually was hills and crags unsuitable to build on. Warren provided a letter from Arizona U.S. Senator Barry Goldwater supporting the land project.

Eventually Arizona cracked down. CMS filed a civil lawsuit in 1972 seeking $2 million in damages. Ray also was a major creditor in the 1970 bankruptcy of Smith's Wendell-West in Washington. Smith told reporters Ray had provided a $1.5 million line of credit for land deals in exchange for an eventual $3.5 million in return.

Arizona Republic newspaper reporter Don Bolles, who wrote about the Arizona land frauds, was killed in a car bombing in Phoenix in June 1976. Police said Bolles was investigating another matter, but was lured to his death on a tip that Goldwater and another congressman were involved in land frauds.

Whether Ray knew some of the land sold by CMS was useless for home construction never was made clear.

What was made clear was that even though Ray's once Midas-touch for making money was eroding, the IRS had him in a box and the Outfit hovered around the corner to kill him, he couldn't give up making deals.

The next one would be in Kentucky.

Chapter 71

RURAL KENTUCKY SANCTUARY

"This bed at home is starting to look real good to him," Helen told a friend around 1971 about Ray.

Helen endured his philandering – whether real or imaginary to her – with young women for years. Now nearing 70, Ray was ready for the quietness of life around Evansville.

He still spent months each year in Palm Springs and the Safari Club but needed an isolated place to relax where he didn't have to worry about the Chicago hoods.

Lake Malone located in rural Muhlenberg County in western Kentucky (between Evansville and Nashville, Tennessee) was an ideal choice. Muhlenberg County was in the middle of nowhere. The closest sign of life was the tiny town of Dunmor.

The only activities at Lake Malone were what Ray loved – fishing, horseback riding and boating. After his successful Duke's Ridge oil wells in Muhlenberg County, he had always wanted to repay the friendly people he met there by buying property in the county.

It was years later that Steve Bagbey got to meet with a group of Ray's friends from the Lake Malone days and understand Ray seeking sanctuary in that rural area of Kentucky. After talking to a dozen of them, Steve believed they saw the softer, generous, funny side of Ray and really liked the guy.

Ray told Bill Gorman, who ran Ray's Evansville oil company, to start looking for land in Kentucky. Gorman called Charles Paschel

"Pack" Stovall, a Greenville oil distributor, to see what properties were for sale in Muhlenberg County.

Stovall suggested the old Malone farm of 10,000 acres. A short time later Gorman called Stovall back and said Ray wanted to purchase the farm and was coming down. Gorman also warned Stovall: "Don't let Ray drive your vehicle, use your boat, even your canoe. Don't let him have anything mechanical because he will tear it up."

Ray showed up and Pack Stovall's son, Charlie, drove Ray around in an International Harvester Scout. Ray liked the vehicle and wanted one. Charlie called the dealer in Central City for a Scout. "Who's going to pay for it?" the dealer asked. The answer: "Don't worry about it." The dealer sent a new vehicle over. Ray also saw a pontoon boat he liked and had one delivered.

Ray already owned a farm on Orchard Road near Evansville with riding horses, but he fell in love with the Lake Malone property that was along two or three miles of shoreline. He said if the property owners along the lake would sell, "I'd buy every foot of it. It's one of the prettiest places in the world." He planned to carve out home sites and an inn nearby.

He needed a place to stay and one of several small cabins along the lake was for sale. Ray dropped by the cabin at 10 a.m. and found the owner Richard Pearson, his wife and kids there swimming.

Pearson showed Ray the cabin and said the price was $23,000. "That's a fair price," Ray told Pearson. "I will give you $25,000 if you get out of here by noon." Pearson turned and yelled to his wife "get the kids. We're leaving. We've sold the cabin." He loaded up his family and left.

Helen began making the cabin ready to live in, bringing in old mops, brooms and other household items she had stored at their Evansville home. They settled in and Ray never felt more at ease than in the two-bedroom cabin. No one, including Ray, locked their doors at night.

Ray needed someone to mow his lawn and Charlie Stovall recommended Hubert Joines, who maintained the lawns of many cabin dwellers along the lake. Charlie said Joines charged $15 or $20.

But the word was out that Ray Ryan, an old man with scads of money, had a lake-side cabin. Joines met with Ray, who asked what he charged. Without blinking an eye, Joines said $50. "Mr. Capitalist," Ray said, smiling and agreeing to the price.

When he was at the cabin and Helen in Evansville, Ray often walked two miles to Charlie's home for dinner. They'd sit, talk and drink for hours. If he had too much to drink, Ray curled up on a sofa in the Stovalls' cabin and spent the night. Ray never felt the need for bodyguards around the cabin even if he could have afforded to pay for them.

Ray's favorite outfit in cool weather was an old gray sweater and tan corduroy pants. The ever-neat Helen hated that ratty outfit and pleaded with the Stovalls to throw the clothes away if they ever had the chance. Charlie Stovall had a beard and Ray grew one, too.

Ray concentrated on building the inn. To design the facility, he brought in George MacLean, a Los Angeles architect and engineer who had designed the homes of many famous people, including the Palm Springs home of Ralph Stolkin, and the Acapulco Princess Hotel in Mexico. Before construction started, Ray wanted to get on the good side of local residents.

Many nights Ray and his new neighbors gathered to play backgammon tournaments for money. Charlie Stovall's wife, Sharon, was a novice at backgammon and wouldn't gamble with the rest but did play in the tournaments.

The group made a pact that if Sharon won any tournaments, everyone had to go to church on Sunday and put money in the collection plate. Sharon won her share of the games and Ray and friends went to local churches, filling a back pew and piling in a couple of thousands of dollars when collection plates were passed down the aisles. At one church, wide-eyed church deacons stared at the full plates in amazement then debated whether to keep the money. They did.

Ray rarely donated to established charities. He liked to say "if you need to help someone you go hand them the money or buy them what they need."

On one of the days Pack Stovall took Ray to the Kiwanis Club in Greenville, a representative of the local high school appealed to the club for donations to buy uniforms for the high school band. The club donated $100.

After the meeting, Ray told the band director he would pay to outfit the entire band.

When Ray flew into Nashville, Pack Stovall sometimes picked him up at the airport and they stopped over at the inn. When they were driving through Amish country along the way, Ray saw a store that sold saddles and they stopped. In the store was a punch bowl seeking donations for a family with a diabetic son needing a dialysis machine.

Ray pulled out a wad of bills from his pocket to pay for the machine, and got permission to meet the family and the boy. Ray was impressed with the family and offered to hand over more money if they needed it.

Chapter 72

THE INN THING

Construction on the inn started in January 1972 and was completed by the fall. MacLean designed the building with an African motif similar to Ray's Safari Club. There were small lakes, swimming pool, tennis courts, parking grounds for campers, miniature golf course and riding stables.

To oversee final construction, Ray hired a couple he met in Kenya who ran a safari tour company. The woman had majored in archaeology in college, and was fascinated by arrowheads she found when wandering the woods. Ray knew a man who made arrowheads on a lathe and ordered a dozen faux arrowheads and Ray spread the phony arrowheads around the area near the inn. The elated woman found them and made them into a necklace that she wore all the time. No one told her the arrowheads were fakes.

Cheap materials were used in the inn's construction because the IRS had the bulk of Ray's cash tied up. Stones from nearby creeks were hauled in by hand and used for the chimneys. The interior was decorated with African items Ray had or could get his hands on quickly.

Gigantic elephant tusks were shipped over from the Safari Club and placed in the inn's lobby. Kenya had a ban on removing elephant ivory but Kenyan President Jomo Kenyatta permitted his friend Ray to ship the tusks to America.

Bill Gorman thought Ray's grand idea for developing homes along the lake a futile project and he was right. Several lots were sold but there were no water lines and the county wasn't willing to extend them to the lake. Ray built the inn but abandoned plans for homes. Ray never asked the county for a favor to bring the lines in. "That's the way Ray was," a friend said. "When he was through with something, he was through with it. He didn't look back."

Accessible only by a winding county road, the 55-room inn quickly attracted guests. Groups from Greenville and Central City came for dinner meetings. Some of Ray's friends showed up.

Palm Springs mayor Charles Farrell, an actor who had played the father on the television show "My Little Margie," visited Ray at the inn. Older women guests oohed and aahed and crowded around to see Farrell, now in his 70s, as he walked through the lobby.

Charley looked older than rain, but was still popular even though "My Little Margie" had been off the air for 15 years. Watching the fawning women, Ray wryly noted: "Don't they know he's not Charley Farrell any more."

Ray befriended Glenn Robertson, a local painter of barns and signs who dabbled in art that he tried to sell for $25 or $30. Ray liked Robertson's work and took him under his wing.

One year Ray decided to take Robertson to Africa, and gave him a trench coat Ernest Hemingway had left at the Safari Club. Robertson returned and completed several large paintings of African scenes that Ray displayed on the inn's walls. Ray set up R&R Art Company to exhibit and sell Robertson's paintings.

Robertson adored Ray and always wanted to be around him. So did Charley O'Curran who frequently showed up to live off Ray's money for a while, playing cards and keeping Ray amused and teaching dance steps to kids who were around.

One friend recalled Ray and O'Curran fishing and playing golf at Lake Malone. "One would get a nibble and the other threw rocks into the water to scare the fish away from the other man's line. They deliberately tangled lines, laughed and kidded around for hours. It was the same when they played golf. They needled each other for errant shots and muffed putts, each trying to out-cheat the other on strokes."

Ernie Dunlevie, Ray's partner in a house development near Palm Springs, also visited the inn and joined in one of the gin rummy games with Ray and O'Curran. Dunlevie had brought along his 10-year-old son and during the evening, O'Curran took time to teach the kid some dance moves. "After a few drinks, Ray tried to learn the dance moves, too," Dunlevie said. "That's another thing Ray couldn't do is dance. He was the clumsiest fellow."

Ray liked to go out on the lake in the pontoon boat. The state prohibited swimming in the lake so he, Helen and friends would find an isolated cove to swim. Ray also purchased a speed boat and raced hell-bent around the lake. "Ray drove us around Lake Malone in that boat," Dunlevie recalled. "We kept running into logs and everything."

Charlie Stovall loved to water ski and Ray would pull him behind the speed boat. Once Ray decided to give Charlie the full treatment and pushed the boat as fast as it could go with Charlie hanging onto the rope for dear life until he hit a wave and was bounced into the water so hard that he lost his swimming trunks. Ray roared with laughter – after making sure Charlie was okay.

Friends across the world dropped into the inn at times to see Ray – Bill Holden, Ernie Dunlevie, singer Don Ho, golfer George Low and others. Rex Rand, "Sexy Rexy" as he was known, came by for more than a week with his Swedish girlfriend Ingrid Lange. Rand was a wealthy flamboyant Englishman, a Florida radio station mogul always chasing women.

Ray had met Rand years earlier in Florida and later in Jamaica where Rand had a home. Rand would die in an aircraft accident a few years later but Ingrid became a family friend of Ray and Helen and may have had advance knowledge of Ray's murder.

Carl Hirschmann also visited from Switzerland. The playful prankster Ray and the sophisticated Hirschmann lolled around Lake Malone reminiscing about the good old days in Europe and at the Safari Club.

They smoked Cuban cigars Ray kept in his cabin. Hirschmann wanted to know where he got them. Ray said he had a local source but wouldn't say who. Hirschmann badgered Ray for days, demanding to know where he got the cigars.

Finally Ray admitted he got them at Woodley's Market in Dunmore. Hirschmann couldn't believe a country store in tiny Dunmore would have such cigar delicacies. "Carl, go to the store and ask for Freddie. He keeps the cigars under the counter," Ray said with a straight face.

Hirschmann hustled to the store and asked for Freddie. The man behind the counter said he was Freddie and the only person who worked at the store. Hirschmann asked for Cuban cigars. "What are you talking about?" Freddie said. "I don't have Cuban cigars."

"Ray said you did," Hirschmann said. "Who's Ray?" Freddie asked. "Ray Ryan," said Hirschmann. "Who's that?" asked Freddie. Hirschmann said the Cuban cigars were kept under the counter. "I got some King Edward cigars right here behind the counter," Freddie said pointing to a row of cigars on a shelf.

Hirschmann argued with Freddie, demanded the Cuban cigars with no luck and stormed out of the store frustrated. When he got back to Ray, he ranted about Freddie playing dumb. A sympathetic Ray listened for a while then broke into laughter. Hirschmann realized there never had been any Cuban cigars at the store. He had been caught in a Ryan practical joke.

Another time when a little girl was left fishing with a pole off the dock while her father went in a boat with pals to fish in the lake, Ray went to a store, bought fish and put them on the girl's stringer. She proudly displayed her larger "catch" when her father returned. Ray just grinned.

While Ray pulled elaborate practical jokes on others, he wasn't immune to being caught in one himself.

As the inn filled with guests, Ray wanted to keep the land along the lake trim and neat. He was told goats would eat the grass and keep the land looking nice and that Hubert Joines had goats. Ray said he'd buy them.

Joines showed up with about 10 goats in the back of his truck. "Ten dollars apiece," he said and Ray handed over $100. Joines drove toward the lake. Later that afternoon, Joines showed up with another load of goats and Ray paid another $100.

Over the next week, Joines showed up once or twice a day with loads of goats and Ray handed over $10 for each goat. A couple of weeks later he decided to see how the goats were doing. He and a friend mounted horses and rode off to the lake.

Ray came back irate. He had found only about 10 goats during his ride. "You know I bought at least 100 or 120 goats," he moaned to friends. "Where did they go? Those sons of bitches, they have drowned, they have drowned in the lake."

His friends grinned at Ray's frustration. They finally told him that Joines had sold him the same 10 goats over and over. Ray roared in laughter. He loved a good practical joke even if it was on him.

When Joines' wife was diagnosed with a tumor a short time later, Helen drove her to Vanderbilt University Hospital in Nashville each week for treatment.

Ray paid for everything.

Chapter 73

THESE GUYS
NEVER FORGET

Ray's Lake Malone friends had heard him talk so much about the famous people he knew around Palm Springs that they had to see for themselves.

Ray and Helen made winter trips to Palm Springs and invited the people from Lake Malone to visit. Several made a few trips to Palm Springs to see Ray and Helen.

There was swimming in the morning, followed by lunch, golfing in the afternoon and dinner. Ray usually treated 20 or 25 guests to dinner daily at the El Mirador, the Racquet Club or other fashionable Palm Springs dining places followed by drinks and dancing.

Ralph Stolkin, Charlie Ferrell, Ardis Holden (the actress Brenda Marshall who was divorced from Bill Holden), wealthy attorney Seymour Lazar (later accused taking millions of dollars in kickbacks as a serial plaintiff in class action suits) and international financier of dubious repute Bernie Cornfeld were among the folks at the dinners with the Lake Malone people.

At one party, they watched as a morose Zeppo Marx leaned against a wall with a drink, oblivious to everyone around him. He was just divorced from his wife Barbara and the settlement had cost him about $6 million. Ray walked past. "What are you doing, Zeppo, looking for your $6 million," said Ray trying to get a smile from the Marx brother. Zeppo stared straight ahead with a blank, sad face.

At another Palm Springs party with Charlie Stovall and his wife, Sharon, Ray had a few drinks under his belt. When the band took a break, Ray headed for the piano and started playing and singing "Ace in the Hole." He was a decent piano player and that night he sang and sang. Helen listened until she had enough. She turned to Stovall and said, "Charlie will you go down and get Raymond John," the name she used when she had enough of Ray's antics.

While Ray feasted on the lofty atmosphere of the Palm Springs scene, Helen didn't. She thought many of the Hollywood crowd and hangers-on were phonies. She preferred the down-to-earth sensibility of folks around Evansville.

Helen told about a time when she had a pink diamond ring that was loose on her finger and she had to wear two other rings on the finger just to keep the diamond from falling off. Once while dancing with a man at a Palm Springs club, the man tried to slip the diamond from her finger.

Helen never again trusted many folks in Palm Springs.

She was happiest with Ray at the Lake Malone cabin. She was surrounded by good friends and they enjoy golfing, swimming and dancing. She was a good listener and had a sense of humor. Ray also enjoyed leisure time at the cabin.

"I think Lake Malone was what Ray was looking for," Sharon Stovall later said. "I think he was tired of the kind of life he had been living. You can't imagine how happy he was when he was on the lake in that two-bedroom cabin."

Lydia Herron, a frequent Lake Malone visitor and Helen's close friend, remembered playing poker with Ray one night, scrounging around for pennies to bet. She couldn't find enough pennies so they used wooden match sticks instead. "I never played poker in my life for match sticks," Ray said.

Later that night, he received a call from friends in Monte Carlo urging him to fly over to the casino to gamble. Ray talked for a while before hanging up. He knew the days of popping off for Monte Carlo on a whim were no more. His lifestyle now was playing for small stakes in Palm Springs or Lake Malone, and sometimes just for match sticks.

He still had a cache of cash secreted away somewhere, but no one knew where. When he first showed up at Lake Malone, Ray brought along a suitcase full of money to deposit in a local bank to meet payroll and other expenses of Ryan Oil Company in Evansville and to finance construction of the inn.

Later when county health officials cracked down on the inn for dumping sewage into one of the nearby lakes, Ray went away for a few days and returned with more than $200,000 in a suitcase to pay for the repairs to the inn's sewage disposal system.

Ray's money supposedly was being watched by the IRS, but no one around Lake Malone asked how he came up with so much cash so quickly. They were just glad he did.

They also enjoyed long evenings over drinks listening to Ray talk about his life and exploits.

He sometimes spoke about gangsters and the danger he faced since testifying against Caifano and Delmonico. Ray claimed he never liked getting into oil leases with mobsters because when wells elsewhere came in, the hoods thought they were due a share of those wells, too.

One evening, he recounted the meeting with Caifano and Delmonico at the Desert Inn during the extortion attempt and his running away to avoid a ride in the desert.

Ray jumped up, became very animated, throwing his arms about, saying he fled through the kitchen, tossing pots and pans around and metal racks behind him to block people chasing him. It wasn't the account in the court records but did make for good theater for his friends at Lake Malone.

But the Stovalls and others knew Ray was convinced Chicago had a contract out on his life. Ray had a fatalistic attitude. "Those guys never forget. It might take a long time but they get you eventually," he told his friends; then a dark mood settled over Ray.

There always seemed to be the thought in the back of Ray's mind that he might be killed in Evansville.

An old oil field friend remembered seeing Ray in Evansville on one of his infrequent visits and asked Ray why he spent so little time in Evansville.

Ray calmly explained. "I know they might try to get me here because they'd think they would get away with it."

Little did he know the groundwork was being laid for such an event.

Chapter 74

MAKING THE HIT LIST

Marshall Caifano walked out of the Atlanta federal penitentiary in December 1972, still seething at spending more than half a decade in prison because of Ray Ryan.

Caifano was released nearly a year early thanks to his cellmate Alva Johnson Rodgers, a long-time criminal who became a fairly knowledgeable jailhouse lawyer. Rodgers managed to find a loophole in Caifano's case that shortened Caifano's sentence.

The veteran Outfit hood immediately set out to renew old friendships in Chicago and attempt to get the lay of the land with the goal of regaining his lost power in that mob's pecking order.

By then, a loss of power was an Outfit problem, too.

In early 1973, federal Justice Department authorities and strike force investigators were cracking down in both Chicago and Florida with probes into gambling, prostitution, racketeering and narcotics.

Outfit leaders deserted or already had left Chicago.

Tony Accardo, Edward "Dutch" Vogel and others were in Palm Springs. Ronald DeAngeles, the electronic wizard and suspected bomb maker, was in New Mexico. Other hoods were in Las Vegas, California and Florida. Joseph "Doves" Aiuppa had to stay to run the Outfit on a day-to-day basis. Many people still believed Accardo pulled the strings from afar.

With the federal heat on, Caifano abandoned Chicago for a while and headed to Florida where federal agencies tracked him meeting with old friends Charles Delmonico, David Yaras and Frank Schweihs, all of whom had homes around Miami and Fort Lauderdale. The Feds believed Caifano lived briefly with Delmonico.

After things in Chicago cooled in a few months, Caifano returned to the city and lived in a townhouse apartment with his mother and brother's family. When Rodgers got an early release for himself in May 1973, Caifano sent him plane fare money to join him in Chicago.

Caifano was determined to have the Outfit sanction a hit on Ray but Ray wasn't considered a priority to anyone in Chicago's hierarchy. Caifano had to do something to make up the mob's mind for them.

He set out to handle he chores he was assigned. He collected street tax from pornographic businesses, kept the owners in line and used muscle to coerce independent porn shop owners into the fold. Outfit capo Joseph "Joey the Clown" Lombardo got Caifano and Rodgers involved in the operation of the Peeping Tom gay pornographic shop.

Also working at the porn shop was William "Red" Wemette. Red had been a secret FBI informant since August 1971. He ran the front section of the porn shop where the videos and sex devices were sold and Rodgers looked after the video machines in the back. Based on a recipe Red provided, Rodgers also manufactured butyl nitrate, an inhalant used by homosexuals to heighten sexual pleasure.

Red met Caifano through Rodgers. When they first got together Caifano was wearing baggy pants and was introduced as Johnny Marshall.

"Everybody had turned their backs on Marshall. They said he had screwed up in Vegas. After he got out, he went to Joey, said he could be useful, be his counselor," said Red, who became friends and had long talks with Caifano.

"Marshall was extremely friendly, open and honest. He told funny stories, goofy ones, and most of the time he talked about everyday life like golf and young ladies. He had a fetish for young girls, 16 and 17 years old. He liked to keep that secret. He had a voice like Peter Lorre. He talked odd. He always had a twinkle in his eye when he looked at me. He was easy going with me because I was on the inside. I never complained, never did anything (to rile the hoods). I was no problem to them and was a steady source of income. I never saw a mean bone in his body but you could tell he was vicious by the way he handled other people."

Having trouble with a man threatening to kill him, a scared Red told Caifano about the situation. Caifano told him to calm down and started laughing. "We'll fix it," he said. Caifano met the man at a restaurant and when Caifano returned, Red asked him what happened. "If the guy bothers you again let me know," Caifano said. Red said a short time later, the guy called him at the shop. "You're trying to get me killed," he said and quickly hung up.

Red knew about Ray Ryan because Rodgers said Ryan had to be killed, that Marshall couldn't sleep at night because Ray took too many years out of Caifano's life. Rodgers "talked more than anyone I ever knew. He just kept telling me stories. Joey hated him. All the guys in that crew hated him. Marshall kept him around," Red said.

Rodgers loved fire and explosives, Red said. "He said his stepfather bought him a chemistry set and the first thing he blew up was a barn when he was 15 years old." When he stopped by Rodgers' home one day, Red saw Rodgers testing a remote control device raising and lowering a garage door. "This is for Ray Ryan," Rodgers told Red. After Ray was killed in the Evansville car bombing, investigators found pieces of a garage door opener in the debris.

When Red talked to Caifano about Ray Ryan, the only thing Caifano would say was "that's unfinished business."

Caifano had more pressing business during those days in 1973 – proving his worth to Lombardo, a rising Outfit thug who had just turned 44. Cops believed that Chicago mob murders during that period were committed, initiated or sanctioned by Lombardo with final approval from Joseph Aiuppa and Tony Accardo.

Caifano once had the clout Lombardo possessed, but now Caifano was a follower not a leader. He wanted Ray dead, but couldn't order it any more. He had to regain his former prestige to exact revenge on Ray.

A step in that direction came shortly before Christmas 1973 with the unwilling help of Richard Cain.

"Only a town like Chicago would spawn a creep like Richard Cain," Chicago Tribune reporter Bob Wiedrich once wrote. "In his own mind, Cain saw himself a soldier of fortune, a daring double agent for the Mafia, a man so clever he could outwit anyone he met along the dangerous path he walked between two worlds – law enforcement and criminality."

Born around 1931 in Chicago, Cain often was identified by the FBI as Ricardo Scalzitte, the family's original name and agents hinted that Cain was the illegitimate son of Sam Giancana. Cain's Italian mother grew up in the Patch around Giancana who was three years older.

Cain attended high school in Michigan, and then went into the military. He was highly intelligent, able to remember details without committing them to paper, and fluent in a half dozen languages. He joined the Chicago police department in the mid-1950s, probably with the help of Giancana.

Cain was an aggressive cop soon assigned to the sex bureau where he directed police crackdowns on non-mob bookmaking and gambling operations, leaving the Outfit enterprises untouched.

He doled out monthly mob payoffs to cops on the take, keeping the figures in his head and reporting directly to Giancana. He ripped off money from madams and drug dealers during raids and shook down street criminals and prostitutes.

Cain's partner in the police department was Gerald Shallow, a union that eventually landed both in prison for different crimes.

Cain and Shallow worked undercover for Republican Cook County State's Attorney Ben Adamoski in 1959 to investigate Irvin N. Cohen, chief investigator for Democratic Mayor Richard J. Daley. Adamoski wanted to root out corruption in the court system.

Once Cain's shadowy work was discovered, he and Shallow cooked up a plan for Shallow to tell the Democrats about the undercover scheme, allowing Shallow to remain a cop and eventually be promoted while Cain was dumped from the force.

In 1961, Cain worked for a private detective with mob connections. Through Central Intelligence Agency contacts, he helped train Cuban exiles in Florida planning to overthrow Cuban dictator Fidel Castro. Returning to Chicago, he organized a group of private detectives supporting Republican Richard R. Ogilvie for Cook County Sheriff.

When Ogilvie was elected in 1963, he hired Cain as his chief investigator. Cain was back protecting the mob's gambling and vice interests under a different guise and in a more powerful role. He cultivated relationships with the city's top reporters. He led reporters and television crews on a raid that recovered less than $50,000 of $250,000 in drugs stolen earlier from a warehouse, allowing the mob to keep the rest.

In 1963, six men were arrested for robbing the Franklin Park Savings and Loan. The Outfit believed one of them had ratted out the rest. Cain had the sheriff department's lie detector equipment used to test the robbers outside the usual police process. One didn't fare well on the test and ended up dead.

After two years, Cain was bounced as chief investigator and started traveling with Giancana, who was in Mexico after leaving as the Outfit's boss. When Cain returned to Chicago in 1967, he was arrested and tried and convicted for his involvement in the savings and loan robbery and sentenced to four years in prison. Released in 1971, he rejoined Giancana in Mexico and they traveled to Europe and Caribbean, setting up casinos, gambling cruise ships, drug running and smuggling.

Cain became an informer and friend of Chicago FBI agent William F. Roemer, Jr. around 1971. Roemer was convinced Cain always told him the truth, but questions remained whether he did.

After a falling out with Giancana, Cain returned to Chicago in 1973, set up burglary and policy numbers operations and talked of taking over the Outfit.

It was then that the mob decided Cain had to go.

Caifano set up the hit by using Ray Ryan's name as bait, just as he and others had done years earlier in Las Vegas with Louie Strauss. It was an easy ploy to use because everyone knew how much Caifano hated Ray Ryan.

Caifano's plot was for Cain to go to Evansville and kill Ray, although no such contract hit was even contemplated at the time by the Outfit.

Cain told his old friend Shallow about meeting Caifano regularly at Adolph's Restaurant or at Rose's Restaurant on West Grand Avenue and about the plan to kill Ray Ryan.

Cain said Caifano told him approval for the contract came from "out west." Shallow assumed that meant the "retired" Tony Accardo living in Palm Springs. Cain didn't mention a specific figure for the hit, but Shallow figured the payoff would be $50,000 to $75,000 which indicated "Marshall must be back in good graces." Shallow didn't tell the FBI about those talks with Cain until eight years later.

Cain and Caifano were to meet on December 21, 1973 and travel to Evansville. Cain planned to use an M-2 automatic carbine for the job. That made Shallow suspicious because Cain had such poor eyesight that he and Caifano often had to drive Cain around the city. Shallow couldn't believe the Outfit would rely on Cain to shoot anybody with a rifle.

On December 20, Caifano and Cain met at Rose's sandwich shop supposedly to lay out the final plans. What they talked about isn't known, but Caifano later walked out of the restaurant.

Shortly after, two men wearing ski masks and carrying shotguns entered and forced patrons to the walls. One man had a walkie-talkie. Patrons heard a lookout outside say over the walkie-talkie that "someone is coming. All right, it's clear now." With Cain and the diners lined against a wall, one gunman placed a shotgun to Cain's head and fired, blowing his face away, then the men left.

Shallow got a call from a police friend and a short time later arrived at the restaurant. He couldn't immediately recognize Cain from what was left of him. Shallow believed the shooters were Joey Lombardo and Frank "The German" Schweihs. Others believed Schweihs was one of the men outside with walkie-talkies watching for cops. Shallow concluded Cain never was supposed to murder Ray and the idea was a ruse to set up Cain to be killed.

Newspapers speculated on numerous reasons for Cain's murder – his burglary operation competed with Outfit crews, members of Caifano's burglary crew had been arrested and Cain had tipped off the cops or Cain was talking too much to Roemer. Shallow would have another reason for Cain's departure.

By setting up Cain, Caifano earned the clout to ask for a contract on Ray Ryan, and pestered for – even demanded – the hit. Caifano apparently asked for the contract to be delayed a year until he completed his probation because he "wanted to be personally involved in the hit," as one FBI report later claimed.

Steve Bagbey learned years later that even when the idea of a contract on Ray eventually was set in motion, Lombardo proposed not killing Ray if Ray paid $1 million with Caifano getting half. Caifano reluctantly agreed.

The question was whether Ray would.

Chapter 75

RAY'S WORLD CRUMBLES

Ray's attorneys Raymond Larroca and Herbert Miller in Washington, D.C., and George Barnett, Sr. in Evansville worked feverishly trying to combat the legal net the IRS and Justice Department tossed around Ray.

They fought government efforts to grant Ray immunity to testify about the money in the Swiss bank and his Kenyan companies.

Federal agents interviewed Bill Holden and sought Carl Hirschmann for questioning. Ray's attorneys tried to negotiate a settlement in the tax case. By the mid-1970s, progress was made with all officials except one – Sommers Brown, who wanted to pursue the case to the end.

Always hanging over Ray's head during those years was the Outfit.

When at home in Evansville, he and Helen feared going to the door at night, never sure if the person there was a neighbor, friend or hit man.

There were periodic phone callers who said "Ray, this is a friend, the mob is after you." He didn't have bodyguards around anymore. He couldn't afford them with his money tied up by the IRS.

Ray felt sure the mob was lurking somewhere around him. "They're going to get me, I know it," Ray told one friend, and "if they get me, they get me," to another.

Concern intensified on May 27, 1974, when Bill Gorman went to the Ryan farm on Orchard Road in Evansville to go horseback riding. Gorman was found a short time later lying on the road with severe head injuries. He lingered in a coma for 26 months before dying on July 23, 1976. The death was ruled accidental.

Most people in the city accepted Gorman's death as a tragic accident but not Evansville FBI agent J. Robert Duvall, who was convinced Gorman was murdered. Gorman had kept Duvall informed of Ray's trips.

Duvall also thought Gorman an honest man who knew the inner workings of Ray's financial dealings and there were mob people who wouldn't want Gorman's knowledge made public. But like his conviction that Charles Delmonico robbed the Evansville bank, Duvall had no proof that Gorman was killed.

Several of Ray's mob acquaintances/friends – whose influence probably kept the Outfit from killing Ray for years – also were dead.

Frank Erickson died in 1969 and Frank Costello in 1973 from natural causes; Thomas "Tommy Ryan" Eboli was gunned down in New York in July 1972. John Rosselli's body, legs cut off to make it fit, was found in a 55-gallon steel drum floating in Dumfounding Bay near Miami in August 1976.

Also gone were other friends. Ralph Stolkin, his RKO partner and fellow Palm Springs resident, died in February 1973. Stolkin went though a 1967 divorce and bankruptcy and was ordered by a court in 1970 to pay $18 million and sell his yacht.

But Stolkin never gave up his flamboyant lifestyle even while dying of cancer. His Palm Springs home parties were lavish even during bankruptcy – Rolls Royces in the garage, expensive furniture in the house, the best of food and drink. "This is the best testimony to bankruptcy that I've ever seen," Bruce Cabot said at one party.

Soon Cabot and H. L. Hunt, two of Ray's closest friends, also were dead of natural causes.

In the summer of 1976, Ray was in Palm Springs when he got word that Benny Binion in Las Vegas wanted to talk to him. Ray and his West Coast business manager Frank Hayden flew to Las Vegas.

Ray went alone to Binion's casino where Binion passed along a message from the Outfit.

"Old friend, the word is out," Binion said to Ray. "Caifano said you caused him to spend 10 years in jail and he wants $1 million or steps will be taken to get even." Ray knew what "get even" meant – kill him.

But Ray couldn't come up with $1 million in cash even if he wanted to. "Tell Caifano he'll have to get behind the 'G'," Ray told Binion and walked away.

Ray paused outside the casino thinking and worrying. He knew this was his last chance to stop a murder contract, but that meant giving those bums his money, something Ray wouldn't do even if the IRS didn't have him hemmed in.

He and Hayden returned to Palm Springs. Hayden said he didn't ask what Binion wanted and Ray didn't tell him.

It was several months before Ray told Rae Jean about the $1 million demand to save his life.

A short time later in 1976, Ray flew to the Safari Club for a long stay. It would be his last visit there alive.

Chapter 76

INFORMANTS GUIDE

Q. Was Marshall more or less possessed with Ray Ryan?
A. Marshall was a very vindictive guy...It ate at him
the whole time that he was in jail (and) it was Ryan who was
still walking around.

Ray's murder had sent Steve Bagbey into an enigmatic world where nothing was as it seemed – a maze where turning a corner led to more turns with no assurance of what was ahead.

It wasn't a simple killing; there were no footprints to follow, no fingerprints that matched. What appeared to be a Chicago organized crime hit had a mind-boggling national and international flavor for the Evansville cop.

But Steve knew somebody had to know something and he had to continue his pursuit for answers.

More than three years after Ray's murder, Steve was reassigned in the city police department to routine bunco/fraud crimes – worthless checks, identify theft and bilking of banks – but called federal agents at times pushing for action to fill in missing details on leads in Ray's murder. He realized he'd have to find out more on his own.

In the summer of 1979, Steve, his wife Lynda and their seven-month-old son Sean visited Lynda's parents, Kellond (Hootch) and Sue Howton in Clearwater, Florida.

Frank Gulledge, by then a lieutenant on the city police force, reached Steve in Florida by telephone to tell him he could interview Alva Johnson Rodgers in Miami. Rodgers was a personal friend of Marshall Caifano, the only one close to Caifano willing to tell what he knew because Rodgers was facing other charges.

Steve and Gulledge had talked about a possible interview with Rodgers before Steve left on vacation. The city couldn't afford a full-blown trip to Florida but could foot the bill for a plane trip from Tampa to Miami for the interview. Evansville FBI agent Gary Perkins got the okay for Steve to talk to Rodgers and to stay at the apartment of Hugh A. Cochran, one of the Miami FBI agents.

The year before, sheriff deputies in Pima County, Arizona, had tracked a vehicle with stolen Illinois plates to a house near Tucson where Rodgers and a 20-year-old woman were arrested. Police found over 100 marijuana plants, a 45-caliber handgun stolen from the U.S. Marine Corps in 1964, a .22-caliber pistol and other items in the house. The charges were dropped after the car owner refused to come to Arizona to testify.

Rodgers and the woman left, traveling to Chicago, Florida and Boston where her parents lived. Later, Rodgers and the woman were arrested in Dade County, Florida, transporting 50 pounds of marijuana. The woman was released and went back to her parents.

Cochran and another FBI agent had questioned Rodgers in October 1978 in the Dade County Jail on the marijuana charge. The 49-year-old Rodgers already had spent more than 22 years in jails across the country on various charges.

The FBI summary of the interview Steve received was a little over one page. It gave brief details of Rodgers' relationship with Caifano after they were released from a federal penitentiary, his stay with Caifano in Chicago and Rodgers' concern the Chicago mob had a contract out to kill him.

ATF agents Frank Cook and David Carman also interviewed Rodgers in November 1978 and wrote a report of a page and a half – another example of two federal agencies covering the same ground and passing along a minimum of information to Steve.

Rodgers seemed like a common criminal to the ATF. He said he left Chicago in June 1977 with the woman, who he said was his wife, busting up the lab where he manufactured butyl nitrate for the Chicago mob as he left.

Rodgers and the woman went to Nevada, returned to Chicago, stole the Illinois car and returned to Nevada. They camped in an old gold field in the Sierra Nevadas until the weather turned cold then went to Los Angeles, staying at a hotel while the woman got a job hustling drinks at 77 Sunset Strip.

Shortly after Christmas 1977, they traveled to Tucson, Arizona, rented a ranch at the bottom of Raggedy Top Mountain and the woman worked at a whorehouse. (During his time with the woman, Rodgers sometimes offered folks around him the chance to have sex with her, which was Rodgers' way of trying to build friendships with people he worked with or met.)

Rodgers told the Feds about meeting Caifano in prison and that the Chicago mob didn't care for Caifano by then because of the bad publicity Caifano had generated. He said Caifano never discussed Ray Ryan and other Outfit members with him because he was an outsider, but he learned about Ryan because he worked on Caifano's legal case in prison. Rodgers told agents he only recently had learned about Ray's murder from an FBI agent, but didn't know who killed him.

Steve remembered mulling over the reports and thinking that Rodgers knew a lot more than he told the ATF and FBI.

Steve was thankful when Gulledge called to say an interview was set up.

Hugh Cochran picked up Steve at the Miami International Airport and drove to the Federal Correction Institute where Rodgers was held. Rodgers wasn't in the Federal Witness Security Program, commonly known as the witness protection program, but later would be after federal agents became convinced the Outfit wanted Rodgers dead. Rodger would become a good federal witness in several future mob trials.

Steve and Cochran watched Rodgers as he entered the room at the federal institution wearing a dark blue jail jumpsuit. He was six feet tall and about 190 pounds, but looked thinner than Steve remembered from earlier mug shots. Rodgers' hair was thinner, his high cheekbones sunken from too many years in prison. He had a long thin face, a sharp-pointed nose and jailhouse pallor.

Rodgers offered a limp handshake to the officers. He was polite, spoke in a soft voice with a Texas twang and seemed half-way cooperative. FBI agents had told Steve one topic was off-limits – that Rodgers and Caifano may have been lovers in the Atlanta penitentiary.

The 1979 interview started at 11:35 a.m. and ended over an hour later. The transcript prepared by Steve would take 29 typewritten pages.

Rodgers had been serving a seven-year sentence in the Atlanta federal prison for possession of counterfeit money and additional years for parole violation on a previous bank robbery charge. He was in an eight-man cell and Marshall Caifano, transferred to Atlanta from the federal penitentiary at Marion, Illinois, was assigned to the cell around 1969 or early 1970.

"I didn't know who he was," Rodgers said. "I knew he was somebody because a guy that I knew out of Miami came to me and told me to look out for him (Caifano), you know. He's a small guy. He's only about five-four and weighs about 140 pounds. I figured that he was organized crime." Over a period of time, they "became very friendly," Rodgers said.

With years in prison, Rodgers had become a reasonably good jailhouse lawyer. Caifano had Rodgers look into his case. Someone in the prison at Leavenworth where Caifano earlier was housed had found a flaw in the case and Rodgers came up with other ways to reduce the remaining two and a half years on Caifano's extortion sentence by a year.

Rodgers said the extortion case was built around Ray. "I believe from everything that I ever talked to anybody about that that Marshall was telling the truth about his case. I believe Ryan lied right down the line to get him convicted, but that is neither here or there."

Rodgers had Caifano's court papers from California and Chicago and talked to prisoners who knew anything about Ray. "I don't know what Ryan's reputation was in Evansville, but he has been a very high-lined professional card cheat all his life and in gambling all his life. What started Marshall's case was apparently Ryan ripping off Nick the Greek for six hundred thousand, and Nick ran to Chicago for muscle to try and get his money back."

Rodgers said Caifano was "a very vindictive guy. No one knows this better than me, you know, because it ate at him the whole time that he was in jail, the whole time I was with him in Chicago. It was Ryan who was still walking around."

Ryan may have gone along with the extortion scheme if it hadn't been for Charles "Chuckie" Delmonico hitting Ryan, Rodgers said.

Caifano told of meeting Ray in the Las Vegas hotel. "Apparently Ryan showed up for the meeting and Ryan saw Phil Alderisio in the hallway and (that) must have scared the shit out of him because he figured that if Phil was there, he was dead. So he ran to the security force of the motel and asked for protection and they called the city police."

Rodgers said he later learned that Caifano "was promised from Day One that Ryan wouldn't appear to testify. Apparently Ryan was tied in with some family in New York. I am led to believe by some New York people that it was Eboli (Thomas "Tommy Ryan" Eboli, acting boss of the Genovese family)."

Rodgers said the New York mob "had promised Chicago that they would pull Ryan off before the case came down and apparently Ryan was so incensed and so obsessed by Chuckie Delmonico slapping him that he didn't give a shit. It was more a matter of pride with him than it was his life. He went ahead and took the stand. Even with the people that he was associated with trying to get him not to take the stand; he (Ryan) did it anyway. And he always claimed that it was because Chuckie slapped him unnecessarily for no reason."

Steve listened intently. Inmates had lied to him dozens of times over the years, but he believed what Rodgers was saying. *Why in the hell hadn't some of this stuff showed up in those earlier federal agents' reports,* Steve wondered.

Rodgers told of being in New Orleans for his own hearing when Caifano was released on December 22, 1972. Caifano wrote Rodgers letters two or three times a week urging Rodgers to come to Chicago when released. "He thought he could help me. I didn't particularly have any place to go, a job or anything to do when I got out." Rodgers got his own remaining sentence reduced and left prison in May 1973, caught a plane and by evening had dinner with Caifano in Chicago.

Rodgers' ex-wife and two children were in Florida and he sometimes visited them. Caifano and his then girlfriend, Jayne Sanders, usually spent a month or six weeks in West Palm Beach and Key West each year. The 48-year-old, petite blond Jayne Sanders was the former wife of William "The Saint" Skally, a thief, gambler, bootlegger, counterfeiter and murder suspect who was found in his car with a bullet in his head on January 5, 1960.

Sanders later told federal agents she had known the Caifano family for 25 years from the Taylor Street area of Chicago. They developed a "relationship" as she put it and she knew Caifano was an underworld figure.

The woman told agents she never met any of Caifano's associates and he had been very good to her when she had surgery.

Chapter 77

TAKE THE MONEY AND KILL HIM

In Chicago Rodgers drove Caifano around. "We just hung out together all the time. We were always together, you know, either playing golf or going to the driving range or just riding or sometimes at his home or my apartment just sitting around bullshitting," Rodgers told Steve Bagbey in the 1979 interview.

Rodgers said that in late 1976 or early 1977 he started manufacturing a product with butyl nitrate called Locker Room, which was inhaled by homosexuals as a muscle relaxant during anal intercourse and to enhance orgasms.

Rodgers got $7,800 from "Marshall's boss" to take over the business. The boss, he later learned, was Joseph "Joey the Clown" Lombardo. Rodgers manufactured butyl nitrate and a portion of the income had to go to Lombardo.

Rodgers once turned $2,000 over to Caifano to give to Lombardo, but a couple of days later Caifano told Rodgers not to say he had given him any money if Lombardo asked. Caifano had used the $2,000 for something else and it put Rodgers "kind of in the middle." He knew he couldn't tell Lombardo about giving Caifano the money.

"Marshall is a very dangerous guy, you know. He gets to sitting around thinking that you might be able to hurt him and he's going to figure out some way that you don't hurt him," Rodgers told Steve. Rodgers also said he didn't want Lombardo mad at him and "it started preying on my mind."

One of the chores for Rodgers and Caifano was to muscle in on the wholesale pornography business in Chicago. Hanging around Caifano brought Rodgers into contact with Lombardo and other mobsters.

"Marshall at one time was on the (Outfit's murder) crew, you know. I don't know for how many years. Obbie (Frabotta) was one of the crew. The Saint (Vincent Inserro) was one of the crew. Giancana was one of the crew. There were five of them. Phil Alderisio was on the crew. Battaglia was the boss of the crew. Marshall told me all this," Rodgers said.

In May 1973, Sam "Teets" Battaglia died. Battaglia was from the old 42 Gang and he and Caifano were considered among the crew that used to handle Outfit murder contracts. Battaglia took over as the Chicago mob boss in 1966 but lasted only a year before being sent to jail for bribing public officials.

While Battaglia was in prison, the Outfit made him the absentee head of the West Side crew. Released after six years, Battaglia died a short time later.

About two weeks after Battaglia's death, Caifano was excited, Rodgers said. "He thought that he was going to get Sam's job (ruling over the West Side crew). They had a meeting. He came back home dejected. He said they gave it to another guy, a lot younger guy."

Caifano told Rodgers he could "get along with" the guy. Rodgers learned a few days later that guy was Lombardo, who was two decades younger than Caifano. Caifano starting hanging out more with Lombardo and pressuring to get Ray Ryan killed.

Two months later Rodgers heard the first conversation between Lombardo and Caifano about Ray. Caifano frequently brought up Ryan's name and the answer was the same, Rodgers said. "I heard Joey at least five or six times tell Marshall that they were working on Ryan. Apparently Ryan was a very paranoid guy with good reason, you know. Ryan expected to get killed the day that he took the stand and I guess up to the day he died he was apparently very hard to set up, you know. He must have been super careful all the time."

Lombardo claimed that while Caifano was in prison the mob was tracking Ryan. "Someone even followed Ryan to Africa or some place trying to set him up. Ryan apparently had some kind of safari partnership with William Holden and they were using it to cheat people at cards, you know. If Marshall was telling the truth, they worked on Ryan for like twelve years, probably not every day but periodically. They would send somebody out to check on him and see what his habits were."

Rodgers said one day Lombardo told Caifano they had come up with an idea to get revenge against Ryan without killing him. That came during one of the frequent meetings of Caifano, Lombardo and others at a driving range in the Chicago suburb of Addison.

"Joey approached Marshall one day and he said 'listen we may be able to approach Ryan for a settlement. There was some talk about Ryan making a settlement for a million dollars for us to leave him alone. If we got the million off of him, we would give you half of it if you want to go for it'."

"Let's take the million and hit him anyway" shot back Caifano. Lombardo said if they gave their word to the go-between making the offer "we're going to have to live up to it. You got to make up your mind to let the guy alone for the rest of his life if the deal goes through."

Caifano eventually told Lombardo to go ahead and get a million dollars from Ryan. "Marshall was hurting for money. Marshall was broke when he came out of the joint," Rodgers said. He said police officials later told him that Benny Binion had pitched the proposal to Ray.

Ryan never agreed to pay the money, otherwise "I would have heard it immediately if there had been a settlement," Rodgers said. "Marshall would have come and told me. Not only that, from his spending every time, if he came into a half a million dollars there would be spending."

Rodgers didn't know who killed Ray. "There is probably any one of a hundred people in this United States that could have wanted to kill Ryan. He has been a card cheat all of his life. But I know positively from first hand knowledge that the Chicago Outfit intended for years to kill Ryan. Whether they did it or not, I don't know. I know that they were working on doing it because I heard not once, but a number of times, promises made to Marshall that he (Ryan) was going to be killed."

If Chicago killed Ryan, Lombardo had to order it, Rodgers said. "Joey is the one that ordered all the hits in Chicago, the one that puts them (contracts) out on the street. If Ryan was killed by Chicago, Joey might not have done it, probably didn't do it, but he ordered it."

Rodgers said Caifano was acting hyper in early 1977 and Rodgers was getting paranoid himself. Working around the butyl nitrate was tearing him up physically. He was bleeding internally, was getting weak and wanted out of the business but Caifano wouldn't let him out.

In June, 1977, "I figured fuck it. I just went and got all my shit and that night I rented a truck and took all my stuff to Reno, Nevada, and stored it. I haven't seen Marshall or anybody else in Chicago since." Rodgers said Chicago put a contract out on him for abandoning the butyl nitrate operation.

Cochran and Steve concluded the interview asking Rodgers about various vehicles witnesses had seen in Evansville at the time of the car bombing and the names of mob members who may have been involved in the murder. Rodgers offered no help in those areas.

Rodgers said ATF agents out of Indiana had told him the bomb that killed Ryan was triggered by radio control and asked if that was true. Cochran and Steve wouldn't comment.

Cochran and Steve thanked Rodgers and left. Steve wished he had asked Rodgers whether he and Caifano had been lovers in prison just to see Rodgers' reaction.

That evening, Cochran took Steve to the Miami Playboy Club. The first club opened in Chicago in 1960 and the second one in Miami in 1961. They sat at the bar and Cochran pointed out FBI agents and Miami mob guys in the crowd.

Next to Steve was an old man. As the man put a drink to his lips, Steve noticed a faded tattoo on the man's arm. It was the first time Steve had been close to anyone from one of the World War II concentration camps. Steve remembered his father talking about his anger at the Germans when he found out about the concentration camps while serving in the military in Europe during World War II.

The old man noticed Steve looking at his arm. "You know what this is," the man asked in a broken accent, pointing to his tattoo. "Treblinka," the man said. He told about the infamous German extermination camp in Poland and his family members who died there. "Young man, I hope you never forget," the man said. "Sir, don't worry. I'll never forget," Steve said.

The man asked what Steve did. Steve said he was a police officer from Indiana working on an organized crime murder. They talked a little longer before the old man got up to leave. "I wish you luck," he told Steve.

As the man walked away, Steve knew the troubles he had with the Ryan murder case paled in comparison to what the old man had been through.

Chapter 78

FIRST CAIN, THEN RAY

Early in the Ryan investigation, Steve Bagbey had heard about Aladena J. "Jimmy the Weasel" Fratianno, but Gerald Thomas Shallow's name didn't pop up until 1981.

Fratianno was the famous one – a mob hitman who, in part because of Caifano, became a FBI informant shortly after Ray was murdered and went on to send major hoods to prison.

Intimate with West Coast, East Coast and Chicago mob inter-actions and even acting boss in Los Angeles for a while, Fratianno had committed a string of gangland murders and knew about more.

Shallow was less visible, his knowledge less expansive, but offered an intriguing look into the Outfit's inner workings.

In the spring of 1981, Chicago FBI agents John J. "Jack" O'Rourke and Robert Pecoraro arrived at Shallow's neat ranch-style bungalow near Chicago to question him about armed robberies and jewelry thefts he was believed involved in.

In his fifties, Shallow was on a leave of absence as a sergeant on the Chicago police department amid an investigation that he stole a car. While on leave, he earned money by stealing. The agents also wanted to ask about a murder in Indianapolis, but planned to wait until later in the conversation.

Chicago reporters called O'Rourke "Father O'Rourke" because of his success in getting criminals to flip and confess to crimes. He didn't have to work hard earning that reputation with Shallow, who sur-prised O'Rourke by his openness.

As the interview progressed, Shallow asked O'Rourke "Jack, aren't you going to ask me about that murder?" Shallow then described the

1972 murder in Indianapolis of a crime syndicate gangster's girlfriend, saying he drove the car and Richard Cain shot and killed the woman.

Shallow couldn't have been more willing. He detailed the crimes he was involved in or knew about, a treasure trove of information from a busy thief, shakedown artist and murderer who doubled as one of Chicago's finest.

O'Rourke grew to have a bit of respect for Shallow over the next few months as Shallow told about his life of crime. "He never bulls-hitted us," said O'Rourke. "I never had a guy more honest who was so immoral."

Shallow told about the crew of thieves he worked with and about a guy he had trouble with over a truck scam. Shallow set up a meeting to kill the guy, but didn't because the man showed up with his wife and kids. Shallow decided to shake the guy down for money instead. He couldn't blow the man away in front of his family.

On April 27, 1981, O'Rourke and Agent John T. Dolan interviewed Shallow at Caesar's Inn motel in a Chicago suburb. The main topic was the December 20, 1973 murder of Richard Cain, one of the most fascinating figures ever to disgrace the Chicago police department.

Shallow had joined the department in 1953, serving as a patrol-man then plainclothes officer until assigned to the detective bureau in September 1955. He worked narcotics, cartage detail and general crime duties until being transferred to the sex bureau in 1957 where he teamed with Cain. They remained partners until Shallow was assigned to the robbery detail in 1960.

Shallow told of him and Cain working with the Republicans against Richard Daley's Democratic city machine, Cain becoming the state attorney office's chief investigator and then joining Sam Giancana in March or April of 1972 in Mexico as his driver, bodyguard and interpreter. Giancana pulled in skim money from Las Vegas, cash from Caribbean gambling boats and the two traveled across the world setting up money-making casinos, scams and drug deals.

When he returned to Chicago, Cain stayed with the nephew of Sam Battaglia, who asked Cain to look after the nephew because he wasn't too smart and needed to be kept out of trouble.

Shallow drove Cain to meals and meetings. Cain told of having frequent meetings with Caifano and that Caifano gave him a contract to kill Ray Ryan. Shallow didn't trust Caifano and warned Cain to "be wary of him."

Cain had his own suspicions about Caifano, recounting driving around one night with Caifano and stopping at Alderisio's house to check on Alderisio's boy who was a drug addict. The house was on a dark street. "I wondered out loud if he intended to murder me or set me up," Cain told Shallow. A car suddenly went past them as they walked along the dark street, but nothing happened. There were no gunshots, but Cain still had doubts about Caifano.

The day before Cain was killed Shallow drove him to Rose's restaurant to meet Caifano around 2 p.m. and talk more about killing Ray. Caifano was to bring the money for the contract to the restaurant the next day.

Shallow didn't drive Cain to the restaurant that fateful Thursday and didn't know how Cain got there. When he went to the restaurant after the shooting, Shallow couldn't recognize Cain because his face was shot away. That vision stayed forever with Shallow.

He believed Cain was killed because he had publicly embarrassed Gus Alex, one of the syndicate's money-makers and political fixers, during a meeting on the city's North Side. Cain called Alex a "jag off," "an asshole" and other disparaging terms in front of other mob members. "That's considered the deepest kind of insult," Shallow said.

Cain had believed he was immune from retribution because of his friendship with Giancana. Shallow knew that was a mistake, later learning from the street that Alex got permission to have Cain killed and Caifano got the contract.

Cain's murder elevated Caifano's standing in the Outfit and, as a reward, the mob authorized the hit on Ryan, Shallow said.[28]

While Caifano's thirst for revenge might have been sated with the bombing of Ray Ryan in 1977, Caifano never again would play a major role in Chicago's mob.

In 1980, Caifano was convicted of conspiracy and interstate transportation of blank stock certificates that had been stolen in 1968 from Chicago's O'Hare Airport. Caifano and other hoods were charged

---

28 In 1982, Shallow pleaded guilty to the Indianapolis murder and was sentenced to 10 years in prison. He went into the federal witness protection program and testified at later mob trials.

with moving the stolen securities a decade later from Florida to Texas and trying to sell them. Caifano also was charged as a dangerous special offender, or a habitual criminal. He received two concurrent 20 year prison sentences and served 10 years.

After Ray's murder, the once deadly Caifano ended up simply a footnote during that period of the Outfit's history.

Chapter 79

THE WEASEL DIDN'T KNOW ALL

Steve Bagbey knew about Aladena "Jimmy the Weasel" Fratianno from newspaper clippings and magazine articles when Fratianno became a federal informer.

Steve's interest in talking to Fratianno himself was heightened after the FBI had debriefed Fratianno following Ray's car bombing. The tidbits that the agency passed along to Steve were about Fratianno's meeting at a Chicago restaurant with Caifano, Lombardo and Frabotta in 1975 or 1976, months before Ray was murdered.

Before the restaurant meeting, the previous time that Fratianno had seen Caifano was around 1954. Caifano had served his prison sentence for the Ryan extortion and by the mid-1970s Caifano's status had plummeted. Fratianno learned Caifano was getting $400 a week, and spending most of his time playing golf. Meanwhile, Lombardo was entrenched near the top of the syndicate's heap; Frabotta was, as usual, a dependable soldier even as his health deteriorated.

At the restaurant, Fratianno thought Caifano was angry at Joey Aiuppa, the Outfit leader, and knew why. "What is happening with Ray Ryan," Fratianno asked. "You know, I am a little peeved because they ain't got him number one on the hit parade," Caifano said. "Don't worry. Take it easy. It will come," Lombardo told Caifano. Nothing else was said about Ray as they ordered something to eat.

Steve wanted to dig deeper into what Fratianno knew and talk to the hood-turned-informer, but federal task force attorneys deflected his inquiries. Fratianno could reel in more important gangsters than a murder in Evansville – and generate a lot more good publicity for the Feds.

Fratianno was a mobster's mobster deeply entrenched in the syndicates and their inner workings. He worked with and for New York and Chicago mobs and tried to put backbone into the sometimes bumbling Los Angeles family.

Born in Italy, Fratianno moved with his family to America when he was four months old. He migrated to Los Angeles in 1946 and got into gambling, shylocking and race track bookmaking. Catching the eye of the Los Angeles crime syndicate headed by Jack Dragna, he became a member in late 1947 or early 1948. Around 1960, Fratianno continued to live in California but was loaned out to the Chicago Outfit at times for jobs, including murder. He was transferred back to the Los Angeles around 1975.

While Steve wanted his own sit-down with Fratianno, there wasn't much Steve could do on his own three years after Ray was murdered. Evansville was running out of money and the city couldn't afford to send Steve across the country for interviews.

Evansville by then was in the same fix as other American cities. Federal funds to local communities, which often were used to pay for day-to-day expenses, had dried up. Now the cities were forced to dip into sparse local tax money to make up the shortfall in revenue.

It would be another two years before Evansville reached the breaking point and had to lay off hundreds of employees along with slapping a moratorium on pay increases and sharply curtailing spending to keep its financial head above water.

The city did send Steve to the FBI National Academy in Quantico, Virginia in June 1980, but instead of paying for him to fly, Steve drove a city vehicle – a 1974 Chevy Nova with a damaged left back fender. The driver's floorboard was gone and a garage worker had welded a stop sign on the floor to prevent Steve's feet from slipping through.

The academy offers training for young FBI agents and local and state police officers from across the country involved in organized crime investigations. Steve had set a goal of getting to the FBI academy before he was 32 years old. He graduated from the 13-week course on September 12, 1980, just days before his 32nd birthday.

Steve's room at the academy was a social hub where officers talked about their cases. Wisconsin officers brought cheese, California cops wines. Steve talked about the Ryan murder several times with Terry Walters, chief deputy U.S. Marshal from Iowa; Richard Wright, a lieutenant with the LA police department's organized crime section; and John O'Brien, then a detective with the New York police department's bank robbery and organized crime task force.

O'Brien filled Steve in on Frank Costello, Wright knew all about the California mob and Walters and another marshal had guarded Fratianno when he was being debriefed at a safe house in the Washington, D.C., area. Steve later learned Fratianno had been at an academy office for one debriefing session at the same time he was on the campus. So close, yet so far.

Steve was delighted, however, when he learned about Fratianno, Alva Johnson Rodgers and FBI agent Jack O'Rourke testifying at Caifano's dangerous special offender hearing in a Florida federal court earlier in 1980.

O'Rourke told the court that Caifano was suspected in the murders of Ray Ryan and Richard Cain and the attempted murder of Louis Barbe in 1964. Steve could only smile. It was the first time a federal agent had indicated Caifano was involved in the murder of Ray Ryan.

O'Rourke testified Caifano returned to illegal bookmaking and gambling within a month of his release from prison, financed illegal bookmaking operations and was involved in extortion of pornography businesses. Alva Johnson Rodgers told the judge that Caifano boasted he was part of the Outfit since he was 19, a hit-man and that Lombardo had killed Cain.

Fratianno testified that he met Caifano, aka Johnny Marshall, in Las Vegas in 1952 where Caifano had an apartment. Louis Dragna, the nephew of Jack Dragna, introduced Caifano, the Outfit's new man in Las Vegas, to Fratianno. Caifano gambled at the Desert Inn, played golf, bought land around Las Vegas and reported directly to the Outfit boss, Fratianno said.

In Ovid Demaris' book "The Last Mafioso" about Fratianno's life, Fratianno described the murder of Louis "Russian Louie" Strauss, who had become a danger to Benny Binion and had to be eliminated.

Fratianno met with Caifano and Alderisio in Las Vegas and was introduced by Caifano to Strauss in the Desert Inn lobby.

Fratianno had to get Strauss to California to kill him because of the mob prohibiting murders in Nevada. Fratianno told Strauss that Ray Ryan owed him $400,000 or so and they would go to Palm Springs to get the money. Strauss, who knew Ray, was to tag along to convince Ray to pay.

When Strauss briefly left the group, Caifano said he wanted a five-carat diamond ring that Strauss was wearing. "Okay, no problem," said Fratianno. Caifano wasn't going along on the ride. "Jimmy, I will send Phillip (Alderisio) with you."

Fratianno and Alderisio drove Strauss to his home to pick up a bag then they drove to a city in California where seven men waited and Strauss was garroted. Fratianno and Alderisio returned to Las Vegas to set up alibis while the other men disposed of the body. Caifano didn't get Strauss' ring. "He left it at home," Fratianno told Caifano. Fratianno was investigated for the Strauss killing, but never charged.

Fratianno had little to do with Caifano for a quarter century after that murder. Fratianno later faced extortion, robbery and other charges and landed in prison several times. After being released in 1973, he took money occasionally from the Feds but made a living on gambling and shylocking.

It was four years later that he seriously considered becoming a FBI informant, thanks to Marshall Caifano.

During late summer or early fall of 1977, Fratianno in San Francisco received word from Frabotta to call Johnny Marshall in Chicago. Fratianno said Caifano asked him to come to Chicago.

The incident was recounted in Demaris' book about Fratianno. "I want you to go see the old man (the Outfit's boss) and talk to him about taking (and introducing) me to Benny Binion. There are some other things that I would like to talk to you about. I will even send you a ticket," Caifano said. That was ridiculous, Fratianno thought. Something wasn't right. Hell, Caifano didn't need him for an introduction to Binion.

"If you want to talk to me, number one you can't call me. You have to go through my boss (James Brooklier, then head of the Los Angeles family)," Fratianno said in the book. "You come out here. I will meet you at the airport, meet you at Palm Springs. You know Benny Binion better than I do." Caifano hemmed and hawed at flying to California. "I'll talk to you later," Caifano finally said.

The hairs bristled on Fratianno's neck. He had been in the mob 32 years. You can't bullshit a bullshitter. He knew the Outfit wanted him dead. Caifano must think he was an idiot.

During the following weeks, a FBI agent friendly with Fratianno warned him that agents had seen a couple of mob hitmen trailing him. One was Joey Hansen, the Chicago mobster sent to California years ago and who may have been involved in the car bombing of Ray Ryan.

Fratianno switched sides and the FBI acquired a valuable informant.

After Quantico, Steve continued efforts to talk to Fratianno. He sent a letter in 1981 to James D. Henderson, the attorney in charge of the U.S. Department of Justice's Los Angeles Strike Force, seeking permission to talk to Fratianno and including a series of questions he wanted to ask.

In April 1981, Henderson responded with a letter that concluded by saying: "In view of the paucity of knowledge he (Fratianno) seems to have concerning your investigation, it would appear that time and expense economies would not dictate a necessity for a specially arranged interview. As an experienced investigator, I know you also understand that marginally necessary and unnecessary interviews of witnesses like Mr. Fratianno can potentially subject significant prospective prosecutions, and, more important, attained convictions to potential additional witness impeachment problems and the possibility of new trial motions which could cause serious problems for the government." What gibberish, Steve thought. He couldn't interview Fratianno. Solving Ray's murder didn't stir a nibble on the federal pond, Steve concluded.

Henderson sent along the transcript of Fratianno's testimony in the Caifano hearing and very brief handwritten responses of Fratianno's answers to the 24 questions Steve had submitted.

Fratianno said he knew Ryan "well from Las Vegas and Los Angeles. Ryan was a hustler and scam artist," didn't have a known role with the Outfit, was acquainted with Johnny Marshall, Johnny Rosselli and Alderisio but had no known ties with Giancana.

Fratianno said Charles Delmonico couldn't have played a role in Ryan's death because Delmonico was not a made member of the Chicago family. Fratianno didn't know who killed Ray, didn't know about Chicago wanting $1 million from Ray, what role Binion had in the Ryan case or if Ray had ties with the New York families. Fratianno didn't have answers to most of Steve's questions.

Even Fratianno didn't know everything, Steve concluded.

Chapter 80

WARMING A COLD CASE

A rejuvenated Steve Bagbey returned from the FBI Academy in 1980 hoping to pick up speed in the Ryan murder investigation.

Those long talks with Dick Wright, John O'Brien and Terry Walters – guys who knew a lot about syndicate hoods who popped up in Ray's case – had opened doors and made Steve think there could be a light at the end of the tunnel.

But there was only so much time – and money – the Evansville police department could devote to one killing no matter how gruesome or how much publicity it generated. The FBI and ATF pursued leads but with less and less enthusiasm. And despite the information from Fratianno and Shallow, the investigation into Ray's murder was heading for the cold case file in the police department's basement.

But Steve kept trying. Every four or five years starting in 1980, he sent partial palm and fingerprints from the car bombing scene to the FBI in hopes of a match as new data was punched into FBI computers. No dice. Periodically, he called Ray Larroca and police officers from the FBI Academy to see if they had any new information.

He remained convinced Caifano was at the scene when the bomb exploded "probably having an orgasm" watching the man he detested die, Steve told an ex-FBI agent. "You show me one other person who stood up to Marshall Caifano. The guy hated Ray so much he'd break the rules and watch." And he prayed for the day an agent would walk into his office and say "Hey Bags, look what we found on the Ryan case." But that hadn't happened.

By the early 1980s, Chicago federal agents moved on to other more high profile murders. Several were names Steve had learned about during his investigation; others weren't. He had the feeling that to the federal agents, those victims were bigger names than Ray Ryan.

Daniel Seifert, who had been slated to testify against Joey Lombardo and others for defrauding the Teamsters Union, was shot down in front of his wife and son in September 1974. Lombard and Frankie Schweihs were suspected in the shooting.[29]

Ousted Outfit boss Sam Giancana was slain in his Chicago home in 1975. Around 1978, hoods who burglarized the Chicago home of Tony Accardo starting showing up dead. Other murders followed: Chicago mobster William Petrocelli, his face mutilated with a blow torch, was killed in 1980 and Nicholas D'Andrea, a mob lieutenant, was found bludgeoned in the trunk of a burning car in 1981.

Allen Dorfman was gunned down in 1983 while walking in a Chicago hotel parking lot. Dorfman, a powerful aide in the 1960s to Teamsters Union President James Hoffa, was facing a 60-year sentence following a 1982 conviction, along with Lombardo and former Teamsters president Roy E. Williams, for trying to bribe Nevada Democratic Senator Howard Cannon to block a truck deregulation bill in Congress. The Outfit feared Dorfman would talk to the Feds for a lesser sentence.

Charles "Chuckie" English was murdered in 1983, Leonard Yaras in 1983, and in June 1986, the bodies of Anthony "Tony" Spilotro, Chicago's kingpin in Las Vegas after Caifano, and his brother Michael were found in a shallow grave in an Indiana cornfield. A dozen or so lower-ranking hoods also were slain during the first half of the 1980s.

Steve's suspicions grew that Ray's murder was going to end up a cold case to the Feds.

That was made clear when Evansville FBI agent Gary Perkins told Steve around 1985 the agency was thinking of closing its books on the car bombing.

In 1988, the Indianapolis FBI office said the Vanderburgh County prosecutor's office "would consider prosecution of this matter, if additional information is developed. However, since all logical

---

29 A mob hitman and informant later said Joey Hansen was there and put a bullet into Seifert's head.

investigation has been conducted with negative results regarding any additional information of value, Indianapolis is placing this case in a closed status."

Washington may pass on Ray Ryan, but Steve couldn't give up on a mob killing in Evansville.

Around that time, another possible suspect's name came to light – Wayne Bock, Jr. The 42-year-old former football tackle at the University of Illinois had spent a year with the professional Chicago Cardinals and became a soldier in one of the Outfit's crews, hooking up with Schweihs. Mob informants concluded that if Schweihs participated in killing Ray, Bock may have been there, too.

In 1987, a decade after Ray's murder, the Chicago FBI office had gained a couple of new mob informers. Agents sent Steve a lengthy report on who the informers thought might have been involved in the car bombing.

Frank Schweihs and Anthony Panzica headed the list of "top suspects in any murder involving the use of remote control explosive devices" but also at the top the FBI listed Wayne Bock. The report highlighted details about the history and current residences of Schweihs and Panzica, but no details about Bock.

Bock had been questioned in the 1965 car bombing murder of a 22-year-old suburban Chicago woman and was believed linked to the 1967 gangland style slaying of Gerald Covelli in Encino near Los Angeles. Covelli was a Chicago hood turned federal informant whose testimony sent James "Monk" Allegretti and three other Chicago hoods to prison. Covelli died when a bomb was exploded by remote control under his car as he left his California home.

Despite crimes comparable to Ray's, Steve learned little else about Bock and his possible involvement in Ray's murder faded into the night, never to resurface.

Ray's killing was ancient history now to federal agencies. Steve was out on the limb alone.

Still, other tidbits caught his attention.

A curious report from the Zurich, Switzerland police arrived in 1985 that offered an insight into why federal authorities thought Ray used sleight of hand in concealing money.

Four men and a woman were arrested for the attempted blackmail in Zurich of Dr. Arthur Wilfried Hunziker and Dr. Thomas Adolph Wach, top officials at Schweizerische Treuhandgesellschaft, a finance company that once represented Ray's business transactions in Switzerland and Kenya. At the heart of the case was a container belonging to Ray supposedly containing $13 million in stocks and securities.

Steve thought Ray secreting $13 million in stocks plausible. He was convinced Ray had hid millions of dollars across the country and the world during his lifetime, including at Hirschmann's Swiss bank. Steve doubted if anyone, perhaps not even Ray, ever knew exactly how much he salted away for a rainy day.

Steve remembered a report that U.S. Customs agents in New York once searched the luggage of Ray and Helen as they were leaving for a trip to Europe a couple of years after the extortion trial and found $1 million in a suitcase. Steve always gave Helen the benefit of the doubt on whether she knew the money was there.

In the documents from Zurich, Moritz Duno Caspar had told police he had been a secretary and chauffeur for Ray after meeting him in 1956, calling Ray "my best friend" and occasional traveling partner. "Ray Ryan left at my residence a container (envelope) which had $13.8 million in stock in it. I kept the container in my residence in a shoebox and later I transferred it to a safe deposit box. Ray Ryan was always traveling. He was associated with the Mafia. He worked with them. He told me that if anything should happen to him to turn the container over to his daughter, Rae Jean, or to his wife."

Four days after Ray was murdered in Evansville, Caspar said Hunziker called to say he needed the container for safekeeping. Caspar said he could turn over the container only to Ray's daughter or wife. "I subsequently telephoned Mrs. Ryan and she told me that I should give the container to Dr. Hunziker." Caspar said, adding he did that in November 1977.

Caspar told Zurich police that three years later he met Helen at Rae Jean's California home and Helen said she never received the container. Caspar said he called Hunziker and was told "that a settlement had not been made because the items in question were too hot."

Hunziker later told him he had given everything to Ray's attorney, Raymond Larroca.

Because of a reported scheme to blackmail Hunziker, Zurich police got involved with Caspar; his wife, Ellen; two car dealers: Georgi Ivanov Georgiev, a Bulgarian, and Osman Massalkhi, a Lebanese; and businessman Ulrich Laager.

Caspar claimed he was approached by two organized crime figures, who demanded $6 million they said Ray owed them. Caspar asked Hunziker to retrieve the stocks but Hunziker said he couldn't help him.

In early 1985, Zurich authorities searched the homes of Caspar and the other men. After an intensive investigation, the group admitted fabricating the story about the syndicate hoods and Massalkhi confessed he placed calls in English to Hunziker pretending to be from the Mafia.

Zurich police sent transcripts and files to FBI agents who passed them on to Steve.

Steve thought Caspar's shakedown attempt a Johnny-come-lately idea to get money and probably had nothing to do with Ray's murder.

But he was intrigued by the idea that Ray may have hid millions of dollars in stocks along with cash in Swiss banks.

He called Raymond Larroca and asked about the envelope containing those stocks. Larroca claimed client-attorney privilege and said nothing.

The Zurich police reports became another footnote in Ray's case.

But a nagging thought remained in Steve's mind.

Had Ray left other "buried" treasure across the world at the time he died?

Had Ray tried to launder organized crime money through stocks and securities? That would explain why some of Ray's close hoodlum friends wanted to keep Ray alive through those turbulent years after the attempted extortion by Caifano.

As usual, more questions than answers.

Chapter 81

A MURDER NEVER GOES AWAY

Over the next five years, Steve was assigned at times to work part time with the Evansville FBI office on joint investigations into state and federal violations. In the summer of 1986, he again was assigned to the FBI office.

This time the case was national in scope – pizza shops used to distribute and sell heroin brought in from Europe, a billion-dollar drug trafficking case that became known as the Pizza Connection. Several pizza shops in Evansville, Kentucky and Illinois were operated by Sicilians and other Italians that the FBI thought linked to the drug ring although the emphasis was on larger cities – New York, Philadelphia, Newark, Chicago and Detroit.

From 1987 to September 1990, he worked full-time with the FBI, cultivating informants, conducting surveillances, tracking telephone records and preparing documents as arrests were made. He worked with John O'Brien in New York on links between Evansville and East Coast Italians in the case.

Forty-three people in the Evansville Tri-State area were arrested for delivery and possession of drugs and conspiracy. Another two dozen were targeted for a second wave of indictments until the Feds closed down the Pizza Connection probe as major trials got under way elsewhere.

In 1990, Steve was reassigned to the police department's white collar crime unit and decided to run for the nine-member Evansville City Council from the city's Second Ward. Raymond Larroca, George

Barnett, Doyle Dressback and Helen Ryan sent checks and donations to Steve's campaign. Another came from Ryan Oil. Steve won the 1991 election, helped by a recent ward redistricting increasing the number of Democrats in the ward and a contested mayoral race that brought more Democrats to the polls.

The southeast side Second Ward faced a multitude of problems, drainage being the foremost due to low-lying areas and poorly designed combination storm sewers that flooded during heavy rains and backed up sewage into streets and homes. Fixing the problems required millions of dollars the city didn't have.

Steve received countless phone calls about crumbling streets, crime, abandoned vehicles, and speeding vehicles. Late nights and early mornings after storms he donned waders and trudged through neighborhoods inspecting flood damage and listening to residents' complaints. He prodded the city to pump more money into sewer, drainage and road projects with some but never enough success.

On council, he was more a cop than a slick politician and struggled at speaking in public. He took a speech class at a local university and got a C grade, and the instructor said he'd never be a public speaker. To improve, he taught college criminal justice classes, discussed unsolved murders with a high school forensic class and gave talks to high school students and sports teams.

Sometimes his Irish temper took over and he had angry outbursts on the council floor for which he never apologized. His enemies thought him overbearing; Steve countered that he was passionate for what was best for his ward and willing to take a stand on unpopular issues. Republicans tried to use his occasional temper outbreaks against him at election time with little success.

His opponents claimed he would rubberstamp whatever the police department wanted but the local Fraternal Order of Police thought he wasn't doing enough for them. The FOP endorsed him in his first two races, but not the last two.

Working with the FBI in the Federal Building also meant Steve spent little time across the street in police headquarters. Younger officers rarely saw him and knew little of what he did. Some veteran officers resented Steve, who was a detective/corporal, getting high profile assignments while they were left on the streets handling domestic disputes and thefts.

Many elected officials from both sides considered Steve a person who listened to their concerns and tried to work out solutions, but there were residents who didn't like him as a cop, councilman or personally and that weighed heavily on him. Still, he continued to win elections by about 60 percent of the votes cast in his ward.

With Indiana's first riverboat casino set to open in Evansville, Police Chief Art Gann in 1994 assigned Steve, detective Larry Sparks and other officers to determine the effect of the riverboat casino on the community, the current status of gambling in the city and organized crime activity. The unit was known as organized crime intell.

Casino Aztar's $17 million riverboat docked at Evansville's riverfront in November 1995. Aztar pumped millions of dollars into local governments and special public projects each year and city officials wanted to ensure the only gambling going on was at the riverboat.

There hadn't been a crackdown on gambling in years. Fraternal and social clubs, bars, taverns and some diners had coin-operated devices called the "poor man's slot machines" where winnings were paid off in cash. Most machines came from Chicago, where the Outfit operated, and Tennessee, where New York's Genovese family had influence.

Sparks met with business and club owners and asked them to voluntarily remove the machines; known bookies were told to shut down. Few complied. Police started making arrests and hundreds of machines were confiscated.

Club members and bar owners berated police for taking away the money-making machines. Steve's house was vandalized, his wife's car forced off the road one day, the tires on his car slashed, BB gun pellets fired at his home. After a while, the attacks ceased.

Whenever possible in the 1990s, Steve picked at the Ryan case, using the internet to dig into organized crime data, court documents and newspapers and e-mailing people familiar with syndicate operations.

On February 28, 1996, Steve got a call from Bill Roemer in response to one e-mail. Steve was a devoted reader of Roemer's books on organized crime and his determination to take on the mob.

Roemer had spent 30 years with the FBI, turning down promotions and reassignments to remain in Chicago to track the Outfit. He knew all the Chicago gangsters – from Accardo to the lowest street hood, had been a thorn in Giancana's side and planted bugs in hoods' hangouts and telephones. He recently was on television documentaries dealing with organized crime.

Roemer was wrapping up his sixth book and was ill with lung cancer. Steve was looking for insight and went over Ray's case with Roemer in detail – Ray's oil and gambling years, Palm Springs, Las Vegas, the murder, statements from Fratianno and other informants. "You're a hard worker. You've done everything that could be done," Roemer said. "It haunts me," Steve said. "I've done everything. I just can't get there." Roemer said he had been a close friend to Richard Cain. "I wish he was alive. He could help you on this," Roemer said.

"You have a great career, but I think the Lord put you on earth to write books for cops. I believe in the message you send – you got to work your hardest, develop your sources and give it your best shot," Steve said. "I think Caifano is just a piece of toilet paper. As a Catholic I believe in Heaven and Hell. I hope he gets some roasting time. I need closure."

They talked about Notre Dame University. Roemer got a law degree there and was an outstanding amateur boxer at the school. His father had been a professor at Notre Dame. Steve grew up supporting Notre Dame. Roemer began to sound tired. He said his sixth book was basically finished but he wasn't pushing it because of his cancer. "You'll be in my prayers," Steve said.

"Steve, keep up the good work. Keep punching and keep the faith," Roemer said before hanging up. Roemer died less than four months later, two days short of his seventieth birthday.

Chapter 82

TIME RUNNING OUT

On December 27, 1998, 89-year-old Helen Ryan died at her home on Lombard Avenue in the same house that her mother had passed away in 38 years earlier. Helen had lived more than two decades as the widow of a murder victim and went to her grave with the killing unsolved.

Steve had heard that Helen was ill with cancer and read of her death in the newspaper, but didn't go to the funeral. His appearance would only remind Rae Jean, the grandchildren and great-grandchildren of that day in October 1977 and he felt there wasn't any need for his presence to bring back those memories.

He reached Rae Jean later by phone at her home in Corona del Mar, California. She thanked Steve for his hard work on her father's case and told him the nice things her mother had said about him. "Helen Ryan was a lady with a capital L," Steve said. Rae Jean said she'd like to have lunch with him when she visited Evansville again. Steve and Rae Jean never had that lunch. Family friends later packed up Helen's belongings and shipped them to California and drove Helen's car to California. The Lombard Avenue house was sold.

In 1999, Steve retired from the Evansville police department and took a job as safety coordinator with the Evansville Catholic Diocese. Between that job and city council duties, he had little time to work on Ray Ryan.

That changed in 2002 when a reporter for the Evansville Courier and Press newspaper began preparing a six-day series marking the 25th anniversary of the Ryan car bombing. *Thank God someone still cares*, Steve thought.

He sifted through the material he had, going through old memories, reliving the past. A shed behind his home was crammed with photographs, witness statements, federal and local reports, yellowing newspapers. His basement was cluttered with manila folders and old briefcases packed with documents.

But all important details were indelibly printed in his mind. No one knew more about Ray's murder than Steve. FBI, ATF and city police investigators when questioned years later about details in the murder all said: "Talk to Bags. He knows everything about it."

In the end, any success in closing the case came back to Bags.

The newspaper series published in October 2002 rejuvenated Steve; this "old dumb cop from Indiana" as he called himself was ready to bounce headlong into a gangland murder just like 25 years before.

Now he was older and heavier, his knees ached from old football injuries and general wear and tear, his dark mustache and hair had turned white. But, the investigative fire still burned inside; yet he knew the federal government had to give a damn – and quickly.

Time was running out – for everybody.

In September 2003, Marshall Caifano died quietly in Florida at the age of 92.

Caifano's death went nearly unnoticed in Chicago except for Chicago Tribune veteran mob-watching columnist John Kass who went to the funeral home and wrote in a column that Caifano looked shriveled, even smaller than he was in real life, and crucifixes adorned the casket and the wall behind.

Kass wrote that it was odd to think that Marshall Caifano would get to die a natural death "because in life he was said to favor the shotgun and the car bomb as one of the most notorious hit men in the history of the Chicago Outfit."

Kass said it was the small in height guys that did the "heavy work" in the Outfit. Caifano's colleague Vincent "The Saint" Inserro "was a shrimp too. If one stood on the other's shoulders, they might have been able to change a light bulb."

Kass recounted the various murders that cops thought Caifano had a hand in, including Ray Ryan. "And after almost a century of blood and fear, there he (Caifano) was in his coffin, the image of a kindly, devout old man, with crucifixes hovering, placed there to protect him. I wonder if they'll protect him where he's going," Kass wrote.

Steve Bagbey's dream of arresting Caifano for killing Ray was gone. He had hoped Caifano might go soft at the end and tell about the murder. But Caifano, who struck terror in so many people over the years went out a professional hood, quiet and obedient to the Omerta code of never informing.

Only a few of the suspected killers of Ray were left – Schweihs, Lombardo and Joey Hansen.

While "The German" Schweihs and "The Clown" Lombardo were familiar mob figures, Joseph H. Hansen always lurked in the background. Hansen grew up in Chicago within a few blocks of Tony Spilotro, attending the same school and hustling the same streets in the 1950s.

In the early 1970s, Spilotro took over as Chicago's man in Las Vegas with the balding Hansen settling in Marina Del Ray in California to handle Outfit chores. Paul John Schiro, also from Chicago, joined them, living in Phoenix. Some investigators believed Schiro and Hansen were guys Spilotro could call on for murder contracts and were among the suspects in the slaying of Sam Giancana in 1975.

It was the FBI spotting Hansen trailing Fratianno in 1978 that contributed to Fratianno turning government informer. Hansen sold jewelry in California and hung around with notorious burglars. Police could find no evidence to arrest him.

Schiro was sent to jail in 2001 for being part of the jewelry theft ring of former top Chicago cop William Handardt.

While Hansen lurked out of the public eye, Lombardo and Schweihs didn't. They would be mentioned as suspects separately or together in the murders of Richard Cain, Daniel Seifert, Allen Dorfman, Charles "Chuckie" English and others.

Steve also was told that John J. Flood, a retired cop and veteran mob watcher, encountered Schweihs and Lombard in 1964 when he was a sergeant with the Cook County Sheriff's Department. On patrol one night, Flood spotted a man carrying a lead pipe and heading toward a parked Thunderbird containing a man and a woman in a motel parking lot near O'Hare Airport. Flood demanded the identification of the armed man, who started wrestling with him.

As they struggled, a car suddenly headed toward Flood trying to run him down. Flood knocked the man to the ground and jumped out of the way as the car sped away. Flood arrested the man, who turned out to be Schweihs. Flood believed, but couldn't prove, that Lombardo was the driver of the car.

The man in the parked Thunderbird was Richard Hauff, the motel owner. Hauff was an Iranian orphan during World War II who was taken under the wing of an American, adopted and brought to the United States. Hauff became a front man for gangsters and a million-aire Rush Street playboy who once dated Zsa Zsa Gabor and Marshall Caifano's ex-wife Darlene. Flood believed Schweihs had intended to kill Hauff for some mob violation.

Schweihs was one of the toughest mobsters Flood ever met, ranking up there with Lombardo, Milwaukee Phil Alderisio and Nicoletti. To Flood, Caifano wasn't in the same league with those hoods.

"Schweihs and Lombardo are mean, tough gutsy guys. Chuckie Nicoletti and Alderisio would wipe the floor with Caifano. Schweihs and Lombardo would, too."

Chapter 83

PROMISE OF
FAMILY SECRETS

Even a quarter-century after Ray's murder, Steve still didn't have a trusted contact within the Chicago police department.

The extent of the mob tentacles into the department was evident in 2001 when federal investigators arrested William A. Hanhardt, who was a cop's cop during his 33 years on the force from 1953 to 1986, advancing to head of the burglary section, chief of detectives and finally deputy superintendent before retiring with the rank of captain.

Hanhardt then became a consultant for the television show "Crime Story" about a team of Chicago detectives battling the mob. He was friends with the show's star, Dennis Farina, a former Chicago police officer in the mid-1960s who went on to make numerous films and play Detective Fontana in the popular television show "Law and Order."

Hanhardt's world tumbled down when he and six other men were indicted for running a nationwide jewelry theft ring that had stolen $5 million in gems since 1984. Federal prosecutors said Hanhardt used old cop friends to gain access to police computers to learn when jewelry salesmen rented vehicles. From California to Wisconsin, Hanhardt's crew ripped off gems from eight salesmen after they left jewelry unattended in cars at lunch or in hotel rooms. Another $1 million was stolen in 1994 from an Ohio hotel's safety deposit boxes during a jewelry sales convention.

In 2002, the 73-year-old Hanhardt was sentenced to 16 years in jail and ordered to pay $4.8 million in restitution. Hanhardt had been in the mob's pocket for decades, taking money from bookies, burglars and jewel thieves and giving a heads-up on police plans.

Little wonder federal agents were leery of Chicago's police department, Steve thought.

But a door opened with the department in 2004 when Chicago police detective Mike Hammond had an informant from a street gang talking about crimes including a wealthy oilman killed in Evansville years ago. Evansville police referred Hammond to Steve, even though he was no longer on the force.

The two men talked several times over the next months. Hammond's informant didn't have any direct knowledge of Ray's murder, but Steve mailed Hammond a large packet of documents about the Evansville murder. He needed to have a working acquaintance with someone on the Chicago force just in case. Steve sent an e-mail in January 2005 thanking Hammond for his efforts. "I want this thing so very much, but maybe the wise guys will win this battle here on Earth," Steve wrote. "I am okay with letting my Dear Lord figure it out at their next stop."

In the meantime, Steve kept in touch with a clique of retired law enforcement officers. Retired FBI agents Jim Beck, J. Robert Duvall, Richard Eisgruber and Tom Page were a telephone call away. Retired city cop Ed Biederwolf was willing to help any time.

Steve also called Dick Wright, who had retired from the Los Angeles police department and was a captain with the Simi Valley Police Department. "I can't believe you crazy bastards are still working this (Ryan murder)," Wright once told Steve. "Bags, I wished I had a bunch of guys like you."

Wright suggested talking to the FBI in Chicago. Beck made a call and learned a large-scale federal investigation known as "Operation Family Secrets" was underway, going after more than a dozen mobsters on nearly 20 unsolved murders spanning two decades..

Two hoods on the list were Lombardo and Schweihs. The only problem was that Ray Ryan's murder wasn't being probed. Still, it was a start.

Wright also passed along another item – Joey Hansen had died in California of cancer. Now only Lombardo and Schweihs were left.

"We are about as close to solving the case as we've ever been and we're about as far from solving the case as we've ever been," Steve told a group of Ray's old friends from the Lake Malone days a short time later. "It has been an up and down roller coaster emotion for me. It's been a lot of work and a lot of effort. No matter what he did, mob guy or not, Ray Ryan did not deserve to die the way he did. I get real passionate about this. I want to bring closure."

Steve was antsy waiting for the Feds to plod along with the Chicago investigation. Days melted into weeks and weeks into months with no indictments. "Operation Family Secrets" wasn't a secret anymore. Chicago Tribune columnist John Kass had reported in early 2003 that a big federal investigation was underway, but it wasn't until near the end of the year that the catchy name of "Operation Family Secrets" appeared.

Reporters already knew the major informant was Nicholas Calabrese, an Outfit killer who had been talking to federal investigators and placed into the witness protection program. Nick Calabrese's brother Frank Calabrese, Sr. was a top syndicate's hood and a key target in the probe.

Big names were thrown around – Lombardo, Schweihs, Calabrese, James Marcello, Paul Schiro, Nicholas Ferriola. "Operation Family Secrets" promised to be a big deal.

One of Dick Wright's detectives in California gave Steve the name of a FBI agent in Chicago to contact. Steve called, but the agent didn't know anything about Ray Ryan, which was expected because it had been more than a quarter century since Ray's murder and the FBI agents around at that time had retired. Steve outlined the case and sent a thick package of documents in hopes of benefits down the road.

He also met with retired Chicago FBI agent Jack O'Rourke in late 2004, picking O'Rourke's brain about Caifano and Schweihs. O'Rourke and fellow retired agents ran an investigation company.

Caifano was "tough as nails, uneducated, vicious criminal," but the guy when he got out of prison on the extortion charge "had lost his clout with the Outfit. He was no longer a heavy hitter," O'Rourke said. "He had been a killer so we thought. He usually was well dressed but when we arrested him (on the stolen securities charge) he was in his pajamas."

While always wanting to know more about Caifano, Steve still had his own investigation to do around Evansville. Two area informants had told Kentucky State Police about a handyman who once worked at the Lake Malone Inn and might be involved in the Ryan murder. Evansville police passed the names on to Steve. The handyman had been Ray's gofer at the inn, running errands, picking Ray up at the Nashville airport and driving him to Evansville and around the city occasionally.

The informants' story was that the handyman told them of once picking up a man at the Nashville airport, driving him to Evansville and going over the routes Ray traveled to the spa and the Ryan Oil company office. The handyman claimed he and the other man parked one evening watching Ray's house, but sped away when a neighbor walking his dog approached the car.

Steve wasn't convinced the informants were correct but the handyman's name never had appeared in the documents he amassed over the years and he had to check it out. He decided to question the handyman, who lived in Muhlenberg County.

Phil Luecke, a veteran Evansville police officer and the city's liaison with the Evansville ATF office, accompanied Steve on the hour trip. On the way, Steve told Luecke, a burly, strong cop with a wry sense of humor, about the latest developments in the case.

The handyman and his wife lived in an old wood frame rural home at the edge of a small collection of houses. A dirty, banged-up car with faded paint and only a rim for a back tire was in the yard. Another vehicle about three or four years old sported a large Harley-Davidson decal. "A man's got to have his dreams," Luecke said looking at the decal.

The handyman was willing to answer questions but his wife yelled she was going to call local sheriff deputies although she never did. Steve questioned the handyman in the yard while Luecke stood a few feet away facing the house in case the wife came out armed. The seemingly slow-witted man admitted driving Ray around and running errands, but denied taking a stranger to Evansville, showing him Ray's routes or parking along Lombard Avenue.

After 30 minutes, Steve and Luecke left. The trip probably was another dead end. On the way back to Evansville, Steve asked Luecke what he thought about the handyman. "It's hard to read a stupid person," Luecke said.

"Damn," said Steve.

The ball was back in the federal government's court.

Chapter 84

ARREST HOPES FADE

On Monday April 25, 2005, grand jury indictments were unsealed in Chicago and federal agents fanned out across the country to arrest 14 men in "Operation Family Secrets."

Steve was driving back from Indianapolis when the Notre Dame fight song blared on his cell phone and an FBI agent told him about the indictments. He thought it might be the break he needed.

Three of the indicted – Frank Calabrese, Sr., his brother Nicholas Calabrese and Paul Schiro – already were in prisons on other charges and another man, Frank Saladino, was found dead of apparent natural causes in a Chicagoland hotel room. Agents and police rounded up eight other defendants within a few days.

Steve followed the progress through Chicago newspapers on the internet. Only two men couldn't be found – Lombardo and Schweihs, who were toddling around somewhere thumbing their noses at the Feds.

"I'm fucking pissed," an irate Steve groused. "Two fucking 75-year-old guys and the FBI can't find them. This blows my fucking mind. Why in the hell wasn't the FBI sitting on those guys. They've been a thorn in the FBI's and Justice Department's sides for umpteen years and the damned FBI wasn't watching them like a hawk. What were these guys doing? I can't believe it."

While he steamed in Evansville, agents pounded pavement in Florida for Schweihs and in Chicago for Lombardo, who had turned 76 in January. A FBI spokesman said Lombardo and Schweihs weren't closely watched for fear of tipping them off that arrests were imminent. The spokesman called getting 14 out of 16 a successful sweep.

The FBI spin was incredible to Steve. The sweep was a dismal failure to him. Lombardo had known he was a target since federal agents took mouth swabs in 2003 to get his DNA. Newspapers also reported the names of many of the other men as under investigation months before the grand jury met.

James Marcello, his half-brother Michael, Lombardo, Schweihs, Frank Calabrese, Sr., Nicholas Calabrese, Frank Saladino, Paul Schiro, Nicholas Ferriola and two former Chicago cops, Anthony Doyle and Michael Ricci, were charged with RICO (Racketeer Influenced and Corrupt Organizations Act) violations. The Marcellos, Thomas Johnson, Joseph Venezia, Dennis Johnson, Frank Calabrese, Sr. and Ferriola faced charges for conducting illegal gambling businesses.

Schweihs, who made sure street tax was paid by owners of pornography and other shops, also was hit with a couple of extortion charges. Obstruction, false statements and tax fraud conspiracy charges also were levied against some of the defendants.

Frank Calabrese, Sr. was accused of murdering at least 13 people; Lombardo and Schweihs of slaying Daniel Seifert; Schweihs and Schiro of the 1986 murder in Phoenix of Emil Vaci, who had testified before a grand jury investigating Las Vegas casino skimming. James Marcello was accused of killing the Spilotro brothers and Nicholas D'Andrea. James Marcello and Frank Calabrese, Sr. also were charged with the attempted murder of another person.

Other criminal activities alleged by the Feds included juice loans at usurious interest rates from one to 10 percent a month, distributing video gambling machines, witness tampering, bribery, violence or threat of violence to extort money from owners of adult entertainment shops and restaurants, bookmaking, filing false income tax returns and cops carrying messages from jailed gangsters back to underlings on the street and keeping the Outfit abreast of police investigations in progress.

Steve's FBI contact in Chicago suggested he call Assistant U. S. Attorney John Scully. Scully wasn't familiar with Ray Ryan and Steve sent him a thick packet of material about the case. Scully wanted to know about the Evansville murder, and kept the door open for further talks. A Chicago FBI agent told Steve "you do have our attention."

"I think they know we are extremely interested and we want to see closure. Maybe we'll get that, maybe we won't," Steve told a friend. A federal reward of $20,000 for Lombardo and Schweihs didn't generate any public response and they remained on the loose for months.

In December 2005, Steve received a call that Schweihs was arrested in Berea, Kentucky, a few days after renting an apartment with a woman in her 60s. One resident said it was the biggest news in Berea since a Cracker Barrel restaurant moved into town.

One down and one to go, Steve thought.

A month later, a shaggy-haired Lombardo looking more like Saddam Hussein was nabbed in Chicago. While in hiding, he wrote letters to his attorney offering to surrender if released on his own recognizance and given a separate trial. He also offered to take truth serum or a lie detector test if FBI agents and informants did too. U. S. District Judge James B. Zagel rejected the offers.

In the summer of 2006 with Schweihs and Lombardo in jail, Evansville police Chief Brad Hill made Steve and retired FBI agent Jim Beck special police officers, a quasi-official status to pursue Ray's murder. No one else had the depth of knowledge that they did.

It would be another year before the Family Secrets trial in Chicago. During that time, Ricci had died and six others pleaded guilty to charges including Nicholas Calabrese, who became a government witness.

Periodically, Steve telephoned Scully, who cryptically said that one of the remaining defendants was ill and may not go on trial. "Schweihs," Steve said, but Scully wouldn't confirm that. Steve knew it had to be Schweihs, who always pretended to have an illness whenever cops nabbed him. When arrested in Berea, he complained of heart problems.

Lombardo, Frank Calabrese, Sr., James Marcello, Schiro and former cop Anthony Doyle went on trial on June 21, 2007 before a jury whose members were known by numbers and not their actual names. The courtroom in the Dirksen U.S. Courthouse was packed.

The judge was told Schweihs was being treated at a federal facility for cancer and was too ill to stand trial at present. Steve called Scully with a special request – if Schweihs is on his deathbed, get a dying declaration about his role in Ray's murder. Scully said he doubted

Schweihs would make such an admission. Steve hoped Schweihs would want to get right with God and confess all before dying. He might avoid years in prison but couldn't avoid years in death.

Scully presented the opening statement at the trial, identifying each defendant to the jury and laying out the prosecution's case. The trial was projected to last four months. Fitting, thought Steve. The 30th anniversary of Ray Ryan's murder also was four months away.

The idea flashed through Steve's head like a dream. *What if? What if? Could it actually happen? Could something come from the trial to solve Ray's murder exactly 30 years later? Could all this work and frustration finally be over?*

He smiled at the thought.

Chapter 85

LOOSE ENDS

Checking the internet for the Chicago newspapers' daily reports on the trial, Steve thought the U.S. attorneys were putting on an efficient and tightly-woven case.

He was excited when Alva Johnson Rodgers, one of the informants in Ray's case, testified. Months ago, Steve was told by a federal agent that Rodgers was dead, but the 78-year-old guy, still an active federal informant, was alive and kicking,. Rodgers outlined his connection with Outfit figures Marshall Caifano and Lombardo and efforts to take over the wholesale pornography business in Chicago.

He also was called to discredit Anthony Pellicano, a Hollywood private investigator who claimed that Lombardo was in an IHOP restaurant in Chicago when Daniel Seifert was killed. Pellicano, a Chicago native who had moved to Los Angeles a quarter century ago, had past links with the Chicago mob and at the time of the Family Secrets trial was in jail for racketeering and illegal wiretapping of well-known Hollywood individuals.

Rodgers didn't mention Ray Ryan in his testimony, but that didn't matter to Steve. He was happy that at least one of the guys tied into Ray's case got to testify. Scully had promised if Ray's name came up in the trial, prosecutors were ready to get into that case. The government moved quickly with witnesses and completed their case in two months.

Family Secrets was a tale of a once great mob syndicate in decline. The Outfit had downsized from six to four street crews with 25 made members and 75 associates, according to FBI estimates. Omerta, the historic Mafia code of silence, had long since vanished. Now Frank Calabrese, Sr., the boss of the 26th Street crew, was ratted out by a mob hitman and brother, Nicholas, and his own son Frank, Jr., who wore a wire in prison to record conversations with his father.

Witnesses detailed grisly murders committed by, or upon the orders of, the men on trial; intimidation of pornography and legitimate businessmen to collect street tax; juice loans at exorbitant interest rates; hanging mice with a tiny noose around their necks from car windshield wipers to discourage someone from talking to the police; and former cops keeping the mob informed of the progress in police investigations.

Relatives recounted the final hours before a husband or father was gunned down before their eyes. Investigators using secretly recorded tapes laid out evidence of code words jailed mobsters used to talk about murders and steps to take for others to avoid prosecution. The prosecutors detailed Lombardo's days as head of the Grand Avenue crew and his alleged involvement in the killing of Daniel Seifert.

When the defense began its case, Lombardo's attorney Rick Halprin said Lombardo would take the stand. Steve had to be there.

A heavy downpour hit Chicago Tuesday morning, August 14, when Steve left a downtown hotel to catch a taxi to the courthouse. The Nigerian cab driver claimed he didn't know the location of the courthouse, a Chicago landmark less than five blocks away. Steve told the cabbie he was a cop and the driver's memory suddenly improved and he sped to the courthouse, turning off the meter after a couple of blocks.

The massive 25th floor courtroom was impressive with dark paneled walls, black and white photographs of former justices ringing three walls and overhead fluorescent lighting filtering through a metal maze. Relatives and friends of the defendants, the murder victims and attorneys packed the seats. They lined up in the hallway two hours before the morning session. Sections of the courtroom were reserved for newspaper and television reporters and authors writing books about Chicago's Outfit.

In the courtroom before Lombardo was to testify, Scully asked Steve "have you seen your man?" "Yeah, what a piece of shit," Steve said. Lombardo looked much older than he had in the old pictures that Steve had seen.

Lombardo leaned back in his wheelchair at his defense table – a 78-year-old guy with a Caesar-style, close-cropped haircut, large round dark eyeglasses – and thumped his cane on the floor. Steve watched Lombardo's constant thumping of the cane. All Steve wanted to do was to take the cane and wrap it around Lombardo's neck for all those people whose lives were forever destroyed by him and his pals.

Steve stared at Lombardo, who looked back for a few seconds, then around to spectators gathering in the courtroom. Lombardo, who would be the first of the defendants to testify, bragged to Marcello at a nearby table. "Wait till I get up there (on the witness stand). Wait till I get up there and show them. I'll show them how this is played. I'll show them how to do it."

The S.O.B. was cocky, real cocky, but Steve expected Lombardo to be that way. That was the image he always had of Lombardo – a tough, arrogant guy who thought he was smarter than the FBI, always ready to take a serious situation and make a funny out of it.

Steve also watched as Anthony "Twan" Doyle, the former cop, came over and hugged Calabrese. Doyle was Sicilian by birth, his family name was Passafiume, but he legally changed it in 1975 to the Irish-sounding Doyle when applying to the Chicago police force. Doyle grew up in the same neighborhood as Calabrese, who took Doyle under his arm when they were kids.

"Seeing a retired cop hugging and kissing on a fucker charged with all kinds of homicides, who's got a dysfunctional family, really disgusted me," Steve said. "He probably disgusted me more than Joey."

Scully also introduced Steve to Al Egan, a retired Chicago cop, and put his arms around both men, a sign that Egan could be trusted – a good guy's version of the Mafia's signal of "a friend of ours" used to introduce made syndicate members. Steve and Egan talked mainly about Doyle.

Several of Lombardo's friends opened that day's testimony by claiming Lombardo was a worker at International Fiber Glass, a company that Daniel Seifert owned, applying fiberglass to sinks. The defense offered a photograph of Lombardo in long sleeves and an apron covered in fiberglass after a day of work.

Following a break, Lombardo was wheeled to the witness stand. His defense was that he never was in the mob hierarchy, did run a dice game for years to make money and had long ago disassociated himself from syndicate activities.

Chicago Tribune columnist John Kass would write that Lombardo in two days of testimony stubbornly clung to his story "like one of those drowning people in cartoons, clutching an anvil."

During pauses in questions from Halprin, Lombardo often leaned back in his wheelchair and gazed almost absent-mindedly at the ceiling, then tried to impress the jury with his memory, rattling off the addresses of businesses he went to, where his family had lived, restaurants he ate at and places where he met people.

He told of being a shoeshine boy for tips as a kid including cops who'd give him a nickel tip. "Very cheap people," Lombardo said, quickly adding to his attorney "you told me to tell the truth." That drew a laugh from the audience and a warning from the judge that there wasn't anything humorous about the case.

Lombardo was into sports in high school – wrestling, fencing, basketball, swimming – and later boxed and played golf, handball and racquetball. He worked as a "dummy waiter" at the Blackstone Hotel, sending food up and down among the floors on the hotel's dumbwaiter. He operated a floating dice game, collecting 25 percent of the profits. He said the game went on with the okay of one of Chicago's "50 bosses" – the city council's aldermen, powerful political figures in their districts.

Questions on whether he killed Seifert or was involved in the Outfit, Lombardo answered "positively no." Lombardo said Alva Johnson Rodgers was "positively a liar" as were all the other people who testified against him.

During his cross examination of Lombardo the next day, Assistant U.S. Attorney Mitchell Mars painted a concise, detailed scenario of a Lombardo knee deep in crime. Mars put on an impressive attack although his closest friends knew he was seriously ill with lung cancer (he died a year later).

When Mars corralled Lombardo on a secretly recorded tape of him threatening a 72-year-old attorney who owed the mob money that he wouldn't reach 73 years of age, Lombardo said he was pretending to be "like James Cagney and Edward G. Robinson," movie gangsters.

On another tape, Lombardo talked with a mob figure about getting rid of an independent massage parlor operating close to a mob-protected parlor, saying "we'll flatten the joint." Lombardo said he was mixed up in using the word "we," like a president who used to mix up his words. Mars shot back that the president doesn't have a crew. "He's got a bigger one," answered Lombardo.

Later Lombardo said there was "a little difference" in his appearance when arrested, a scraggy beard and wild hair similar to Saddam Hussein, and what he normally looked like. Mars asked if Lombardo thought that was funny. "A little joke every once in a while isn't going to hurt," Lombardo said.

He admitted buying police scanners and other electronic devices but said he did so for bondsman Irvin Weiner. Lombardo said his thumbprint found on the registration in a car used in the Seifert murder came from him touching documents when he visited Weiner's office.

The prosecution claimed Lombardo's mob connections resulted in him getting a windfall from sale of a Florida hotel. Lombardo said his family put up $100,000, of which $57,000 was returned at the time of closing, to buy the hotel which then was sold for $1.4 million.

Lombardo said he knew Marshall Caifano, who helped collect juice payments, and Caifano was a friend but never worked for him.

He said his being in the famous 1976 "Last Supper" photograph at an Elmwood Park restaurant with the Outfit's top hoods – Tony Accardo, Joseph Aiuppa, Jackie Cerone, Joseph "Little Caesar" DiVarco, James "Turk" Torello and others – was a coincidence and that he was in the area, stopped off for a meal, saw the men at the table and ended up in the picture.

Steve listened stoically to Lombardo and didn't see how anyone in the courtroom believed him. Joey was an absolute embarrassment, shooting himself in the foot with every word. Jury members seemed bored as Lombardo droned on, denying everything, calling everyone against him a liar. *The dumb bastard should have kept his mouth shut*, Steve thought.

During a courtroom break, the Chicago FBI agent Steve had talked to by phone several times told Steve "I wish there was something I could do to help you." He said the FBI had tried to approach Schwiehs about talking to them, but was told to go pound sand. Steve asked if Lombardo might talk if he was convicted. "No way," said the agent.

Steve knew all the loose ends remaining in the Ray Ryan murder were going to stay that way.

Chapter 86

THE FACE IN THE MIRROR

Steve left Chicago impressed with the government's case and with a good feeling of at least seeing Lombardo in a courtroom, even if it wasn't for Ray's murder.

Other defendants followed Lombardo to the stand as federal prosecutors during cross examinations highlighted the hoods' pasts, tightening the noose around each defendant's neck.

The case went to the jury in early September 2007. The jury deliberated about 20 hours over three days and announced its verdicts on the RICO portion of the case on Monday, September 10.

"Hoooorrrraaaayy," Steve yelled when he got the telephone call back in Evansville that the jury had found all five defendants guilty on RICO charges. "It's a great day for the Irish. It's vindication. Those federal prosecutors did a wonderful job. They've made my day. I couldn't be happier than if one of the murders they were convicted of was Ray Ryan."

It was one of the best days of his life.

The jury took a break before returning several days later to deliberate on whether defendants should be convicted in any of the 18 murders. On Thursday September 28, the jury deadlocked on whether Schiro was guilty of murder but found Frank Calabrese, Sr. guilty of seven murders (the jury deadlocked on six other murders against Calabrese), James Marcello guilty in the killings of the Spilotro brothers and Joey Lombardo guilty in the murder of Daniel Seifert. The decisions meant the three men would spend the rest of their lives in prison.

Now Steve's handcuffs, which he had hoped to slap on the murderers of Ray Ryan, could be stored with all the thousands of documents he had amassed on the case. He knew Lombardo would die in jail and Schweihs would die before being tried, or in prison if he did go before a jury.

"What's unfortunate is that Mrs. Ryan is not here to see this, but I think the community of Evansville and a lot of us old-timers who are still interested in the case can take great pride in that we did everything we could," Steve said. "It wasn't for us to solve but we know who did it."

If Lombardo or Schweihs would want to talk, Steve would "do a Rule 20" to charge them with Ray's death but any sentence would run concurrently with the time they received in "Operation Family Secrets." But he knew they wouldn't talk. He had to close out the case in his own mind and people still would say he didn't solve it and they would be right.

"Yeah, it didn't work out like we'd all liked for it to work out, but we never shirked our responsibility. We tried. We got ridiculed a lot, but I don't think we have to take a back seat to anybody in our efforts," Steve said. "I feel okay about it. A little cocky? Maybe. I'd feel cockier if I got the opportunity to put the bracelets on somebody but I didn't have any control of that. Caifano is rotting in hell. I know as a Christian that Lombardo and Schweihs will be going there, too."

Steve knew the face in the mirror was satisfied with what he had done. He often used the poem "The Man in the Glass" when speaking to high school students – do your best, try your hardest, and don't cheat the person in the mirror.

He always remembered the poem's final passages:

"He's the fellow to please – never mind all the rest,
For he's with you clear to the end,
And you've passed your most dangerous, difficult test
If the man in the glass is your friend.

You may fool the whole world down the pathway of years
And get pats on the back as you pass.
But your final reward will be heartache and tears
If you've cheated the man in the glass."

Steve Bagbey didn't feel cheated.

EPILOGUE

On Tuesday, June 10, 2008, Frank "The German" Schweihs was wheelchaired into the federal courtroom in Chicago. He was gaunt, ashen-faced, looking like death warmed over. Although Schweihs was under a death sentence from cancer, federal prosecutors wanted to get the ball rolling on a trial for Schweihs should he live that long.

While his body was weak, Schweihs' voice and mind weren't. He knew this might be his last chance to go out as the meanest S.O.B. the Chicago Outfit ever had and he played it to the hilt. He snarled at one prosecutor. "You making eyes at me? Yeah you, you making eyes at me. Do I look like a fag to you?" He called another prosecutor an asshole.

Lombardo, Marcello and Calabrese might play nice-nice in the courtroom, but not Schweihs. He had nothing to lose. Everything already was lost. The judge set a trial date of mid-October. Schweihs' attorney told reporters after the hearing that his client was usually very polite, but anyone, who had listened to the hours of tapes that the government had of Schweihs' fucking-laced chatter and promises of doing harm to someone, saw little politeness in The German.

Six weeks later, Schweihs was rushed from the Metropolitan Correction Center to Thorek Memorial Hospital on the city's North Side where he died on Wednesday, July 23. His family hadn't been able to work out arrangements with the government in time to be at his bedside and he died alone. The families of people Schweihs was believed to have murdered had no sympathy for his passing.

On Monday about a dozen people gathered at a funeral home, but Schweihs' body wasn't there. It had been confiscated by the county medical examiner's office, which hadn't been properly notified that Schweihs had died and had to do its own examination of the remains before releasing it to the family. The funeral service was held without a body. Schweihs was buried the next day. The federal judge formally dismissed the indictment against him.

Steve Bagbey and his wife were visiting relatives in Florida when he learned of Schweihs' death. He felt compelled to contribute to an internet blog about a Chicago newspaper's article about Schweihs dying.

"The death of Schweihs closes an era for me," Steve wrote. "I am deeply pissed I never got to put bracelets on their wrists (Schweihs, Marshall Caifano, Lombardo). Let us never forget the pain, loss these lowlife people like Schweihs did to the innocent and not so innocent folks. Justice was denied with Marshall and Schweihs for their murders but those of faith know where they might be. Never forgive or forget the pain felt by the relatives of the murder victims!"

U.S. District Judge James Zagel, who presided over the Family Secrets trial, never forgot the pain of the victims' relatives.

On January 26, 2009 when Paul Schiro, convicted of racketeering by the jury which deadlocked on the murder charge, appeared for sentencing, the judge said the prosecution in the trial had proven by a preponderance of the evidence that Schiro had participated in the killing of Emil Vaci and sentenced the 71-year-old Schiro to 20 years in prison. Zagel said Schiro showed no hesitation when asked by the Outfit to kill his friend Vaci and served as a lookout during the murder.

After hearing of the sentence, Steve wanted to meet Zagel. "That guy has balls. I have got to send him a thank you note."

Two days later, Zagel sentenced the 71-year-old Calabrese to life in prison. While the jury found Calabrese guilty of seven murders, the judge said the preponderance of the evidence showed Calabrese also was guilty of the six murders that the jury deadlocked on. "Your crimes are unspeakable," Zagel said. On Thursday February 5, 2007, James Marcello was sentenced to life in prison for the murder of the Spilotro brothers.

Three days earlier on February 2, Joey Lombardo had been sentenced to life in prison with the prosecutor calling Lombardo "an Outfit boss with no remorse." Judge Zagel was equally harsh. "The worst things you have done are terrible and I see no regret in you," the judge said. While "The Clown" had some ability to charm people, in the end life is about actions and "not about our wits and our smiles," Zagel said.

Lombardo now is in a federal prison. Lombardo is the last person alive who can tell Steve the details about the murder of Ray Ryan.

Even after 35 years, Steve hasn't given up trying to wrap up everything. It's something he feels he needs to do. After all, the case is personal.

He has instigated efforts to talk with Lombardo in prison, but so far has met with no success. Even with an interview, Lombardo may not want to say anything.

Who knows?

But, Steve Bagbey plans to keep trying.

It's that bulldog in him.

ACKNOWLEDGMENTS

Tracking Ray Ryan was a trail across the country from Watertown, Wisconsin, to Chicago, New York, Miami, Arkansas, Texas, Las Vegas and Palm Springs. Boxes of documents were accumulated over the past 30 years since I arrived at the Olympia Health Spa on October 18, 1977 and began chronicling the investigation into Ray's murder as a reporter first at the Evansville Press then eventually at the Evansville Courier and Press.

The journey was all-consuming at times, but always fascinating. The greatest pleasure was meeting dozens upon dozens of old-timers, folks in their 70s, 80s and even 90s who lived through the oil boom days in Evansville, East Texas and West Texas; the never-to-be-seen-again gambling days in Hot Springs, Chicago and Miami; and those who knew Ray in Watertown and his glory days in Palm Springs.

Many of their stories are recounted in this book. No matter whether they played small or large roles in Ray's life, they were delightful people to meet with remarkable memories and the ability to vividly recall those days. It was a part of their lives they never could forget and never should. Not all of the people interviewed could be mentioned in this book, but the willingness of all to talk was appreciated.

Some broke no new ground but helped line up others who did. One led to Tony Montana from Las Vegas, who arranged a meeting at a Starbucks on West Taylor Street in Chicago and for four hours calmly told of growing up in the city's Italian Patch among the street and high-ranking hoods of Chicago's Outfit.

Who really made this book possible was Steve Bagbey with his pack-rat collection of documents – local police reports of the investigation, correspondence and reports from the FBI, ATF and other federal agencies and photographs picked up along the way – and his reliable memory of past events, his eagerness to put everything on record and his never-ending desire to solve a murder.

Some people in Evansville may resent Bagbey for the way he handled some investigations as a cop, his occasional sharp-tongued outbursts as a city councilman and his leadership in banning smoking in city restaurants. But what they should admire is his dedication in trying to bring the murderers of Ray Ryan to justice.

I appreciate the help received at the Chicago Crime Commission, the Palm Springs Historical Society, the National Archives in Washington, D.C., the Nevada State Museum in Las Vegas, and the public libraries and historical societies in Watertown, Milwaukee, Chicago, Evansville, Miami, Hot Springs, Ontario in California, and Midland, Snyder and Tyler in Texas.

Thanks go to Thomas Schultz of the Watertown Daily Times whose columns about my early research life generated tips from people who had known Ray. Joycelyn Winnecke of the Chicago Tribune helped over the years by providing important articles about Ray. John J. Flood, a retired Chicago cop and modern day mob watcher, offered frequent insights.

A thank you also goes to Andrew Murray, Bagbey's nephew, for allowing us to use several photographs from his Ray Ryan collection. Additional thanks also to Mary Ann Hughes with the Evansville Catholic Diocese and Steve Halbig, former Evansville Courier copy editor, who read book versions and suggested corrections. Any mistakes that remain are mine alone.

The deepest gratitude, however, goes to my wife, Judy, who painstakingly went through old newspapers, baptismal records, school and church records and historical documents in Watertown, Milwaukee, Chicago, the National Archives, Las Vegas and Palm Springs and endured the months, make that years, required to put this book together. Without her, the book and none of the other joys in my life – especially sons Mark and Ross – would have been possible.

Herb Marynell

Although I failed to make an arrest in the Ray Ryan murder, I did try and that was important. The case was difficult, demanding and extremely frustrating. At the time, I was personally ridiculed by peers for constantly pursuing the investigation, being told I was "beating a dead horse" and "you're never going to solve it." This only added to the frustration.

But I got to delve into the life of the most fascinating man I never met and whose manner of death wasn't deserved. The investigation was the most rewarding I had ever done and allowed me to meet wonderful, extremely talented law enforcement officials across the country. It also strengthened my belief that the Evansville police department took a back seat to no one when it came to such cases.

I could never have had the career I did without the mentors, friends and supervisors who helped shape my investigative skills from the Evansville police department: Gene Martin, Dick Tenbarge, Frank Gulledge, Larry Sparks, Bob Overby, Gary Sprinkle, Don Erk, Barry Hart, Ron Clark, Ed Biederwolf, Ted Mattingly and Richard Morris. Also, special thanks go to former EPD Chief Brad Hill and Assistant Chief Rob Hahn for their support in this investigation.

Many times local and state officers across this country have been very critical of the FBI. I was never exposed to this opinion. If I could go back in time, I might have looked at joining the FBI. Their pay and retirement benefits are usually much better than us locals. The agents I met were good men and I owe them my thanks – Richard Eisgruber, Gary Perkins, Rob Brannon, Bill Wagner, Jack O'Rourke, Jim Beck, Tom Page, Tom Van Wormer, Karen Elmendorf and Robert Duvall. There are many federal agents I never met and some I have who did a tremendous job on the Family Secrets investigation that was based in Chicago.

At the U. S. Attorney's office for the Northern District of Illinois, thanks to U.S. Attorney Patrick J. Fitzgerald and his staff for an outstanding effort with Family Secrets. Very special thanks to Assistant U.S. Attorney Mitch Mars, who died so soon after his hard work on the mob in Family Secrets. Thanks also to Assistant U.S. Attorney John Scully, who I had the most contact with during the Family Secrets trial. He was guarded in our conservations at the outset but was eager to learn about the Ryan case and was willing to help in my investigation. He was an outstanding prosecutor who also turned out to be a classmate of my brother-in-law Judge Hagel (USMC Ret.) at the U.S. Naval Academy. And on a personal note, thanks to John for the introduction to Al Egan, retired Chicago police department officer and a fine man. Mike Hammond with the Chicago police department also helped in my investigation.

Great assistance in the investigation came from Dick Wright, a retired Los Angeles police department captain who went on to join the Simi Valley police, the late John O'Brien from the New York police department and Terry Walters with the U. S. Marshal Service, my peers from the FBI National Academy. I can't say enough about what I learned from them. Thanks also go to John Bizzack and Drexel Neal of the Lexington, Kentucky, police department, who helped in tracking down leads in that city.

Thanks also to Herb Marynell who did a fantastic job in capturing Marshall Caifano and Ray Ryan in this book. I have never agreed with him about highlighting my role in this project but it was his idea.

It is nearly the 35th anniversary of Ryan's murder. A lot has happened with the birth of two sons, the death of parents. I would like to thank my family for all of their support throughout the years. Our son Sean and his lovely wife Carla gave us a beautiful grandson, Noah Bagbey, who now is four, and granddaughter Ainsley, who was born on St. Patrick's Day 2011. Our second son Chris, like his brother, continues to dedicate himself to the medical service.

My friends and I are still running down information in the Ryan case. We shall see what happens in the future. I looked forward to the day that Joe Lombardo was sentenced to jail for the rest of his life for his criminal activity. I just wished the Ryan case had been included in Family Secrets. Frank Schweihs died before the trial. I hope he enjoys his new warm home.

In closing, I want to say a special thanks to my teachers, coaches, relatives and friends: Bob Hargrave, Gene Logel, Ralph Weinzapfel, Ron Wannemuehler, the Brothers of Holy Cross, my grandfather Frank Riger, uncle John R. Bagbey, uncle Bobby Riger, uncle Harry Bagbey. I say thanks again. You really helped in my journey through life. If I am a success, it is because of all of you.

Peace

Steve Bagbey

Badge number 2x679

442

4

CPSIA information can be obtained at www.ICGtesting.com
Printed in the USA
LVOW01s2004090713

342082LV00005B/8/P